TOWARD
Natural Right and History

TOWARD *Natural Right and History*

Lectures and Essays by Leo Strauss, 1937–1946

EDITED BY
J. A. Colen and Svetozar Minkov

THE UNIVERSITY OF CHICAGO PRESS
Chicago and London

The University of Chicago Press, Chicago 60637
The University of Chicago Press, Ltd., London

Published 2018
Printed in the United States of America

27 26 25 24 23 22 21 20 19 18   1 2 3 4 5

ISBN-13: 978-0-226-51210-5 (CLOTH)
ISBN-13: 978-0-226-51224-2 (E-BOOK)
DOI: 10.7208/chicago/9780226512242.001.0001

Library of Congress Cataloging-in-Publication Data

Names: Strauss, Leo, author. | Colen, José, editor. | Minkov, Svetozar, 1975– editor.
Title: Toward Natural right and history : lectures and essays by Leo Strauss, 1937–1946 / edited by J. A. Colen and Svetozar Minkov.
Description: Chicago ; London : The University of Chicago Press, 2018. | Includes bibliographical references and index.
Identifiers: LCCN 2017044565 | ISBN 9780226512105 (cloth : alk. paper) | ISBN 9780226512242 (e-book)
Subjects: LCSH: Political science. | Natural law. | Social sciences. | Strauss, Leo.
Classification: LCC JA66 .S87 2018 | DDC 320.01—dc23
LC record available at https://lccn.loc.gov/2017044565

♾ This paper meets the requirements of ANSI/NISO Z39.48-1992 (Permanence of Paper).

Contents

Foreword

MICHAEL ZUCKERT

Forty-five years after his death and we are still reading Leo Strauss. We are now reading him rather differently from the way he was read in his lifetime. He was seen then by his detractors as a kind of throwback, as a thinker who had not heard that the old-time philosophy of thinkers like Plato, Aristotle, and Thomas Aquinas had been superseded. To his supporters and admirers, he seemed a great defender of old-fashioned virtue and Truth. Both groups were of course correct to some degree. Strauss did call for a return to the classics, most especially to Plato and other Socratics. As he himself pointed out, such a call for a return was then extremely unusual outside of Roman Catholic circles. It is far less uncommon today, for we have experienced a major revival of interest in classical authors since Strauss wrote, as in the movement to revive virtue ethics. Strauss still remains somewhat outside this revival, for he was committed to a return not so much to Aristotle as to Plato and Socrates. Those who saw Strauss as an ally in the battle against relativism, nihilism, and some forms of existentialism were also correct, for these were his opponents as well.

But forty-five years later things look more complex. Themes in his work that were mostly passed over or ignored have now begun to receive more attention. Among other matters, readers of Strauss are now more struck by the role of Martin Heidegger in his thinking—both the influence Heidegger had on him and the degree to which his corpus was an attempt to counter or overcome Heidegger. Strauss's claim that Heidegger was "[t]he only great thinker" of his age is now taken far more seriously than it was in his lifetime. Likewise, as Strauss has been increasingly seen as a great thinker, more of his early writings have been brought to light—writings from his pre-America days in Germany, France, and England, as well as writings from his pre–University of Chicago days at the New School for Social Research. With the publication of his "pre-Strauss" writings and of his correspondence, interest in his "development" as a thinker has grown, along with recognition that he must be considered as starting out from within the intellectual milieu of interwar Weimar Germany. Thus, there is now interest in his neo-Kantian education, his youthful political Zionism, his relations to the circles of Edmund Husserl and Heidegger from which emerged so many other eminent German thinkers of his generation. His relations not only to Heidegger and Husserl, but to others from that milieu—Hans-Georg Gadamer, Jacob Klein, Hannah Arendt, to name a few—are of increasing interest.

The collection of essays compiled and edited by J. A. Colen and Svetozar Minkov fits into the frame of these new or modified themes of interest in Strauss. Indeed, the editors add substantial new materials from one phase of Strauss's career so far little explored, his years at the New School. Colen and Minkov's selection of six essays by Strauss relate to Strauss's *Natural Right and History*, the book that in his lifetime was surely his best-known and most widely read. One of the revisions that has occurred in the years since Strauss's death is not so much to lessen appreciation for *Natural Right and History* but to elevate the importance of his later writings, such as *The City and Man*, *Thoughts on Machiavelli*, and his late writings on Xenophon. But none of this is to deny the significance of *Natural Right and History*, which Colen and Minkov bring into much sharper focus with the materials they have gathered into this volume. They put it well when they speak of these materials as offering a peek into Strauss's workshop, for here we see him thinking his way toward *Natural Right and History* and some of the positions for which he became best known—his opposition to historicism, his attempt to recapture ancient thought, his shifting interpretations of the nature of modern political philosophy. It is no denigration of Strauss's mature thought to say that he had a development—how else could he have arrived at a position so different from the starting points he shared with contemporaries like Gadamer and Arendt?

In addition to the hitherto unpublished essays by Strauss, the editors have presented an introductory essay to each of the Strauss essays, each written by a scholar with expertise in Strauss's thought. These essays begin to draw forth what is of value in each of the Strauss essays by discussing how the essay relates to *Natural Right and History* and more broadly to Strauss's mature thought. The introductory essays give us a welcome tour, so to speak, of Strauss's workshop, and, without interrupting him as he sits at his desk, allow us to look over his shoulder and see what work he is doing.

Abbreviations

CM	*The City and Man*
FRSS	"The Frame of Reference in the Social Sciences"
H 1941	"Historicism"
HPP	*History of Political Philosophy*
LAM	*Liberalism Ancient and Modern*
LIG	"The Living Issues of German Postwar Philosophy"
NR 1946	"Natural Right"
NRH	*Natural Right and History*
OMPT	"The Origin of Modern Political Thought"
OSCPP	"On the Study of Classical Political Philosophy"
OT	*On Tyranny*
PAW	*Persecution and the Art of Writing*
PL	*Philosophy and Law*
PPH	*The Political Philosophy of Hobbes*
RCPR	*The Rebirth of Classical Political Rationalism*
SPPP	*Studies in Platonic Political Philosophy*
TOM	*Thoughts on Machiavelli*
WCL	"What Can We Learn from Political Theory?"
WIPP	*What Is Political Philosophy?*
WL	Walgreen Lectures

Editors' Note

We have transcribed these lectures and essays written or corrected by Strauss's hand, standardized spelling and punctuation, indented paragraph beginnings, italicized titles and foreign words, corrected a few grammatical errors, inserted a few words (signaled in the endnotes), and used endnotes to indicate Strauss's own changes. We italicized all underlinings, both typed and manuscript. When "e.g." came at the end of a phrase, we moved it to the beginning of the phrase or replaced it with "for example." We kept Strauss's square brackets around some paragraphs in his texts; their meaning is unclear, but they probably marked sections to skip or to expand in oral delivery. We avoided using square brackets to insert missing words in the transcripts but not in the essays. We took the text corrected in handwriting by Strauss as the intended final version but kept as endnotes the typed alternatives in all instances, except the obvious typographic corrections. All Strauss's own notes and marginalia were kept as footnotes to the text and marked as such, when an exact positioning of the notes was possible, and we also used footnotes to provide relevant information about specific passages or to complete references.

Two of the articles by Strauss included here have been previously published. "What Can We Learn from Political Theory?," edited by Nathan Tarcov, appeared in the *Review of Politics* 69, no. 4 (October 2007): 515–29. "The Frame of Reference in the Social Sciences," edited by J. A. Colen and Svetozar Minkov, appeared in the *Review of Politics* 76, no. 4 (October 2014): 619–33.

In addition, part of the introduction, chapter 6, and the afterword are abridged and modified from a text previously published in J. A. Colen, *Facts and Values* (London: Plusprint, 2010, 2017).

Introduction

J. A. COLEN AND SVETOZAR MINKOV

Toward Natural Right and History brings together lectures and essays that Leo Strauss wrote between 1937 and 1946.[1] During this prolific period at the New School for Social Research, after his decisive turn toward classical thought, but before the publication of his major works, Strauss was writing extensively. At the University of Chicago in the fall of 1949, just after leaving the New School, he gave his first series of Walgreen Lectures, a set of six lectures that in revised and expanded form was eventually published in 1953 as *Natural Right and History*. The book was essentially faithful to the texts he prepared for the Walgreen Lectures, lectures that, owing to time constraints, he considerably abbreviated while delivering them. The lectures and the book took shape over a long time, beginning, in a way, at least as early as the 1930s.[2] But his first decade in the United States can be regarded as the period during which the mature Strauss was working out the details of the arguments that would be expressed in *Natural Right and History*. Strauss developed its fundamental structure, wrote "drafts" of the work, and prepared a number of lectures in which he established the central arguments of the future book, though not always with the same emphasis or along the same lines as in the final version.

This volume presents six of these drafts and lectures, previously unpublished in book form, with brief interpretative essays that try to establish their relation to or to clarify the ideas pervading *Natural Right and History*. In chronological order, the texts and essays included in this book are: "The Origin of Modern Political Thought" (1937); "On the Study of Classical Political Philosophy" (1938 or 1938–39) followed by an undated commentary of the *Education of Cyrus*; "Historicism" (1941); "What Can We Learn from Political Theory?" (1942); "The Frame of Reference in the Social Sciences" (1945); "Natural Right" (1946). Was it because Strauss struggled to develop them into the longer text, which he carefully revised from 1949 to 1953, that these lectures were never included in any of his collections of essays? Or because these "collections" are not mere anthologies but unified works, whose purpose could not allow a place for these unpublished lectures? Or because he changed his mind about some of their content? Many other lectures were prepared and not published during this period, so in response to these questions it is best to acknowledge our ignorance. One of the main conclusions of our research and of the reading of these essays, however, is that many of the distinctive ideas that pervade Strauss's more famous works were already fully formed in this period.

Texts and Context

There are several reasons for making these precursor texts available now to a broad readership. On one hand, some of them can easily be counted among the most attractive of Strauss's lectures. Some texts have the brevity, the incisiveness and emotion of his later speech in Jerusalem[3] and the depth of his most extensive published works. In general, Strauss's texts that began as courses or lectures are always livelier than his texts conceived from the beginning for publication. Furthermore, his relentless revisions made the published versions both more accurate and more difficult, in such a way that in the final version Strauss is already almost hidden, and it is not he who speaks but rather his Plato or his Hobbes. The texts presented here, by contrast, are still almost "unadorned," and for this very reason are, or appear to be, more direct and accessible.

On the other hand, most of these lectures have not been published and have been ignored for a long time by scholars, partly because they seem to have been intended for merely oral presentation. Moreover, not all of the texts presented here are completely finished. It may be argued that some curiosity is always aroused by unfinished or provisional versions of a philosopher's work. Their incompleteness is therefore not a reason to think that they will not be of interest to many readers. In fact, the unpolished character of some of the essays and lectures even has a certain appeal, because readers get something of a "behind the scenes" look at Strauss as he was thinking things through, also provided by including his revisions. The very indiscretion involved in reading increases one's interest, and these kinds of sketches, handwritten notes, and texts therefore have their own charm.

But there is an additional reason to read and reflect on these specific texts roughly corresponding to the main sections of *Natural Right and History*. The papers and essays in question have been selected because they each, in different ways, show Strauss in his workshop, so to speak, thinking through the themes—historicism, social sciences, classic natural right, the origins of modern thought, the quarrel between ancients and moderns—that are central to the first set of Walgreen Lectures given in 1949.[4] According to Strauss's own advice, preference should be given to the work that an author chooses to make public, and so these texts should be understood as supplements to the published version of the book. For this reason, these texts will appear here as reflections on the road "toward" *Natural Right and History*, a claim that is perhaps too bold. However, to make possible this indiscreet glimpse, it is necessary to proceed with as much caution as audacity, because these very texts emphasize with vehemence the careful reading Strauss always recommended.

In order to proceed carefully, it is necessary furthermore to be aware that the connection between the historical context and the ideas is merely "accidental." According to Strauss, we must distinguish the validity of a theory from the conditions in which it emerges.[5] The centrality of natural right in Strauss's work becomes clearer, however, when we bear in mind how a significant part of his work at the New School for Social Research in the 1940s was incorporated into the Walgreen Lectures at the University of Chicago. It is useful to recall briefly that the lectures brought to light here were written during what was perhaps the most important period in the formation of Strauss's thought and teaching.

It is generally said that Strauss seldom expressed his views on specific political issues or American politics, however pressing or urgent. Even if this is generally accurate, at least in this period at the New School it was difficult for him to avoid commenting on the current situation, and a salient feature of his teaching in this context is the attention devoted to contemporary problems.[6] Most of the graduate school faculty were émigrés who had escaped from Nazi Germany. In fact, alongside the original vocational school, Alvin Johnson, an enthusiast of European social sciences and a firm advocate of interdisciplinary work, set up a "University in Exile," bringing together a number of European scholars versed in different areas of the humanities. The faculty naturally reflected on totalitarianism and the causes of war, and some (including Leo Strauss) formed the "Study Group on Germany."[7] Members of the New School also decided to make their studies public and gave lectures in general seminars directed at all the students and teaching staff at the School.

Strauss's own declarations in these texts also make clear that he is not thinking in a virtual vacuum. In the first of these texts, "What Can We

TABLE 1. New School Lectures Printed in Strauss's Lifetime

Year	*Lectures*
1939	"The Spirit of Sparta" (*Social Research*)
1941	* "Persecution and the Art of Writing" (*Social Research*)
	"The Literary Character of the Guide" (*Social Research*)
1943	* "The Law of Reason in the *Kuzari*"
1945	* "Farabi's Plato"
	** "On Classical Political Philosophy" (*Social Research*)
1946	"On a New Interpretation of Plato's Political Philosophy" (*Social Research*)
1947	"On the Intention of Rousseau" (*Social Research*)
1948	* "How to Study Spinoza's *Theologico-Political Treatise*"
	On Tyranny
1949	** "Political Philosophy and History"

* marks articles reprinted in *PAW* 1952; ** marks those reprinted in *WIPP* 1959.
This list, however, is misleading since much of this work, on Hesiod, Homer, Thucydides, the pre-Socratics, Plato, Aristotle, etc., remained unpublished until after his death. In Strauss's archives many more texts can be found. To name just a few, most of which have been or are on the verge of being published: 1938 "On the Study of Classical Political Philosophy"; 1939 "Hesiod and the Pre-Socratics"; 1939 "Exoteric Teaching"; 1940–41 "The Origins of Economic Sciences: Xenophon's *Oeconomicus*"; 1940 "The Living Issues of German Postwar Philosophy"; 1941 "Historicism."

Learn from Political Theory?," Strauss asserts that if an intelligent policy (and he points out the broad lines of what such a policy should be) could dispense with the use of political philosophy, it remains the case that liberal democracies that protect civil liberties would be "unthinkable without the tradition of political philosophy and the concept of natural right." And in the introduction to the second text, "Historicism," he mentions that his own lecture was delivered between someone else's lectures on "historical sociology" (by Max Weber and Georg Lukács) and on Plato and Aristotle. In fact, Strauss often shared courses and seminars with other professors at the New School, despite important differences between their fields and even their views. This was very common since the New School was conceived according to the interdisciplinary model of Johnson, the creator of the graduate school.

Strauss shared and co-organized joint seminars, with among others Solomon Asch (1907–96), a pioneer in social psychology;[8] Alexander Pekelis (1902–46), a jurist and social activist;[9] Alfred Schütz (1899–1959), a sociologist from Max Weber's school and a scholar on Husserl's phenomenology;

Kurt Riezler (1882–1955), a statesman but also a scholar and "humanist"; and the historian of science Alexandre Koyré (1892–1964).

Curiously, some of these courses and joint seminars did not deal exactly with Strauss's colleagues' areas of expertise, but with famous philosophical works: Aristotle's *De anima* and Descartes's *Passions of the Soul*, or Plato's *Theaetetus*. Strauss also co-taught several seminars with now lesser-known colleagues, such as Phillips Bradley (1894–1982), later an officer of the United States Information Service. Little is known about their relationship to Strauss, but Strauss was "*The* Philosopher"[10] of the School, and there are signs of a certain intellectual "partnership" between the members of the faculty.[11] Among those who shared courses with Strauss, only Howard White (1902–72) was in fact a student under Strauss at the New School, and he assisted him in some seminars in Strauss's final years there.[12] But Strauss attracted a first generation of students: Henry Magid, who would study John Stuart Mill; Harry V. Jaffa, who wrote on Aristotle and Saint Thomas, before devoting himself to Lincoln; and especially Joseph Cropsey, who was not actually a student but also attended Strauss's seminars on the suggestion of his friend Jaffa. Jaffa later described the Wednesday seminars held by Strauss as "a convocation on Mount Olympus."[13]

Although the lectures and talks presented here are somewhat marked by the spirit of the age, the bulk of Strauss's teaching concerned topics of political philosophy where ancient authors dominate. Later, Strauss indicated the core of his pedagogy: "The teachers themselves are pupils and must be pupils. But there cannot be an infinite regress: ultimately there must be teachers who are not in turn pupils. Those teachers who are not in turn pupils are the great minds or, in order to avoid any ambiguity in a matter of such importance, the greatest minds." He continued that "[s]uch men are extremely rare. We are not likely to meet any of them in any classroom,"[14] requiring therefore the reading of the books that carry their voices from the past. Starting in 1938 he taught courses titled "Greek and Roman Political Philosophy," usually taking two semesters, with Plato almost always at the center: even a course called "Utopias and Political Science" (1939, 1941, etc.), whose title is enigmatic, was apparently dedicated to Strauss's new reading of the *Republic*.[15] The fourth piece in this volume, "On the Study of Classical Political Philosophy," shows how distinctive Strauss's approach to the classics had already become.

Most of Strauss's seminars at the New School were indeed centered on single texts, but others were dedicated to problems or themes, such as "Political Theory: Selected Problems." His later writings showcase some of the problems that we see him addressing in his courses: "Persecution of Freedom of Thought in Classical Antiquity"; "Continental Champions of Freedom of Thought"; "Philosophy and Revelation"; or "The Philosophy of Aristotle and the Teaching of the Bible."

Strauss's interest, however, was not restricted to the ancients. The fifth essay included here, "The Origin of Modern Political Thought," shows that Strauss kept very much alive his interest in the moderns. In these courses, Strauss begins to treat topics that he later addresses in the Walgreen Lectures of 1949. For example, he gave courses called "Writings and Speeches by Edmund Burke," "The Philosophy of Spinoza," and, perhaps most surprisingly, "Rule of Law and Constitutionalism." Strauss taught one course focused only on the Declaration of Independence, while others dwelt on the influence of Locke on American ideals: "The Constitution of the United States: Philosophical Background" and "The Social Philosophy of Early Capitalism: Analysis of Locke's *Civil Government*."[16] Some other titles also anticipated issues directly related to the Walgreen Lectures: "Natural Law and the Rights of Man," "Justice and Political Necessity," "Religion and the Rise of Modern Capitalism: The Weber-Tawney Controversy," renamed later "Religion and the Rise of Modern Capitalism."

The last text in this volume, from 1946, shows Strauss using the bulk of his teaching at the New School to tackle the problem of "natural right." Strauss invested so much of his energy in the 1940s in this topic that its culmination, *Natural Right and History,* Strauss's most famous book on a subject he considered of the utmost importance, deserves special attention.

Toward *Natural Right and History*

The end result of the texts gathered in this volume was, indeed, the Walgreen Lectures and the book *Natural Right and History. Natural Right and History* is one of Strauss's longest works on a single topic. It is therefore appropriate that the particular set of texts included in this book, which cast a special light on the Walgreen Lectures, should again be presented to the general public, inasmuch as a lively debate, not always devoid of malice, persists around Strauss's thought on natural right. And the book is, in fact, in some cases deliberately elliptical, if not ambiguous. Even in 1949, some readers and reviewers[17] expected the book to be soon followed by a

TABLE 2. New School Courses

Year	Semester/ Quarter	Courses
1938	Fall	Greek and Roman Political Philosophy: Plato and His Predecessors; Plato's *Laws*
1939	Spring	Greek and Roman Political Philosophy: Aristotle and Later Ancient Political Thought; Utopias and Political Science
	Fall	Political Philosophy from Hooker to Spinoza; Persecution of Freedom of Thought in Classical Antiquity; Political Philosophy[1] and the Study of History in Antiquity
1940	Spring	Political Philosophy and the Study of History in the Modern World; Continental Champions of Freedom of Thought; European Thought from Locke to Burke
Strauss did not teach the courses scheduled for the 1939–40 academic year. See the appendix for detailed course descriptions and additional courses.		
1941	Fall	History of Political Ideas (I); Joint Seminar: History of Psychology and the Doctrine of Man—Albert Salomon, Leo Strauss; Absolutism and Constitutionalism, Ancient and Modern
1942	Spring	History of Political Ideas (II); The Political Philosophy of Aristotle
	Fall	History of Political Philosophy (I); Natural Law and the Rights of Man; Readings in Political Philosophy: Reason of State and the Absolutist Concept of Government
1943	Spring	Religion and the Rise of Modern Capitalism: The Weber-Tawney Controversy; Modern Political Philosophy; Political Theory: Selected Problems; Readings in Political Philosophy: Rule of Law and Constitutionalism; **412-S Readings in Political Philosophy; Utopias and Political Science; History of Political Philosophy (II)
	Fall	History of Political Philosophy—Basic Course; The Political Philosophy of Plato and Aristotle—Graduate Course; The Philosophy of Aristotle and the Teaching of the Bible
1944	Spring	Political Theory: Selected Problems—Graduate Course; The Declaration of Independence—Graduate Course; Readings in Philosophy: Philosophy and Politics—Open Course
	Fall	Joint Seminar: Religion and the Rise of Modern Capitalism; Joint Seminar: Theory of Knowledge—A. Koyré, K. Riezler, L. Strauss. Idealism and Empiricism on the basis of Plato's Dialogue *Theaetetus*; History of Political Philosophy—Open Course; Readings in Political Philosophy: Basic Problems in Democracy
1945	Spring	Readings in Political Philosophy: Justice and Political Necessity; The Constitution of the United States: Philosophical Background—Graduate Course; Readings in Philosophy: An Introduction to Philosophy in General and Political Philosophy in Particular—Open Course; Joint Seminar: The Forerunners of Modern Psychology—S. E. Asch, K. Riezler, L. Strauss; The United States Constitution: Theory (new) and Practice—Phillips Bradley and Leo Strauss—Open Course; Readings in Political Philosophy: Justice and Political Necessity

TABLE 2. *Continued*

Year	Semester/ Quarter	Courses
	Fall	History of Political Philosophy—Open Course; Readings in Political Philosophy; Utopias and Political Science: Interpretation of Plato's *Republic*; Political Philosophy: Its Problems and Its Development—Graduate Course
1946	Spring	Readings in Political Philosophy: The Social Philosophy of Early Capitalism; Analysis of Locke's Civil Government; Human Nature in Politics—Solomon E. Asch and Leo Strauss—Seminar; Readings in Philosophy: An Introduction to Philosophy, Especially Political Philosophy—Open Course; Morals and Politics in Plato's *Protagoras*; Moral Philosophy: Its Problems and Its Development—Graduate Course
	Fall	Human Nature and Human Institutions (I)—Solomon E. Asch, Alexander H. Pekelis, and Leo Strauss—Graduate Course; History of Political Philosophy—Open Course; Readings in Political Philosophy: Political Liberty and Separation of Powers—Leo Strauss, assisted by Howard B. White; Socrates and the History of Philosophy—Leo Strauss—Graduate Course
1947	Spring	Readings in Political Philosophy: The Social Philosophy of Thomas Aquinas—Leo Strauss, assisted by Howard B. White—Seminar; Readings in Philosophy—An Introduction to Philosophy, Especially Political Philosophy; The Declaration of Independence—Graduate Course; Readings in Political Philosophy: The Social Philosophy of Thomas Aquinas—Seminar
	Fall	History of Political Philosophy—Open Course; Readings in Political Philosophy: Principles of Liberal Democracy; Philosophy and Revelation
1948	Spring	Plato's Political Philosophy and Its Metaphysical Foundations—Graduate Course; Interpretation of Plato's *Republic*; Readings in Political Philosophy: The Aristotelian Principles—Seminar; Readings in Philosophy: An Introduction to Philosophy, Especially Political Philosophy—Open Course; Interpretation of Two of the Smaller Platonic Dialogues; Readings in Political Philosophy: The Aristotelian Principles—Seminar; Readings in Philosophy: An Introduction to Philosophy, Especially Political Philosophy
	Summer	Research in the History of Political Ideas
	Fall	History of Political Philosophy (I)—Open Course; Readings in Political Philosophy: The Problem of Equality; The Moral Principles of Politics—Seminar
1949	Spring	Readings in Philosophy: An Introduction to Philosophy—Open Course; Interpretation of a Platonic Dialogue; Readings in Political Philosophy: The Problem of Theory and Practice—Seminar; Analysis of Selected Writings and Speeches by Edmund Burke; The Philosophy of Spinoza—Graduate Course

[1] Elsewhere listed as "political science."
Compiled on the basis of the catalogues available in: http://digitalarchives.library.newschool.edu/index.php/Detail/collections/NS050101

systematic exposition of the content of natural right—perhaps in the tradition of Hugo Grotius, or Althusius, or even akin to Otto von Gierke's historical presentation.[18] In its absence, a debate emerged that endures to this day. The express purpose of the Walgreen Lectures is to recover a forgotten and, nowadays, even incomprehensible problem. Strauss speaks of natural right without suggesting that man's need for natural right in any way implies that such a need can be satisfied: a wish is not a fact,[19] and it is not clear if one can move beyond merely recollecting an almost forgotten problem.

Given Strauss's initial modesty, one might also think that the work has only a "tentative" character, that is, that it is an incomplete sketch, so to speak. Indeed, just one year after the Walgreen Lectures he wrote in a letter that he had just presented the question of natural right as "an unsolved problem."[20] One could therefore easily be led to see *Natural Right and History* as merely a history book that does not contain Strauss's own teaching on natural right—or even to suppose that Strauss has no such teaching.[21] Strauss, however, defends the philosophical significance of this work. According to Strauss himself, even the historical content of the book is in some way philosophical.

In another article published in 1949, Strauss asserts that historical knowledge is important for political philosophy, but "is only preliminary and auxiliary to political philosophy; it does not form an integral part of it."[22] He nevertheless concludes that it is needed today for recovering problems that before were clear, "explicit and in the center of consideration and discussion," and even "perfectly lucid,"[23] but have now become abstract and secondary. Plato ignored history in the study program in the *Republic*, Aristotle disregarded it as being less serious than poetry, and everyone who considered Aristotle's discussion to be the basis for knowing the truth dispensed with historical research. The situation has changed, given that the foundations of truth are now hidden, and for this reason, "within limits," a certain "fusion" of history and philosophy is "inevitable on the basis of 'modern political philosophy'" or "modern science." Research aimed at reawakening memory and the problems hidden by progress is needed today. "This philosophical inquiry is the history of philosophy or of science."[24]

It is best not to lose sight of the fact that such inquiry would be an attempt to transform inherited knowledge into genuine knowledge. Is the 1953 book primarily philosophical?[25] Or is it merely a historical study? It is certainly obvious to any reader that the historical studies in *Natural Right and History* do not appear in the work in a conventional manner. The book as a whole is organized in pairs: the first two chapters are contemporary, the two central chapters are ancient, and the last two are modern,[26] but even if we ignore the peculiar "flashback" from contemporary thought, this is a work whose straightforwardness is only apparent. Strauss begins with a critical "summary" of historicism and then presents Max Weber as a representative of positivism in the social sciences. He then turns to the prephilosophical era and the classics (balanced between pre-Socratics and post-Socratics). The chapter on classical natural right takes several turns, the most significant being the presentation of the classics as a coherent whole that is nevertheless split into multiple strands. Only beginning with the moderns does the book begin to follow an approximately chronological order. Even then, the brief reference to Machiavelli within the chapter on Hobbes (or the repeated references to Hobbes himself in those on Locke and Rousseau) and the dissolution of modern natural right hardly follow a clear timeline—going from Rousseau and Burke, for instance, back to Epicureanism—finally coming full circle with the emergence of historicism.

The reading we intend to suggest of *Natural Right and History* upholds the idea that the work embodies an important part of Leo Strauss's teaching,[27] the whole of which is imbedded in suggestive and provocative historical studies, conducted in a philosophical and nonhistoricist vein. These studies should be measured not against a standard of historical accuracy that easily succumbs to what Strauss refers to as "the weakness of the flesh" that tempts accurate historians, but against a standard of philosophical depth. This explains why he continues to inspire and provoke strong reactions, while almost no historical studies from the 1940s, which are necessarily outdated, deserve to be read today.[28] It is in a *précis raisonné* of the history of natural right, one that aims to present natural right as a problem, that Leo Strauss reveals his thoughts about the most serious subjects: the appeal to higher principles (and their limits) and the very possibility of philosophy. In the final essay, we will try to summarize the core of such thoughts through the examination of his intention and teaching in the work.

Doubts about the intention and teaching of the work are compounded by the fact that few philosophers have paid so much attention as Strauss to the problem of identifying an author's intention.[29] In these essays (and many other texts), Strauss explains that in identifying the "deeper" teaching of an author, it is necessary not to iron out its rougher edges and to be aware of manifest blunders, as well as digressions and apparent contradictions, which may in fact be deliberate and serve to indicate the author's intention.

It certainly accords with Strauss's art of writing that the philosopher can use silences and puzzles, "studied ambiguity or imprecision."[30]

The beginning of the book is itself surprising since, in the version given to the press, the two epigraphs are biblical quotations about justice that Strauss, at first glance, does not comment on either in the book or in the 1949 lectures. They are perhaps examples of "those simple experiences regarding right and wrong which are at the bottom of the philosophic contention that there is a natural right,"[31] but only later does he explain his reading of their content.[32] The theologico-political problem suggested by these quotations, which is the symbol of the human condition, is neither entirely apparent nor wholly absent from the book, but kept in the background. It appears instead as simply a set of digressions. Strauss says, however, that digressions are often where the author explains his deepest ideas. In the oral version of the Walgreen Lectures, Strauss deviates leisurely from his analysis of Max Weber's thought to present philosophy as an alternative to revelation[33] before returning from these "awful depths" to something that promises a quiet sleep. This is one of his most complete statements on the conflict between philosophy and revelation.[34] Strauss's texts in this volume explain why the question cannot be ignored.[35]

Now, the first indication of Strauss's intention is that the work begins by exalting, "for more reasons than the most obvious one," the words of the Declaration of Independence as "self-evident" truths.[36] Is he merely wondering whether belief in these truths still endures? He was clearly aware that "it was as obvious to the drafters of the Declaration as it is to us that not all human beings understand government as they did."[37] The weight of these words and their immunity to the degrading effects of familiarity are perhaps best explained by their power to command the allegiance of American citizens and turn their country into the most powerful and prosperous nation on earth.[38] To invoke the modern rights of man in the introduction is, notwithstanding, paradoxical because to do so sanctions from the start that notion of "individualism" which "is the hitherto most powerful solvent of natural right."[39]

Strauss also states that "in the present state of our knowledge, it is difficult to say at what point in the modern development the decisive break occurred with the 'unhistorical' approach that prevailed in all earlier philosophy."[40] That is to say, it is difficult to determine with precision; and the assumption appears to be that Burke (or maybe Rousseau) paved the way for the historical approach—but no name is put forward at this point in the book.[41] In Strauss's talk titled "Historicism" in this volume, the difficulty is presented in this way: "Things changed fundamentally since the sixteenth century only. No earlier political philosopher known to me ever spoke of history with so much emphasis as did Machiavelli, Bodin and Bacon and even Hobbes."

There is a very important difference between claiming the authority of history and radical historicism, but Strauss is almost blunt in linking the two: "Historicism cannot be understood but as a reaction to the rationalism of the seventeenth and eighteenth centuries." The difficulty is explained in the 1937 text "The Origin of Modern Political Thought." After considering various definitions and criteria of modernity, Strauss does not hesitate in identifying Hobbes as having completed the break with the ancients, sowing seeds in the field that Machiavelli had prepared. This revelation was already apparent in 1936, in *The Political Philosophy of Hobbes,* where Strauss's main concern is to recall how Hobbes begins his theory not with a model of science but through history.[42] Strauss's later, quasi-Hobbesian reading of Locke is not naïve but deliberate. Nor is his presentation of Rousseau naïve. These liberties taken with historical "exactness" to reawake the memory of a philosophical problem are not a complete surprise: Strauss's 1953 subchapter on Rousseau in *Natural Right and History* is quite distinct from Strauss's 1947 text "On the Intention of Rousseau."[43]

These brief indications, following Strauss's own guidelines, are meant only to recall that *Natural Right and History* hides as much as it shows. The "ambiguities," "paradoxes," and "digressions" alert us to Strauss's intention. Strauss's intention is an important interpretive key to his work as a whole. Max Weber must be pursued far beyond his "explicit" statements. The teachings of Hobbes, Locke, and Rousseau should be presented as true teachings and in accordance with their intentions, often *against* their most frequent and explicit assertions. The historical studies in the book "are emphatically not studies of History with a capital H."[44] Provocative historical studies within a less than obvious plan for the book appear a questionable venture and seem to leave Strauss's work exposed to easy criticism. This would be more easy to understand if in the essay in this volume on how to study the classics,[45] Strauss did not clearly assert that "a good book may be compared with a healthy animal, i.e. with a self-sufficient being with a head and feet and middle parts of its own, which is capable of locomotion without needing crutches: a good book will fulfill its specific function, i.e., education and teaching, only if it is understood exclusively by itself."

The Precursor Texts to *Natural Right and History*

Strauss's essays in this volume are arranged according to their correspondence with chapters or parts of *Natural Right and History*. But if one considers the essays in their chronological order, one would see better the way in which they constitute a vector toward *Natural Right and History*. Such a consideration would begin with the 1937 "Origin of Modern Political Thought." In examining this lecture, it becomes quickly apparent that it is the one furthest removed from *Natural Right and History*, not only in time but in content. Yet for that very reason, it is also a clear marker in the trajectory of Strauss's engagement with Hobbes: it is part of a long transition to the statement on modern political philosophy found in *Natural Right and History*.[46] This longer trajectory reveals the Hobbes subchapter in *Natural Right and History* as a provisional stage in Strauss's understanding of Hobbes, and in fact one already surpassed in 1953, as is evident from Strauss's course on Hobbes in the autumn of 1953. The pivotal change in Strauss's understanding concerns the question whether Hobbes is a "subconscious" believer in justice in the full or original sense, as well as a "secularized" or disappointed believer in God. The 1937 lecture is closer to the early Hobbes book in suggesting that Hobbes is such a believer. *Natural Right and History* turns away from this view—the anguished Hobbes of the lecture is a far cry from the impish iconoclast of *Natural Right and History*—a turn that is completed in the Hobbes chapter in *What Is Political Philosophy?*[47] It is perhaps of more than merely biographical or antiquarian interest to note that this turn corresponds to a greater appreciation on Strauss's part of Machiavelli as a founder of modernity.

While Strauss's understanding of modernity may have undergone significant shifts in the 1940s and 1950s, his fundamental approach to the classics may have been formed in its essentials since the 1930s. The 1938 "On the Study of Classical Political Philosophy" lays the textually interpretive groundwork for *Natural Right and History*: it considers the question of how one should read the book of a philosophical thinker, a question to which *Natural Right and History* gives only an implicit answer through its extraordinary use of citations in the footnotes. In Strauss's published career, *Persecution and the Art of Writing* serves as that hermeneutical and methodological foundation, and it is not accidental that Strauss published that book before he published *Natural Right and History*.[48] In chapter 4 of *Natural Right and History* Strauss refers back to *Persecution and the Art of Writ-*

ing;[49] it is likewise in the chapter on classic natural right that Strauss uses the expression "exoteric," which is otherwise conspicuously absent from *Natural Right and History* (together with its counterpart, "esoteric," which is altogether absent). This hermeneutical groundwork is essential because without it Strauss's approach in *Natural Right and History* could have been easily characterized as a kind of "higher criticism"—the authors under consideration are treated in light of major themes and historical movements, a treatment that is open to the objection that it constitutes an unnecessary "surgery," which might do a healthy body "only harm."[50] The books behind the major issues are not studied in light of their "organic," fundamental design. By contrast, the 1938 lecture shows the extraordinary care Strauss took in approaching the books of classical political philosophy as if they were "healthy animals." Strauss's hermeneutical comments in 1938 could also serve as a guide to appreciating the living unity of Strauss's own books.

The 1941 "Historicism" essay is closer to the 1952 *Persecution and the Art of Writing* (most of which was composed in the early 1940s) than to *Natural Right and History* also with respect to another feature: the stark dismissal of historicism. According to *Persecution and the Art of Writing*, historical understanding used to be a "liberating force," but it lost its power "by becoming historicism, which is nothing other than the petrified and self-complacent form of the self-criticism of the modern mind."[51] In "Historicism," Strauss similarly calls even historicism itself a former "truly liberating force" but regards its current incarnation as a "blinder, for it has become a prejudice itself."[52] In the title essay of *Persecution and the Art of Writing* (likewise dating from 1941), Strauss also laid bare the inadequacy of the exactness of historical understanding. True exactness requires not missing the forest for the trees: paying scrupulous attention to each explicit statement, but not overlooking its modification, and sometimes even retraction, by the fundamental design of the work, the action of the argument and the argument of the action.[53] In a similar way, Strauss remarks in "Historicism": "While the modern historian accepts as binding the rules which I have intimated, he very rarely lives up to them."[54] The approach in *Natural Right and History* is substantially different. As Strauss takes on Heidegger in chapter 1, he does not rush to the conclusion that historicism is the product of intellectual laziness, a mere prejudice, or a smug and petrified form of self-criticism. In fact, in *Natural Right and History*, Strauss at least acts as if he cannot even discuss the more fundamental "theses" of historicism, which appear to expose "the dogmatic character of the basic premise of philosophy": "the whole is actually always incomplete and never truly a whole"; it is essentially changing; it is unintelligible; "human thought essentially depends on something that cannot be anticipated"; "to be" does not necessarily mean "to be always."[55] There is indeed a clear bridge between the 1941 "Historicism" lecture and chapter 1 of *Natural Right and History*, found in Strauss's statement that "there has always been a glaring contrast between the way in which historicism understands the thought of the past and genuine understanding of the thought of the past; the undeniable possibility of historical objectivity is explicitly or implicitly denied by historicism in all its forms."[56] And precisely because Strauss takes historicism more seriously in *Natural Right and History* than he does in the "Historicism" lecture, he is able to raise radical questions about the validity of the much-vaunted "experience of history."

The 1942 "What Can We Learn from Political Theory?" gets closer to the center of gravity of *Natural Right and History*. The lecture as a whole is a prolegomenon to or a vindication of the enterprise contained or furthered by *Natural Right and History*. In particular, it is a warning against intruding overly theoretical considerations into the realm of practical politics.[57] The resistance to an excessive harmonization of theory with practice is directly relevant to Strauss's critique of modern political philosophy and its attempted politicization of philosophy, with potentially detrimental effects to both philosophy and politics.[58] Strikingly, in this 1942 lecture Strauss suggests that modernity—or at least modern utopianism—is founded as "a compromise between Machiavelli and the tradition." Whether this statement diverges from the estimation of Machiavelli's role as founder provided in *Natural Right and History* is unclear, especially since modern utopianism is not an explicit theme in *Natural Right and History*. But if modern utopianism is represented in *Natural Right and History* by Hobbes's project to "guarantee the actualization of the right social order,"[59] then *Natural Right and History* holds similarly that not Machiavelli but a successor of his is the founder of modern utopianism: "No Scipionic dream illumined by a true vision of the whole reminds his readers of the ultimate futility of all that men can do. Of political philosophy thus understood, Hobbes is indeed the founder."[60]

The lecture from 1945, "The Frame of Reference in the Social Sciences," pulls together several threads in the fabric of *Natural Right and History*. Strauss's concern with a comprehensive frame, framework, or scheme for analyzing political (and natural) phenomena is clearly visible in *Natural*

Right and History, especially in his confrontation with Heidegger and Weber in chapters 1 and 2. In the 1945 lecture, however, Strauss all but identifies "divine law"—understood as the common ground between the Greek way and the Hebrew way—as the appropriate starting point for just such an analysis. Aided by the powerful and lucid presentation in the "Frame" lecture, one might begin to see all of *Natural Right and History* as devoted to the recovery of that frame of reference, if that recovery is understood to include the demonstration of its necessity, as well as a confrontation with the obstacles that face it. The idea of an appropriate frame of reference fits well with the end of chapter 2 of *Natural Right and History*: "The information that classical philosophy supplies about its origins suffices, especially if that information is supplemented by consideration of the most elementary premises of the Bible, for reconstructing the essential character of 'the natural world.'"[61]

The 1946 "Natural Right" lecture, the one closest in time to *Natural Right and History*, is likewise close in spirit to it, but it has telling differences of emphasis. Reading the 1946 lecture alongside *Natural Right and History* raises fundamental questions about the relations among conventionalism, historicism, and philosophy. While it is still "on the way" to *Natural Right and History*, it may, in one respect, get even more directly to the heart of the matter than the book does. Insofar as it is not as polemically engaged with historicism and positivism, it appears to state more starkly the fundamental alternative between conventionalism and natural right. On the other hand, since *Natural Right and History* does present the *philosophic* conventionalism of the first philosophers, as well as of a philosopher such as Lucretius,[62] Strauss's view in the book may be that while conventionalism is *the* alternative to natural right, it is not the alternative to philosophy. It is also possible, as one can see from the development from the 1941 "Historicism" to *Natural Right and History*, that the 1946 lecture is a way station to Strauss's greater appreciation of the challenge of historicism as the alternative to philosophy. Moreover, one also cannot leave out the role of divine revelation. In this connection, we observe that the book and the 1946 lecture treat somewhat differently the debate between the Averroists and the Thomists as to how to read Aristotle on natural right. Both here and in *Natural Right and History*, Strauss looks for a "safe middle way" between Averroes, whose interpretation is in "manifest conflict with Aristotle's explicit statement that there is a natural right," and Thomas Aquinas, whose interpretation is in "manifest conflict with Aristotle's explicit statement that *all* natural right is changeable."[63] As distinguished from *Natural Right and History*, however, the 1946 lecture concludes that if *Aquinas* is right in asserting the existence of natural right, *Averroes* is right "regarding *any* unqualified rules of natural right."[64] He follows this conclusion by minimizing the difference between Averroes and Thomas Aquinas: "Thomas can afford to assert the immutability of the principles of natural right *merely* because he admits a *divine* right in addition to natural right."[65] The 1946 formulation leaves open the possibility that Thomas used the article of faith in divine intervention as a kind of exit clause to his unconditional assertion of an immutable natural right (or, more precisely, natural law).

To sum up: these hitherto ignored texts of Strauss, and the interpretative essays we include alongside them, will contribute to a revival of a study of the book as a healthy and self-sufficient whole and exclusively on its own. The introductory essays that precede each of Strauss's lectures or manuscripts do not merely indicate their context or the circumstances in which they emerge but are intended to guide the reader through Strauss's arguments, making explicit certain aspects that might otherwise go unnoticed.

It is now time to give the word to Leo Strauss himself, caught unawares in his workshop or in the middle of his lectures.

Notes

1. We would like to thank John Tryneski, Nathan Tarcov, and Charles Myers for their unfailing support of this project, in some cases since 2012. We are also grateful to the two anonymous reviewers for a number of good suggestions and criticisms, as well as to friendly criticism by Catherine Zuckert, Susan Shell, and Timothy Burns, among others. The responsibility for any remaining flaws is our own. Valuable support for this book was provided by the James Madison Program in American Ideals and Institutions at Princeton University, and the hospitable environment provided by the program for J. A. Colen's work on this book, which was mainly funded by Fundação para a Ciência e Tecnologia. Svetozar Minkov's work was supported by a research leave from Roosevelt University.

2. See "An Introduction to Natural Right (1931)" in Strauss, *Hobbes's Critique of Religion and Related Writings*, ed. Gabriel Bartlett and Svetozar Minkov (Chicago: University of Chicago Press, 2011).

3. Leo Strauss, during a 1954–55 lecture series in Jerusalem, declared that political philosophy was "in a state of decay and perhaps of putrefaction, if it has not vanished altogether" (*WIPP*, 17.). The lecture was first published, in part and in English, only in 1957, as "What Is Political Philosophy?," in the *Journal of Politics* 19, no. 3 (August). According to an accompanying note, it was "a revised version of a portion of the Judah L. Magnes Lectures which were delivered at the Hebrew University in Jerusalem in December 1954

and January 1955. A Hebrew translation with English summary of this version appeared in *Iyyun*, April 1955." It is one of his more moving texts.

4. The second set of Walgreen Lectures was given by Strauss in 1954, in which he pursued "the problem of Machiavelli." It was eventually published as *Thoughts on Machiavelli*.

5. See Strauss to Helmut Kuhn, *Independent Journal of Philosophy* 2 (1978): 24.

6. Posthumously published lectures that date from 1941, 1942, and 1943, for example, include "German Nihilism," "What Can We Learn from Political Theory?," "The Living Issues of German Postwar Philosophy," and "The Re-education of Axis Countries concerning the Jews." And there were certainly many others.

7. Peter M. Rutkoff and William B. Scott, *New School: A History of the New School for Social Research* (New York: Free Press, 1986), 84–106 and 137–43. For a few corrections of this valuable book, see the review by Strauss's friend, Hans Speier, in *Contemporary Sociology* 16, no. 3 (May 1987): 278–79.

8. We know very little about their relationship, but in 1953, Strauss wrote to Seth Benardete that Asch was "a very decent chap," a "'psychologist'" who "feels the need to study Plato's and Aristotle's doctrine *peri psyches* with [Strauss]." Strauss and Asch applied for a grant from the Ford Foundation (in the section on behavioral social studies!) to study this doctrine in "some quiet place or places" for a whole year (Florence is mentioned). Strauss to Asch, February 17, 1953, Leo Strauss Papers, box 4, folder 18, Special Collections, University of Chicago Library.

9. Cf. *Encyclopedia Judaica*: https://www.jewishvirtuallibrary.org/jsource/judaica/ejud_0002_0015_0_15530.html (accessed June 1, 2016).

10. Rutkoff and Scott, *New School*, 143.

11. "A new booklet, 'Plato's Theory of Truth' by Heidegger, has appeared. Strauss says it is the most brazen thing he has run into." Alfred Schutz to Aron Gurwitsch, February 4, 1948, in *Philosophers in Exile: The Correspondence of Alfred Schutz and Aron Gurwitsch, 1939–1959*, ed. Richard Grathoff (Bloomington: Indiana University Press, 1989), 97.

12. In 1951, he was called back to the Graduate Faculty. For twenty-three years there, he taught classical and modern political philosophy, including American political thought. White was the undergraduate teacher of Werner Dannhauser, Richard Kennington, and Thomas MacDonald, among others. From 1961 through 1966, during a difficult period of transition for the New School and the Graduate Faculty, he served as dean of the faculty. His contributions to *Social Research* were perhaps more numerous than those of any other faculty member.

13. Interview quoted in Steven Smith, *The Cambridge Companion to Leo Strauss* (Cambridge: Cambridge University Press, 2009), 25.

14. *LAM*, 3. Yet "[e]ach of us here is compelled to find his bearings by his own powers, however defective they may be" (*LAM*, 8). See chap. 11, "Strauss as an Educator," from Michael P. Zuckert and Catherine H. Zuckert, *Leo Strauss and the Problem of Political Philosophy* (Chicago: University of Chicago Press, 2014), 289–310.

15. In 1943, it was renamed "Readings in Political Philosophy; Utopias and Political Science. Interpretation of Plato's *Republic*" and in 1948 received its definitive name:

"Plato's Political Philosophy and Its Metaphysical Foundations. Interpretation of Plato's *Republic*."

16. " Absolutism and Constitutionalism, Ancient and Modern," or "Readings in Political Philosophy: Reason of State and the Absolutist Concept of Government"; "Basic Problems in Democracy" or "Principles of Liberal Democracy"; "The Problem of Equality." Assisted by Howard White, Strauss taught about "political liberty and separation of powers," and "The United States Constitution: Theory (new) and Practice," a course that was co-taught with Phillips Bradley.

17. Leo Strauss Papers, box 26, folders 10–11: reviews and letters to Strauss about *Natural Right and History*, 1953.

18. The famous quote from Ernst Troeltsch in *NRH*, p. 2, is taken from a translation of Otto von Gierke's work *Natural Law and the Theory of Society*, translated with introduction by Ernest Barker (Cambridge: Cambridge University Press, 1934), 1: 201–22. Gierke's theory of society inferred from natural law many social institutions, including a theory of corporations.

19. *NRH*, 6.

20. In the letter to Eric Voegelin dated October 12, 1950, Strauss responds to Voegelin's criticism of Strauss's "nondialectical" mode of presentation in this way: "[the Walgreen Lectures] did not do more than present the problem of natural right as an unsolved problem." *Faith and Political Philosophy: The Correspondence between Leo Strauss and Eric Voegelin, 1934–1964*, ed. Peter Emberley and Barry Cooper (Columbia: University of Missouri Press, 2004), 151.

21. In fact, years later, faced with Helmut Kuhn's criticism of the book, Strauss conceded in a letter: "I had to write a *précis raisonné* of the history of natural right." Strauss to Kuhn, undated (but likely from 1957), in *Independent Journal of Philosophy* 2 (1978): 23. See, however, how Strauss dismisses "the assumption that the Platonic dialogues do not convey a teaching" as "absurd." *CM*, 51.

22. "Political Philosophy and History," *Journal of the History of Ideas* (January 1949): 30.

23. Ibid., 47.

24. Ibid., 49 and 50.

25. J. A. Colen would like to thank Catherine Zuckert for helping him clarify these ideas and even expressions—and for an amazing time spent reading Plato's *Republic*—as well as seemingly stern advice.

26. In Richard Kennington's formulation, in each pair the first is "the root of which the other is the florescence." See Kennington, "Strauss's Natural Right and History," *Review of Metaphysics* 35, no. 1 (September 1981): 62.

27. We should note that it is far from certain that Strauss's "teaching" was unambiguously reflective of his most important concerns.

28. It is pertinent here to recall what Strauss says about Xenophon. Xenophon allows himself to use the "specific immunity of the commentator or historian to show what he has in mind regarding serious issues in his 'historical' works rather than in the works where he presents his doctrine" (OSCPP). Cf. also Strauss, "Farabi's Plato," in *Louis Ginz-*

berg: Jubilee Volume on the Occasion of his 70th Birthday, ed. Saul Lieberman, Shalom Spiegel, Solomon Zeitlin, and Alexander Marx (New York: American Academy for Jewish Research, 1945), 375. Eugene R. Sheppard, *Leo Strauss and the Politics of Exile* (Hanover, NH: University Press of New England, 2006), 93 and the reference on 168n67. In a similar vein, in order to identify Strauss's own intention, we too must take his venture seriously. As he says (H 1941), Averroes or Aquinas understood Aristotle better than most modern authors despite their ignorance of Greek and of the many facts about Aristotle and the Greeks that the average historian knows today. Their superior understanding rests on the fact that their reading was guided by their desire to discover the essential truth of the doctrines contained in Aristotle's works. They were interested in the truth in Aristotle because they approached his thought "philosophically," not in a historical way but as natural men.

29. Cf. not only *PAW*, 24ff., but also, e.g., the first chapter of *TOM*.

30. But not lying. Even the pious ascetic was able to leave the city under siege telling the truth about himself. "Farabi's Plato," in *WIPP*, 135–37.

31. *NRH*, 31–32.

32. The first—and most famous—biblical story of David and the prophet Nathan establishes the parallel between the prophet and the philosopher: the prophet's censorship of King David finds its "nearest parallel . . . in the Socratic writings" when Socrates reproves "his former companion, the tyrant Critias." Strauss, "Jerusalem and Athens," *SPPP*, 173. The second one, taken from the book of Kings, chapter 21, reappears as a vivid example in Strauss's 1962 seminar on natural right (lecture 8, October 31, Leo Strauss Papers, box 79, audiocassette). Strauss explains that "the ground given by Naboth is the sacredness of the inherited estate or lot . . . And this is obviously not a universally valid principle . . . In all modern societies this has long been abolished . . . Now Plato would say the principle to which Naboth appeals is the sound one . . . [since] the polity of Plato's *Laws* is based on this principle that the inherited lot cannot be alienated." Cf. "Jerusalem and Athens: Some Preliminary Reflections" (*SPPP*, 172–73) and Xenophon, *Memorabilia* 1.2.32–33. But there are limits to this parallel, a fact that also emerges in "Progress or Return" (*RCPR*, 251). Here Strauss contrasts the passage with Simonides in the *Hiero*: Nathan's rebuke is serious and ruthless, Simonides' playful and elegant. Strauss goes further in his analysis: kingship was established for the common good, and if the vineyard was needed for something in favor of the commonwealth, the king could have disposed of it through compensation. Now: "This sacredness of the inherited estate is the most wise institution possible . . . [although] no one can deny that Jezebel acted illegally and Naboth and Ahab acted legally. But the positivists will say, why should one prefer acting legally to acting illegally? Ultimately that's a non-rational preference. Some like legal action; others don't. Conventionalists, with whom Socrates argues in the *Gorgias* and the *Republic*, would say this: 'The case for law as a necessary evil for the many is very strong, but it is, indeed, only a case for a law as a necessary evil for the many, not for the really—for the *hombres*, for the he-men'" (seminar on natural right [1962]).

33. WL, lecture 2, pp. 5–6 and 7, Leo Strauss, "Natural Right and History: Six lectures delivered at the University of Chicago, Autumn, 1949, under the auspices of the Charles R. Walgreen Foundation for the Study of American Institutions," Regenstein

Library, University of Chicago; the same passage is fully stated in *NRH*, 74–76. We think it is significant, especially since the digression compelled Strauss to abridge the last lectures.

34. And is similar to what is said in the lectures of 1946 and 1948: "Jerusalem and Athens" (1946), a paper made available to us by Nathan Tarcov, and "Reason and Revelation" (1948), in Heinrich Meier, *Leo Strauss and the Theological-Political Problem* (Cambridge: Cambridge University Press, 2006).

35. See in FRSS: "Our frame of reference is the outgrowth of the combination of two radically different traditions [Greek and Hebrew]." In addition, *the* problem of Strauss's investigations reappears in the last words of the first lecture in this volume: "we have to choose between philosophy and the Bible" (WCL).

36. See *NRH*, 1. However, in *CM* he explains that the right to life, liberty, and the pursuit of happiness is just "the means" or condition for virtue, which the modern state provides without fostering virtue (*CM*, 32).

37. Michael Zuckert, *Natural Rights and the New Republicanism* (Princeton: Princeton University Press, 1994), 3. If these rights are here implied not to be self-evident, Strauss looks like even less a fan of modern human rights than MacIntyre. Compare *NRH*, 1 and ff., with 224ff.

38. See Lincoln's Second Inaugural Address.

39. Kennington, "Strauss's Natural Right and History," 60. Cf. final paragraph of *NRH* on the centrality of the "status of 'individuality.'"

40. *NRH*, 13.

41. Ibid. According to Kennington, however, there is no doubt that Strauss thought this break occurred long before Locke and the philosophers who inspired the words Strauss commends. Obviously, Rousseau and/or Burke did indeed pave the way for extreme versions of historicism.

42. *PPH*, chap. 6, "History." However, we are not conflating modernity with historicism: Strauss speaks of different waves, but there may be good arguments for Hobbes's making the fate of reason/philosophy depend on a historically unfolding project. We should point out as well that the image of Locke in this essay, and its dependence on Hooker and the tradition of natural law, also appears to be placed within a broader and substantially different context from that of the image found in the Walgreen Lectures: "Condorcet believed that modern political philosophy was founded by Locke. Now, it is well-known how much Locke owed to the judicious Hooker; Hooker, in his turn, follows, as far as principles are concerned, Thomas Aquinas and the Fathers; the latter do nothing other than expound the views of the Bible on the one hand, and of Greek and Roman philosophy and of the Roman lawyers on the other" (OMPT).

43. Heinrich Meier, *Leo Strauss and the Theologico-Political Problem*, trans. Marcus Brainard (Cambridge: Cambridge University Press, 2006), 67; see also the following pages.

44. Susan Shell, "Natural Right in the Face of History: Comments on Chapter One of *Natural Right and History*" (unpublished lecture), p. 28.

45. See OSCPP.

46. To understand the status of this lecture by Strauss, it helps to look back to 1936

and *The Political Philosophy of Hobbes* while looking forward to *Natural Right and History*, as well as to the 1954 Hobbes essay in the 1959 *What Is Political Philosophy?*

47. The 1964 course on Hobbes does not constitute, we believe, a major advance in Strauss's understanding of Hobbes.

48. In an archival note from the 1940s, Strauss anticipates publishing *Natural Right and History* in 1951–52 and *Persecution and the Art of Writing* in 1951; the dates ended up being 1953 and 1952. Leo Strauss Papers, box 18, folder 15.

49. An important note in *NRH*, 158n32.

50. See OSCPP and the final essay in this volume.

51. *PAW*, 158.

52. See H 1941.

53. *PAW*, 30.

54. See H 1941 and Tanguay's essay in this volume. Strauss adds: "That study known to me which comes nearest to the goal of historical exactness, is J. Klein's analysis of Greek logistics and the genesis of modern algebra"; cf. *NRH*, 78n34, and *WIPP*, 75n4.

55. *NRH*, 31.

56. *NRH*, 32.

57. Developed in the introduction to *Natural Right and History* and in chapter 6B of the same book.

58. *NRH*, 34.

59. *NRH*, 186, 191, 194.

60. *NRH*, 177.

61. *NRH*, 80. Chapter 3 of *Natural Right and History* does, however, go further in the direction of a *critique* of divine law than what we find in the "Frame" lecture.

62. *NRH*, chap. 3; also p. 11.

63. See NR 1946.

64. In *NRH* Strauss is, in a sense, bolder since he supports that statement by reference to his own interpretation of Halevi in his *Persecution and the Art of Writing.*

65. This formulation—and Strauss's reference to Thomas's "falling back on *Divine* dispensation"—either sheds prospective light on, or provides an interesting contrast with, this statement in *Natural Right and History*: "the ultimate consequence of the Thomistic view of natural law is that natural law is practically inseparable not only from natural theology—i.e., from a natural theology which is, in fact, based on belief in biblical revelation—but even from revealed theology" (*NRH*, 164). See NR 1946.

1

Introduction to Political Philosophy

Leo Strauss on the Relation of Theory to Practice

NATHAN TARCOV

Leo Strauss wrote "What Can We Learn from Political Theory?" for delivery at the General Seminar of the Summer Course at the New School on July 17, 1942. The theme of the course was "Social Science and Political Action in Relation to the Present Situation."[1] Strauss's lecture includes what may be his fullest statement about the relation of political philosophy to political action as well as rare statements about what he considered would be reasonable political action in the then-current situation. The lecture was evidently carefully considered, composed, and corrected, though Strauss did not attempt to publish it. He may have had second thoughts about some of the arguments he advanced in it, or he may merely have chosen to concentrate his literary efforts in other directions.

Theory and Practice in *Natural Right and History*

The question of the relation of theory to practice, specifically the relation of political philosophy, that is, of what Strauss called classical political philosophy, to political action, only occasionally rises to the surface of *Natural Right and History*. The introduction to the book argues negatively that the rejection of natural right seems to lead to "disastrous consequences," and that its contemporary social scientific rejection leads to nihilism,[2] but it does not promise that a recovery of natural right would provide positive concrete guidance for political action. At the end of the first chapter, "Natural Right and the Historical Approach,"[3] Strauss laments that in modernity "philosophy as such had become thoroughly politicized," that it had become a weapon and an instrument.[4] He contrasts that with the original character of philosophy as "the humanizing quest for the eternal order" and "a pure source of humane inspiration and aspiration." This contrast leaves open whether before its modern politicization philosophy actually "humanized" political practice, rendering it more humane, or merely rendered the practitioners of philosophy and those affected by it more fully human. In the fourth chapter, "Classic Natural Right," Strauss goes so far as to identify prudence with obedience to the law of the cosmos ruled by God rather than with wise political action in any actual political community ruled by human beings.[5]

One should not hastily conclude from this fantastic statement, however, that the argument of *Natural Right and History* renders philosophy or classic natural right irrelevant to prudent political action. Toward the end of that chapter on classic natural right, Strauss attributes to both Plato and Aristotle the view that "there is a universally valid hierarchy of ends, but there are no universally valid rules of action." As a result, in deciding what to do "here and now," one has to consider not only which end is "higher in rank, but also which is most urgent in the circumstances."[6] Thus it appears that theory or philosophy provides the hierarchy of ends but that is "insufficient for guiding our actions," which must depend on prudence to judge urgency in particular circumstances.[7] The chapter concludes by indicating that the classics shared with Montesquieu a concern for maintaining the latitude for statesmanship not unduly trammeled by supposedly universal rules.[8]

Strauss returns to the issue of the relation between theory and practice or prudence toward the end of *Natural Right and History*. Strauss warns there that the distinction between theory and practice is blurred if one understands all theory as essentially in the service of practice. Although science may be concerned with "truth as such, regardless of its utility,"[9] political theory is concerned not only with understanding the actual but with "the quest for what ought to be," and is "'theoretically practical' (i.e., deliberative at a second remove)."[10] I take this obscure statement to refer to the sort of theory he attributed to the classics that elaborated a hierarchy of ends but left to prudence the practical guidance of our actions. Still Strauss insists, however paradoxically, that prudence cannot be seen properly without genuine *theoria*.[11] Genuine practice entails the possibility of "a human life which has a significant and undetermined future," denied by the historicism that also denies the possibility of theory.[12]

The Situation, Title, and Form

Since Strauss wrote this lecture with an eye to the contemporary situation as required by the theme of the summer seminar, it may be helpful to remind ourselves that he composed it at a time when Allied victory in World

War II was by no means assured. Axis armies were continuing to advance into the Soviet Union and in North Africa, and Japanese gains in Asia still overshadowed the recent American victory at Midway.

Strauss makes clear at the start of "What Can We Learn from Political Theory?" that the title was at least in part assigned rather than of his own choosing. He would have preferred to speak of political *philosophy* rather than political *theory*. The term political theory implicitly denies the traditional division of the sciences, according to which political science is practical not theoretical, implying instead that all science is ultimately practical or that pure theory is the basis and safest guide for reasonable political practice.[13] Strauss's terminological preference therefore points directly to the question of the practical bearing of political philosophy. For Strauss takes the question "What can we learn from political philosophy?" to mean, in line with the overall title of the summer course, what can we learn from political philosophy that can serve *to guide political action*?

Strauss gives a definition of political philosophy that might lead one to expect it to provide guidance to political practice: "the coherent reflection carried on by politically minded people concerning the essentials of political life as such, and the attempt to establish, on the basis of such reflection, the right standards of judgment concerning political institutions and actions . . . to discover *the* political truth."[14] Strauss's preliminary remarks conclude by distinguishing political philosophy from political *thought*, which is coeval with the human race.[15]

The deliberately scholastic form of Strauss's lecture is striking. As in Aquinas's *Summa Theologica*, Strauss first presents the negative arguments (that we can learn *nothing* from political philosophy), followed by an argument "to the contrary" taken from "authority" (Plato), and then the positive arguments (what we *can* learn from ancient political philosophy).

The Case against Learning from Political Philosophy

Strauss argues the negative case on three grounds: (1) there are many contradictory political philosophies, so political philosophy can be at best clear knowledge of the problems or questions, not of the solutions or answers, and so cannot be a safe guide for action; (2) practical wisdom, shrewd estimation of the situation, rather than political philosophy is needed for reasonable political action; and (3) political philosophy is ineffectual, merely reflecting rather than guiding political practice, since all significant political ideas come from statesmen, lawyers, and prophets rather than from political philosophers.

In the second negative argument, that practical wisdom rather than political philosophy is needed to guide action, Strauss avers the following:

> I have not the slightest doubt as to the possibility of devising an intelligent international policy, for example, without having any recourse to political philosophy: that this war has to be won, that the only guarantee for a somewhat longer peace period after the war is won is a sincere Anglo-Saxon–Russian entente, that the Anglo-Saxon nations and the other nations interested in, or dependent on, Anglo-Saxon preponderance must not disarm nor relax in their armed vigilance, that you cannot throw power out of the window without facing the danger of the first gangster coming along taking it up, that the existence of civil liberties all over the world depends on Anglo-Saxon preponderance—to know these broad essentials of the situation, one does not need a single lesson in political philosophy. In fact, people adhering to fundamentally different political philosophies have reached these same conclusions.

Having first sketched the negative case, Strauss then in good scholastic fashion presents an argument "from *authority*": "quite a few men of superior intelligence were convinced that political philosophy is the necessary condition of the right order of civil society." He quotes "the most superior and the most famous of these men, that evils will not cease in the cities until the philosophers have become kings or the kings have become philosophers," referring, of course, to *The Republic* of Plato. He goes on to quote Pascal to the effect that for Plato and Aristotle political philosophy is of some practical use in minimizing the harm done by the madmen who rule us.

The Case for Learning from Political Philosophy

In the third, longest, and final part of the lecture Strauss makes his positive argument for the practical utility of what turns out to be *classical* political philosophy. This positive argument turns out to be not a refutation but a *modification* of the negative arguments. It concedes the force of the first two negative claims, that political philosophy is knowledge of the problems, not of the solutions, and that common sense or practical wisdom, not political philosophy, is the guide for reasonable political action. Thus the scholastic form of Strauss's lecture brings out the peculiar character of his view of the relation of theory to practice or of political philosophy to political action: his case for the relevance of political philosophy to political action rests on views of political philosophy and the role of prudence that share common ground with the case against the relevance of political philosophy to political action. Strauss's positive argument adds, however, that although reasonable political action is discovered by prudent statesmen without the need for political philosophy, political philosophy is needed to defend such action when it is challenged by erroneous political teachings.[16] This may be related to what Strauss means near the end of *Natural Right and History* when he calls political theory "deliberative at a second remove."[17]

Strauss illustrates this role for political philosophy with reference to what he characterized in the negative section as an intelligent international policy that could be arrived at without any recourse to political philosophy. He restates this policy as follows:

> human relations cannot become good if the human beings themselves do not become good first, and hence it would be a great achievement indeed if foundations for a peace lasting two generations could be laid, and hence the choice is not between imperialism and abolition of imperialism, but between the tolerably decent imperialism of the Anglo-Saxon brand and the intolerably indecent imperialism of the Axis brand.

Strauss's point here seems to be that since human beings are *not* going to become good, we cannot expect international relations to become simply good and must accept tolerably decent imperialism (perhaps the British Empire or American administration of the Philippines). For the same reason, his first statement requires armed vigilance and even preponderance of power by Britain and the United States to maintain civil liberties around the world after the war.[18]

Strauss notes that such a policy is attacked not only by those who would shirk the burdens of "a decent hegemony," but also by "infinitely more generous political thinkers" with utopian views of human nature that render power irrelevant and hegemony dispensable. (This particular danger is explained further in Strauss's succeeding contrast between ancient and modern utopianism.) Such prudent policy arrived at without the aid of political philosophy needs to be protected against such utopian illusions by "a genuine political philosophy reminding us of the limits set to all human hopes and wishes." Strauss further illustrates the role of political philosophy in protecting prudence against erroneous teachings by asserting: "If the sophists had not undermined the basic principles of political life, Plato might not have been compelled to elaborate his *Republic*." (I take this remarkable statement to refer to the defense of political justice rather than that of the philosophic life in *The Republic*.) Similarly, Strauss claims that the policy of religious toleration inaugurated by reasonable statesmen in the sixteenth and seventeenth centuries would not have been accepted if political philosophers had not enlightened public opinion and convinced people that it was not their religious or moral duty to rebel against heretical governments. (It should not be but is nonetheless necessary to note that Strauss here characterizes religious toleration as a reasonable policy.)

Although Strauss's positive argument accepts and modifies the second negative argument, that prudent policy is derived from practical wisdom not political philosophy, his positive argument denies the third negative claim, that all significant political concepts are the work of political men rather than philosophers. One fundamental political concept, the concept of natural law or natural right, is of philosophic origin. Natural right is the standard by which classical political philosophers judged all actual political orders and is their guide for reform and improvement. In contrast to natural right, all actual orders are imperfect.[19] This contrast is what Strauss here calls "the legitimate utopianism" of Plato and Aristotle's political philosophy. They did not believe that the perfect condition could be brought about by political action. Strauss admits that we do not need lessons from the tradition of political philosophy to discern the soundness of Churchill's approach, but he adds that "the cause which Churchill's policy is meant to defend would not exist but for the influence" of this tradition. The liberal democratic polities that protect civil liberties would be unthinkable without the tradition of political philosophy and the concept of natural right.

Utopianism Ancient and Modern

In a foreshadowing of a claim made famous in *Natural Right and History*,[20] in "What Can We Learn from Political Theory?" Strauss identifies Machiavelli as the great turning point in the replacement of the traditional utopianism by a new, modern utopianism. More broadly, this contrast between ancient and modern utopianism anticipates the contrast between ancient and modern political philosophy given prominence in that work, though with a distinctive emphasis. Strauss claims here that modern utopianism lowered the standards of conduct to guarantee their realization, but here he attributes this attempt not to Machiavelli himself but to a *reaction* to his teaching that effected "a compromise between Machiavellianism and the tradition."[21] Modern utopianism reduced virtue to enlightened self-interest, and eventually assumed that enlightenment would gradually make the use of force superfluous. Strauss contrasts modern utopianism's assumption that social harmony would follow if all men were interested in raising their standard of living with the view of older philosophers who held that enlightened self-interest would lead to social harmony only if all men could be satisfied with the truly necessary things.

Strauss argues against modern utopianism on several grounds. The appeal to enlightened self-interest weakens the moral fiber that enables men to make sacrifices. Furthermore, enlightened self-interest is in conflict with the desires of at least some people for power, precedence, and dominion. Modern utopianism forgets the existence of evil, as if "all wickedness, nastiness, malevolence, aggressiveness were the outcome of *want*" and could be cured by satisfying men's wants.[22] Strauss therefore rejects the economism, whether in its liberal or its Marxist form, that he regards as inseparable from modern utopianism. He predicts that "the withering away of the State . . . will still be a matter of pious or impious hope [a] long time after the withering away of Marxism." Strauss concludes that the ancient philosophers' insistence that the realization of the ideal is a matter of chance and the theologians' insistence that providence is inscrutable were more realistic than the modern utopian assumption that the realization of the ideal is necessary.

Strauss's thumbnail survey of the history of political philosophy, emphasizing the contrast between classical and modern, enables him to respond to the hitherto neglected first negative argument, that there is such a variety of contradictory political philosophies that there is no political philosophy from which we can learn anything. His survey is meant to show instead that there is a single tradition of political philosophy, "whose adherents were in agreement as regards the fundamentals . . . founded by Socrates, Plato, and Aristotle . . . transformed but not broken under the influence of the biblical virtues of mercy and humility," that "still supplies us with the most needed guidance as regards the fundamentals." That guidance, however, is imperiled by the "spurious utopianism" of modernity that "makes us underestimate the dangers to which the cause of decency and humanity is exposed and always *will* be exposed." He concludes: "The foremost duty of political philosophy today seems to be to counteract this modern utopianism."

Although Strauss diagnoses modern utopianism as the foremost threat to prudent political practice that political philosophy must counteract in his time, he argues that political philosophy is needed "at all times." It is needed to teach us how difficult it is to protect the minimal decency, humanity, and justice taken for granted in free countries and not to expect too much of the future. Political philosophy protects us both against smugly thinking our own society is perfect and against recklessly dreaming we are achieving a future perfect society. Common sense is proof against neither danger but requires the support of political philosophy.

Strauss does not spell out in this lecture precisely how political philosophy knows such things as the existence and persistence of evil, the eventual decay of every human institution, the continuing importance of power, the precariousness of decency, humanity, and justice, the impossibility of permanently abolishing war, or the absolute limits to human progress. Nor does he explain in what way political philosophy knows such things differently from how they might be known through common sense, experience, and history. It would seem to be from a knowledge of human nature, part of the knowledge of nature or the natures. Strauss suggests that such insights come from looking at political things "philosophically, i.e., *sub specie aeternitatis*," seeing that political things in contrast to the whole are "essentially *perishable*," contain the germ of their ultimate destruction, and are therefore not capable of sustaining all our will, hope, faith, and love.[23]

Strauss insists that philosophic recognition of these limits is not pessimistic. He asks: "Do we cease living, and living with reasonable joy, do we cease doing our best although we know with absolute certainty that we are doomed to die?" The lecture concludes by saying that whereas the philosophers advise us to love fate and the Bible promises us God's mercy, the flesh wants an impossible "man-made eternal peace and happiness." The issue of reason and revelation that surfaces only occasionally in *Natural Right and History*[24] appears in the last words of the lecture: "we have to choose between philosophy and the Bible."

What Can We Learn from Political Theory? (1942)

LEO STRAUSS

Lecture to be delivered in the General Seminar of the Summer Course, July 1942[a]

The title of this lecture is not entirely of my own choosing.[25] I do not like very much the term political *theory*;[26] I would prefer to speak of political *philosophy*. Since this terminological question is not entirely verbal, I beg leave to say a few words about it.

The term political theory implies that there is such a thing as *theoretical* knowledge of things *political*. This implication is by no means self-evident. Formerly,[27] *all* political knowledge was considered *practical* knowledge, and *not* theoretical knowledge. I recall the traditional division of the sciences into theoretical and practical sciences. According to that division,[28] political philosophy, or political science, together with ethics and economics, belongs to the practical sciences, just as mathematics and the natural sciences belong to the theoretical sciences. Whoever uses the term political theory tacitly denies that traditional distinction. That denial means one of these two things or both of them: (1) the denial of the distinction between theoretical and practical sciences: *all* science is ultimately *practical* (*scientia propter potentiam*); (2) the basis of *all* reasonable practice is pure theory.[b] A purely theoretical, detached knowledge of things political is the safest guide for political action, just as a purely theoretical, detached knowledge of things physical is the safest guide toward conquest of nature: this is the view underlying the very term political theory.

The term political theory has another important implication. According to present-day usage, theory is essentially different, not only from practice, but above all from *observation*. If a man is asked "How do you account for this or that event?," he may answer: "I have a theory," or "A number of

[a] This lecture was transcribed and annotated by Nathan Tarcov. Steven Smith drew the lecture to his attention. The typescript can be found in the Leo Strauss Papers, box 6, folder 12, Special Collections, University of Chicago Library.

[b] The following handwritten note was added at the bottom of the page: Science, d'où prevoyance; prevoyance, d'où action (Auguste Comte, *Cours de philosophie positive*).

theories may be suggested"; sometimes one is asked: "What is *your*[29] theory?" What is meant by "theory" in such cases is the essentially *hypothetical* assertion of a *cause* of an observed fact. The assertion being essentially hypothetical, it[30] is essentially *arbitrary*: *my* theory. What is *seen*—Hitler's rise to power, for example—is *not* a theory, but our differing *explanations* of Hitler's rise to power are our *theories*. This use of the term theory is of fairly recent date. The original meaning of the Greek verb θεωρεῖν, with which "theory" is connected, is to be an envoy sent to consult an oracle, to present an offering, to be present at festivals;[31] to look at, to behold, to inspect, contemplate, consider, compare . . . ,[a] i.e., the original meaning of the term does not warrant at all the distinction of theory from observation; it rather excludes it; it certainly does not justify the identification, or almost identification, of theory with an essentially *hypothetical* kind of knowledge.

I have some misgivings as regards these two connotations of the term theory, which are, to repeat, (1) the implication that a purely theoretical discussion of political questions is possible, and (2) the view that political knowledge as a whole consists of observation of "data" and hypothetical explanation of these "data"; I prefer therefore the term political philosophy which does not imply these assumptions. By political philosophy, we understand the coherent reflection carried on by politically minded people concerning the essentials of political life as such, and the attempt to establish, on the basis of such reflection, the right standards of judgment concerning political institutions and actions; political philosophy is the attempt to discover *the* political truth. Accordingly, I would not speak of the political philosophy of Hitler, for example, Hitler being not interested in truth and relying on intuition rather than on methodic reflection. It is legitimate, however, to speak of the political *thought*, or of the political *ideas*, of the Nazis. All political philosophy is political thought, but not all political thought is political philosophy.[32] (E.g., the very terms "law" and "father" imply political thought, but not political philosophy. Political thought is as old as the human race, but political philosophy emerged at some definite time in the recorded past.) I think we owe it to philosophy that we do not use its noble name in vain.

I. I shall then discuss the question "What can we learn from political *philosophy*?" For the purpose of a summary discussion, it is advisable to

[a] Strauss takes these definitions from the entries for θεωρέω and θεωρόσ in *Greek-English Lexicon*, Henry George Liddell and Robert Scott (Oxford: Clarendon Press, 1941).

sketch first the arguments in favor of the negative. It seems as if we can learn *nothing* from political philosophy. For: (1) one may doubt whether there exists[33] such a thing deserving to be called political philosophy; (2) even if there were a political philosophy in existence, we would not need it; (3) even if we would need it, its lessons would necessarily be ineffectual.

1. There is *no* political philosophy, because there are *many* political philosophies; only one of them, if any, can be true; and certainly the layman does not know which is the true one. When we ask what can we learn from political philosophy, we mean, of course, what can we learn from the *true* political philosophy? We can learn nothing *from* the wrong political philosophies, although we may learn something *on the occasion* of them. The situation in political philosophy is not fundamentally different from that in the other branches of philosophy. Philosophy means the attempt, constantly renewed, to *find* the truth; the very term philosophy implies that we do *not possess* the truth. Philosophy is at best possession of clear knowledge of the *problems*—it is not possession of clear knowledge of the *solutions* to the problems. The basic questions in all branches of philosophy are as unsolved today as they were at all times; new questions have been raised from time to time; the interest has shifted from one type of questions to others; but the most fundamental, the truly philosophic questions remain unanswered. This is, of course, no objection to philosophy as such: but it *is* an objection to the expectation, or the claim, that philosophy is a safe guide for action. One may try, and people did try, to seclude from the realm of philosophy the questions which do not seem to permit of a universally acceptable answer, but in doing so, one is merely *evading* the questions, not answering them. I have been trying to remind you of that melancholy spectacle called the anarchy of the systems, a phenomenon which is almost as old as philosophy itself and which seems to have so profound roots in the nature of philosophy and of its objects that it is reasonable to expect that it will last as long as philosophy itself. That spectacle becomes perhaps even more melancholic if one considers political or social philosophy by itself.[34] One could take almost any fundamental question of political philosophy, and one could show that no answer exists which is universally accepted by honest seekers of the truth, to say nothing of the partisans of the various camps. (E.g., is justice of the essence of the State?)[35]

2. But even if we could be reasonably certain that a given political philosophy is the true political philosophy, one could say that one cannot learn anything important from it as far as political action is concerned. For that

kind of knowledge which is indispensable for reasonable political action is not philosophic knowledge: practical wisdom, common sense, horse sense, shrewd estimation of the situation, *these* are the intellectual qualities which make up the successful man of affairs: he does not require political philosophy for his guidance. I may refer to the story told in England of H. G. Wells meeting Winston Churchill and asking about the progress of the war. "We're getting along with our idea," said Churchill. "You have an idea?" asked Wells. "Yes," said Churchill, "along the lines of our general policy." "You have a general policy?" Wells persisted. "Yes," answered Churchill, "the K. M. T. policy." "And what is the K. M. T. policy?" asked Wells. "It is this," replied Churchill, "Keep Muddling Through." The fact that this muddling through led to disaster in the case of Singapore and Libya[a] is evidently not a proof of the necessity of political philosophy, considering that neither the Japanese generals[b] nor Rommel are political philosophers to speak of. I have not the slightest doubt as to the possibility of devising an intelligent international policy, for example, without having any recourse to political philosophy: that this war has to be won, that the only guarantee for a somewhat longer peace period after the war is won is a sincere Anglo-Saxon–Russian entente, that the Anglo-Saxon nations and the other nations interested in, or dependent on, Anglo-Saxon preponderance must not disarm nor relax in their armed vigilance, that you cannot throw power out of the window without facing the danger of the first gangster coming along taking it up, that the existence of civil liberties all over the world depends on Anglo-Saxon preponderance—to know these broad essentials of the situation, one does not need a single lesson in political philosophy. In fact, people adhering to fundamentally different political philosophies have reached these same conclusions.

[a] "Gallipoli" and "Egypt" crossed out and "Singapore" and "Libya" handwritten. Gallipoli in particular is known as "Churchill's folly": he tried to open a second front during World War I, which proved an ambitious disaster. The attack on Gallipoli began on the morning of February 19, 1915, and the Gallipoli Campaign lasted nine months before the evacuation in January 1916. Each side sustained 250,000 casualties. "Fortress Singapore" against Japanese invasion turned out to be a myth, with the city taken in 1941. Strauss may have changed Gallipoli to Singapore to stick to cases during World War II. Rommel's victory at Tobruk with the surrender of 35,000 Allied troops on June 21, 1942, lost Libya to the Axis, but Egypt was saved by the Allied victory at the First Battle of El Alamein in July. Strauss was keeping up with the progress of the war.

[b] "Tojo" was crossed out and "the Japanese generals" handwritten. Tojo was the prime minister of Japan during much of World War II, from October 17, 1941, to July 22, 1944.

3. But even if it were true that we could not find our bearings in the political world without being guided by political philosophy, i.e., by the one true political philosophy, the possibility would still remain that the orientation supplied by political philosophy would be ineffectual: political philosophy might teach us what should be done, and yet we might be certain that this knowledge would not have the slightest influence on the unpredictable course of events: a set of microbes killing Hitler may seem to have an infinitely greater political significance than the clearest and best demonstrated lesson in political philosophy. If we look at the whole course of the history of political philosophy, we seem to learn that "it is almost a law of the development of political thought that political conceptions are the by-product of actual political relations" (McIlwain, *Growth*, 391).[a] As Hegel said, the owl of Minerva starts its flight in the dusk: philosophy comes *always* too late for the *guidance* of political action; the philosopher *always* comes *post festum*; philosophy can merely *interpret* the result of political action; it can make us *understand* the State; it cannot teach us what should be *done* with regard to the State. One may wonder whether there are any significant political concepts, or ideas, which are the product of political philosophy: all political ideas seem to go back to political fighters, statesmen, lawyers, prophets. Would philosophers have spoken of mixed constitutions but for the fact that such constitutions had been devised by such nonphilosophic lawgivers as Lycurgus?[36] Would Montesquieu have taught in 1748 that the separation of executive, legislative, and judicial power is desirable but for the fact that such a separation had been effected, to a certain extent, in England by the Act of Settlement of 1701? What is the political philosophy of Plato and Aristotle but a reflection of the Greek political reality? The influence on political events of Alexander the Great is infinitely greater than that of his teacher Aristotle—and Alexander's political activity is diametrically opposed to the principles laid down by Aristotle.

II. Now, even if we have no knowledge *of our own* to oppose to these arguments, we cannot help being impressed by an argument to the contrary which is taken from *authority*. If political philosophy is an evident failure, how is it understandable that quite a few men of superior intelligence were convinced that political philosophy is the necessary condition of the right order of civil society—or, to quote the most superior and the most famous

[a] Reference to Charles Howard McIlwain, *The Growth of Political Thought in the West, from the Greeks to the End of the Middle Ages* (New York: Macmillan, 1932).

of these men, that evils will not cease in the cities until the philosophers have become kings or the kings have become philosophers? Shall we say with Pascal that Plato's *Republic* was meant by Plato himself as a joke? It would certainly be rash to take this for granted. All the more so since Pascal himself continues his remarks on Plato's and Aristotle's political philosophies as follows: "They wrote on politics as if they were organizing an insane asylum; and they pretended to consider politics as something grand, because they knew that the madmen to whom they were talking believed themselves[37] to be kings and emperors. They accepted the assumptions of these madmen, in order to make their madness as harmless as might be." (*Pensées*, Brunschvicg, n. 331.)[a] Even according to Pascal, Plato and Aristotle *did* believe[38] that political philosophy is of *some* practical use.

III. Let us then consider first the second argument, which was to the effect that we can know without any political philosophy what should be done in the political field, as regards international policy, for example. Now, a reasonable policy, I take it, would be along these lines: human relations cannot become good if the human beings *themselves* do not become good first, and hence it would be a great achievement indeed if foundations for a peace lasting two generations could be laid, and hence the choice is not between imperialism and abolition of imperialism, but between the[39] tolerably decent imperialism of the Anglo-Saxon brand and the[40] intolerably indecent imperialism of the Axis brand. Such a policy, as we all know, is[41] by no means generally accepted; it is attacked not only by those who dislike the burden, and the responsibility, which go with a decent hegemony, but above all by a group of infinitely more generous political thinkers who deny the assumptions, implied in that reasonable policy, concerning human nature. If for no other purpose, at least in order to defend a reasonable policy against overgenerous or utopian thought, we would need a genuine political philosophy reminding us of the limits set to all human hopes and wishes. In other words, *even if it were true that man does not need political philosophy absolutely speaking, he does need political philosophy as soon as reasonable political action is endangered by an erroneous political teaching.* If Zeno

[a] Reference to Blaise Pascal, *Pensées* (Paris: Brunschvicg, 1897). The preceding portion of the text reads: "On ne s'imagine Platon et Aristote qu'avec de grandes robes de pédants. C'étaient des gens honnêtes et, comme les autres, riant avec leurs amis; et, quand ils se sont divertis à faire leurs Lois et leurs Politiques, ils l'ont fait en se jouant; c'était la partie la moins philosophe et la moins sérieuse de leur vie, la plus philosophe était de vivre simplement et tranquillement."

had not denied the reality of motion, it would not have been necessary to *prove* the reality of motion. If the sophists had not undermined the basic principles of political life, Plato might not have been compelled to elaborate his *Republic*. Or, to take another example, people would not have been willing to accept the policy of toleration which was the only way out of the religious wars and hatreds of the sixteenth and seventeenth centuries if they had not become convinced by political philosophers that it was *not* their religious or moral duty to rebel against heretical governments; the political philosophers did not *inaugurate* the policy of toleration; *this* was done by reasonable statesmen, but these statesmen never would have succeeded but for the help of the political philosophers who enlightened public opinion.

These and similar examples merely show that political philosophy is necessary to *defend* a reasonable course of action which was discovered, and embarked upon, independently of political philosophy, against allegedly true political teachings which endanger that reasonable course of action; these and similar examples, I say, merely show the necessity of political philosophy as a sort of political *apologetic*. Such apologetics are evidently useful, and since they are bound to be backed by the politicians or statesmen whom they support, they are not necessarily ineffectual. The *difficulty* concerns political philosophy proper, which is not the *handmaid* of a reasonable policy, but its architect, as it were.

Let me put the question this way: Is it true that all significant political concepts or theses are the by-product of political life, or the work of statesmen, politicians, lawyers, prophets, and not of philosophers? For argument's sake, I will assume that it is true in all cases in which it could seem to[42] be true before one has sifted the evidence. There is certainly one fundamental political concept which is necessarily of philosophic origin, because its very conception is, so to speak, identical with the emergence of philosophy as such. This concept is the concept of *natural law* or *natural right*. For "nature" is *the* fundamental philosophic discovery. Truth, Being, even World, and all other terms designating the object of philosophy are unquestionably older than philosophy, but the first man who used the term "nature"—I think it was Odysseus or Hermes, the god of thieves, merchants, and Athenian democracy—was the first philosopher. The only contribution of philosophy to politics of which we can be absolutely certain is the concept of natural law or natural right, a law or right which is not made by man nor by gods, which has the same force everywhere, and which sets an absolute limit to human arbitrariness.

"Nature" was the first and decisive and, I think, the most unambiguous discovery of philosophy. But one does not understand the meaning of the term nature if one does not bear in one's mind that from which nature is distinguished and to which it is opposed. If everything were nature or natural, nature would be a very empty concept. The men who discovered "nature" conceived of nature as the opposite of *convention* or *law*. Natural things, they observed, are everywhere the same, but the conventions vary from country to country, from city to city. Fire burns in Persia as well as in Greece, that fire burns is *necessary*; men are generated by men, and dogs by dogs—these things are *necessary*, but the laws concerning inheritance, theft, sacrifices, etc., are different in different countries and even in the same country at different times: these laws are essentially *arbitrary*, they are conventions. On the basis of that distinction the idea arose that it should be possible to discover such an order of life as is good and right *everywhere*, because it is in accordance with the one and unchangeable *nature* of *man*; this *natural* order is the only truly legitimate standard for judgments on the arbitrary enactments of monarchs and republics, and it is the only reliable guide for reform and improvement. Up to then, people had tacitly or expressly identified the good with the inherited or the old; from that moment, men began to *distinguish* the good from the old: "We are seeking the good, and not the old" (Aristotle).[a] With regard to this fact, we may say: philosophy is *the* antitraditional force; the liberation from the opinions of the past, the opening up of new vistas is, and always has been, of the essence of philosophy. As long as philosophy was living up to its own innate standard, philosophers as such, by their merely being philosophers, prevented those who were willing to listen to them from identifying *any actual* order, however satisfactory in many respects, with the *perfect* order: political philosophy is the eternal challenge to the philistine. There never has been and there never will be a time when this medicine administered by political philosophy has been and will be superfluous, although it must always be administered, as all medicine must, with discretion. This holds true in particular of our time; for in our time we are confronted not merely with the philistines of old who identify the good with the old or the actual, but with the philistines of progress who identify the good with the new and the future. But of this I shall have to speak somewhat later.

If it is true that the concept of a natural law, or of a natural order, is

[a] *Politics* 1269a4–5.

coeval with philosophy itself, we are justified in speaking of the legitimate utopianism inherent in philosophy as such. *This* utopianism is the very soul of Plato's and Aristotle's political philosophy, whose primary and guiding purpose is to discover that "constitution," that order of civil society, which is "natural." And this utopianism is *legitimate* because it is not *deceptive*: the philosophers I am speaking of call the perfect order of society an object of εὐχή, which means both wish and prayer; that perfect order is the object of the wish, or the prayer, of all *decent people*. Since it is acceptable, and meant to be acceptable, to decent people only, it is *not a theoretical* construction, but a *practical* ideal. By calling it candidly an object of wish or prayer, they left no doubt as to the gulf separating the ideal from reality; they considered that the realization of the ideal is a matter of *chance*, of lucky circumstances which may, or may not, arise. They did not make any *predictions*. While completely suspending their judgments concerning the *realization* of the ideal, they were definite as to the ideal itself: this ideal was, and was meant to be, the standard of sincere, uncompromising judgments on the real. The practical meaning of this utopianism was not, to repeat, to make any predictions as to the future course of events; it was merely to point out the direction which efforts of improvement would have to take. They did not seriously believe that the perfect order of society would ever become a reality, for being an object of wish or prayer, there is[43] no necessary reason why it should; but they felt that *any* actual order could bear improvement, *substantial* improvement. The relation of the ideal, or the utopia, to reality, as they conceived of it, may be described this way: there is a common, ordinary civil justice which consists in obedience to the law of the land and just administration of that law; that justice is not concerned with the justice of the law itself; it is for this reason a very imperfect justice, for every law, every legal order is bound to be only imperfectly just; therefore justice must be supplemented by *equity*, which is the correction of *legal* justice in the direction of perfect justice; the equitable order, or, as we might prefer to say, the order of charity is the utopian order; that utopian order by itself is essentially the object of *wish* or *prayer*, and not of political action; equity, or charity, by itself is[44] not able to subsist on this earth without the solid, somewhat brutal, imperfectly just, substructure of common justice; common justice must be "completed," corrected by considerations of equity or charity—it can never be supplanted by them, although all decent men would wish, or pray, that it could.

It is for this reason that traditional political philosophy, or moral philosophy, frequently took on the form of exhortation, or moral advice. For if you do not believe that the perfect condition can be brought about by political action, you cannot hope for more than that one or the other of those in power might be induced, by moral appeal, by advice, by exhortations, by *sermons*, to do his best in his station along the lines of decency and humanity. This approach was underlying one special genre of political literature in particular, the mirrors of princes.

While mentioning the mirrors of princes, I have come to the great turning point in philosophy, to the starting point of the development in the course of which[45] the traditional utopianism of the philosophers and, we may add, of the theologians was gradually replaced by the *modern* utopianism of the *social engineer*. The mirrors of princes provoked the displeasure, the disgust, the passionate reaction of Machiavelli. Opposing the whole tradition of political philosophy, he did not wish to study any longer how men *ought* to behave, but how they *do* behave. He felt, not without good reason, that princes are not likely to listen to moral advice. From this he drew the conclusion, which no good man would have drawn, that he ought to teach princes how they could be efficient, if wicked. Machiavelli is the father of modern political philosophy, and[46] in particular of that trend of modern political philosophy which came into being as a *reaction* to his teaching. For very few philosophers were prepared to follow him on his dangerous course. The general trend was along these lines: people accepted Machiavelli's critique of the utopianism of the philosophic and theologic tradition; they admitted that the traditional ideals are too lofty to be put into practice; but, they argued, one cannot limit oneself to merely describing how men are and behave; men must be taught how they *should* be and behave. Thus a compromise between Machiavellianism and the tradition came into being: the idea to *lower* the traditional standard of conduct in order to *guarantee* the realization of these lower standards. Political philosophy attempted therefore to discover standards whose realization would be *necessary*, or automatic, and hence no longer an object of mere wish or prayer. The natural standard of human societies is the common good; the problem was to reconcile the common good, the common interest, with the private good, the private interest. The answer which was given was this: the common good is the object of *enlightened* self-interest; or virtue is identical with enlightened self-seeking. Accordingly, the primary task of political philosophy became to enlighten people about their self-interest. The idea was that the necessary outcome of general enlightenment about self-interest would be that people would no longer interfere with that natural, automatic process which would bring about social harmony but for people's foolish interference with that process.

The guiding motive of all men—this is the "realistic," "Machiavellian" assumption underlying this modern utopianism—is self-interest. Self-interest as we actually find it, unenlightened self-interest, necessarily leads to conflict, to the war of everyone against everyone, but this conflict is by no means necessary: everyone can be brought to realize that he would be better off in peace. What you have to do is to enlighten people about their self-interest: enlightened self-seekers will be as cooperative as unenlightened self-seekers are untractable. Enlightenment will gradually make superfluous the use of force.

The trouble with this idea, or rather the fallacy underlying this idea, is this: however enlightened a man may be about his self-interest, the object of his enlightened self-interest is not necessarily identical with the object of his strongest desires. This means the original conflict between moral demands and desires remains intact—it merely becomes much more difficult to cope with. For the conflict between moral demands and desires has its natural remedy, which is the appeal to sense of duty, honor, or however you might like to call it. The appeal to the enlightened self-interest necessarily lacks that moral sting. Enlightened self-interest requires as much sacrifice as justice itself—but the exclusive appeal to enlightened self-interest weakens the moral fibers of men and thus makes them unable to bring *any* sacrifice. Things become, not better and clearer, but worse and more confused, if self-interest is replaced by self-realization.

Another implication of this utopianism is the assumption that people really and basically want the object of their enlightened self-interest, that only lack of information prevents them from willing it. Actually, at least *some* people want *more*: power, precedence, dominion. And these dangerous people, even if few in number, are able to counteract the whole effort of enlightenment by employing[47] various devices, which sometimes are more effectual than the quiet voice of enlightening reason. What I am alluding to is the well-known fact that this modern utopianism naturally forgets the existence of the "forces of evil" and the fact that these forces cannot be fought successfully by enlightenment. We know a number of people who were honest enough to admit that they had forgotten the existence of evil; we can only hope that they will never do it again. One sometimes hears this kind of reasoning: during the last century, man has succeeded in conquering nature; natural science has been amazingly successful; all the more striking, and all the more regrettable, is the failure of the social sciences; the failure of the social sciences to establish social harmony, when contrasted with the success of the natural sciences, appears paradoxical. But it *is* paradoxical on the basis of the modern utopianism only. For what is the human meaning of the success of the natural sciences? That man has become enormously more powerful than he has ever been. But does a man necessarily become a better, a nicer man by becoming more powerful?

Let us consider for one moment under what conditions it would be reasonable to say that man becomes better by becoming more powerful. This would be reasonable if all wickedness, nastiness, malevolence, aggressiveness were the outcome of[48] *want*. For as far as this is the case, one could make men better by satisfying their wants. This view is underlying the famous theory of frustration and aggression. The decisive fallacy expressed in this theory is the assumption that frustration is avoidable, that a life without some sort or other of frustration is possible at all, or that full satisfaction of wants is possible. I must try to explain this somewhat more fully.

The view that enlightened self-interest leads to public-spiritedness and even to social harmony, whereas only unenlightened self-interest leads to social conflict, is not altogether erroneous. The error creeps in as a consequence of the ambiguity of the term "wants." Which are the wants whose satisfaction is the object of enlightened self-interest as distinguished from the object of unenlightened self-interest? Philosophers of former times used to distinguish between the necessary and the superfluous things. And they held that if all men were satisfied with the necessary things, with the *truly* necessary things, with what the body really and absolutely needs, the products of the earth would be sufficient to satisfy *these* wants without any fight among human beings becoming necessary. In other words, they held that the only guarantee of universal harmony is universal *asceticism*. Accordingly, they believed that the basic vice, the roots of all social conflict, is the desire for superfluous things, for *luxury*.[a] Now, one of the first actions of modern utopianism was the *rehabilitation* of luxury. It was assumed later on[49] that if all men were interested exclusively in raising their standard of living, their comfort, in the *commoda vitae*, social harmony would follow;

[a] [LS handwritten note] Plato's *Republic*—the true city, the healthy city, called by Glaucon the city of pigs—Glaucon is dissatisfied with the vegetarian food of the nice peaceful people—he gets his meat—and together with the meat: war.

it was assumed that the object of enlightened self-interest is, not the bare minimum of subsistence, but the highest possible standard of living. No sensible person can be unmindful of the great blessings which we owe to the victory of this tendency, but one is justified in doubting that it has brought about any higher degree of social harmony, or that it has brought us any nearer to universal peace. The number and the extension of the wars of the nineteenth and twentieth centuries is not sensibly smaller than the wars of earlier ages.

The curious thing about the present-day utopist is that he appears in the garb of the most hard-boiled realist. He does not speak of moral ideals—he speaks of economic problems, economic opportunities, and economic conflicts. He has learned in the meantime that mere enlightenment, that mere change of opinions would not do; he insists on the necessity of changing of institutions; he does not hesitate to recommend social revolution, unbloody[50] or otherwise. I am aware of *that.* Nevertheless, I must insist on the basic agreement between him and his grandfather of the eighteenth century.

No one will misunderstand me as if I were saying anything against economists. I still remember the papers read by Drs. Feiler and Marschak[a] in last year's summer course, papers which culminated in the thesis that the most important economic problems necessarily lead beyond the sphere of economics into the sphere of moral decisions.

But to come back to the trend of my argument, modern utopianism is not without good reason inseparable from economism as distinguished from economics. For modern utopianism ultimately rests on the identification of the common good with the object of enlightened self-interest understood as a high standard of living. The original thesis was that man *would* be determined by economic impulses, *if* he were enlightened, whereas actually he is determined by such foolish impulses as pride, prestige, etc. The next step was the assertion that man is in fact decisively determined by economic impulses and economic factors. The basic social or political facts are the economic facts: "the first private owner is the true founder of the State," "power goes with property." In its fully elaborated form, it is the economic interpretation of history which boasts of its more than Machiavellian realism, and which has nothing but contempt for the utopian socialism which it

[a] Arthur Feiler and Jacob Marschak were economists and colleagues of Strauss at the New School.

supplanted. But to say nothing of the withering away of the State, which will still be a matter of pious or impious hope a[51] long time after the withering away of Marxism will have been completed, what is more utopian than the implication of Marx's famous sentence: "Hitherto, the philosophers have limited themselves to *interpreting* the world; what matters is that the world be *changed*."[a] For why did the philosophers limit themselves to interpreting the world? Because they knew that the world in the precise, unmetaphoric sense of the term, the universe, cannot be changed by man. Marx's innocent-looking sentence implies the substitution of the little world of man for the real world, the substitution of the whole historical process for the real whole, which by making possible the whole historical process sets absolute limits to it. This substitution, a heritage from Hegel's idealistic philosophy, is the ultimate reason of Marx's utopian hopes. For is it not utopian to expect a *perfect* order of society which is essentially *perishable*? To expect men to put all their will, hope, faith, and love on something which is admittedly not eternal, but less lasting than this planet of ours? To mistake eternity for a time of very long duration, for some billions of years, is the privilege of nonphilosophic men, it is the mortal sin for a man who claims to be a philosopher. If all human achievements, the jump into liberty included, are not eternal, the germ of ultimate destruction will be noticeable even in the highest human achievements, and hence the so-called perfect order on earth is bound to be a delusion.

Much more realistic were the philosophers of old who insisted on the fact that the realization of the ideal is essentially a matter of chance, or the theologians of old[52] who insisted on the fact that the ways of providence are inscrutable to man. Modern utopianism is based on the assumption that the realization of the ideal is necessary, or almost necessary. By "almost necessary" I mean that but for an avoidable human shortcoming the ideal would necessarily be realized. The peak of modern utopianism was reached in the apparently least utopian political philosophy of the last centuries, in the political philosophy of Hegel. For, contrary to Plato and Aristotle and their followers who had insisted on the fundamental difference between the ideal and the real, the reasonable and the actual, Hegel declared that the reasonable is the actual and the actual is the reasonable.

A general survey of the history of political philosophy is apt to create the impression that there is no political philosophy from which we can

[a] "Theses on Feuerbach" XI.

learn anything because there is a disgraceful variety of political philosophi*es* which fight each other to the[53] death. Deeper study shows that this impression is misleading. It would be absurd to say that deeper study shows us all political philosophers in perfect agreement; it does show us, however, that there was a tradition of political philosophy whose adherents were in agreement as regards the fundamentals, the tradition founded by Socrates, Plato, and Aristotle, which was transformed but not broken under the influence of the biblical virtues of mercy and humility, and which still supplies us with the most needed guidance as regards the fundamentals. We do not need lessons from that tradition in order to discern the soundness of Churchill's approach, for example, but the cause which Churchill's policy is meant to defend would not exist but for the influence of the tradition in question.

This tradition is menaced today by a spurious utopianism. No one will deny that the basic impulse which generated that utopianism was generous. Nevertheless it is bound to lead to disaster because it makes us underestimate the dangers to which the cause of decency and humanity is exposed and always *will* be exposed. The foremost duty of political philosophy today seems to be to counteract this modern utopianism.

But to describe the service which political philosophy can render, not merely today, but at all times, one would have to say that political philosophy teaches us how terribly difficult it is to secure those minimums of decency, humanity, justice which have been taken for granted and are still being taken for granted in the few free countries. By enlightening us about the value of those apparently negligible achievements, it teaches us not to expect too much from the future. In the last analysis, political philosophy is nothing other than looking philosophically at things political—philosophically, i.e., *sub specie aeternitatis*. In thus making our hopes modest, it protects us against despondency. In thus making us immune to the smugness of the philistine, it makes us at the same time immune to the dreams of the visionary. Experience seems to show that common sense left to itself is not proof[54] against these faulty extremes: common sense requires to be fortified by political philosophy.

Man's modern venture, which has been amazingly successful in many respects, makes us distrustful of all teachings which insist on the fact that there are certain absolute limits to human progress: have not many of the allegedly existing limits proved to be surmountable? But the question is whether the price which had to be paid for these conquests was not, in some cases, too high; in other words, whether it is not still true that man can indeed expel nature with a hayfork, but that nature will always come back with a vengeance.[a] By erecting the proud edifice of modern civilization, and by living within that comfortable building for some generations, many people seem to have forgotten the natural foundations, not dependent on human will and not changeable, which are buried deep in the ground and which set a limit to the possible height of the building.

In practical terms this means that the task before the present generation is to lay the foundations for a long peace period: it is *not*, and it cannot be, to abolish war for all times. To quote a great liberal of the last century, Henry Hallam: "the science of policy, like that of medicine, must content itself with devising remedies for immediate danger, and can at best only retard the progress of that intrinsic decay which seems to be the law of all things human, and through which every institution of man, like his earthly frame, must one day crumble into ruin." (*Const. Hist.* 1182.)[b]

This sounds pessimistic or fatalistic, but it is not. Do we cease living, and living with reasonable joy, do we cease doing our best although we know with absolute certainly that we are doomed to die?

At the end of the third part of *King Henry VI*, after the victory of his house, King Edward IV says: "For here, I hope, begins our lasting joy." All the commentary that is needed is implied in the fact that Edward's brother Richard, afterward King Richard III, is silently present. At the end of *Richard III*, after that bloody tyrant has been slain, the victorious Henry VII concludes his speech by saying: "peace lives again: That she may long live here, God say amen!" The prudent Henry VII, the favorite of Bacon, was wiser than the ill-fated Edward IV. A wise man cannot say more than the father of Henry VIII did, and he cannot seriously *hope* for more. To what God did say amen after the victory of Henry VII is recorded in the histories.

It is hard to face these facts without becoming cynical, but it is not impossible. The philosophers advise us to love fate, stern fate. The Bible promises us God's mercy. But the comfort which comes from God is as little pleasant to the flesh as is the love of fate. For the flesh which is weak wants tangible comfort. That tangible comfort—a man-made eternal peace

[a] Horace, *Epistles* i.x.24.

[b] Henry Hallam, *The Constitutional History of England from the Accession of Henry VII to the Death of George II* (New York: A. C. Armstrong and Son, 1880).

and happiness—*non datur*. We have to choose between philosophy and the Bible.

Notes

1. The schedule of the lectures was as follows:

July 10 Albert Salomon, "The Task of the Scholar"
July 17 Leo Strauss, "What Can We Learn from Political Theory?"
July 24 Erich Hula, "Planning for World Order"
July 31 Adolph Lowe, "What Can We Learn from the British War Effort?"
Aug. 7 Arthur Feiler, "The Problem of Demobilization"
Aug. 14 Felix Kaufmann and Paul Schrecker, "Problems in Social Science"

Compiled on the basis of the catalogues available at http://digitalarchives.library.newschool.edu/index.php/Detail/objects/NS050101_gf1942sp (accessed April 27, 2016).

2. *NRH*, 3–5.
3. *NRH*, 34.
4. He alludes here to Julien Benda's *La trahison des clercs* (Paris: Grasset, 1927), translated into English as *The Treason of the Intellectuals*, trans. Richard Aldington, introduction by Roger Kimball (New Brunswick, NJ: Transaction, 2007).
5. *NRH*, 150.
6. *NRH*, 162.
7. Ibid.
8. *NRH*, 164.
9. *NRH*, 258.
10. Ibid.
11. *NRH*, 321.
12. *NRH*, 320–21.
13. On the traditional (Aristotelian) division of the sciences and the implications of its denial compare *LAM*, 205–6.
14. This definition should be compared with those in *WIPP*, 10–12 and 93–94. Passages in "On Classical Political Philosophy" also suggest that the primary concern of classical political philosophy was the right guidance not the understanding of political life (*WIPP*, 88).
15. Strauss makes this distinction more fully in *WIPP*, 12–13.
16. Compare *LAM*, 206. In the chapter on Aristotle's *Politics* in *CM*, Strauss first avers that the sphere ruled by prudence is closed by principles fully evident only to gentlemen and its ends are known independently of theoretical science (25), but then concedes that the natural end of man becomes genuinely known through theoretical science (26) and the practical sphere is not unqualifiedly closed to theoretical science (28). This discussion is conducted, however, within the Aristotelian framework that considers theory to be physics and metaphysics rather than political philosophy. Strauss contrasts

that view with the view of Plato and Aristotle that "philosophy as prudence is the never-to-be-completed concern for one's own good" (29).

17. *NRH*, 320.

18. I discussed some possible contemporary implications of Strauss's presentation of these policies in "Will the Real Leo Strauss Please Stand Up?" in *American Interest* 2, no. 1 (September/October 2006): 120–28.

19. Compare *NRH*, 13 and 151.

20. *NRH*, 177–79.

21. Here Strauss writes of lowering the standards of conduct, whereas later he wrote of modernity lowering the goals. He himself in a sense recommends lowering the goals in this lecture, e.g., not aiming at the abolition of war or imperialism.

22. Compare *CM*, 5: "no bloody or unbloody change of society can eradicate the evil in man: as long as there will be men, there will be malice, envy and hatred." Similarly, Strauss writes in *WIPP* that classical political philosophy is "free from all fanaticism because it knows that evil cannot be eradicated and therefore that one's expectations from politics must be moderate" (28).

23. Strauss does not explicitly respond to the part of the first negative argument that maintains that philosophy is at best only clear knowledge of the problems, not of the solutions. It is worth noting that Strauss himself makes such statements later, e.g., *NRH*, 125, and *WIPP*, 11, 39, 116.

24. Most manifestly in the sections on Weber and Locke, *NRH*, 74–76 and 202–20.

25. "making" was crossed out and "choosing" inserted by hand.

26. "theory" was underlined by hand.

27. "Originally" was crossed out and "Formerly" inserted by hand.

28. "distinction" was x'ed out and "division" typed above it.

29. "your" was underlined by hand.

30. "it" was inserted by hand.

31. "hence" was crossed out by hand.

32. Under the term "philosophy" the word "thought" was x'ed out and vice versa, both in typing.

33. "is" was crossed out and "exists" handwritten.

34. "themselves" was crossed out and "itself" handwritten.

35. This parenthetical sentence was added by hand.

36. This sentence was added by hand at the bottom of the page.

37. We have added the word "themselves" to Strauss's direct translation from the French edition.

38. The word "then" before "believe" was crossed out by hand.

39. "a" was crossed out and "the" handwritten.

40. "a" was crossed out and "the" handwritten.

41. "is" was inserted by hand, replacing the "is" typed and crossed out after "Such a policy is."

42. "seem to" was typed above the line.

43. "is" handwritten replaced "was" crossed out.

44. We changed from "by themselves are."

45. Strauss replaced "point when" with "starting point of the development in the course of which."

46. "and" was handwritten.

47. "employing" was handwritten.

48. "of" was handwritten.

49. "later on" was handwritten.

50. "bloody" was x'ed out and "unbloody" typed above the line.

51. We have inserted the word "a" before "long time."

52. We have changed from "the old."

53. We have inserted the word "the" before "death."

54. "a sufficient guarantee" was crossed out.

2

The Historical Approach

Breaking Free from the Spell of Historicism

DANIEL TANGUAY

Strauss's lecture on historicism represents an important stage in his reflection on this concept, which is as widespread as it is vague. In it he puts forward for the first time in English what will become classic arguments in his effort to break the spell exercised by the dominant opinion of our era. We find in it a sketch of the genesis of historicism in its two forms as well as an attempt to elaborate a more precise definition of this doctrine. According to this definition, historicism wishes to erase the distinction between philosophy and history by completely fusing the two disciplines. In Strauss's view, this fusion necessarily leads to the disappearance of philosophy to the extent that the eternal horizon of philosophy is reduced to the contingency of history. In this dense discussion of historicism, we see the fundamental intention that will guide Strauss in his later works taking shape: keeping alive the possibility of philosophy against all forms of dogmatism, and, in particular, against the dogmatic skepticism that belongs to historicism. This struggle against historicism leads Strauss to formulate a paradox that runs through his entire body of work: only history rightly understood can liberate us from the modern presuppositions that belong to historicism. A true and objective understanding of the ancients will compel us to admit the possibility of a nonhistorical understanding of the world. In the same way, if we understand the ancient philosophers as they understood themselves, we must recognize that history played only a secondary role for them, and that they were completely unaware of the historical consciousness. In this way, Strauss wants to turn historicism against itself, and compel us to examine once again the presuppositions that are at the origin of the dominant spirit of our times. This critical reflection on historicism was supposed to lead to the opening of a new chapter in the "quarrel of the ancients and moderns." The outcome of this quarrel cannot be decided in advance, as was maintained by the defenders of historicism. Philosophy, not history, Strauss maintains, will henceforth be its judge.

The problem of historicism is at the heart of Strauss's magnum opus *Nat-*

ural Right and History and of his thought as a whole. However, every reader of the short chapter in *Natural Right and History* where Strauss tackles this problem directly is struck by the simultaneously dense and elliptical character of his argumentation. In twenty-five pages, the philosopher sketches a portrait of the genesis and evolution of historicism while at the same time carrying out a thoroughgoing critique of its philosophic presuppositions.[1] This level of concision is surprising to the reader, above all if he has already immersed himself in the immense literature to which historicism gave rise in the German philosophic tradition. Strauss's analysis appears inadequate next to the eight hundred pages of Ernst Troeltsch's unfinished classic on the question, *Der Historismus und seine Probleme*.[2] However, one could quite rightly point out that Strauss comes back to the question of historicism in his criticism of the thought of Max Weber in chapter 2 and in the final chapter on Burke. One could also show that large parts of the section devoted to Rousseau retrace the philosophic genesis of historicism, and that such a philosophic genesis is also subtly sketched in the chapter on Hobbes. Indeed, as its title invites us to do, the whole work can in fact be read as a veritable *Auseinandersetzung* of Strauss with the problem of historicism.

The Emergence of Historicism

The reader who wishes for more after reading *Natural Right and History* will read with interest the lecture on historicism that Strauss delivered on November 26, 1941, at the Graduate Faculty of Political and Social Science in the New School for Social Research. This lecture was delivered as part of a "General Seminar" that allowed various professors and researchers attached to this institution to discuss a theme of general interest. In his introductory pages, Strauss mentions that his lecture will be delivered between that of Dr. Albert Salomon on historical sociology and that of Dr. Ernst Karl Winter on Plato and Aristotle. He then explains in what seems to be a different version of the same introduction that this order is significant insofar as historical sociology is based on historicism, and also because Plato and Aristotle could constitute a response to the crisis of modern rationalism provoked by historicism. It would thus be a matter of returning to a classical form of rationalism in order to surmount the crisis of reason provoked by modern rationalism and historicism. Here we have, in a nutshell, Strauss's philosophic project. We will return later to the spirit of this solution.

Another remark concerning the context can help us to understand Strauss's text. It is noteworthy that the members of the New School decided to devote a General Seminar to historicism at such a date. In November 1941 Hitler and Nazi Germany were at the summit of their power and the outcome of the war was far from being certain. Most of the teaching staff at the New School were German or Austrian émigrés who had fled Nazi Germany. The New School had truly become a "University in Exile."[3] It was therefore completely natural that numerous researchers at this institution would reflect on the causes of the war. A number of them—Eduard Heimann, Erich Hula, Carl Mayer, Albert Salomon, Kurt Riezler, Leo Strauss, Horace Kallen, and Felix Kaufmann—formed a group named "The Study Group on Germany," whose principal goal was to reflect on the philosophic and political sources of the German catastrophe and, more largely, on the "crisis of European liberalism."[4] Even though there is only an indirect allusion to the war in Strauss's text ("Those who did not know it before can learn it today that the victorious cause is not *necessarily* the good cause"), one can refer to the lecture that he gave in February 1941 entitled "German Nihilism" in order to see the profound connection between historicism and German nihilism. The latter, in its most elevated philosophic expressions, is a result of the more general crisis constituted by historicism, and can be understood both as an aggravation of this crisis and as an attempt to find a solution to it. However, the defect of this "solution" is precisely that it abandoned reason along the way, and soon all moral and political decency, in favor of a destructive and irrationalist philosophic activism.

It is this process of the self-destruction of reason with its disastrous political consequences that Strauss will seek to describe and explain. Now, it should be noted that this process found its most radical expression in German philosophy, even if it is a phenomenon that affects all of Western rationalism. This point is essential in order to understand the climate of urgency that runs through Strauss's lecture and in order to correctly situate the very location of the problem of historicism. One cannot insist too strongly on the fact that in many ways Strauss remained, even after his forced exile first in France, then in England, and finally in the United States, profoundly marked by his human and intellectual experiences in Germany under the Weimar Republic. In reading Strauss one sometimes even gets the impression that he never really left the Germany of the Weimar Republic. The point of departure of his thought is a series of questions that were posed with great urgency in the climate of cultural and political crisis that prevailed in the Germany of that era. Among these questions, there was one that had been especially prominent since at least the end of the nineteenth century, and that had taken on new dimensions after the First World War: that of historicism or, more precisely, the question posed by the "crisis of historicism."[5]

We cannot discuss here the complex history of this crisis and the multiple meanings of the concept of historicism.[6] Certain summary indications can, however, shed light on certain aspects of Strauss's lecture. One can first of all speak of the crisis of historicism in the sense of a crisis of a particular practice of history or of a particular way of understanding history. Strauss describes the genesis of this first form of historicism both here and in *Natural Right and History*.[7] It was born in reaction against the abstract ideals of the modern Enlightenment, and in particular of the French Revolution. It has a profound affinity with romanticism, with which it shares the worship of the particular and of individuality as against cold and abstract universals. The representative par excellence of this historicism, the German historian Leopold von Ranke, through wanting to understand "the past as it really was," was led to substitute a belief in the value in itself of each epoch as an expression of divine providence for the Enlightenment's belief in progress. According to Strauss, this historicism is the origin of the enormous development of historical science in Germany in particular, and also of the formulation of the ideal of the historicist: "A historicist, we may say to begin with, is a man who devotes all his intellectual powers to the contemplation and the understanding of that all-embracing texture, or of single phases and aspects of it, or of any significant individual phenomenon of human life of the present or of the past, but preferably of the past, with no other intention except to understand the past."

The first attack this first form of historicism had to undergo was that of Nietzsche in the second of his *Untimely Meditations*: "On the Uses and Disadvantages of History for Life."[8] This attack was devastating and definitive according to Strauss. Nietzsche's attack set out to show that objective history, the history practiced by scrupulous and impartial historians, was contrary to life. Every affirmation of life, every serious engagement in life, in fact presupposes forgetting and a closed horizon. But historical science overloads the memory and multiplies horizons to infinity. It makes us observe all the histories of the world as spectators. The modern individual emerges paralyzed and confused from such a spectacle: he no longer knows how to choose and how to devote himself to a cause larger than himself. He becomes blasé about history and loses himself in skeptical contemplation of the past. This is why Nietzsche's critique prefigures the apparition of a second form of historicism, a historicism that will henceforth put history into the service of life, action, and the needs of the present time.

Beyond this moral critique, Nietzsche revealed a second aspect of the crisis of historicism. It is this second aspect that is at the heart of the crisis of historicism in its deepest sense, and it is this second aspect that interests Strauss above all. History or historical consciousness arrived at maturity reveals, according to Nietzsche, a truth with enormous implications: everything is swept along by becoming, and man cannot find a stable and fixed point in this incessant flux. One must therefore understand the crisis of historicism to mean the crisis engendered by man's becoming conscious of the uniquely and exclusively historical character of all forms of knowledge and all values. This becoming conscious of the temporal and thus contingent character of all truth can in turn lead to moral relativism or even to nihilism.

Strauss presents this view of historicism in very clear terms at the beginning of his lecture:

> If I understand the usual view of historicism correctly, historicism is the doctrine that "everything is historical," i.e., that it is not possible to make a clear-cut distinction between the invariable ("eternal") and the variable elements of human things; that doctrine is based on the observation, or assertion, that any such distinction between invariables and variables is itself determined by the historical situation of the scholar who makes it; therefore, all knowledge, all beliefs, all standards, all institutions are of a limited validity, of a validity limited by the historical situation to which they belong: there is no knowledge nor standard of conduct valid for man as man; the historical situation limiting the claim of a doctrine to be true, for example, may be of a very short duration, but it may also be an epoch of two millennia.

It is worth noting, however, that he presents this view as the "usual view." This usual view is certainly not false, but it anticipates a wider and more comprehensive definition of historicism. However, this wider definition is, at the same time, as he presents it to us, "somewhat more vague." According to this latter definition, "historicism is the tendency to overemphasize history to the detriment of philosophy." The crisis of historicism is thus above all according to Strauss a crisis of philosophy, or, at least, a crisis of philosophers who have lost confidence in the powers of reason to discover the one and eternal truth.[9]

Historicism thus understood—"that trend of human thought which tends toward the merging either of philosophy and history in general or of philosophy and intellectual history in particular"—is the dominant opinion of our era. It embodies the "spirit of our time." Everyone from the youngest to the oldest is under the spell of this idea according to which all philosophy is nothing but the expression of its era, there is no unchanging human nature, and our "nature" itself is a product of history and culture. Everyone knows as well that all moral and political doctrines are relative to their era and thus that that which is true for us was not true for the eras that preceded us, is not true for other societies, and probably will not be true for the humanity of the future. In sum, the truth about the most important things is relative.

It goes without saying that such a historicist conception risks leading to an anarchy of values and convictions or, more precisely, to the impossibility of establishing a yardstick that would permit us to distinguish between good and bad actions in the moral and political sphere. As we mentioned above, this moral and political dimension is not, to be sure, absent from Strauss's reflections at that tragic moment of history, but it is not in the foreground, despite appearances to the contrary. The fundamental subject with which he is preoccupied is the possibility of philosophy or, even more precisely, of the philosophic quest. According to him, historicism attacks the traditional intention of all science and philosophy: to reach a truth that is universally valid independently of the particular conditions that engendered it.

The 1941 lecture thus brings to light Strauss's fundamental intention in his discussion of historicism. On the other hand, a certain rhetoric characteristic of *Natural Right and History* tends to disguise this primary intention in that work. Indeed, this rhetoric has enjoyed a success perhaps even beyond Strauss's expectations. He has been seen as a defender of natural right in a sense that was above all moral and political, whereas his intention was fundamentally other. Strauss certainly judged the moral and political consequences of historicism to be disastrous, but he also was not unaware that a political or moral need does not constitute a philosophic response to the historicist argument. In other words, political communities' legitimate need to refer to a universally valid natural right or to transhistorical values in order to ensure their own survival does not in and of itself constitute an argument against historicism. Strauss clear-sightedly faces up to the fact that historicism could be a deadly truth. This is why a genuine refutation of the historicist thesis cannot be reduced to a moral condemnation, but must examine the philosophic presuppositions of historicism in a critical fashion. The true question historicism poses is that of the very possibility of philosophy. Already in this lecture we see the terms of the problem that will be at the heart of *Natural Right and History* clarifying themselves: the problem of the possibility of philosophy as an essential condition for the reopening of the question of natural right.

The Paradoxical Refutation of Historicism

This refutation of historicism takes on a paradoxical character of which Strauss is very conscious.[10] It begins with a historical argument. Strauss wants to turn the weapons of historicism against historicism itself. In order to do this, he pushes the logic of historical inquiry and of concern for historical veracity to its utmost limit. He therefore gives us a small treatise on historical method as applied to the understanding of authors of the past. In order to understand an author, one must understand him in his own terms: "each author of the past must be interpreted, as much as possible, by himself." This means that the historian must refrain from introducing terms and concepts that do not belong to the author under study and that he must scrupulously restrict himself to what the author explicitly says. For example, he will be forbidden to speak of Plato's "metaphysics" or again of Socrates as the founder of "ethics." The modern historian nevertheless rarely lives up to this historical demand. He frequently succumbs to the temptation to understand authors in the light of his own historically determined categories.

But the historicist's "sin" is more serious than a simple failure to live up to the demands of historical objectivity that he pretends nevertheless to scrupulously follow. The historian generally fails in his effort to understand the authors of the past because he is not impelled by a sufficient desire for knowledge. To the extent that an author and a work are for him only the expression of the truth of a particular historical era, he does not expect to find in them the truth and nothing but the truth. He is not open to the possibility, while reading Plato, Aristotle, Descartes, or Spinoza, that they might have been able to discover the comprehensive truth. In fact, he does not seek such a philosophic truth but rather a "historical" truth, that is, the truth that belonged to a given era. He does not envisage the possibility that this truth could be addressed to him, or even reveal to him an eternal wisdom for the conduct of his own life. Because his historical interest is purely antiquarian, he can look with indifference at all that human culture has produced. In his eyes, everything is of equal worth, and everything deserves to become an object of historical curiosity.

The historian's historicist prejudice thus prevents him from taking the truth seriously and, in particular, the truth that can be discovered in the authors of the past. This is why, Strauss provocatively asserts, an Averroes or a Thomas Aquinas understood Aristotle better than most modern authors. They did not know Greek, or again were ignorant of facts about the Greeks or Aristotle that any modern historian of ancient philosophy knows, but their reading was guided by the idea that essential truths for them were contained in Aristotle's works. They were interested in the truth present in Aristotle's philosophy because they approached his philosophy in a nonhistorical manner. They approached the truth not as "historical" men but as "natural" men.

It is this natural state that Strauss wanted to make us recover, beyond the deformations inflicted on it by the "historical consciousness." And yet only history can lead to our liberation from the historicist spell. Indeed, it is historical knowledge that can bring out the fact that in other historical eras and for other civilizations, history did not have the central role it occupies for us. For an Aristotle or a Plato, and for their numerous followers in antiquity and the Middle Ages, history is merely a secondary discipline that has more to do with rhetoric than with science. An adequate historical comprehension of most of the Western scientific and philosophic tradition requires us to embrace the nonhistorical attitude that fundamentally characterized it. Understanding Plato and Aristotle as they understood themselves means understanding the fundamentally ahistorical essence of their thought. Thus a truly "objective" understanding of the past leads for Strauss to an overcoming of historicism:

> Generally speaking, we can say: if we take historicism seriously, if we take seriously the view that the whole past must be understood adequately, we are on the best way of overcoming historicism. For historicism is a very recent thing: practically the whole past thought and thinks nonhistorically. By understanding the premodern past, we familiarize ourselves with an essentially nonhistorical approach. By assimilating ourselves to that nonhistorical approach, we are learning gradually, slowly, not without pains, to

> look at things with the eyes of nonhistorical human beings, with the eyes of *natural* human beings . . . But let me hurry back from that utopia to our imperfect present.

The final sentence of this quotation indicates that Strauss is very conscious of the paradox contained in such an approach. It is utopian, because in order to be carried out successfully, it would require a considerable effort to liberate oneself from the bonds that shackle us to contemporary prejudices. Such an effort to liberate oneself is indeed the same effort that is at the origin of philosophy. It reproduces the original impetus of philosophy, but in very different circumstances. In its original meaning, philosophy is the attempt to replace opinions with knowledge. The Greek philosophers took the opinions that presented themselves to them in the city as their point of departure. It is this natural condition of philosophic reflection that is disrupted by historicism. The natural condition of man transforms itself into a restrictive historical condition once philosophy has made a detour from which it was spared for most of its history. The philosopher must first of all make himself into a historian in order to attain, thanks to history, the original grounds for philosophic questioning.

It follows that the philosopher today finds himself in a paradoxical situation: the only way for him to liberate himself from historicism is through an excess of history. The philosopher must become a historian of philosophy, for it is only by means of history that he can recover a nonhistorical way of philosophizing. Strauss is conscious of the dangers such a position represents for philosophy. It risks encouraging even more the tendency to historicize philosophy that has been under way since the nineteenth century. Moreover, propaedeutic by means of the history of philosophy can lead to a purely antiquarian practice of philosophy where the goal becomes to know what the great philosophers of the past thought rather than to think through the questions their texts treat. It is in order to avoid these pitfalls that Strauss insists on the fact that "[w]e do not assert an *essential* connection between philosophy on the one hand and historical studies concerning philosophy on the other—for, if we did, we should beg the decisive question; we merely assert an *accidental* connection."[11]

In the same spirit, Strauss emphasizes that this historical propaedeutic work cannot be entrusted to "classical scholars" but rather must be entrusted to "philosophic historians." "Classical scholars" are too imprisoned by modern presuppositions to understand ancient philosophers as they understood themselves. Only "philosophic historians" will be up to the task of liberating themselves from their presuppositions and thus be able to attain the requisite degree of historical exactness. As Strauss admits in a passage that is both surprising and not without a certain degree of arrogance, such philosophic historians are a very rare species indeed: "As a matter of fact, I do not know of a single historical study which is beyond reproach from the point of view of exact historical research. That study known to me which comes nearest to the goal of historical exactness is J. Klein's analysis of Greek logistics and the genesis of modern algebra."[12]

Isn't there a certain circularity in the argument Strauss presents here? In order to emancipate oneself from historicism and to examine it from the outside, it is necessary to undertake historical studies with the aim of finding a forgotten point of view, that of philosophy in its original meaning. However, these studies must be carried out by a mind that has already been liberated from modern presuppositions because it is these presuppositions that prevent one from understanding the authors of the past as they understood themselves. So it is necessary that the philosophic historian have carried out a radical critique of historicism before he sets out. But such a critique is possible only after one has been able to confront historicism with a nonhistoricist understanding of the world, which presupposes that by means of history one has been able to attain a point of view that has been freed from history.

Learning to Philosophize Again

We mentioned above one of the approaches Strauss adopted in order to avoid this circularity. It is historicism itself, pushed to its extreme limits, that constrains us to reconsider its own presuppositions and to experience its internal weakness.[13] An objective historical understanding of past eras makes us discover the novelty and the exceptional character of the "historical consciousness." This historicization of the "historical consciousness" opens up a formidable question for the historicist: what exactly is the status of his thesis according to which all truth depends on history? If the historicist is true to his principles, he must admit that his own historicism is itself historical, and thus that its truth value is relative to a contingent historical context. It is at most his truth, it is surely not the truth.

In the two final pages of his lecture, Strauss once again seeks to weaken the historicist's position by denouncing what he calls the "historicist fallacy." This is the fallacy of confusing the question of the genesis of a doctrine with that of its truth. One cannot judge the truth of a doctrine on the basis of the historical conditions of its emergence. These are two different questions that belong to two different fields of inquiry. One finds this argument among the neo-Kantian philosophers, and then in the celebrated text of the early Husserl entitled "Philosophy as Rigorous Science."[14] Strauss alludes to this argument in an earlier part of his lecture. This argument is of capital importance for Strauss because it rests on a certain idea of philosophy and of truth that constitutes the heart of his thought. The study of the context of the emergence of a philosophic doctrine tells us nothing about its truth or falsity. In fact, a philosophic doctrine must be evaluated according to criteria that belong to philosophy as rational discourse, and these are independent of history. In addition, the famous "anarchy of the systems" is not a conclusive argument for denying the possibility of attaining an absolute truth in philosophy. Even if it is true that philosophic doctrines contradict one another, one cannot exclude from the outset that one of them could be the true doctrine while the others could be false or incomplete. Judgments about the value of various doctrines depend on an examination everyone must undertake for himself. Even if we recognize the diversity and contradictory character of various philosophic doctrines, we are not freed from the obligation to undertake a serious examination of each of them to the extent that they state propositions with a claim to universal validity. Only philosophy can judge the value of doctrines, and arguments drawn from history miss the essential problems.

Whether it wishes to be one or not, historicism is also a philosophic doctrine. While it is taken to be an open-minded and tolerant doctrine, according to Strauss it is in fact a form of dogmatic skepticism that "betrays a lamentable or ridiculous self-complacency." It would nevertheless be an error to believe that Strauss's primary response to this dogmatic skepticism is to set up an antihistoricist dogmatism in opposition to it. From this point of view, it is very interesting that Strauss initially refuses to identify his position with one of the three tendencies of contemporary philosophy he presents at the very beginning of his lecture. The first tendency consists of philosophers who believe that philosophy must remain loyal to the ideal of modern natural science as it has been elaborated since Descartes. The second tendency is that of philosophers who accept modern philosophy's break with ancient and medieval philosophy, but who judge that this break was not radical enough. This is why they propose a new type of philosophy, a philosophy of the future whose principles would be brought out on the basis of a radical critique of the Greek bases of philosophy and modern science. Strauss counts Bergson, Heidegger, and also William James among these "ultramodern" philosophers. A third tendency consists of philosophers who judge that modern philosophy does not represent a progress for thought, and that it is therefore necessary to return to the philosophy that preceded it. These are the antimoderns: neo-Thomism, Third Humanism, and Nietzsche's return to the pre-Socratics.

Everyone knows that Strauss's final position will be identified with the third tendency, that of the antimoderns. This is in large part true, but it is much more difficult to determine the nature of the return to the ancients Strauss proposes. In a passage where he is most likely speaking about the path followed by a part of his intellectual generation, he returns precisely to the antimoderns and, in particular, to neo-Thomism, which at the beginning of the 1940s was the most powerful philosophic movement in the antimodern tendency: "The success of neo-Thomism is a byword. But neo-Thomism is merely the most popular form of a much broader trend whose most powerful and most profound representative was, and still is, the unknown Nietzsche." The association of the "unknown Nietzsche" with neo-Thomism is strange, but it permits Strauss to situate his thought in a larger movement that aims at surmounting what it perceives as the dead ends of modern thought. Strauss is very much conscious that in the eyes of modern thought and of its *enfant terrible*, historicism, such a return must appear utopian, because it denies both historical and spiritual progress. In his lecture, Strauss responds to this objection by emphasizing that the new quarrel of the ancients and the moderns that he wishes to open does not judge in advance the final outcome of this quarrel. He wishes to give the ancients another chance, and in order to do this, he invites us to read them without our modern historicist glasses. The reopening of the quarrel of the ancients and the moderns therefore presupposes a reeducation of our way of looking at things, a separation from our prejudices, which will permit us to correctly depict the positions under consideration, and thus to examine the arguments of one and the other. We cannot help being intimidated by this new "Battle of the Books" to which Strauss invites us, first of all as spectators, then eventually as participants. Despite its relativism and skepticism, historicism offers us a comfort Strauss persistently denies us: that of being in possession of a truth—the "historical consciousness"—that grants us a form of superiority over all past forms of humanity and installs us comfortably at the summit of human history. Strauss's calling into question of historicism is thus therapeutic in nature, to the extent that it aims to cure us of the intellectual laziness engendered by our "self-complacency" and invites us to leave the comfortable shores of history in order to set out on the high seas in the hope of finding a passage toward the truth.

Historicism (1941)

LEO STRAUSS

Graduate Faculty of Political and Social Science[a]
New School for Social Research, 66 West 12 Street, New York, N.Y.
General Seminar: Social Research
November 26, 1941
Historicism—Dr. Leo Strauss

[Plan of the Lecture]

1. Historicism is provisionally defined as the tendency to overemphasize history to the detriment of philosophy.
2. Historicism may be said to be the spirit of our age. This thesis will be illustrated by a cursory survey of the progress of historical thought.
3. Historicism has a certain justification as the attitude permeating genuine historical research.
4. The meaning of "exactness" in historical studies.
5. The philosophic question concerning historicism is whether philosophy is essentially separated from, and superior to, history of any kind, or whether the traditional separation of philosophy from history ought to be abandoned.
6. The philosophic question mentioned is only one aspect, if probably the most important aspect, of "*la querelle des anciens et des modernes*" as seen from today.
7. Historicism is in many cases a polite description of what is properly to be called intellectual laziness.
8. The question of "historical objectivity" and the original meaning of history as political history.[b]

[a] This typescript can be found in the Leo Strauss Papers, box 6, folder 14. It was transcribed by Scott Nelson and J. A. Colen and reviewed and annotated by Daniel Tanguay.

[b] [LS handwritten remark] History of human thought is based on specifically *modern* assumptions; hence it becomes *problematic* as soon as these assumptions become problematic;

Introduction

The intention of this lecture is to submit to you certain general[15] considerations concerning[16] historicism. The question of historicism was brought up in this seminar by Dr. Heimann,[a] who contrasted the historical approach in economics with the classical, nonhistorical approach; and, more directly, by Dr. Salomon,[b] who read a paper on historical sociology. Thus, it can hardly be denied that my subject is germane to the broader subject of this seminar. I should like to discuss it in a very broad, and even in a sweeping, manner. For I am afraid that we might forget the wood for the trees. No doubt, one cannot know the wood without knowing the trees; but it is doubtful whether one must know, or describe, each individual tree if one wants to know, or to describe, the wood. Unfortunately, my subject is so comprehensive that I cannot even *mention* certain extremely important aspects of the question: I had to limit myself to those aspects which, to my mind, are most apt to be overlooked. What I regret most is that I am unable to discuss in my paper the application of the principles to such[17] questions as are of immediate concern[18] to every social scientist. Opportunities to do[19] this will no doubt arise in the discussion, or else in later meetings of this seminar.

[20]My paper is most closely related, as far as its topic is concerned, with the paper of Dr. Salomon on the one hand, and with that of Dr. Winter[c] on the other. Dr. Salomon spoke on historical sociology, and Dr. Winter is going to speak on Plato and Aristotle today. I shall start where Dr. Salomon left off, and I shall leave off where Dr. Winter will start. Dr. Salomon's thesis, as far as it is relevant to *my* thesis, amounted to this: Historical sociology is not a new subdivision of sociology, such as rural sociology, but rather a reinterpretation of sociology as a whole. Just as historical jurisprudence was a reinterpretation of jurisprudence as a whole, and historical economics was a reinterpretation of economics as a whole. But "reinterpretation" is a some-

---

yet: *precisely* if these assumptions become problematic, history of human thought becomes of *utmost* urgency; only on the basis of this doubt can history of human thought live up to the highest standards of *exactness* (for as long as one believes in the superiority of modern thought, one does not pay the highest possible attention to the past) and thus become what it intends to be: adequate understanding of the thought of the past in the service of philosophy.

[a] Eduard Heimann (1889–1967), a German economist and sociologist, taught at the New School from 1933 to 1958.

[b] Albert Salomon (1891–1966), a German sociologist, taught at the New School from 1935 to 1966.

[c] Ernst Karl Winter (1895–1959) was an Austrian sociologist and politician.

what misleading expression: just as the relation of historical jurisprudence to nonhistorical jurisprudence was one of *antagonism*, historical sociology implies a *criticism* of sociology as usually understood. Historical sociology is the revolutionary attempt to make sociology radically historical. Historical sociology is therefore one form of historicism.

Historicism cannot be understood but as a reaction to the rationalism of the seventeenth and eighteenth centuries. Modern rationalism and historicism belong together. If historicism should prove to be untenable, some doubt is cast on modern rationalism which paved the way for it. Since we cannot possibly take leave of reason altogether, the question arises: whether rationalism is necessarily *modern* rationalism. In other words: whether premodern rationalism, classical rationalism, is not preferable to modern rationalism and all its descendants, one of which is historicism. It is for this reason that my paper leads from the historical sociology of Dr. Salomon's paper to the Plato and Aristotle today of Dr. Winter's paper.

Lest I should be completely misunderstood, I must say a word about my starting point. In the thought of our time, we can discern three fundamentally different trends: (1) The numerically most powerful group of scholars consists of those who believe that the tradition of modern natural science, which was the backbone of the philosophic development since Descartes, should *remain* the backbone of philosophy—the modern ones.[21] (2) Another group (Bergson, Heidegger) believes that the break, effected by Descartes and his successors, with the classical tradition was a decisive progress, and that a return to pre-Cartesian philosophy is impossible; but, they add, that break was not radical enough; they demand a new type of philosophy, based on a radical criticism of the Greek foundations of modern philosophy and modern science. This demand for a *new* philosophy, for a new *type* of philosophy, for a philosophy of the *future* was heard for the first time in the generation succeeding Hegel (Feuerbach)—the ultra-modern ones.[22] (3) A third group consisting of people who doubt that the philosophic development since Descartes is a progress in any philosophically relevant sense: neo-Thomism, Third Humanism,[a] Nietzsche's return to the pre-Socratics—the antimodern ones.[23]

I believe it is reasonable not to take sides in this controversy before one

[a] Third Humanism was an intellectual movement that emerged in Germany around 1930. It attempted to restore classical humanism by giving it a strong political dimension. One of its proponents was the classicist Werner Jaeger. See in particular *Humanistische Reden und Vorträge* (Berlin/Leipzig: Walter de Gruyter, 1937).

has studied *afresh* all the evidence pro and con. But I believe also that the mere fact that a tradition of three centuries is now seriously doubted is a real *boon* for philosophy. For the beginning of philosophy is wonder, and there are too many things which have ceased to be a matter of wonder and surprise since generations—which have been taken for granted since centuries.[24]

Historicism

(Lecture to be delivered in the fall of 1941 in the General Seminar)

1. As far as we can speak at all of the spirit of a time, we can assert with confidence that the spirit of *our* time is historicism. By "historicism" we understand to begin with that trend of human thought which overemphasizes[25] "history" in the double meaning of that term: "history" as historical *knowledge* and "history" as the *object* of historical[26] knowledge which is the all-embracing and yet unfinished and fragmentary,[27] constantly changing texture made up by human actions, human productions, human habits,[28] human sufferings, human institutions, and, last but not least, human thoughts and speeches. A historicist, we may say to begin with, is a man who devotes all his intellectual powers to the contemplation and the understanding of that all-embracing texture, or of single phases and aspects of it, or of any significant individual phenomenon of human life of the present or of the past, but preferably of the past, with no other intention except to understand the past.[29] Historicism thus understood was attacked in the year 1872 by Friedrich Nietzsche in the[30] second of his *Reflections Out of Season: On the Advantage and the Disadvantage of History for Life,*[31] with such a success that it is no longer a force with which we have to reckon. Today, it is fairly generally admitted that history, historical knowledge, is not an end in itself; that it is not only desirable but necessary that history should be in the service of life, of action. From this point of view, "historicism" came to mean that trend of human thought which overemphasizes the *past*, the usual domain of history, to the detriment of the *present*; which forgets *action* which always is concerned with the present or future, in favor of contemplation of, or longing for, the irrevocable past. Yet, as I said before, "historicism" thus understood is no longer a serious danger. To describe that historicism which confronts us today, we need a broader definition of historicism, a definition equally applicable to nineteenth century *and* to[32] twentieth-century historicism. We shall then say that historicism is that trend of human thought which overemphasizes history to the detriment of more important things. And when we use the term "historicism" emphati-

cally, we mean by it the tendency to overemphasize history to the detriment of *philosophy*. In the extreme case, which is evidently incapable of realization, historicism would be the tendency to *replace* philosophy by history. In the *typical* case, historicism is the tendency to *obliterate* the fundamental *difference* between philosophy and history, and in particular between philosophy and *intellectual* history. In the most *common* case, it is the tendency on the part of philosophers to devote their attention to the past or to the present or to the future rather than to what is always or the eternal.

The definition which I suggest is preferable to[33] the usual one because it is more comprehensive than the latter. If I understand the usual view of historicism correctly, historicism is the doctrine that "everything is historical," i.e., that it is not possible to make a clear-cut distinction between the invariable ("eternal") and the variable elements of human things; that doctrine is based on the observation, or assertion, that any such distinction between invariables and variables is itself determined by the historical situation of the scholar who makes it; therefore, all knowledge, all beliefs, all standards, all institutions are of a limited validity, of a validity limited by the historical situation to which they belong: there is no knowledge nor standard of conduct valid for man as man; the historical situation limiting the claim of a doctrine to be true, e.g., may be of a very short duration, but it may also be an epoch of two millennia. The[34] propositions of science, it is asserted, are not absolutely true, or eternally valid; for, it is argued, how can that be *true* which is not even *meaningful*?[35] Now, the propositions of modern science, for example,[36] would not even be meaningful to the ancient Greeks, for example. Thus, *modern* science is essentially "relative" to *modern* man. This view has been stated[37] with unusual clarity and sincerity by Spengler,[a] but it is held by many people who reject, or believe that they reject, Spengler's doctrine. For how else can we account for the fact that it has become customary since some time to speak of "modern science," or "Western science," or "classical science" or "Babylonian science," to say nothing of "capitalist" science and "Aryan" science?[38] This manner of speaking implies that there is not one human science valid for all times and nations, if actualized[39] only by[40] certain people in certain periods. It reduces *science*, i.e., *true* knowledge of causes, to the level of *doctrines*, which as such are not necessarily true but may be a conglomeration of superstitions.

[a] Strauss probably refers here to Oswald Spengler, *The Decline of the West* (New York, Alfred A. Knopf, 1937), vol. 1, chap. 2, sections 3 to 5, pp. 59–67.

When what *we* call *modern* science emerged, the champions of that science attacked, not ancient *science*, or scholastic *science*, but what they believed to be[41] a *pseudo*-science, and they attacked it in the name, not of *modern* science, but of the *only true* science. The view that all science and all other "ideas" of the human mind are historical, i.e., relative to definite historical situations and not meaningful beyond those situations, is what is[42] usually meant by the term "historicism." For my present purpose, I am in need of a more comprehensive if somewhat more vague[43] definition. According to that definition, historicism is the tendency to overemphasize history to the detriment of philosophy.

2. Historicism in the sense defined is the spirit of our time. *History* in the sense of *knowledge* of the past, or *records* of the past, or *memory* of the past, may be said to be[44] almost as old as the human race. But it never played such a role as it plays today. It is a matter of course to us that history—history of all kinds, political history, social history, economic history, history of art, history of religion, history of civilization, history of literature, history of philosophy, history of science, history of medicine, history of history—is taught at the universities, but it was only about a few centuries[45] ago that chairs for history, i.e., for political history only, were established for the first time in European universities. Most[46] other sections of our historical teaching and training are of a still more recent origin. It was the romantic movement in Germany which brought about the substitution of *historical* jurisprudence, *historical* political science, *historical* economic science for *natural* jurisprudence (i.e., natural law), *natural* political science, *natural* economic science. When we look up the plans of studies which Plato sketches in his *Republic* and[47] in his *Laws*, we find mathematics, astronomy, and dialectics[48]—we do not find the slightest trace of history. There is no difference in this respect between Plato and Aristotle: Aristotle said that poetry is more philosophic, i.e., more scientific, than history.[a][49] This attitude is characteristic of all philosophers of antiquity and of all their followers throughout the Middle Ages. History was not a part of the highest kind of learning up to the sixteenth century, and even in important respects up to the eighteenth century. History was highly praised, not by the philosophers, or men of science, but—by the rhetoricians. It is perhaps not out of place to mention the facts that Augustine, who is frequently referred to as a "philosopher of history," was originally a teacher of rhetoric, and that Giambattista

[a] [LS note] Cf. Aristotle, *Poetics* 9.51b5.

Vico, one of the most renowned precursors[50] of historicism, was a professor of rhetoric. The words of high praise[51] which Cicero bestows upon history occur in his rhetorical rather than[52] in his philosophic writings. It is true, Jews and Christians were deeply interested in biblical history. But—to say nothing of the fact that Jews as Jews and Christians as Christians are not necessarily philosophers[53]—they were interested in biblical history[54] not *as* history, but as legal, moral, and theological documents of a revealed, and therefore absolutely true, character.[a] It was rather[55] philosophers *attacking* the absolute claims of the Bible who[56] engaged, for that limited purpose, in truly historical observations concerning the Bible and the biblical tradition. Things changed fundamentally since the sixteenth century only. No earlier political philosopher[57] known to me ever spoke of history with so much emphasis as did Machiavelli,[58] Bodin and Bacon and even Hobbes. And yet it was for Bacon still a matter of course that the seat of historical learning is memory, and not reason, whereas the seat of philosophic learning, the highest type of learning, is reason, and not memory. As regards the time after Bacon, one may say that the interest in history increased almost from generation to generation at an ever-accelerated pace. Since the end of the seventeenth century, people started to speak of "the spirit of a time."[59] Toward the middle of the eighteenth century, *Voltaire* coined the *paradoxical*[60] term "philosophy of history" (1756, introduction to *Essai sur les moeurs*). In the philosophy of Hegel, philosophy and history have completely merged. Similarly, the central thesis of Comte's positivist philosophy cannot be stated but in historical terms. As far as human things are concerned (human knowledge, ideals, institutions), the same holds true of the evolutionism of the second half of the nineteenth century. The exact sciences and the philosophic schools most closely related to them had become, by the end of the nineteenth century and the beginning of our century, the last bulwark of a relatively nonhistorical[61] attitude; those schools insisted against historicism on the fundamental difference between the philosophic question of the *validity* of knowledge and science, and the historical question of the *origin* of knowledge and science, and on the superior dignity and importance of the philosophic question. The attack for example on that particular brand of historicism which calls itself sociology of knowledge was based on that distinction between the philosophic[62] question of validity and the historical[63] question of origin. How terrible must have been the shock

[a] [LS note] cf. Thomas, *S. Th.* I qs. 1 [art. 2 ad 2.].

to the nonhistorical epistemologists, when the most profound and most radical epistemologist of our century, Edmund Husserl, rejected what he called "the predominant dogma of the fundamental separation of epistemological elucidation and historical explanation" (*das herrschende Dogma von der prinzipiellen Trennung von erkenntnistheoretischer Aufklärung und historischer Erklärung*).[a]

Historicism is then that trend of human thought which tends toward the merging either of philosophy and history in general, or of philosophy and intellectual history in particular. Of that trend, it can safely be said that it is today all-pervasive. It is characteristic not only of phenomenology, but likewise of Hegelianism, Marxism, sociology of knowledge—of the adherents of Dilthey and Spengler as much as of those of Dewey. It expresses itself in very many different ways, and it justifies itself on the most different intellectual levels. But it is essentially the same trend in all cases: the trend toward the merger of philosophy and history.

Today, we all are historicists to begin with. Where are the liberals who dare appeal to[64] the *natural* rights of man? They prefer to appeal[65] to the *tradition* of liberalism. Historicism is the basic assumption common to present-day[66] democracy, communism, fascism. Before we have read any philosopher, we know already from hearsay that every philosophy is essentially historical, i.e., the expression of its time, of the *spirit*, or *soul*, of its time, or of the *socioeconomic situation* of its time. Almost before we can read and write, we are told that there is no such thing as an unchangeable human nature; and since a moment's reflection is sufficient to refute this analphabetic assertion, we are told when we are changing over from the kindergarten to the first grade that the unchangeable nature of man consists in his being "historical," i.e., in his being *actually*, so to speak, nothing, but *potentially* almost everything, or that the changing aspects of human life are more important than the invariable ones, for, it is argued, the orientation by the invariable aspects leads one to an "abstract" view of human na-

[a] [LS note inside the text] "Die Frage nach dem Ursprung der Geometrie als intentional-historisches Problem," p. 220.] Strauss quotes here the first edition of this text published in *Revue internationale de philosophie* 1, no. 2 (1939): 203–25. It appears subsequently in Walter Biemel's edition of *Die Krisis der europäischen Wissenschaften und die transzendentale Phänomenologie* (The Hague: Martinus Nijhoff, 1954) as *Beilage III*, pp. 365–86. For an English translation, see *The Crisis of European Sciences and Transcendental Phenomenology: An Introduction to Phenomenological Philosophy* (Evanston, IL: Northwestern University Press, 1970), 370.

ture, and the "concrete" meaning of the invariable factors *entirely* depends on the variable historical settings.

In order not to be misunderstood, I must mention in passing that the term "unchangeable human nature" is ambiguous. In a sense, no one can deny that man can change, and does change, his nature. Even the nonhistorical philosophers of antiquity knew this much. One of their pupils went so far as to assert that man can even *expel* nature with a *hayfork*; he added, however, that nature will always[67] come back.[a]

3.[68] However historicism may be understood, the historicism of the kindergarten as well as the historicism of the highest possible level have this in common, that they presuppose, or demand, the merging of philosophy and history. Historicism leads to a historical philosophy and—in a sense—to[69] a philosophic history. To speak first of the last aspect: one is justified in saying that at no earlier epoch did man devote so much intelligence and zeal to the investigation of the past as such, of all phases and aspects of the past, as he does since the nineteenth century. Never before was there at work such a truly universal interest in each significant individual phenomenon of human life, of the past as well as of the present. Therefore, one may expect that, generally speaking, our understanding[70] of the past is superior to that of any earlier age. This is not in itself something to boast of:[71] erudition does not teach to have sense, as Heraclitus said.[72] It became of decisive importance merely because of the particular circumstances in which historicism arose.[73]

The position which preceded historicism was the belief in progress: the belief in the superiority, say, of the late eighteenth century to any earlier age in all important respects, and the hope for still further progress in the future. The belief in progress stands midway between the nonhistorical view of the philosophic tradition and historicism. Belief in progress agrees with the philosophic tradition in so far as both admit that there are universally valid standards [of truth and justice],[74] standards which are not susceptible of[75] any historical justification.[76] The belief in progress deviates from the philosophic tradition, in so far as it is essentially a view concerning "the historical process": it stands and falls with the thesis that there is such a thing as "the historical process" and that that process is, essentially and generally speaking, a progress, an increasing approximation to the universal

[a] See Horace, *Epistles* 1.10.24.

standards of truth and justice. As a consequence, the belief in progress, as distinguished from the view of the philosophic tradition, can legitimately be criticized on purely historical grounds. This was done by early[77] historicism, which showed in a number of important cases—the most famous example is the interpretation of the Middle Ages—that the progressivist *view* of the past was based on an utterly insufficient *understanding* of the past. And this was fatal to progressivism, in so far as it was an assertion concerning the *past*.[78] It is evident that our understanding of the past, and of each individual period of the past, will tend to be the more adequate, the more we are *interested* in the past; but one cannot be seriously interested, *passionately* interested in the past if one knows beforehand that the present, the modern period, is superior in the most important respects to the past. Historians who started from this assumption felt no necessity to understand the past *by itself*; they understood it as a preparation of the present only. (A glance at almost any textbook of the history of political and social ideas suffices to see that this approach is still, to put it mildly, lingering on.)[79] The progressivist,[80] when studying a doctrine of the past, will not ask primarily, what was the conscious and deliberate intention of the originator of the doctrine in question? but rather, what is the meaning, *unknown* to the originator, of the doctrine from our present point of view? What is the contribution of that doctrine to our present beliefs?[81] The progressivist takes it for granted that he can understand the phenomena of the past better than the contemporaries could [he is convinced in spite, or because, of his being a man of mediocre intelligence that he can understand Plato better than Plato could understand himself].[82] The historicist on the other hand tries to revitalize that understanding of each period of the past which that period itself had. This truly universal interest in the past as past, or, more precisely, in each significant individual phenomenon of human life as individual phenomenon, is opposed not only to the belief in progress, but likewise to the philosophic tradition which was concerned, not with individuals, but with types, not with the *history* of *individual* phenomena (e.g., of the modern state), but with the *natural genesis* of *typical* phenomena (e.g., of the political community). These prehistoricist positions were not interested in understanding the past as it really was, "*wie es eigentlich gewesen ist*," as it appeared to the people who lived it, who experienced it; they did not understand the past from *its* point of view, but from an allegedly, or really, superior point of view. By rejecting the belief in progress in particular, in favor of the belief that "each period is immediate to God," historicism paved the way for a much higher degree of historical exactness than was considered necessary in former times.[a] Today, after a century and more of passionate discussions concerning the right method of historical studies, all true historians submit, in principle, to rules such as these: (1) Each period of the past must be understood by itself, and must not be judged by standards alien to it. (2) Before one can *judge* a phenomenon of the past, or before one can *explain* it in terms of its socioeconomic determinants, for example, one must have *understood* it thoroughly by itself: adequate interpretation is the indispensable prerequisite for *judgment* or *explanation*. (3) Only such presentations of the views of an earlier author can be accepted as true as are ultimately borne out by explicit statements of the author himself: the true historian, when confronted with an image invented by a superior man—the character of Falstaff, the knocking at the gate in *Macbeth*, Faust's descent to the mothers, the adventures of Don Quixote, the travels of Odysseus[83]—will suppress those dreamy thoughts of his or others which are aroused by the image in question, but will not rest nor remit until he has brought to light that lucid thought which the author wanted to convey by that image[84] to his sober and serious[85] readers.[86] (4) Each author of the past must be interpreted, as much as possible, by himself: no term of any consequence must be used in the interpretation of an author which cannot be literally translated into the language of the author, and which has not been used by the author himself or which was not in fairly common use in his time.

The up-to-date historians are very exacting people. They forbid themselves many easygoing habits of the former generations. They forbid themselves to speak of a *system* of philosophy if the author of a philosophic doctrine did not consider his doctrine a "system"; or to speak of Plato's "metaphysics" or of Socrates as the founder of "ethics," or of the Greek "theory of the State," or of Greek "religion," or of the "religion" of the Bible or of the "philosophy of history" of the Bible, since terms such as these do not occur in the vocabulary of the books or men in question. For Plato never spoke of "metaphysics," Socrates apparently never spoke of "ethics," the Greek language has no words which could be translated by "State" or

[a] Strauss quotes two famous dictums of the German historian Leopold von Ranke. The first dictum, "wie es eigentlich gewesen ist" (how it really happened), is an excerpt of the *Preface to the First Edition of Histories of the Latin and Germanic Nations*, in *The Theory and Practice of History* (Indianapolis: Bobbs-Merrill, 1973), 137. The second dictum, "each period is immediate to God," can be found in the *First Lecture to King Maximilian of Bavaria "On the Epochs of Modern History,"* in ibid., 53.

"religion," nor are there words in biblical Hebrew which could be translated by "religion" or "philosophy" or "history." The historians argue that the great men of the past showed themselves perfectly able to express every thought which they had and which they *wanted* to express, and if the[87] language of their nation lacked a term which could express a thought of theirs, they were perfectly able to coin a new term; therefore, if they did not use a certain term, the specific thought abbreviated by that term never occurred to them; consequently, if we should use that term in the interpretation of their thoughts, we would substitute more often than not a modern cliché for a living thought of antiquity; in any case, we would impute to them a thought alien to them, and grossly neglect our duties as historians. The modern historians who know their duties know from experience that whenever they catch themselves in the act of uncritically applying a modern term to a premodern phenomenon, they are led to see a very serious philosophic[88] problem which up to then escaped their notice.

While the modern historian accepts as binding the rules which I have intimated, he[89] very rarely lives up to them, owing to the weakness of the flesh. As a matter of fact, I do not know of a single historical study which is beyond reproach from the point of view of exact historical research. That study known to me which comes nearest to the goal of historical exactness is J. Klein's[90] analysis of Greek logistics and the genesis of modern algebra.[a][91]

When making a serious effort to live up to the standards of historical exactness, the historian is bound to have, sooner or later, an interesting experience. One notices, e.g., that in many important cases the medieval interpreters of Aristotle who were living in historical surroundings essentially different from those in which Aristotle had lived, and who did not even know the Greek language,[92] were better able to understand Aristotle than are most[93] modern historians. Now, the medieval commentators, such men as Averroes and Thomas Aquinas, were not historicists. This shows[94] that, in order to understand adequately a phenomenon of the past, one need[95] not be a historicist, nor need[96] one possess a "philosophy of history": one merely must use one's eyes and one's head, and one must be animated by a serious interest in that phenomenon of the past with which one happens to deal. Thus, the claim of historicism to have opened up a more adequate understanding of the past becomes more and more doubtful. One finally

[a] [LS note] It is only fair to add that I have not yet been able to read Prof. Koyré's work on Galilei. (Strauss probably refers to Alexandre Koyré, *Études galiléennes* (Paris: Hermann, 1939).

arrives at the suspicion that, in the most important cases, historicism *prevents* one from understanding the past. For to understand a phenomenon, one must take it seriously; one must be willing, for example, to consider it possible that a certain doctrine of the fifth century BC or of the twelfth century AD is *the* true doctrine; one must familiarize oneself with the outlook of the author by *practicing* it; one has not understood an author of the past as long as one does not know from intimate knowledge how he would have reacted to our modern refutations of his doctrine. Now, historicism denies,[97] by its definition, the reasonableness[98] of a nonhistorical philosophy; it denies, a priori, that any doctrine of the past can be *the* true doctrine.[99] Accordingly, the historicist is per se unable to understand adequately a nonhistorical position:[100] as little as according to the predominant view[101] the dogmatic Aristotelians of the seventeenth century were able and willing to understand Galileo, as little is the historicist of our day able to understand Plato or Aristotle or the Bible. Historicism once acted as a truly liberating force when it was dissolving certain specific prejudices of the European past; today, it is acting as a blinder, for it has become a prejudice itself. This is not to deny, nor necessarily to assert, that historicism understands other phenomena, in which no one was seriously interested in former ages, much better than did the greatest men of earlier times; no conceivable harm is done if we admit that certain contemporaries of ours[102] understand the plastic art[103] of the African Negroes better than Plato or Aristotle or Thomas Aquinas or Descartes or Kant could have done.[104]

Generally speaking, we can say: if we take historicism seriously, if we take seriously the view that the whole past must be understood adequately, we are on the best way of overcoming historicism. For historicism is a very recent thing: practically the whole past thought and thinks nonhistorically.[105] By understanding the premodern past, we familiarize ourselves with an essentially nonhistorical approach. By assimilating ourselves to that nonhistorical approach, we are learning gradually, slowly, not without pains, to look at things with the eyes of nonhistorical human beings, with the eyes of *natural* human beings. I.e., historicism considers each historical individuality as something which can be measured only by its *own* standard; he does *not judge*; but a rational human being *does* judge: foolishly, if he is a fool, wisely, if he is wise.[106] But let me hurry back from that utopia to our imperfect present.

4. The radical problem of historicism is *not* whether or not historicism enables us to understand adequately the past, but whether and how far

historical knowledge has philosophic relevance. As regards *that* question, we are confronted with the suggestion, which in certain quarters has degenerated[107] into a foregone conclusion, that the traditional separation of philosophy and history should be abandoned[108] once and for all. We are then confronted with the *alternative* of a nonhistorical philosophy and an intrinsically historical philosophy. The question as to what approach—the nonhistorical approach or the historical approach—is the *right* approach is a *philosophic* and not a *historical* question. But if we want to answer that philosophic question, if we want to know adequately what can be said *pro et con* each side of the alternative, if we want to *elaborate* that *philosophic* question, we cannot help engaging in *historical* studies. For there does not exist any longer any significant philosophic position which is not tinged by historicism: if we want to know what nonhistorical philosophy really means, we have to go back to the past.

If we could trust certain romantic writers, we might expect to find a truly nonhistorical or unhistorical position in eighteenth-century rationalism. For one of the most successful charges brought against eighteenth-century rationalism is precisely this, that it utterly lacked "historical consciousness": not only did it believe in an eternal natural right, it even indulged in such utterly unhistorical conjectural accounts of the origin of society and government as are the doctrines of a presocial[109] state of nature.[110] [The implication of such charges is that up to the emergence of the revolutionary philosophy of the seventeenth and eighteenth centuries, man possessed "historical consciousness." This romantic view is based on a[111] grave mistake:[112] it mistakes[113] traditionalist thought, the habit of thought characteristic of former ages, for[114] historical thought. Actually, traditionalist thought presupposes the belief, irreconcilable with historicism, that the tradition to which one happens to adhere is absolutely superior to any other tradition; the Romanist jurists of former ages, for example, accepted Roman law, not so much[115] for historical reasons as[116] because they considered Roman law the *ratio scripta*, human reason itself in its utmost perfection laid down in writing.] Actually, however,[117] the thought of eighteenth-century philosophy was much more historical than that of any earlier philosophy. The clearest sign of that historical trend is exactly the doctrine of the state of nature, which may be historically erroneous but which was meant to be a *historical* account, if a hypothetical account,[118] as distinguished from, and opposed to, a *miraculous* account, of the origins of civilization, an account which should be the *introduction* for[119] a coherent account of the *one* process of civilization itself. The only justification of the romantic verdict is contained in the fact that eighteenth-century rationalism was as convinced of the superiority of the present to the whole past as no earlier philosophy had been. But *contempt* of the past is not in itself a sign of a nonhistorical way of thinking. On the contrary: if that low view of the past is an integral part of one's philosophy, it is a sign that one's philosophy is essentially historical. Closer study shows that not only eighteenth-century philosophy, but above all that of the seventeenth century presupposes a turn from philosophy to history which has taken place in the sixteenth century, and whose greatest exponents were Bodin and Bacon. Therefore, if we want to get hold of an unambiguously nonhistorical philosophic position,[120] we have to go back to ancient and medieval philosophy. And we have *got* to get hold of such a position, if we want to elaborate the *philosophic* question as to what approach—a nonhistorical approach or a historical approach—is the right philosophic approach.

This means: as matters stand *today, in our time,* one is unable to elaborate, and to answer, a fundamental *philosophic* question without actually becoming a *historian* of philosophy. This may be called a historical justification of historical studies; it certainly is not, and is not intended to be, a philosophic justification. We do not assert an *essential* connection between philosophy on the one hand, and historical studies concerning philosophy on the other, for if we did, we should beg the decisive question; we merely assert an *accidental* connection: since certain possibilities have been *forgotten* since some time (and there was no inescapable necessity of their being forgotten), they must be recovered by means of historical research. Nothing prevents us from visualizing a time when history will again have sunk back into its former philosophic insignificance. For does not historicism itself assert that every human doctrine as a *historical* phenomenon is "historically relative," and is not historicism a human doctrine?

5.[121] *In our time,* the elaboration of the elementary philosophic questions requires serious and intensive historical studies. Until a generation ago, the superiority of the modern approach, i.e., of the habits of thought which have emerged since the Renascence, to the earlier approaches was generally taken for granted. Those philosophers who were in opposition to the predominant trend of modern thought—such men as Bergson and W. James—demanded an essentially *new* kind of philosophizing, a kind of philosophy which should be still more different from premodern thought than from the thought of the seventeenth till nineteenth centuries. In the meantime, the essential superiority of modern philosophy to premodern philosophy has become doubtful to an ever-increasing number of people. The success of neo-Thomism is a byword. But neo-Thomism is merely the most popular form of a much broader trend whose most powerful and most profound representative was, and still is, the unknown Nietzsche. The question as to whether the moderns are superior to the ancients, or the ancients are superior to the moderns, has again become a *question*, and even the most fundamental question: for it concerns the *approach* to *all* philosophic questions, it concerns the *method* of all philosophic investigations. That question has been the topic of a famous discussion at the end of the seventeenth and the beginning of the eighteenth century, of *la querelle des anciens et des modernes*. Most of you will remember Swift's *Battle of the Books*, in which the moderns are compared to the spider which "boasts of being obliged to no other creature, but of drawing and spinning out all from itself," and the ancients to the bee "which, by a universal range, with long search, much study, true judgment, and *distinction of things*, brings home honey and wax," "thus furnishing mankind with the two noblest of things, which are sweetness and light."[a] [That controversy, it was believed, has been decided by "*history*" in favor of the moderns. But the verdict of "*history*," i.e., of the public opinion of two centuries, is not decisive. Those who did not know it before can learn it today that the victorious cause is not *necessarily* the good cause.][122] The question of the ancients and the moderns remains then an open question to which only a fool will offer a ready-made answer. To answer that question, and indeed to understand what it means, we need historical studies: *exact* confrontations of the ancient and the moderns. I say, *exact* confrontations, i.e., such confrontations as present the ancients from *their* point of view, and *not* from the modern point of view. For if we were to[123] present the thought of the[124] ancients from the point of view of the moderns, we should beg the decisive question: we should tacitly presuppose the superiority of the modern approach. But these historical studies are not an end in themselves, they are merely preparatory to a future attempt to settle the *philosophic* question.

[Someone might object that we do not need new historical studies since we *know* the ancients: are their doctrines not clearly and adequately set forth[125] in the books of the great scholars of the nineteenth and twentieth

[a] See Jonathan Swift, *A Tale of a Tub with Other Early Works 1696–1707* (Oxford: Basil Blackwell, 1965), 150–51. The emphasis is Strauss's.

centuries, and especially of[126] the classical scholars of our time? The answer must be in the negative. For it is impossible that a classical scholar, as far as he is a classical scholar, should understand ancient thought. The classical scholar is not an ancient thinker, he is a modern man: his modern prejudices are bound to interfere with his understanding of the ancients, if he does not methodically reflect on the modern presuppositions as such. Such a reflection transcends the limits of classical scholarship, and must be entrusted to philosophic historians.][127]

6.[128] We are then confronted with the paradoxical fact that extensive studies in the field of *history* of philosophy, the full-time job of more than one generation of scholars, have become a prerequisite of *philosophic* studies. This paradoxical fact is the necessary outcome of the modern development, and in particular of the belief in progress which is characteristic of the predominant trend of modern thought. The founding fathers of modern philosophy, while being no doubt genuine philosophers, conceived of philosophy in such a way that a degeneration of philosophic thought became unavoidable. Philosophy, we may say, is the attempt to arrive at a free, unbiased understanding of all things, or the most important things; i.e., philosophic understanding is fundamentally distinguished from, and opposed to, a *traditional* understanding. Philosophy and a given tradition *may* agree, but this is purely accidental from the point of view of philosophy. When the founding fathers of modern philosophy opposed scholasticism as a *tradition*, they did merely what any genuine philosopher would have done. But they went much beyond that. They may be said to have started from the following fact. It seems necessary that the knowledge of a man who is equally intelligent and diligent as his teacher, if external conditions are the same, should become greater, more advanced, than the knowledge which his teacher possessed. Now, everything depends on what we understand by "greater" knowledge. If we understand by greater knowledge more *extensive* knowledge, the knowledge of the pupil will necessarily be greater than that of his teacher. But if we understand by greater knowledge a knowledge which is more *profound*, the knowledge of the pupil is *not* necessarily greater than that of the teacher. For it may very well be that the teacher devoted all his intellectual powers to elucidating the most fundamental question, and that the pupil simply *took over* his teacher's answer to that question without bothering too much about the question. The founding fathers of modern philosophy asserted not merely that, all other things being equal, the knowledge of the perfect pupil will finally be superior to the knowledge of the perfect teacher; they went so far as to assert that, just as the knowledge of each individual progresses in the course of his life, the knowledge of the whole human race necessarily advances from day to day, i.e., from generation to generation. In asserting this, they underrated the difference between inherited knowledge, i.e., the knowledge which one acquires in schools and universities, and independently acquired knowledge, i.e., knowledge acquired by a mature scholar. Thus it came to pass that inherited knowledge was given the same cognitive status as independently acquired knowledge. (Witness the phrase: the results of modern research.)[129] Whereas, actually, inherited knowledge is hardly distinguishable from prejudice: inherited knowledge is, in the typical[130] case, a collection of true prejudices.[131] This is the ultimate reason why all modern philosophy and all modern science, as distinguished from premodern philosophy and premodern science, absolutely *depends* on history of philosophy and history of science: since modern knowledge consists to a considerable extent of inherited knowledge (this is implied in the very concept of progress of knowledge as we usually understand it), it is indispensable that that inherited knowledge, or our true prejudices, be transformed into genuine knowledge; and in order to do this, we have to go back to the point when that knowledge which *we* have inherited was originally acquired. In some cases, it so happens that what, to begin with, is supposed to be inherited[132] *knowledge* or *true* prejudice proves to be an *inherited error.*

If the question of the ancients and the moderns is a *question*, it follows that we cannot take it for granted any longer that there is such a thing as History, i.e., an object or field or a dimension fundamentally distinguished from Nature. For History as the object of historical knowledge is a discovery, or invention, of *modern* thought. One of the most urgent duties of the philosophic scholar would be to describe in terms of ancient thought what we, in our language, call History. When this has been done, we shall be in a position to discuss the question whether the ancient view of the matter is inferior, or superior, to the modern view.[133] It is hardly necessary to add that the term "philosophy of history" is subject to the same grave doubt as "History" itself.

7.[134] Our very admitting the possibility that the question of the ancients and the moderns is an open question presupposes a break, not only with the belief in necessary progress of thought, but likewise with historicism in the usual sense of the term. For historicism asserts that every philosophy is essentially related to the *time* in which it emerged. Accordingly, restorations of earlier positions are considered impossible. [Every renascence, it is asserted, is a transformation. In many cases, it could be shown that what claims to be a restoration is merely a transformation of an earlier doctrine. But this does not prove that restorations in the strict sense are *impossible.* More's *Utopia*, for example, is a perfect restoration of classical principles. That these principles are applied by Thomas More to the economic situation of sixteenth-century England does not affect at all the principles themselves.][135]

Let us consider from this point of view the example of neo-Thomism. The historicist would say that the venture of neo-Thomism is absurd, for neo-Thomism is the attempt to restore a medieval position in the modern world, but a medieval position is *per se* inapplicable to modern conditions. But even if the essentially medieval character of all essential tenets of Thomism were demonstrated, the question would still remain whether the Middle Ages were not just the period *most favorable* for the emergence of *the* true doctrine, so that modern man could do nothing better than to take his bearings by the most elaborate medieval position. Some people would argue: Thomism is merely an interpretation of Aristotle, and Aristotle's philosophy has been refuted by modern science; even if we know nothing of modern science, we know at least this much, that it *works*. But does it really work? I am not competent to say a single word about modern natural science. But as regards modern *social* science, can it be said to work, as long as its very objectivity is an unsolved problem, as long as we are confronted with the choice between an objective social science which does not lead to any "value judgments" and irresponsible personal "decisions"?

We may speak of *the* historicist fallacy, which is that history proves anything as to the truth or falsehood of any doctrine, that *a tempore ad veritatem valet consequentia*. History proves nothing, so to say, because the relation between a doctrine and the time of its emergence is essentially *ambiguous*: the time at which a doctrine emerged may have been *favorable* to the discovery of a truth, and it may have been unfavorable. Only the philosophic study of the doctrine by itself with a[136] view to its truth or falsehood or one-sidedness permits us to *interpret* the relation between a doctrine and its historical setting. Another form of the historicist fallacy is the assertion that the history of ethical or metaphysical doctrines supplies us, as such, as history, with the refutation of the "absolute" claim of all ethical or metaphysical doctrines; it is asserted that[137] the mere spectacle of the anarchy of the systems proves that all of them are invalid. Actually, the different doctrines merely *contradict* each other. And it is incumbent, not on the historian, but on the philosopher, to find out which of the two contradictory doctrines is the true doctrine, or perhaps whether the evidence at our disposal permits us at all to answer that question but compels us rather to engage in other philosophic studies. Historicism in the usual sense is merely the fashionable form of intellectual laziness.

History does not prove the historical relativity of all philosophy: it would prove, in the best case, that *hitherto* all philosophy has been historically relative, i.e., that all philosophies known to us have been a failure—that all attempts, *hitherto made*, to discover the truth about God, the universe, and man have failed. But what else does this mean except that philosophy, quest for truth about the most important things, is as necessary as ever? And this is so far from being a new insight, due to historicism, that it is implied in the very *name* "philosophy," which means that no man is wise, knowing the truth, but in the best case a seeker for truth. Historicism might[138] offer us[139] a proof of our ignorance concerning the most important subjects—of which ignorance we can be aware without historicism—but by not deriving from that insight into our ignorance the urge to seek for knowledge, for philosophic knowledge, historicism betrays a lamentable or ridiculous self-complacency.[140]

Notes

1. *NRH*, 9–34. See also *WIPP*, 25–27 and 56–77, and "On Collingwood's Philosophy of History," *Review of Metaphysics* 5, no. 4 (June 1952): 559–86.

2. Ernst Troeltsch, *Der Historismus und seine Probleme* (Tübingen: J. C. B. Mohr-Paul Siebeck, 1922).

3. Rutkoff and Scott, *New School*, 84–106.

4. Ibid., 137–43.

5. The young Strauss had already presented the general contours of this crisis in three texts dating from the end of the 1920s and the beginning of the 1930s: "Der Konspektivismus" (1929), "Religiöse Lage der Gegenwart" (1930), and "Die geistige Lage der Gegenwart" (1932). These texts can be found in the second volume of Heinrich Meier's edition: Leo Strauss, *Gesammelte Schriften, Philosophie und Gesetz—Frühe Schriften*, ed. Heinrich Meier and Wiebke Meier (Stuttgart: J. B. Metzler, 1997), 365–75, 377–91, and 441–64.

6. For a well-documented synthetic presentation of the concept and its history, see George G. Iggers, *The German Concept of History: The National Tradition of Historical Thought from Herder to the Present* (Middletown, CT: Wesleyan University Press, 1983), 124–228. See also the same author's "Historicism: The History and Meaning of the Term"

(*Journal of the History of Ideas* 56, no. 1 [January 1995]: 149–152) as well as Otto Gerhard Oexle, *Geschichtswissenschaft im Zeichen des Historismus: Studien zur Problemgeschichten der Moderne* (Göttingen: Vandenhoeck & Ruprecht, 1996).

7. *NRH*, 12–20.

8. Friedrich Nietzsche, *Untimely Meditations* (Cambridge: Cambridge University Press, 1983), 59–123.

9. The real question that historicism poses is that of the very possibility of philosophy. Already in this lecture one sees the terms of the problem that will be at the heart of *NRH* clarifying themselves. For Strauss, the question of natural right is thus subordinated to the more fundamental question of the possibility of philosophy.

10. Strauss says: "Our must urgent need can only be satisfied by means of historical studies which would enable us to understand classical philosophy exactly as it understood itself, and not in the way in which it presents itself on the basis of historicism." *NRH*, 33.

11. On this question, see *PAW*, 155–58.

12. Strauss is obviously referring here to the work of his friend Jacob Klein: cf. Jacob Klein, "Die griechische Logistik und die Entstehung der Algebra," in *Quellen und Studien zur Geschichte der Mathematik, Astronomie und Physik* (Berlin), Abteilung B: *Studien*, vol. 3, no. 1 (1934): 18–105; vol. 3, no. 2 (1936): 122–235, translated later as *Greek Mathematical Thought and the Origin of Algebra* (Cambridge: MIT Press, 1968).

13. In *Natural Right and History*, Strauss relativizes the ultimate philosophical value of this argument when he discusses what he calls "radical historicism." This more philosophically conscious form of historicism seems untouched by the internal logical contradiction of the "vulgar" historicist thesis. See *NRH*, 25–33.

14. "Philosophy as Rigorous Science," in *Phenomenology and the Crisis of Philosophy* (New York: Harper and Row, 1965), 49–51. See Strauss's commentary on this text: "Philosophy as Rigorous Science and Political Philosophy," in *SPPP*, 29–37. Strauss indicates that Husserl subsequently renounced his original critical position in, among other places, one of the philosopher's last essays, which Strauss quotes on page 10, "Die Frage nach dem Ursprung der Geometrie als intentional-historisches Problem," *Revue internationale de philosophie* 1, no. 2 (1939): 203–25. For an English translation, see the appendix of Edmund Husserl, *The Crisis of the European Sciences and Transcendental Phenomenology: An Introduction to Phenomenological Philosophy* (Evanston: Northwestern University Press, 1970), 352–78.

15. "general" was inserted by hand.

16. "concerning" was inserted by hand replacing "on."

17. "Such" was inserted by hand to replace "concrete."

18. "As are of immediate concern to every" was inserted by hand to replace "interesting the."

19. "to do" was inserted by hand to replace "of doing."

20. Square bracket was inserted by hand.

21. "—the modern ones" was inserted by hand.

22. "ones" was inserted by hand.

23. "—the anti-modern ones" was inserted by hand.

24. The part of the sentence reading "too many things . . . since centuries" was inserted by hand.

25. "over" in "overemphasizes" was inserted by hand.

26. "historical" in "historical knowledge" was inserted by hand to replace "that" which was crossed out.

27. The words "yet unfinished and fragmentary," was inserted by hand.

28. The words "human habits," were inserted by hand.

29. In "except to understand the past" the words "the past" were added by hand.

30. "the" was inserted by hand replacing "his."

31. "of his *Reflections Out of Season*" was inserted by hand to replace "*Untimely Reflections*" which was crossed out.

32. "to" was inserted by hand.

33. "is preferable to" was inserted by hand to replace "differs from."

34. Strauss capitalized "The" in "The propositions of science" in order to mark the beginning of a new sentence, after an illegible word crossed out.

35. ", it is asserted," and ", it is argued," were inserted by hand.

36. "E.g." after "modern science" was inserted by hand.

37. "stated" was inserted by typewriter to replace "held" which was crossed out.

38. The part of the sentence reading "to say nothing of 'capitalist' science and 'Aryan' science" was added by hand in the margin.

39. "actualized" was inserted by hand to replace "actually accessible," which was crossed out.

40. "by" was inserted by hand to replace "to," which was crossed out.

41. "believed to be" was inserted by hand to replace "called," which was crossed out.

42. "what is" was inserted by hand.

43. "if somewhat more vague" was inserted by hand.

44. "may be said to be" was inserted by hand to replace "is" which was crossed out.

45. "a few centuries" was inserted by hand to replace "300 years," which was crossed out.

46. Above "The" the word "Most" was added by hand, possibly as an alternative.

47. "and" was inserted by hand to replace "or" which was crossed out.

48. "dialectics" was inserted by hand to replace "philosophy," which was crossed out.

49. Above the words "Plato and Aristotle: Aristotle" the words "One cannot quote often enough" were added by hand, while above "said" the word "saying" was inserted by hand, possibly as an alternative.

50. The part of the sentence reading "of place to mention the facts . . . one of the most renowned pre-" was added by hand at the bottom of the page.

51. Between "The" and "words of high praise," the word "high" was crossed out.

52. The words "rather than" were inserted by hand to replace "not," which was crossed out.

53. The words "—to say nothing of the fact . . . philosophers—" were added by hand at the bottom of the page, with a sign indicating where they should be inserted in the text.

54. "Biblical history" was inserted by hand to replace "it," which was crossed out.

55. "It [were] rather" was inserted by hand to replace "Only," which was crossed out.

56. "who" between "Bible" and "engaged" was added by hand.

57. Between the words "earlier" and "philosopher" the word "pol." was added, presumably to be read as "political." It is unclear, however, whether it was intended to be an insertion.

58. Above "Bodin" "Machiavelli" was added by hand. It is unclear, however, whether it was intended to be an insertion.

59. This sentence was inserted by hand.

60. "*paradoxical*" was inserted and underlined by hand.

61. "non-" in "nonhistorical attitude" was inserted by hand to replace "a-" which was crossed out. Since Strauss systematically changed "ahistorical" to "nonhistorical" throughout the remainder of the typescript, the editors have opted not to mention these changes in further footnotes.

62. "philosophic" was inserted by hand.

63. "historical" was inserted by hand.

64. "appeal to" was inserted by typewriter to replace "invoke" which was crossed out.

65. "appeal" was inserted by typewriter to replace "invoke" which was crossed out.

66. Between "present-day" and "democracy," the word "liberal" was crossed out.

67. "always" was inserted by hand.

68. "3." was inserted by hand.

69. "—in a sense—to" was inserted by hand.

70. "understanding" was inserted by hand to replace "knowledge," which was crossed out.

71. "this is not in itself something to boast of" was inserted by hand to replace "a decisive advantage," which was crossed out.

72. The words "erudition . . . Heraclitus said." were inserted by hand at the bottom of the page, with a sign indicating where they should be inserted in the text. Heraclitus, fragment 40 [Diels-Kranz]; see also Charles H. Kahn, *The Art and Thought of Heraclitus: An Edition of the Fragments with Translation and Commentary* (Cambridge: Cambridge University Press, 1979), 36 [fr. 18].

73. "of" following "became" was inserted by hand to replace "a," which was crossed out. "importance" was inserted by hand to replace "advantage," which was crossed out.

74. Square brackets were inserted by hand.

75. Above "do not require," the words "are not susceptible of" were inserted by hand, possibly as an alternative

76. Above "justification," the word "legitimation" was inserted by hand, possibly as an alternative.

77. Above "by" in "by historicism," the word "early" was added, but without any sign indicating it should be inserted.

78. The sentence reading "And this was fatal . . . *past*." was added by hand at the bottom of the page, with a sign indicating where it should be inserted in the text.

79. In the typescript, the bracketed sentence reading "A glance . . . lingering on." was also bracketed by hand. For reasons of readability, the editors have chosen to omit the latter bracketing. In the same sentence, the words ", to put it mildly," were inserted by hand.

80. Above "The progressivist" the words "They did not ask" were inserted by hand, but without a sign indicating it should be inserted as a replacement.

81. This sentence was inserted by hand.

82. The sentence reading "he is convinced in spite . . . understood himself." was bracketed by hand.

83. "the travels of Odysseus" was inserted by hand

84. "by that image" was inserted by hand

85. "sober and serious" was added by hand to replace "earnest" which was crossed out.

86. Following "serious readers," the words "by that image" were crossed out.

87. "their" was crossed out.

88. "philosophic" was inserted by hand

89. "he" was inserted by hand to replace "they," which was crossed out

90. Between "J. Klein's" and "analysis" the word "study" was crossed out.

91. The passage reading "While the modern historian . . . modern algebra," including the handwritten insertion, was bracketed by hand.

92. The passage reading "and who . . . Greek language" was inserted by hand.

93. "most" was inserted by hand to replace "the," which was crossed out.

94. "shows" was inserted by typewriter to replace "implies," which was crossed out.

95. "need" was inserted by hand to replace "must," which was crossed out.

96. "need" was inserted by hand to replace "must," which was crossed out.

97. "denies" inserted by hand to replace "excludes," which was crossed out.

98. "reasonableness" was inserted by hand to replace "possibility," which was crossed out.

99. The sentence reading "it denies . . . true doctrine" was inserted by hand. For reasons of readability, the editors have added a full stop and rendered the following sentence as a new sentence by capitalizing "accordingly."

100. "position" was inserted by hand to replace "philosophy," which was crossed out.

101. "according to the predominant view" was inserted by hand.

102. "certain contemporaries of ours" was inserted to replace "we," which was crossed out.

103. Following the word "understand," the word "to-day" was crossed out. We have added the word "art" after "plastic."

104. Above "ever did" the words "could have done" were added by hand, possibly as an alternative.

105. "thought and thinks" was inserted by hand to replace "was" which was crossed out. "Nonhistorical" was changed by hand to "nonhistorically."

106. Sentence was inserted by hand as a note.

107. "degenerated" was inserted to replace "declined," which was crossed out.

108. "abandoned" was inserted to replace "given up," which was crossed out.

109. "a pre-" in "a presocial state" was inserted by hand to replace "an a-," which was crossed out.

110. Following the words "state of nature," the passage "The implication of such charges . . . Actually, however" was bracketed by hand. Since Strauss replaced the previous last five words, "But quite apart from this this" by "Actually, however," he may have intended to leave this section out, at least during delivery.

111. "a" was inserted by hand to replace "the," which was crossed out.

112. ":" was added by hand.

113. "it mistakes" was inserted by hand to replace "that," which was crossed out.

114. "for" was inserted by hand to replace "is the same as," which was crossed out.

115. "so much" was inserted by hand.

116. "as" was inserted by hand to replace "but," which was crossed out.

117. "But quite apart from this" was typed and not obviously crossed out, but we are presenting the handwritten alternative "Actually, however."

118. "if a hypothetical account," was inserted by hand.

119. "which should be the *introduction* for" was inserted by hand to replace "to be succeeded by," which was crossed out.

120. "position" in "philosophic position" was inserted by hand to replace "question," which was crossed out

121. "5." was inserted by hand.

122. The passage reading "That controversy . . . the good cause" was bracketed by hand.

123. "were to" was inserted by typewriter to replace "should," which was crossed out.

124. "thought of the" was inserted by typewriter.

125. "Set forth in the books of" was inserted by hand to replace "expounded by."

126. "Of" was inserted by hand to replace "by,"

127. The entire paragraph was bracketed by hand.

128. "6." was inserted by hand.

129. The sentence reading "Witness . . . research." was added by hand at the bottom of the page, with a sign indicating where it should be inserted in the text.

130. "typical" was inserted by hand to replace "best," which was crossed out.

131. Following "a collection of true prejudices" there is a sign referring to a note added by hand at the bottom of the page, but the note was crossed out.

132. "inherited" was originally underlined by typewriter. The underlining was crossed out by hand.

133. Following "the modern view." the beginning of a sentence was crossed out by typewriter: "For the time being, it would be wise."

134. "7." was added by hand.

135. Following "principles themselves," a sentence was crossed out by typewriter: "Yet, it is asserted that any restoration is condemned to sterility." The passage reading "Every renascence . . . principles themselves." was bracketed by hand.

136. "a" was inserted by hand to replace "the," which was crossed out.

137. "it is asserted that" was inserted by hand.

138. "might" was inserted by hand.

139. Following "offer us," the words "in the best case" were crossed out by hand.

140. Beneath the text, the word "Dixi—" was added by hand.

3

Facts and Values

Is There a Natural Framework for the Social Sciences?[1]

J. A. COLEN

At the end of the introduction to *Natural Right and History*,[2] Leo Strauss speaks of two opponents of natural right: historicism and the distinction in the social sciences between facts and values. In the first two chapters of the book, accordingly, he directs his attention to these two authorities of our time,[3] "the twin-sisters called Science and History."[4] The transition between the introduction and the first chapter is smooth and subtle—and points immediately to the classics[5]—while the transition from chapter 2 to the study of "the origin of the idea of natural right" is somewhat abrupt[6] and loosely articulated around the return to the commonsense or prescientific world.

It is as if the crisis of historicism had opened the door to the return to the classics, only to stumble on the unsolvable conflict of the many and contradictory principles "of right or of goodness"[7] that tormented Max Weber. We contend here that the connection—between the paradoxes pervading modern social sciences and the return to the discovery of the idea of nature—is more than a mere literary device, or a "flashback" to the past where the idea of nature and thus that of philosophy emerged. The connection is this: the cure for the delusions of the social sciences regarding the separation of facts and values requires the recovery of the fundamental "light of the ideas of nature and science" that grounded the investigations by the Greeks of "various tribes to which they had access." The classics were confronted with the many ways and contradictory conceptions of the "divine law." In their investigations of the diversity of "ways," the classics resorted to "a clear and simple scheme" elucidating the many ways under the light of the ideas of *nature* and of *science*. This scheme "is still immediately intelligible to us" and therefore represents our best chance to "recover the natural frame of reference." The frame of reference of the classics may provide us a way out of the "learned parochialism" of present-day social sciences as represented by Max Weber.

Weber is, indeed, the only author who seems to deserve a full chapter in *Natural Right and History*. As Strauss sees it, Weber is the paradigm of the school upholding the separation between facts and values. Although he also considers him "the greatest social scientist of our century," Strauss is blunt in his accusation: "I contend that Weber's thesis necessarily leads to nihilism or to the view that every preference, however evil, base, or insane, has to be judged before the tribunal of reason to be as legitimate as any other preference."[8] Harsh words that need to be explained, especially since in 1940 he describes Weber's *Science and Learning as a Vocation* as "the most impressive defense, offered in postwar Germany, of modern science and philosophy."[9] He also expresses a seemingly friendlier criticism of the man in the 1919 "turmoil" caused by the aftermath of German defeat and the Spartacist uprising that almost turned the country to communism. He describes Weber as an unusually qualified scholar, who "was not merely a theoretician of the social sciences," but someone who had "enriched the social sciences themselves."[10]

In truth, Strauss never questioned Weber's "probity."[11] The mystery that Strauss wishes to clarify is how Weber was able to hide the consequences of this doctrine from himself.[12] According to Strauss, there is indeed a second form of nihilistic relativism, along with historicism, that is commonplace in current social sciences.[13] Paradoxically, Weber departs from historicism or does not follow it to the end, not exactly because historicism rejects the reference to natural standards, but because he considers that historical standards have a pattern that binds them to historical situations.[14] For Weber the reality is always individual and can only be understood as a partial phenomenon devoid of references to general laws or underlying forces. There is no other meaning than the subjective one, that is, the intentions that actors of history attribute to situations, although—paradoxically—the actors' view of history is so limited that unintended consequences of their actions tend to prevail. The historical situation determines not only life but also thought and human ideals.[15]

If Weber does not accept historicism without qualification, it is because he writes under the strong impression provoked in him by the successes of empirical science. The natural sciences appear to be independent of "world views" and valid for both Westerners and Chinese, with a superiority that can be established by reference to the "rules of logic."[16] Even the social sciences, which are very different from the natural sciences, are a corpus of true propositions independent of any viewpoint. Only the questions that a researcher raises depend on his viewpoint, and this viewpoint upon his own values. Strauss notes the weakness of such a position: the substance of the social sciences is radically historical because its conceptual framework is ephemeral—it depends on a scholar's "values," and these are constantly changing. For the social sciences, it is unthinkable to "expect a final system of the basic concepts"[17] that is a "natural frame of reference"—an expression he uses without further comments in *Natural Right and History*.

However, Leo Strauss in the following text discusses in a leisurely fashion the discovery of a possible natural frame of reference independent of the modern observer.[18]

The Natural Frame of Reference vs. the Psychologist's Frame of Reference

In 1944–45, at the New School, Strauss co-taught courses with Solomon Asch (1907–96) on philosophical anthropology. As regards "philosophical anthropology," Strauss wrote to Asch, "after reading Allport's *Becoming*, [I think] that there is an important lesson to be learned for psychology by these efforts, although they in their turn are subject to legitimate criticism."[19] In fact, just after Strauss's arrival at the New School, in September 1939, Gordon Allport had delivered a famous lecture at Berkeley entitled "The Psychologist's Frame of Reference." Strauss's essay included here, "The Frame of Reference in the Social Sciences," whose title is a direct reference to Allport's lecture, paves the way for such a legitimate criticism. It shows in fact that social scientists' diligent positivism necessarily ends in historicism.

The text itself is the direct result of Strauss's reflections on the approach to the problem of the unity of human sciences of another colleague with whom Strauss also taught about psychology and human nature, Kurt Riezler. Riezler (1882–1955) was a remarkable man, and Strauss seems to have been interested in examining the position that he upheld, which Strauss sometimes characterized as "humanism."[20] In a note written in December 1945, Strauss comments on Riezler's "Some Critical Remarks on Man's Science of Man,"[21] a paper published in the journal of the New School for Social Research. Strauss, Asch, and Riezler shared courses related to the possibility of a science able to deal with human phenomena and human affairs.

The problem of acquiring scientific knowledge of human (political and social) affairs is the starting point of Strauss's text. Strauss tackles the problem by adopting the point of view of modern social sciences. Social sciences, he asserts, are a branch of empirical knowledge that deals with facts and causes without questioning what a fact or a cause is. But social scientists cannot deal with all facts, which are infinite in number. The problem of the social scientist faced with an overwhelming mass of data was not of recent provenance: Ranke's solution had been simply to collect and record as much of it as concretely possible in order to decipher divine providence, since to God all civilizations are immediately present.[22]

There are no concrete references in the text to any authors. The phrasing, however, is clearly neo-Kantian. Heinrich Rickert and the Southwest German School of neo-Kantians tried to find the "categories of understanding" of the social sciences—as Kant did before with Newton's physics—and this attempt was pervasive in the Marburg school that Strauss frequented in his German years. Rickert proposed a criterion for the objective selection of facts. According to him, selection depended on their "relevance" or "significance," i.e., on *values*, a universality principle because values are rooted in a certain collective consensus. As Strauss explains in the text, "relevance," however, "presupposes then *criteria* of relevance." The system of those criteria is in essence, according to Strauss, what may be called a frame of reference.[23] Without a frame of reference, social science would have no subject matter: "[w]ithout a frame of reference, no facts."

A sensible framework would not be arbitrary or circumstantial. The opposite of circumstantial and arbitrary, according to Strauss, is "natural." It would be best, Strauss says in his own name, if we could find the natural frame of reference—a "conceptual scheme that mirrors or articulates the essential structure of society as such." The problem that Strauss points out is that "[p]resent-day social science is inclined to reject the very notion of a natural frame of reference [because] society as society doesn't have a permanent or unchangeable character or structure." Society changes radically during history: "That is to say, its very structure differs from period to period or from civilization to civilization." There is no natural or universal conceptual scheme common to all humanity. Wilhelm Dilthey, in fact, objected to Rickert that we could not sift through the data by resorting to the value system provided by the normal consciousness of humanity, because all collective consensus depends on an always-changeable "worldview." Furthermore, after Dilthey, portraying value systems as always changeable and all the works of the human spirit as essentially dependent on the hidden assumptions of *Weltanschauung*, Georg Simmel insisted, on the impossibility of isolating a "historical atom" that would be the equivalent of the atom of the physical sciences and stressed a limit to the cutting-up operation carried out on the past: a war may be cut into battles, battles into individual combats, and even these in human actions during the combat. After that, to recover the historical account, there has to be a minimum of duration and singularity; it is necessary to restore continuity of facts in time, from which he concluded that there were no conceivable scientific "laws of history." Weber still maintained that in spite of an essentially subjective choice of data, objectivity could be attained by establishing causal relations between the facts.

For Weber, as for the social scientist facing a mass of relevant and irrelevant facts, the "frame of reference of the social sciences is the totality of fundamental questions we address to social phenomena. These questions depend upon the point of view, or the direction of interest," and this depends on the historical situation. The questions are subjective and historical, while the facts and causes seem objective. However, as Strauss notes:

> The scheme doesn't reflect the essential nature of society. It reflects the questions which we here and now are forced to address to social phenomena. The scheme does not correspond to the structure of the subject matter. Compared with the subject matter our scheme has the character of a construction, of an artificial model: our scheme consists of ideal types. Our scheme is then a mere tool for the articulation of social reality, it has no cognitive value in itself.

Weber's position could not be, therefore, consistently defended. Strauss shows in the text how from positivism or empirical social science we are necessarily led to historicism, since "our present scheme will be replaced by another one as soon as our age has ceased to be. The scheme [is] imposed upon us by our situation, by our historical fate." Moreover, even if awareness of this historical fate could deliver us from the evils of the obsolete past, the social scientist is bound to the present point of view. Even if there is a transhistorical core "man in society," it is impossible to grasp and express that core in a permanently valid manner, since approaching that core depends on questions posed from a fundamentally variable point of view.[24]

Strauss spells out the inevitable defeat of social science if this prejudice in favor of the present is adopted: we will never understand any other society but remain "enmeshed in a learned parochialism." Using models, ideal-types, and concepts or whatever tools the social scientist uses that are forced on the past by "the Procrustean bed of our conceptual scheme," we are blinded by our time to a parochial understanding of others. Like a delusional Tartarin de Tarascon, who chased lions in the corridors of his own house that he took for the jungle, the social scientist risks never really leaving his home or his own framework of thought, while thinking to study distant tribes. Strauss, who often speaks only through his Socrates or his Plato, is very direct here: "Is social science possible on the basis of such a type of frame of reference? My answer is no."

In contrast with ever-changing historical "schemes," a "natural frame of reference" is a mere scheme, but a scheme that serves to guide the social scientist and draws a line between the important and unimportant, not to mention telling him "what is good and bad." It will not always have an absolute value as regards action. Some circumstantial things, such as a battle or famine, may deserve "careful attention of the statesman or citizen" and of other groups of people, whereas social scientists do not die in battle and do not starve, but are either detached observers or the advisors of princes. They are not involved in the "accidental and ephemeral" and have no country: they are true citizens of the world. The character of the dictator, chosen by Strauss as an example of the ephemeral and accidental that escapes any historical or sociological laws, is the most paradigmatic accidental factor: men's personalities, incapable of changing the great forces of destiny or the nature of tyranny, but of great practical importance since "the idiosyncrasies of a dictator are terribly important for all who have to live with that dictator."

Sciences of Man between Universal Understanding and "Humanism"

Strauss returns therefore to an idea that historicism could never dismiss entirely: there is a core "man in society." Even if this is inaccessible in a universally valid way, he observes, all the various societies are still *societies.* Restating "society" to mean "we here with our way" and "they there with their way," Strauss raises a related problem, a problem with which his colleague Kurt Riezler was especially concerned.

This problem may be articulated as follows: would not our very attempt at objectivity alter the object of our examination? "By getting a glimpse of the idea of science, of the disinterested pursuit of knowledge," the people whom the scientist is examining "cease to be the people they were." The full understanding of a society would indeed consist in understanding it in its truth *and* its appearance to its ordinary members. However, "it is impossible to leave it at trying to understand other societies as they understand themselves": we "are forced to transcend the self-understanding of the various societies." Perhaps we cannot and should not make ourselves more ignorant than we are and should acknowledge our superiority to tribes who take tin cans to have magic powers. In the essay below, Strauss upholds an orientation of social sciences toward the "in itself," to "universal intelligibility," sacrificing, as he says elsewhere, if need, be the "advantages of existentialism."[25] What is this universal understanding or what is the natural frame of reference Strauss searched for? In trying to rediscover this frame, Strauss, in the last paragraphs of the paper below, returns to Martin Buber's idea of society as "I-Thou" and to the language of "our way" as opposed to "their way."[26] Our particular frame of reference has two ancestral roots. Overcoming the ancestral was the achievement of the Greeks investigating the various tribes through a "simple and clear scheme which is still immediately intelligible to us," based on the *new vistas* of nature and science.

An objection may be immediately raised: has not modern science, which so much impressed Weber, defeated the Greek idea of nature? After all, Aristotle himself defined the battlefield: "the issue between the mechanical and the teleological conception of the universe is decided by the manner in which the problem of the heavens, the heavenly bodies, and their motion is solved."[27] The solution of modern men is to accept a hybrid of (quasi-Epicurean) materialism in the view of the cosmos, while preserving ends and intentions in human affairs. Strauss, however, suggests some reservations about the prevailing modern dualism.

Man and the Idea of Nature

What light, if any, do these reflections throw on the problem of such "typically modern dualism of a nonteleological natural science and a teleological science of man"? Strauss has in mind an "Aristotelian cosmology [that] is in harmony with what we may call the commonsense understanding of things in general, and of human and political things in particular." Even in the course in which he makes that statement, however, he articulates only the *starting* point from which cosmology must begin: "all cosmology, Aristotelian or modern or what have you, must start from the world as given, from the world in which the sun rises in the east and sets in the west and the earth is stationary. It must arise from the world as given to its causes. Aristotle takes this starting point, the world as given, more seriously than all other cosmologies; and for this reason Aristotelian cosmology, regardless of whether it is tenable in its details, has a kind of theoretical superiority."[28]

This theoretical superiority rests on taking the world and society as seen by man, that is, pervaded by ends or purposes. Considering the triumph of mechanical natural science, the question is "whether a better understanding of our frame of reference, in its particular character," will or will not "liberate us from its limitations" in social sciences. Here, in the beginning, Strauss appears to be sanguine:

> The best solution would be a frame of reference . . . , that is to say, a conceptual scheme that mirrors or articulates the essential structure of society as such, and therefore of every *possible* society. This essential structure would be defined by the *purpose* of society, or by the natural *hierarchy* of its purposes.

Here in "The Frame of Reference in the Social Sciences," Strauss indicates the access through "a more thoughtful expression of what all peoples originally mean when they speak of their way." And in the end, he concludes: "It seems to me that we would recover the natural frame of reference by recovering the frame of reference used by the classics," which keeps him busy in the two central chapters in *Natural Right and History*. But in the book, Strauss never explains the alternative to Max Weber's concept of the social sciences, which the text below alone clarifies.

The Frame of Reference in the Social Sciences (1945)[a]

LEO STRAUSS

Social science is an empirical science dealing with facts and their causes, and nothing but facts and their causes. Let us assume that we know what a fact is and what a cause is. Then the first difficulty arises from the circumstance that social science doesn't want to[29] deal with *all* social facts, but only with *relevant* facts. It presupposes then *criteria* of relevance. The system of those criteria may be called the frame of reference. Without a[30] frame of reference social science would have no subject matter. Without a[31] frame of reference, no facts. The question then is, how do we get a sensible frame of reference? The best solution would be a frame of reference which is in no way arbitrary and accidental: the *natural* frame of reference, that is to say, a conceptual scheme that mirrors or articulates the essential structure of society as such, and therefore of every *possible* society. This essential structure would be defined by the *purpose* of society,[32] or by the natural *hierarchy* of its purposes. The essential structure and the hierarchy of the purposes would guide the social scientist, they would tell him what is essential and therefore important, and what is accidental and therefore unimportant, to say nothing of the fact that it would tell him what is good and bad. The accidental would not be regarded as absolutely unimportant. It would be of *crucial* importance for a given group of people here and now, that is to say, for *action*, and therefore it deserves the most careful attention of the statesman or citizen. But from the point of view of the social scientist—who as such is not a statesman or citizen but a *teacher* of statesmen or citizens; who as a scientist is a citizen of the *world*, not of any particular country—the practically important things which are accidental and ephemeral would have to be kept in their place, in a subordinate place.

An example: the idiosyncrasies of a dictator are terribly important for

[a] This typescript can be found at Leo Strauss Papers, box 14, folder 10. The transcript was prepared and annotated by J. A. Colen and Svetozar Minkov.

all who have to live with that dictator, but these idiosyncrasies are not the essence of dictatorship.[33]

Present-day social science is inclined to reject the very notion of a natural frame of reference. It is inclined to think that the notion of a natural frame of reference is based on a fundamental delusion, or on blindness to an all-important fact. That fact is called history. There cannot be a natural frame of reference if society as society doesn't have a permanent or unchangeable character or structure. But, it is argued, society changes radically. That is to say, its very structure differs from period to period or from[34] civilization to civilization. Furthermore: there cannot be a natural frame of reference if man is not able[35] to raise himself[36] above his historical situation to a realm of "essences" which is not affected by historical change. But, it is argued, human thought itself is radically historical; man doesn't think in a vacuum, human thought always belongs to a historical and dynamic context, with whose change human thought itself changes. Accordingly, there are as many frames of reference as there are historical situations. Even granting that in every historical situation the core is "man in[37] society," that is to say, something which is permanent, it is impossible to grasp and to express that permanent thing in a permanently valid manner, in a manner which in principle is valid for all men and all times. Man's understanding of man and society is always bound up with a historical situation to which the individual thinker happens to belong. Or, to state it more simply, the frame of reference of the social sciences is the totality of fundamental questions we address to social phenomena. These questions depend upon the point of view, or the direction of interest, of the questioner. But the point of view or the direction of interest depends upon the social situation, that is to say, on something radically changing or historical. Hence there cannot be a natural frame of reference, that is to say, a conceptual scheme which in principle is final, valid once and for all. The only scheme which is possible is a[38] scheme belonging to our situation, our age—a scheme which is, strictly speaking, ephemeral. Our present scheme will be replaced by another one as soon as our age has ceased to be. The scheme imposed upon us by our situation, by our historical fate, has to be made explicit, it has to be clarified, it has to be liberated from the residues of earlier and obsolete ways of thinking. After this treatment, our scheme permits us to study social phenomena in a scientific manner, it allows us to study the social phenomena which are relevant from our present point of view and *as* they are relevant from our present point of view. The scheme doesn't reflect the essential nature of society. It reflects the questions which we here and now are forced to address to social phenomena. The scheme does not correspond to the structure of the subject matter. Compared with the subject matter, our scheme has the character of a construction, of an artificial model: our scheme consists of ideal types. Our scheme is then a mere tool for the articulation of social reality; it has no cognitive value in itself.

Is social science possible on the basis of such a type of frame of reference? My answer is no. For this kind of frame of reference admittedly reflects the way in which our own society understands itself in our own time. Accordingly, by using such a frame of reference we interpret societies other than our own in terms that are wholly alien to those societies. We force those societies into the Procrustean bed of our conceptual scheme. We do not understand those societies as they understand themselves. But the way in which a society understands itself is an essential element of its *being*, not to say that[39] it is the very essence of each society. Hence we shall not understand those societies as what they *are*. And since we cannot understand our own society adequately if we do not understand societies other than our own, we will not be able to understand even our *own* society. We have then to liberate ourselves from the frame of reference that fate has imposed upon us, so that we can understand societies other than our own as they understand themselves, and therewith, ultimately, our own society. Otherwise, by going to remote times and countries, we shall never leave our here and now, we shall remain enmeshed in a learned parochialism.

If our frame of reference essentially belongs to our historical situation, it is a *hindrance* to our understanding of *other* societies. If we want to understand other societies, we have to understand them in terms of *their* frames of reference. After having abandoned the notion of a natural frame of reference, we have now to abandon the view that any single frame of reference will do. We shall have to have a *variety* of frames of reference in accordance with the[40] variety of societies. Social science has to become strictly historical or interpretative. For example, we must not impute the notion of "state" [a typically modern notion][41] or the distinction between "state" and "society" to any society which doesn't know of it. Or the notion of "art," and the implied distinction between "art," "religion," "morality," and "science." Needless to say, this[42] would apply to the key concept "civilization" itself. No society but Western society of the nineteenth and twentieth centuries ever understood itself as "*a* civilization." We must open our minds to the possibility that concepts of an entirely different type would have to become our guiding notions.

But it is impossible to leave it at that.[43] However great and deep the variety of societies, they all are societies. If the term social science is to have any meaning, it must be concerned ultimately with one self-identical object. We express this identity by speaking of societies. But the question arises whether the notion "society," while less *dated* than the notion "civilization," is not also bound up with a specific orientation. One merely has to try to translate the term[44] "societies" as we use it into Greek to see this. We seem to penetrate to a deeper or more elementary stratum by substituting for society "we here with our way," as distinguished from "they there with their way." It would seem that this orientation is truly universal, that is to say, it is universally *understood*. By making the notion "we here with our way" the key concept, we might seem to keep within the horizon, the *conscious* horizon, of every possible society. A notion of this kind would meet the two decisive conditions: universal applicability, and universal *intelligibility*.

But still, however careful and ascetic we might try to be, we cannot help adding something of our own and therewith interfering with the object of our studies. The study of societies has frequently been guided by the distinction between environment and civilization. Students have tried to understand a civilization, or the world of a people, as a product of its environment. This approach has been questioned because it didn't take into consideration the element of freedom underlying the emergence of a civilization or a world. One conceives therefore of a civilization as a product of a *response* to the environment. To this view one rightly objects by saying that the various societies do not conceive of their world in that manner. What we call their environment, meaning by it the *condition* of their world, is for them a *part* of their world. Mr. Riezler has[45] illustrated this occasionally by the example of the tin cans and the Andaman Islanders.[a] The tin cans are not tin cans for the Andaman Islanders. If we want to understand the world

[a] See Riezler, "Some Critical Remarks," 490: "An anthropologist reports that the Andaman Islanders collect (empty) tin cans. He can be said to describe the life of the Andaman Islanders in terms of his own environment. But these are tin cans, 'objectively'; they are manufactured in Philadelphia, as tin cans. Yes, but this kind of objectivity is irrelevant. They are what they are in the environment of the Andaman Islanders—rare, round, shiny objects—by virtue of the role they play in Andaman life."

of the Andaman Islanders, we have to understand those objects which we know as tin cans, exclusively, in the way in which the Andaman Islanders understand them. Still, we have to admit that we understand the situation *better* if we take into consideration the fact that the objects in questions *are* tin cans. Can we make ourselves more ignorant than we are? And if we could, why should we? Knowing that the objects are tin cans, whereas the Andaman Islanders do not know it, we are forced to understand those people *better*[46] than they understand themselves. We have to *transcend* their world in order to *understand* their world. In the language of a famous[47] philosopher, social science has to understand both how things are *in* themselves, and how they are *for* a given people: the full understanding of a society comprises both, the "in itself" and the "for them."

An anthropologist comes to a tribe never visited before by anthropologists. By some means, he has acquired adequate knowledge of the language of the tribe before joining them. He has an open mind. By living with these people, by avoiding leading questions, he will try to find out gradually what *their* frame of reference is: what *they* consider most important or most fundamental. They may not know that there is *anything* which they consider most fundamental or most important; as M. Jourdain did not know that he was talking prose all his life,[a] their frame of reference is only implicit. The mere fact that he wants to know something from them that[48] they do not really know [they know it only implicitly][49] affects[50] the situation. By bringing something to their attention which was not a theme for *them*,[51] he alters the way in which they understand themselves. That is, he alters their *world*. The mere fact that he has come to them to *understand* their *way*, and not to spy on them, nor to trade with them, nor to hide among them, affects the situation. By getting a glimpse of the idea of science, of the disinterested pursuit of knowledge, they cease to be the people they were.

To sum up: it is impossible to leave it at trying to understand other societies as they understand themselves. We are forced to transcend the self-understanding of the various societies.

We cannot understand societies other than our own with the help of *our* frame of reference. We cannot understand them[52] through *their* frame of reference. Is there any alternative? Is there a frame of reference which is neither ours nor theirs? Only a frame[53] of reference which does not belong

[a] This reference to Molière's *Le bourgeois gentilhomme*, act 2, scene 4 has been added by hand.

to any particular society, only a *natural* frame of reference will do. How are we to obtain such a frame of reference?

To *find* a way let us return to the point where we *lost* our way. Everything seemed all right as long as we could leave it at *our* frame of reference, at our *Western* frame of reference, which seemed to correspond to the last and richest stage of the cultural development of mankind from its beginning till now. I am referring to the scheme that is underlying the notion that the way of a people is a *civilization*, and that a civilization consists of art, morality, religion, economics, law, science, etc. This scheme became doubtful because we realized that it is essentially related to a peculiar civilization, and truly adequate only when applied to that particular civilization. We can state this somewhat more precisely. Our frame of reference is the outgrowth of the combination of two radically different traditions [Greek and Hebrew],[54] of a *peculiar combination* of two *peculiar ways*. The question is, whether a better understanding of our frame of reference, in its peculiar character, will not liberate us from its limitations.

Our frame of reference, to repeat, is the product of a[55] combination of two peculiar ways. Yet the two radically different ways, the Greek way and the Hebrew way, have a common basis. This common basis shows itself if we go back from the peaks to the roots: from Plato's dialogues to Lycurgus as the Spartans saw him, from Jesyah[56] or Paul to Moses as the Hebrews saw him. Provisionally expressed, the common basis is the notion of a divine law, a notion that can be shown to be a necessary consequence or a more thoughtful expression of what all peoples originally mean when they speak of their way. For "our way" is the ancestral way, the way of our ancestors, but it doesn't make sense to cling to the way of our ancestors if our ancestors were not superior to us. And superiority to *us* ultimately means superiority to human beings as such, that is to say, divinity.

The notion of divine law became questionable in the moment when man became sufficiently familiar with the variety of ancestral or divine ways, or with[57] the contradiction between these ways. Out of this experience, there arose the idea of nature and the idea of science. In the light of the ideas of nature and science, the Greeks investigated the various tribes to which they had access. For these investigations they used a clear and simple scheme which is still immediately intelligible to us. At the same time that scheme is historically so close to what was originally common to all peoples that it is least likely to be based on any particular and questionable assumptions. It seems to me that we would recover the natural frame of reference by recovering the frame of reference used by the classics.

Notes

1. This essay is based on a chapter of José Colen, *Facts and Values* (London: Plusprint, 2010, 2017) and on a text prepared for a seminar at Notre Dame University that was modified and included in an essay that was co-authored with Svetozar Minkov (see note 18).

2. *NRH*, 8.

3. Cf. however *PAW*, 156: "The authorities to which these people [those who deny the possibility of a final account of the whole] defer are the twin-sisters of Science and History," with *WIPP*, 259: modern physics and its "twin sister, 'the historical consciousness.'"

4. *PAW*, 156.

5. *NRH*, 34–36.

6. Despite a rationale being provided for the transition at the end of chapter 2.

7. *NRH*, 36.

8. *NRH*, 42.

9. LIG, 118. See the whole of "The Living Issues of German Postwar Philosophy" (1940), Leo Strauss Papers, box 8, folder 14. Pages and quotes are from Meier, *Leo Strauss and the Theologico-Political Problem*.

10. LIG, 126.

11. Cf. Leo Strauss, "Existentialism," *Interpretation* 22, no. 3 (1995).

12. LIG, 126–29.

13. Cf. on Strauss and social sciences and Max Weber in particular: Nasser Behnegar, *Leo Strauss, Max Weber and the Scientific Study of Politics* (Chicago: University of Chicago Press, 2003).

14. *NRH*, 35–37.

15. *NRH*, 38.

16. Ibid.

17. *NRH*, 39.

18. On the circumstances of this piece, see José Colen and Svetozar Minkov, "A Controversy about the Natural Frame of Reference and a Universal Science: Leo Strauss and Kurt Riezler," *Kairos: Revista de Filosofia & Ciência* 10 (2014).

19. See Strauss to Asch, February 17, 1953. I thank Svetozar Minkov for this reference.

20. On Strauss's longer discussion of Riezler in *WIPP*, cf. Susan Shell, "'Kurt Riezler: 1882–1955' and the 'Problem' of Political Philosophy" in *Leo Strauss's Defense of the Philosophic Life*, ed. Rafael Major (Chicago: University of Chicago Press, 2013), 191–214.

21. Kurt Riezler, "Some Critical Remarks on Man's Science of Man," *Social Research* 12, no. 4 (1945): 481–505.

22. See Leopold von Ranke, *Sämtliche Werke*, ed. Alfred Dove (Leipzig: Duncker & Humblot, 1867–1890); Ranke, *Das Briefwerk*, ed. W. P. Fuchs (Munich: Hoffmann und

Campe, 1949); Heinrich Rickert, *Grundprobleme der Philosophie* (Tübingen: Mohr, 1934); Max Weber, *Gesammelte Aufsätze zur Wissenschaftslehre*, 4th ed., ed. J. Winckelmann (Tübingen: Mohr, 1973). Cf. Raymond Aron, *La philosophie critique de l'histoire* (Paris: Seuil, 1970), especially the chapter on Rickert. Max Weber considers the problem on Rickert's terms and tries to address it on the basis of two different criteria: the selection of facts, necesary from the present viewpoint, depends on relevance and on posterity.

23. On "frame of reference," "horizon," "comprehensive view," see *NRH*, 26, 39, 125.

24. Cf. "On Collingwood's Philosophy of History," *Review of Metaphysics* 5, no. 4 (June 1952): 559–86.

25. As Strauss says in 1955, "Universal sympathetic understanding is impossible": "To speak crudely, one cannot have the cake and eat it too; one cannot enjoy both the advantages of universal understanding and those of existentialism." "Social Science and Humanism," *RCPR*, 11.

26. See *NRH*, 82–83 and footnote 3 on that page. The influence of Martin Buber's language is apparent.

27. *NRH*, 8, referring to *Physics* 196a25 and ff., 199a3–5.

28. Seminar on natural right, 1962, lecture 2.

29. "want to" was inserted by hand.

30. "a" was inserted by hand.

31. "a" was inserted by hand.

32. "the" before "society" was crossed out.

33. Strauss wrote by hand but then crossed out the following sentence: "What is essential is that in dictatorship the idiosyncrasies of a single man have a terrible effect."

34. "or from" was typed over a crossed-out word.

35. We have changed "capable" to "able."

36. "himself" was inserted by hand.

37. Strauss crossed out "and" and inserted by hand "in."

38. "the" before "a" was crossed out.

39. "that" was inserted by hand.

40. "the" replaced the "a" previously typed.

41. The square brackets are Strauss's.

42. "that" was crossed out and replaced by "this."

43. We have replaced the comma by a period, since the following word is capitalized.

44. "the term" was inserted by hand.

45. "has" was inserted by hand.

46. "better" was inserted and underlined by hand.

47. A handwritten "famous" replaced a crossed out "[a]n earlier."

48. "that" was inserted by hand.

49. The square brackets are Strauss's.

50. "affects" was typed over the line, replacing "alters" crossed out.

51. "them" was inserted by hand.

52. We have replaced "then" by "them."

53. The word "frame" was repeated and crossed out.

54. The square brackets are Strauss's.

55. "of a" was inserted by hand.

56. Strauss crossed out "Jo" and "Jesaya." Strauss may be referring to Joshua (of Exodus, Numbers, and Joshua), as a peak in the sense of entering the promised land as Moses' successor; another possibility is that the reference is to Jesus.

57. Strauss crossed out "between" and inserted by hand "with."

4

Recovering the Classics

A Presentation of Exotericism in Classical Political Philosophy

CHRISTOPHER LYNCH

Leo Strauss wrote "On the Study of Classical Political Philosophy" shortly after "Strauss became Strauss," that is, as he emerged from a nine-year period of reorientation during which he had rediscovered or invented political philosophy as the eccentric core of philosophy; had worked out the fundamental implications of his rediscovery of exotericism; and had come to recognize the need to understand thinkers as they understood themselves.[1] It was then, in 1938, that he was charting the course for extending his discoveries and presenting them to the world.

"On the Study" anticipates in compressed form and in occasionally blunt—even hyperbolic—tones the key subjects and themes of the first three books of Strauss's maturity, *On Tyranny*, *Persecution and the Art of Writing*, and, most important for our present purposes, *Natural Right and History*. For the piece treats Xenophon at greater length than any other writer, reflecting the fact that Strauss would publish "The Spirit of Sparta or the Taste of Xenophon" just a year later, and representing an early attempt at what would become in *On Tyranny* his deliberately "cumbersome" introduction to "Xenophon's art."[2] The date of "On the Study" coincides with his composition of the article that would become the central chapter of *Persecution and the Art of Writing*; even more explicitly than in *Persecution*, in the 1938 lecture Strauss lays out the centrality of education and persecution as they function within the tense relationship between freedom of thought, on the one hand, and society, on the other, in both classical and modern philosophy. Finally, the distinctions that divide the periods of the history of political philosophy that structure *Natural Right and History* are sharpened here, with special emphasis on how to approach the study of the "classics" examined in the central chapter of Strauss's most-read work.

The piece is divided into two main sections, one that asserts the pervasiveness and importance of exotericism among the classical writers and another that seeks to make plausible that assertion by means of an interpretation of the *Education of Cyrus*. As presented here, the piece is in fact an amalgam of three distinct components: (1) a one-and-a-half-page, handwritten outline consisting of twelve numbered points ranging from terse bullet points to a full paragraph in length; (2) a ten-page typescript, dated November and December of 1938, bearing detailed additions, subtractions, and modifications in Strauss's own hand; (3) an eight-page manuscript in Strauss's hand beginning with the same three words with which the ten-page typescript ends and fulfilling the purpose laid out at the end of the typescript, thereby linking the two.

The handwritten outline clearly sketches an entire argument, but only half of the argument is actually followed in the lecture. The ten-page typescript that makes up section 1 closely follows the outline up through its sixth point and somewhat loosely follows its seventh. In brief, the section first considers two entirely inadequate modern approaches to the study of classical political philosophy as well as Aristotle's philosophical approach; the latter is the "eternal model" for the study of classical political philosophy notwithstanding its apparent inadequacy due to Aristotle's neglect of the exoteric form of Plato's political teaching, an exotericism shared by Herodotus, Thucydides, and Xenophon albeit in different ways. Strauss asserts the need to supply the apparent defect of Aristotle's approach by explicitly stating the reasons for the exotericism of Plato, namely, the inevitable need to avoid persecution and the desire to educate potential philosophers; at the end of the section Strauss explains that myth and history were the original methods of exotericism, dilating more on the ironies employed by the historians than on the stories told in myths.

Had Strauss continued to construct his argument as sketched in the outline, he would have discussed briefly Socratic exotericism and then settled into a lengthy consideration of Plato's exotericism, with two small asides given to Xenophon. From the outline one can surmise that Strauss planned to write something along the lines of the opening paragraphs of the central chapter of *The City and Man*. For the outline ranges over a number of dialogues and includes a stark reference to "*logographike anangke* [logographic necessity]" as well as explaining the chief characteristic of Plato's dialogical form: in his dialogues "Plato never sets forth the truth in a plain way, but he always distorts it with regard to the "*tropoi* [ways of life] of the individual interlocutors," such that one must "deduct in each case the distortion" in order to arrive at the truth.[3] Strauss thus concludes the outline of what would have been the second section with: "Exoteric books [are] more difficult to understand than esoteric books." Instead of this treatment of Plato, Strauss devotes the new section to the *Education of Cyrus*. Although this second section offers a sweeping account of the ironic character of the *Education*, thereby accomplishing its purpose of making plausible the assertions of the first section, the second section ends even more abruptly than it began, breaking off in the midst of a more detailed analysis of key parts of the text.

Why Strauss deviated from the outline is nowhere indicated; nor is it clear why the second section breaks off. It is clear, however, that Strauss intended two numbered sections of exactly this character to constitute parts of a whole presentation on how to study classical political philosophy. What, then, do we gain from this presentation? The chief gains may be said to be the following: Aristotle served as a kind of model *and* anti-model for Strauss's own philosophical politics, at least in this early stage of development; a relatively unguarded account of the causes and the importance of exotericism is offered; and put on display by Strauss is a reading of a classical exoteric text designed to gauge the degree and kind of precision and explicitness required to convince readers of the exoteric character of classical political philosophy.

Aristotle as Model and Anti-model

Aristotle as both model and anti-model emerges from Strauss's dialectical treatment of the inadequate alternatives for the study of classical political philosophy. Strauss first agrees with the criticism of what he calls the dogmatic approach put forth by what he labels the historical approach. The former lays out the apparent teachings of the thinkers of the past and judges each in turn, using as its criterion a standard that tacitly and thoughtlessly assumes the superiority of the reigning thought of the current moment, thereby depriving its practitioners of the incentive truly to understand the teachings of old. The historical approach judges this dogmatic approach to be insufficiently historical, insufficiently true to the historical realities that supply the background of the thought being studied. According to it, what is needed to supply the defect of this approach is an interest in history as such: the desire to know the historical truth will lead to a true understanding of thinkers of the past. In a manner that anticipates, most notably, the first chapter of *Natural Right and History*, Strauss shows in a few paragraphs how this approach undermines itself, since it begs two decisively important questions: that one can understand forthwith that which is to be explained by the historical or sociological explanation, namely, the writer's thought as he understood it, and that the writer's thought was decisively determined by his background. As to the first assumption, what if in "important cases the attempt at understanding the doctrine takes up so much time that practically none is left for . . . sociological explanation"? In addition, what if the thought was written in such a manner as to be "inaccessible to ordinary reading, and therefore to society"? Even if these objections could be met, the second assumption of the historical approach seems far from safe; for what if the thinkers in question engaged in thinking "in order to be able to look at things and men freely, in freedom, that is, from their background, from the prejudices of their time"? In light of this possibility, the author must be understood as he understood himself for historical understanding to be genuinely historical; in all interesting cases, *first* an understanding of how the author in question understood himself must be attained *before* one can adduce an explanation of the historical background that accounts for that self-understanding better than it accounts for itself.

This effort reveals itself to be a philosophic effort, one that requires a philosophical approach that does not, like the dogmatic approach, assume the truth of its own present understanding *and* that does not, like the historical approach, beg the decisive questions. In his treatment of his predecessors, Aristotle—of acknowledged importance to the historical, sociological approach if for no other reason than as a precursor of the current social sciences—provides *the* model for exactly this approach. Aristotle's "discussion of earlier political views does not follow the establishment of the true doctrine, but it precedes that establishment and paves the way for it." Aristotle's objection to the dogmatic approach "is then not that that manner was unhistorical, but that it was unscientific."

Just when he seems to have anointed Aristotle in this manner, Strauss pronounces his approach to be vulnerable to the objection of being "notoriously deficient" owing to "well-known shortcomings of his presentation of Plato's political teaching." While casting doubt on the assumption that putative deficiencies are true simply because they are widely acknowledged, Strauss raises the stakes still further by distinguishing Aristotle's merely putative shortcomings from "the *actual* shortcoming of Aristotle's method."[4] He says,

> In order to understand Aristotle's apparently strange presentation of Plato's political teaching, and thus to realize what the actual shortcoming of Aristotle's method is, we need only to consider the most striking difference be-

tween Aristotle's presentation of Plato's political teaching and Plato's own presentation of it: Aristotle ruthlessly omits all the solemn, all the impressive, all the poetic features of Plato's teaching.

In the very moment of providing a parenthetic escape hatch from this censure of Aristotle, Strauss goes still further in his criticism of Aristotle, identifying the "omission for which Aristotle is to blame": his failure to "explain to us why Plato chose to present his political teaching in a poetical form." To be sure, in the same breath that he says "Aristotle is to blame," he adds, "if he is to blame for it at all,"[5] thereby illustrating that both he and Aristotle had their own ways of being "playful" while "presenting the serious and sober truth." Nonetheless, he then indicates the serious sense in which Aristotle stands in essential need of change: "This is the only essential supplement which the Aristotelian method of presenting, and discussing, the political doctrines of the past requires: we have to consider certainly in a more explicit and coherent way than Aristotle himself has done the presentation of political teaching as it was practiced by Plato." The change required is indeed "essential," but it is also clear that it is merely supplemental and that the necessity is due not to a defect of Aristotle's understanding but to what *we* stand in need of here and now. Strauss sets out a crucial task of his own enterprise: to state more explicitly and more coherently than has been done in the past the reasons for exotericism.

The Idea of Exotericism

Strauss contributes to that enterprise straightaway by stating the reason in very general terms: "The emergence of science in Greece was, in a sense, disastrous to political life" since the man of science, the philosopher, was by definition a critic not just of the law or custom of his city and its gods but of law or custom as such. When Strauss states in general terms the question that necessarily arises for such a man, he understandably notes the difficulty and desirability of establishing some sort of harmony between the philosopher's life and that of the city, given that the philosopher's is essentially unpolitical. But when he gives specifics, two things worthy of note occur: first, he asserts in passing that the superiority of the philosophic life is "indisputable." This is noteworthy because it marks a high point of confidence in the period before Strauss suffers the "shipwreck"[6] that requires him to begin over from the very beginning in an effort to justify precisely what he here says is indisputable and therefore in no need of justification for the sake of the philosopher himself. But when he states the reasons for persecution and the need for careful writing "in other words," he seems not just to restate but to leap: from standing in need of "a certain harmony"—a harmony, we add, that could perhaps be gained by going to ground or "adapt[ing] to the popular mind" without actively seeking to guide it—Strauss jumps to asking, "how can the benefits of proceeding from insight into the nature of things be made fruitful for the guidance of the unphilosophic multitude?" What, we wonder, of the solution offered by Plato's Socrates in the *Republic* of weathering the storms generated by public ignorance as best and as quietly as one can?[7]

The ambiguous or potentially confusing character of his account is to some degree resolved when Strauss injects without preparation the information that the modern world answered the question of how to guide the unphilosophic multitude by "devising popular science." The "classical thinkers," for their part, "answered it by devising exotericism," which was "adapted to the popular mind" while also leading the capable to the philosophic life. Thus, the question stated in terms of how to guide the unphilosophic multitude is the question the moderns posed to themselves, leaving the possibility that the classical thinkers sought instead to establish "a certain harmony" that involved a bifurcated approach that accommodated without necessarily positively guiding the multitude while actively guiding a few to philosophy. As if aware that further clarification is required, Strauss, as it were, tears out a page of *Persecution and the Art of Writing* in advance and inserts it into his lecture.[8] He literally does insert an extra typed page.[9] It begins: "We usually underestimate the bearing of what may fairly be called the most epoch-making event in the history of literature as such in general." This "most epoch-making event" is nothing like the invention of the printing press or of writing as such; nor is it the publication of a particular great book or the creation of a new genre like the novel or the first publication of a philosophical treatise or a political tract. It is, rather, the discontinuation of a particular, essentially brutal—even when practiced with subtlety—political practice that occurred at a particular point in time: the event is the discontinuation in the eighteenth century of "the persecution of free thought."

Strauss is careful to qualify his claim about the epochal character of the end of persecution by placing it within the context of two other important points. The first such qualifying point is that the *essential* motivation of the classical writers was not to avoid persecution; similarly, not merely incidental was the education of potential philosophers that occurred in and through their efforts to unlock the meanings of exoteric writings. Indeed, Strauss suggests the reverse, that the chief purpose of exoteric writing was just such an education, while the avoidance of persecution was an incidental result of the efforts to educate philosophers, albeit a significant result that was both foreseen and desired. For "it is highly probable," Strauss avers, "that they hid their views in order to select and to test and to educate a small minority rather than in order to protect themselves or their doctrines against persecution." Strauss does not go on, as he does when conveying the same thought in *Persecution*,[10] to state its fuller implications, that philosophers constitute a class with one and only one interest: the preservation of philosophy. He does, however, all but state these implications when he supplies a crucial piece of information: it is not so much independent thinkers like Socrates who speak face to face in public and private about human things—and more than human things—who face the most relevant type of persecution, but "those independent thinkers who had the desire of transmitting their views to people whom they did not happen to know even by name, and who, therefore, had no choice but to publish the results of their reflections" in books that could be read by anyone.

The second point that qualifies his claim about the epoch-making character of the end of persecution is that exoteric writing was by no means the exclusive practice of classical writers, since Voltaire as much as Herodotus wrote books whose "heterodox statements were to be read between the lines." It is not as though all exotericism vanished from the earth on a particular date in the eighteenth century; writing between the lines continues into the modern age.

Even if avoidance of persecution was not the chief purpose of classical exotericism, and although modern writers practiced an exotericism of their own, the discontinuation of persecution could still fairly be called "the most epoch-making event in the history of literature as such in general." The reason inheres in the following difference between ancient and modern writers. Whereas classical writers appealed from "the eternal majority" of the unphilosophic multitude to "the eternal minority" of the potential philosophers, modern writers appealed from the unphilosophic "majority of today" to the philosophic "majority of tomorrow," that is, to a humanity that will one day be enlightened by philosophic insight into nature. This event resulted, among other things, in a further discontinuation: that of exotericism as practiced by the "great political thinkers of classical Greece." The end of persecution brought the end of the Greek art of writing designed to elude persecution. Thus, if we wish for whatever reason to gain access to classical political philosophy, we must reawaken ourselves to this forgotten kind of writing.

Exotericism Applied: Xenophon's *Education of Cyrus*

Strauss explains how myth and history are the "two ways open for teaching the truth [to] a minority, while hiding it from the vulgar": Both teach moderation in light of the fragile and changing character of human things. Both teach by deeds rather than words: great characters come to sad ends owing to hubris. Otherwise put, they teach the moderation that attends knowledge of the truth about the fleeting character of human things without teaching that knowledge itself—let alone the source of that knowledge in the additional knowledge of the cold nature of all things. But to do so effectively, to purify their readers of hubris, such writers must first show in all its splendor the greatness that will eventually be brought low. When Strauss turns in section 2 to the *Education of Cyrus*, he shows first how one could easily come to think that Cyrus' fictional empire represents Xenophon's political ideal. Then, almost exclusively on the basis of considerations of the work's title and of what he calls the general internal economy of the work as a whole, he argues that it is anything but his ideal.

Crucial to his argument is an increasingly precise analysis (which he explicitly identifies as such) of the question of whether the Persian Cyrus was corrupted by the Median component of his education. The argument issues in the conclusion that the "apparent praise of Cyrus' apparently marvelous achievement actually is a most stringent censure of a thoroughly bad management of public affairs: the whole *Education of Cyrus* is thoroughly ironical." Strauss would seem to have proven his point: Xenophon teaches moderation by first charming his readers with the splendor of his main character and then dispelling that charm by, most superficially, showing Cyrus' empire evaporate upon his death, but also by allowing a discerning reader to consider the political—if not the ultimate—causes of that evaporation.

Not stopping here, however, Strauss carefully and explicitly gauges what readers will and will not be convinced by. He says, "Most readers will not be convinced by considerations based on the title and the general economy of a book, and on the general assumption that a good writer is very careful in choosing his title and in arranging the economy of his book, if the result of those considerations seems to be in obvious contradiction to every individual statement occurring in the book in question." His whole interpretation is exposed to the charge of importing the arbitrary assumption that Cyrus was indeed corrupted by his Median education rather than demonstrating that corruption and therewith the ironical character of the book; Strauss increases the appearance of his vulnerability to this charge by noting that Xenophon seems to contradict the claim with the delightful story of Cyrus' discussion with his mother regarding how he will learn justice while in Media when his teachers are in Persia. To avoid engaging in the doubly loathsome business of explaining Strauss's explanation of Xenophon's joke, suffice it to say that Strauss concludes his treatment of the story by asking, "Can anybody bring himself to believe that any intelligent writer can have written the sentences quoted without ironical intention? Not to mention," he mentions, "the fact that Xenophon was, after all, the pupil of Socrates." What is important to note here is Strauss's own explicit tracking of the level of explicitness that he is engaged in as he proceeds. He produces a kind of meta-demonstration that marks the distance between Aristotle's ruthlessly scientific approach and his own more gentle but no less scientific approach to the study of classical political philosophy.

At the end of Strauss's outline of the lecture as initially planned, he suggests that there simply is no alternative to this approach. The dogmatic and historical approaches fall beneath the weight of their own contradictions, and Aristotle's will not do in an age that is no longer able even to recall the most epoch-making change in the history of literature, let alone the art of writing that predated it. It is hoped that the publication of this lecture will help to further clarify Strauss's rediscovery that "a good book will fulfill its specific function, i.e., education and teaching, only if it is understood exclusively by itself."

On the Study of Classical Political Philosophy (1938)

LEO STRAUSS

[Plan of the Lecture][a]

On the study of classical political philosophy[b]

1. Three approaches to it: dogmatic, historic, and philosophic.
2. Aristotle the model of philosophic approach.
3. Essential shortcoming of Aristotle's method: his neglect of the form in which Plato's political teaching is presented.
4. The form, i.e., exotericism, is characteristic not only of Plato, but likewise of Herodotus, Thucydides, and Xenophon.
5. Reason of exotericism: opposition between theoretical and political life.

   To explain both the reason leading to exotericism and the fact that it is usually not sufficiently considered somewhat more fully, we may say that we usually understand that bearing of what may fairly be called the most epoch-making event in the history of literature as such in general. Persecution and education.
6. The original methods of exoteric presentation: myth and history.
7. Exotericism and irony: irony of Herodotus, shown by the use of an archaic

[a] Both the handwritten plan and the typescript that follows can be found in the Leo Strauss Papers, box 6, folder 6, and were transcribed by J. A. Colen, reviewed by Christopher Lynch and Svetozar Minkov, and annotated by Christopher Lynch.

[b] Immediately to the right of this handwritten title, in the upper-right-hand corner of the page, is the handwritten note: "The dialectic of the dialogues is only an imitation of the *true* dialectics (Cf. *Rep.* 348a–b)." The identical title also appears in typescript at the beginning of section 1 but is not reiterated here; above and to the left of that typed title is written by hand, "Not more than 27 pages." Above and to the title's right is written by hand, "22.11–27.11.38," and beneath that, "27.12.38–," indicting that some portion of the lecture was written between November 22, 1938, and November 27, 1938, and that another portion was written (or intended to be written) between December 27, 1938, and some later date, probably early in 1939. We nonetheless take 1938 as the year of composition since Strauss supplied no end date and since the extant lecture is incomplete.

language (see Regenbogen)[a] *tetharsekotes toisi ornisi*:[b] irony of Thucydides (see Marcellinus).[c]

The exoteric speech is a speech which gives the untruth an apparent [unreadable][11] over the truth. → Aristotle's definition of the *eiron*.[d]

8. The Socratic method: having talks on the market about things human exclusively, i.e., dialogue.

   The evidence of the *Memorabilia* in favor of another interpretation of Socrates (cf. H. Weissenborn, Xenophon).[e]

9. The Platonic method: combinations with drama, more exactly with comedy.

   Drama and hiding.

10. The fact that Plato discusses the methods of writing and speaking compels us to devote particular interest to him—not to mention the fact that the *Republic*, the *Politicus*, and the *Laws* surpass in importance for the history of political philosophy everything written by Herodotus, Thucydides, and Xenophon.

    —*logographike anangke*[f]

    Plato never sets forth the truth in a plain way, but he always distorts it with regard to the *tropoi* of the individual interlocutors. We must deduct in each case the distortion caused by the nature of the interlocutors. Application to *Republic* and *Laws*: truth distorted with regard to Glaukon or to two old Dorians, in particular Kleinias.

11. Silence: the absence of something

    —e.g., the total absence of Athens and letters in the *Cyropaedia*.

    the absence of Kephalos in the *Republic* and the absence of Alkibiades and Critias in *Laches*.

    the absence of Athens in the *Laws*.

    The peculiar importance of the *Symposium*, where *the* representative of the *political* life has the last word.

    The solitary meditation: cf. Socrates in the *Symposium*. Exoteric books more difficult to understand than esoteric books.

[a] Apparently a reference to an article by Otto Regenbogen, *Herodot und sein Werk: Ein Versuch*, published in the journal *Die Antike* in 1930.

[b] In Greek script; translation: "emboldened by the birds" (see Herodotus 3.76).

[c] A reference to the *Life of Thucydides* by the Roman Marcellinus (consider especially lines 35 and 53).

[d] In Greek script; translation: the ironic one, dissembler; an apparent reference to Aristotle, *Nicomachean Ethics* 4.7.

[e] Apparently a reference to Hermann Weissenborn's 1910 commentary.

[f] In Greek script; translation: logographic necessity.

12. Conclusion: the suggestion made in the present essay is the only alternative I can see to the method still predominant of subjecting the writings of Herodotus, Thucydides, Xenophon, and Plato to what still is called higher criticism. The so-called results of higher criticism have been contested and refuted in a number of important instances by outstanding classical scholars, and we may notice that the view gains in strength that, in the absence of sufficiently clear and complete extant evidence, thorough interpretation and thorough understanding has to precede any attempt of higher criticism.

    Yet we rarely meet with the admission that the very principle of higher criticism prevents its application to the works of masters of the art of writing. For higher criticism may be likened to a sort of surgery[12] or some other sort of medical treatment, which a healthy body is not in need of, but which without it do it only harm. But a good book may be compared with a healthy animal, i.e., with a self-sufficient being with a head and feet and middle parts of its own, which is capable of locomotion without needing crutches: a good book will fulfill its specific function, i.e., education and teaching, only if it is understood exclusively by itself.[13]

I

The traditional method of presenting the history of social or political ideas is more and more considered by modern historians to be inadequate. That method may be described as follows: the social and political doctrines of the various writers are summarized or analyzed, and[14] the summary or analysis of each individual doctrine is followed by a definite judgment on the value of the doctrine in question. The assumption which underlies the use of that method by the modern historian is the opinion that he possesses a clear and distinct knowledge of the standard with reference to which he can judge the doctrines of the past.[15] Now, knowledge of the standard is incomparably more important than is knowledge of earlier writers' right or wrong views of the standard. Consequently, these[16] adherents of the traditional method whose knowledge of the standard precedes their study of the doctrines of the past[17] are not compelled to study these[18] doctrines[19] with that high degree of interest, and therefore of attention and care, which an adequate understanding of them requires. Thus, the interpretation, given by[20] followers of the method, of the doctrines of the past cannot possibly be satisfactory. This censure is fully justified since it is directed against scholars who write books on history: on the history of social or political ideas.

The opponent of the traditional method whom I followed up to this point[a] suggests that the shortcomings of that method cannot be avoided but by students who are "interested in history *qua*[21] history." Two consequences, or presuppositions, of his suggestion deserve to be emphasized. He asserts that the historian of social or political doctrines ought to take into account "their context in time and place, their context in society and culture."[22]

He naturally is aware of the two conditions which must be fulfilled before one can proceed along that line. First, one must dispose of a sufficiently detailed and well-established knowledge of the lives of the thinkers whose doctrines are to be explained with reference to their background; before one attempts a sociological explanation of the doctrines, the doctrines themselves must have been understood.[23] Whether a satisfactory knowledge of the lives can be obtained in all important cases may here remain an open question. But it may safely be said that in some important cases the attempt at understanding the doctrine takes up so much time that practically none is left for their sociological explanation;[24] or, in other words, in those cases the gradual[25] understanding of the doctrine makes us realize the redundancy of any explanation of the doctrine in terms of its social environment: a doctrine inaccessible to ordinary reading, and therefore to society, is for that reason proof against sociological explanation. But let us assume that the two conditions mentioned are fulfilled in all important cases: even then the fruitfulness of the approach suggested entirely depends on whether "the cultural and social background" of the political thinker in question actually had a decisive bearing upon the substance of his doctrine. The background[26] doubtless had such a bearing in the case of a number of outstanding modern political thinkers. But[27] those thinkers themselves had consciously and deliberately subjected their thought to social and political "reality" and, consequently, to the social and political "reality" of their time or of their nation: or is it because of their desire[28] to express "reality" that they became the competent spokesmen of their background?[29] At any rate,[30] it is largely due to the preponderant influence of Hegel's view of philosophy on the history of philosophy that we are inclined to assume from the outset[31] that Aristotle's *Politics*, for example,[32] is nothing other than an expression, or an analysis, of Greek political "reality." But is the background necessarily decisive for the substance of man's thoughts?[33] Would it do any

[a] [LS note] Carl Mayer [review of *A History of Social Philosophy*, by Charles Ellwood)] in *Social Research*, vol. 5, [no. 3], Nov. 1938, pp. 490–93.

harm if one would stoop to reconsider the view, somewhat pushed into the background, that there was a time when men, if a rather limited number of men, did not think in order to express the "reality," or the hopes and fears, of their time or of their nation or of their class, but in order to be able to look at things and men freely, in freedom, that is, from their background, from the prejudices of their time and of their nation and of their class? It seems as if the feeling that the great political thinkers of classical Greece were such men is[34] underlying the opinion, still cherished by a number of people, that those thinkers are teachers of mankind at large and for all times. As a matter of fact, their books show that they were such men, and that, therefore, no considerable profit accrues to the understanding of their teaching from musing over the political and learned affiliations, not expressly emphasized in their books, which they have had or may have had: their books must be understood, and can be understood, from themselves. For they have written them not for the delight, or for the profit, of the then present time only, but they have destined them to be, as one of them puts it, possessions for everlasting.[a] And since they constantly had in mind "the end," or "the beginning," i.e., since they knew the instability of all things merely human, they looked beyond the boundaries not only of their Greek present, but likewise of a future which was merely Greek.[b]

The demand that the student of the political doctrines of the past ought to be interested in "history *qua* history" contains the further implication "that the study of the great social philosophies of the past is of the highest significance and that they themselves are to be taken most seriously." The opponent mentions in this connection with special emphasis the study of Aristotle, which "may be felt to be *directly* important for an understanding of the nature of the social sciences." It is true, a strong case can be made for the view that Aristotle is *the* classic of political science. Yet, if we are truly willing to learn from Aristotle, we must be prepared to learn from him even such things which run counter even to the most impressive of our modern prejudices, i.e., to the historical prejudice. For is not Aristotle, whose views we are to take most seriously if we are to be real historians, the originator of that very traditional method which is combated in the interest of a historical approach? This is not to deny that there are differences between the

[a] A reference to Thucydides 1.22.4.

[b] [LS handwritten note] Cf. the remark of Hans Speier, "The Social Determination of Ideas," *Social Research*, vol. 5 [no. 2, Summer 1938], especially pp. 194f. and 202f.

way in which Aristotle uses that method and the way in which it was used during the nineteenth century: Aristotle did not write a history of social or political ideas. That is to say, when discussing[35] the doctrine of an earlier writer on constitutions or on laws, he did not merely assert, by referring himself to the present stage of social or political research, the deficiency of the doctrine in question, but, in the spirit of the adage *Hic Rhodus, hic salta*,[a] he took the trouble of proving his assertion; in other words, his discussion of earlier political views does not follow the establishment of the true doctrine, but it precedes that establishment and paves the way for it. What he would have objected to the manner in which his method of discussing earlier doctrines was used during the nineteenth century is then not that that manner was unhistorical, but that it was unscientific.

We may thus distinguish three different approaches to the study of classical political philosophy: the dogmatic approach, which was prevalent in the nineteenth century; the historical approach, which is prevalent in our time; and the philosophical approach. The eternal model of the third approach is Aristotle's discussion of the doctrines of his predecessors. This assertion is open to the objection that Aristotle's method is notoriously deficient, and that objection seems to be proved by the well-known shortcomings of his presentation of Plato's political teaching. It cannot be denied that[36] at a first glance we hardly recognize Plato's famous teaching when we read Aristotle's analysis of it. It would, however, be rash[37] to presume that Aristotle did not understand Plato; nor would it be less dangerous[38] to suggest that he was not fair to his teacher. In order to understand Aristotle's apparently strange presentation of Plato's political teaching, and thus to realize what the actual shortcoming of Aristotle's method is, we need only to consider the most striking difference between Aristotle's presentation of Plato's political teaching and Plato's own presentation of it: Aristotle ruthlessly omits all the solemn, all the impressive, all the poetic features of Plato's teaching. But Plato himself does not leave us in any doubt concerning the fact that he did not think very highly of solemn, and of impressive, and of poetical presentations of the truth. For he was no less interested than was Aristotle in the truth, the adequate presentation of which does not permit of the lies of poets or of orators or of sophists both recent and old. For one reason

[a] A proverbial expression, translated literally, "Rhodes is here, jump here," and meaning: Stop boasting and prove your point. It is derived from Aesop's fable of a traveler who returns home from Rhodes to boast of his long-jumping victories there, only to be chastened by demands that he demonstrate at home what he claims to have done in Rhodes.

or the other, however, Plato chose to use playful and enthusiastic lies for presenting the serious and sober truth. The omission for which Aristotle is to blame—if he is to blame for it at all—is then simply this: he does not explain to us why Plato chose to present his political teaching in a poetical form. And this is the only essential[39] supplement which the Aristotelian method of presenting, and discussing, the political doctrines of the past requires: we have to consider certainly in a more explicit and coherent way than Aristotle himself has done the presentation of political teaching as it was practiced by Plato, for instance.

For it must be added at once that Plato was not the only teacher of political principles[40] in classical Greece who presented the truth, or what he believed to be the truth, in an unscientific manner: what holds true of Plato holds equally true of Herodotus, of Thucydides, and of Xenophon. Herodotus does not tire of telling us unbelievable stories invented either by others[41] or by himself; Thucydides composes speeches of the most famous men of his time, which are too revealing of Thucydides' own judgment about those men to be true accounts of what these men actually said;[42] Xenophon presents his political views most exhaustively in a life of Cyrus which is almost completely fictitious. All those writers, whose dominant interest was an interest in truth, chose for one reason or the other to teach the truth not in the form appropriate to truth, i.e., in scientific form, but by making use of an ingenious mixture of truth with fiction or lie. Presenting truth by such a mixture was called in antiquity exoteric presentation. The question with which the student of classical political doctrines is confronted at the threshold of his understanding those doctrines is the question of the reason leading to exoteric presentation of the truth.

To answer that question, one must have grasped first the esoteric teaching which is embedded into the exoteric speech, and which, to begin with, is almost completely hidden by the latter. By raising that question and by attempting to answer it, one does not, however,[43] go beyond the sphere of classical political thought. For it was precisely a political difficulty which the ancients overcame by devising exoteric presentation of truth.

The emergence of science in Greece was, in a sense,[44] disastrous to political life: the man of science, or the philosopher, was as such, i.e., as far as he lived a theoretical life, no longer a citizen of his city and a believer in the gods of his[45] city. Science made him critical not only of such and such a custom or law, but of custom and law as such: *nature*, the object of science, is distinguished from, and opposed to, *law*.[a] Yet man is a political being, and the philosopher is a man. He is therefore confronted with the question: how can the indisputable superiority of the theoretical life, which is essentially unpolitical, be brought into a certain harmony with the unavoidable necessity of leading a political life of some sort?[46] In other words, he is[47] confronted with this[48] question: how can the benefits proceeding from insight into the nature of things be made fruitful for the guidance of the unphilosophic multitude? The modern world has answered that question by devising popular science.[49] The classical thinkers answered it by devising exotericism, i.e., by devising a[50] disguised presentation of truth which is adapted to the popular mind, and yet at the same time appropriate for leading on those who are naturally able to become philosophers to a philosophic life.[51]

We usually underestimate the bearing of what may fairly be called the most epoch-making event in the history of literature as such[52] in general.[53] That event was the[54] discontinuation of persecution of free thought which has taken place in[55] the eighteenth century. During the preceding periods, and in some countries even until a more recent date, persecution was, as it were, the natural condition to which public expression of free thought had to adapt itself. Expression of independent thinking was naturally discouraged and even prohibited, since such thinking is incompatible with the unreserved acceptation of the dominant beliefs, whatever those beliefs may be. Under those circumstances, an independent man was compelled to hide his thoughts more or less[56] carefully. Those independent thinkers who had the desire of transmitting their views to people whom they did not happen to know even by name, and who, therefore, had no choice but to publish the results of their reflections, were then confronted with this dilemma: how can one publish one's views and yet at the same time hide them? The solution which they discovered was based on a rather common observation, on the observation, that is, that most people are very poor readers: very few people are able[57] or willing to read between the lines. They became then

[a] [LS note] This statement requires three explanatory remarks which are not meant to be restrictions. 1. The philosophers naturally preferred the rule of law to lawlessness. 2. *Nature*, being the order of things, could metaphorically be called *law*, with the understanding that that true law, which is nature, is distinguished from, and opposed to, law in the original sense of the word. 3. What Plato objects to is not the antithesis *nature-law*, or else he would not have written the *Crito* or the *Politicus*, but the pre-Socratic view of nature.

able to publish the results of their reflections, while hiding them, by writing books the lines of which were filled with orthodox statements, whereas the heterodox statements were to be read between the lines.

Generally speaking, that device was used in the same way by a man like Voltaire as by Herodotus,[58] for example. There is, however, one great and even decisive difference between the exoteric writers who are characteristic of the seventeenth and eighteenth centuries and the exoteric writers of classical antiquity.[59] Whereas the former appealed from the majority of today to the majority of tomorrow, the latter appealed from the eternal majority to the eternal minority. That is to say, the former assumed that the reign of persecution would be superseded in the near or distant future by a reign of freedom of expression; the latter, however, had no such beliefs in the future:[60] they thought that only a minority of mankind is, and always will be, susceptible of true education. Consequently, the classical writers were able or compelled to hide their thoughts much more artfully than the champions of modern enlightenment. By thus compelling their readers to read most carefully, they gave them a kind of education which is perhaps not equaled in quality by any other kind of education devised ever since. Those writers were aware of the educational value of their manner of writing, and it is highly probable that they hid their views in order to select and to test and to educate a small minority rather than in order to protect themselves or their doctrines against persecution. But however this may be, one cannot understand the classical books in question adequately if one does not stop to consider the original occasion which brought men to hide their thoughts. For a close connection exists between the occasion, i.e., the fact of persecution, and the goal of true education: men were persecuted for independent thinking, and independent thinking is the goal of true education.

To begin with, there were two ways open for teaching the truth to[61] a minority[62] while hiding it from the vulgar, or, in other words, for teaching the truth in a manner consciously and deliberately adapted to the popular prejudices.[63] The first way was the discriminate use of myths or stories. From a practical point of view, the most important consequence of the discovery of *nature*, and of science, is the insight into the insignificance of human greatness and of human aspiration to greatness as compared with the truly great order of the universe. Insight into that order leads to moderation (*sophrosyne*), which as is shown by the experience of all men—of men of all times, and of all nations, and of all classes—is the *conditio sine qua non* of human happiness, or of all dignity[64] of both individuals and communities. Now, man can be taught moderation by certain myths as well, by the myth, e.g., that the gods are jealous of human greatness or[65] of human aspiration to greatness, or by the myth that the naked soul of man, the soul deprived of all earthy goods,[66] has to give an[67] account of his deeds[68] after death. By the use of such myths, man can be taught "civil" moderation, i.e., a moderation which is indispensable for man as far as he is a citizen. But "civil" moderation is not true moderation, and the myths educating man in "civil" moderation are not true. In order to show this, i.e., in order to lead a minority of readers to the philosophic life, the exoteric writer inserts into the myths, or into their context, some subtle hints which will be grasped by those only who are fit to become philosophers.[69]

The second way of teaching men moderation without disclosing to them the true view of nature, and the implications of that view, is writing history. Being under the spell of a tradition of historiography which goes back to an almost immemorial past, and of a less old tradition, which originally was a tradition of orators, of preferring history to philosophy, we naturally assume that the illustrious founders of historiography proper—such men as Herodotus, Thucydides, and Xenophon—took historiography as such to be an important and serious enterprise. Yet the strikingly unhistorical features of their works—features which in the case of such masters of historiography[70] cannot be explained as unintentional and unconscious deficiencies—ought to make us distrustful of our initial assumption. The more or less historical works of those masters appear at a first glance to be descriptions of great deeds of individuals or of communities. For the popular mind judges deeds to be more important than speeches, and within certain limits that judgment doubtless is sound. But it so happens that the truth cannot be attained or transmitted by deeds, but only by speech (*logos*).[a] The true education to moderation would then be an education by true speech, by a speech revealing the nature of the universe and thus of man. But if one wants to teach the unphilosophic multitude moderation, one must show them by deeds rather than by speeches where *hybris* leads to, i.e., what the end of *hybris* is. It is for this reason that Herodotus describes the end of Persian *hybris*, and that Thucydides describes the end of Athenian *hybris*, and that Xenophon lets us have a glimpse at the end of the Spartan constitution and of Cyrus'

[a] [LS note] The bearing of the *deed-speech*-antithesis for classical thought can most clearly be seen from a comparison of Plato's *Apology* 32a4–5 with *Crito* 52d5. Those passages explain the cryptic statement of Socrates about his *daimonion* in *Apology* 31d3–4.

empire.—[71] The teacher of moderation would be a mere preacher if he limited himself to a description of the end of *hybris* only. He will not effect purification (*katharsis*) from hybris[72] but by first imitating, and thus letting[73] us experience in a concentrated manner, the incredible charm exercised by successful *hybris*; he has thus[74] to show to begin with[75] the greatness of the allegedly great men or communities in all its splendor, just as if he were fully convinced of the solidity of that greatness, without doing the least thing which could destroy our illusion; that is to say, he has to show us first that greatness in[76] the splendor of its gradual growth, a splendor which everybody would be inclined to compare with the rise of the sun. It is for this reason that Herodotus gives us such a vast description of the rise, which nobody could stop, of the Persian empire, and Thucydides gives us such a condensed and forcible description of Athens's inevitable rise to power, and Xenophon deals almost exclusively with Cyrus' brilliant ascent.—None of those masters discloses the end before its time has come: by only gradually disclosing the truth about *hybris*, he imitates the way in which the vulgar comes to realize that truth, for the vulgar does not realize it but by seeing the end "in deed, and not in speech." Yet the end of hybris can be seen from the very beginning, not, it is true, "in deed," but "in speech." It is for this reason that Herodotus, Thucydides, and Xenophon disclose the end, which "in deed" is not shown before the end of their Histories, "in speech" from the very beginning of their works: they do this by using strange words or expressions, for example,[77] which are easily overlooked or misunderstood (and therefore mistranslated or emended or deleted) even by very learned readers.[78]—The popular mind of ancient times knew of a kind of speeches which disclose the end a[79] long time before it has come about: the oracles were such speeches. Divination claims to be knowledge of the end. That claim is futile; yet divination may be used as a symbol, appealing to the popular mind, of that true science of the end which is rather knowledge of the nature, or of the "beginning" (*archê*), of man and of things. It is for this reason that we read so much in Herodotus and in Xenophon, and even in Plato, about oracles.—Teaching moderation by writing history is teaching by deeds, and not by speech. But as is indicated by the fact that the classical[80] teachers of moderation insert a considerable[81] number of speeches into their accounts of deeds, teaching by deeds alone is hardly possible. And we may even doubt whether teaching by deeds is possible at all. For what else are those histories which apparently teach the truth by deeds only[82] if not speeches? Those histories teach the truth—the truth about man in particular, but therewith the truth about nature in general—by speech, if by exoteric speech.

II

To make the foregoing assertions somewhat more plausible than they may appear to be at first sight, they shall be illustrated by a brief discussion of the meaning of Xenophon's *Education of Cyrus*. It is generally[a]

[a] The typescript ends abruptly at this point.

[On Xenophon's *Education of Cyrus*][a]

It is, I believe, generally[b] recognized that that book (sc. Xenophon's *Education of Cyrus*) is not a historical work, but a fictitious presentation of what Xenophon considered to be a perfect government. The book opens with the question whether lasting rule[83] of men over men,[84] as distinguished from rule[85] of men over animals, is possible at all,[86] and with the answer that such government[87] is not impossible and not even difficult to achieve, provided it is practiced in an intelligent, a "scientific," way. This answer is based on the observation that King Cyrus of Persia was able to rule, with the free consent of his subjects, over an extremely vast empire consisting of heterogeneous nations which had not even a language in common. Cyrus represents, then, the model of intelligent or "scientific" rule. Now, Cyrus eventually was an

[a] This manuscript can be found in Leo Strauss Papers, box 6, folder 11. This transcription was produced by Christopher Lynch and Svetozar Minkov and annotated by Christopher Lynch; it benefited from comparison with the transcription included in Emmanuel Patard, *Leo Strauss at the New School for Social Research (1938–1948): Essays, Lectures, and Courses on Ancient and Modern Political Philosophy*, edited with an introduction (n.d; n.p.). The same author completed a doctoral dissertation at the Université Paris I (Panthéon-Sorbonne), in March 2013 entitled *Leo Strauss à la New School for Social Research (1938–1948). Essais, conférences et cours sur la philosophie politique ancienne et moderne.*

[b] A manuscript begins just as the typescript ends, with the words, "It is generally"; in addition, the words "I believe" are written above with a caret after "is" indicating their later insertion. The remainder of this document is a transcription of the manuscript. Because the manuscript is untitled, undated, and currently located in a folder that contains Strauss's work on Xenophon, especially the *Oeconomicus*, from 1940–42, rather than with the typescript of OSCPP, we cannot be certain that this particular version of Strauss's *Education of Cyrus* interpretation was the one initially meant to form a part of OSCPP or whether what we offer is a version written at another time, such as the 1940–44 period. It is certain, however, that the manuscript begins with the words with which the typescript ends and that the manuscript performs exactly the function the typescript lays out for section 2: to make plausible Strauss's assertions in section 1 by means of a discussion of the meaning of the *Education of Cyrus*. We therefore offer the two pieces together here in what may have been the exact form intended by Strauss or, at the very least, as the best available representation of Strauss's intention.

absolute monarch.[a][88] Thus, we are led to believe that Xenophon judged a vast empire,[b] ruled by an absolute monarch of outstanding moral and intellectual capacities—by a born king,[c] who is most willing to learn and most benevolent toward all men[d]—to be the best polity.[e] Two things are[89] certain: Xenophon ranks foremost among the writers who bestowed high praise upon[90] an individual absolute ruler, or absolute rule in general; and nothing which has been written by Romans in praise of the Roman empire, or by English in praise of the British empire, excels, and it hardly equals, what the Athenian Xenophon says in praise of Cyrus' Persian empire.

The fact that the Greek Xenophon holds up a Persian king, and a Persian king whom he had to magnify much beyond the limits of truth in order to make him fit for that purpose, as the model of a ruler is highly perplexing. Was he a lover of Persians or a hater of Greeks? This is rather unlikely; for when praising the Spartan King Agesilaus, he asserts, if in conditional clauses, that it is noble for a Greek to be a lover of Greeks and a hater of Persians.[f] It is understandable that he did not use the Athenian empire, the downfall of which he witnessed, as the starting point for his description of a perfect polity: being a decided adversary of democracy, and realizing the connection between Athenian democracy and Athenian sea power, he had to choose an empire, such as his Persian empire was, which had no navy at all.[g] But why did he not stick to the undemocratic government of Sparta, which he praises so highly in his *Constitution of Lacedaemon*? Did he believe that that polity[91] would gain in value by assuming the dimensions of[92] a vast empire and by being transplanted into a barbarian atmosphere?[93]

Unfortunately, the very standards with reference to which he praises

[a] [LS note] See especially [*Education of Cyrus*] VIII 1.17–20, 1.22; 1.48–2.4; 2.10–12; 3.13–15.

[b] [LS note] Cf. [*Education of Cyrus*] VIII 2.5–6. I 4–11.

[c] [LS note] [*Education of Cyrus*] I 4.9 and VIII 1.37.

[d] [LS note] See e.g. I 2.1.

[e] [LS note] Cf. Alfred Croiset, *Xénophon*, Paris, 1873, pp. 144f., 156, 160, who however adds the remark that Xenophon never expressly asserts the kind of rule exercised by Cyrus to be the best form of government.

[f] [LS note] *Agesilaus* VII 4.7; cf. VIII 4.—To the same connection belongs his praising the Spartan law forbidding sojourns in foreign places, and the Spartan usage of expelling foreigners (*Rep. Lac.* XIV 4), as well as his praising Lycurgus' refusal to imitate any other city (ibid. I 2). Cf. also the praise of Greek liberty (as opposed to Persian despotism) in *Anab.* III 2.13.

[g] [LS note] Navy in *Rep.*, *Legg.*

Cyrus' empire on the one hand, and the Spartan commonwealth on the other, are not exactly the same. He praises the former for the large number of nations of which it consists, and he praises Sparta rather for the smallness of its population.[a] He praises the Spartan institutions because of their great antiquity;[b] he praises especially the fact that the lineage of Spartan kings has always been continuous, a fact which is all the more conspicuous since no comparable continuity is to be found in any other commonwealth, whether ruled by monarchs or otherwise: as regards in particular the dynasty which started with[94] Cyrus, it scarcely lasted longer than his life.[c95] But, above all, the Spartan constitution is not only no absolute monarchy, but hardly a monarchy at all; it might more appropriately be called an oligarchy.[d] On the basis of Xenophon's praise of Sparta, we have to say that for him the political ideal, far from being a vast empire ruled by an absolute monarch however enlightened and benevolent, was rather a small if very powerful commonwealth governed by a small number of highly trained, or educated, men. And we may be tempted to explain the contradiction between the *Constitution of Lacedaemon* and the *Education of Cyrus* by assuming that Xenophon's political views underwent a profound change:[96] that at one time of his life he preferred the Spartan constitution, and at another Cyrus' Persian empire.

That explanation would not, however, solve the difficulty. For the contradiction between the ideal of Spartan oligarchy and the ideal of Persian absolute monarchy occurs within the *Education of Cyrus* itself: the original constitution of Persia under which Cyrus grew up, as distinguished from the eventual constitution of his empire, is an idealized Spartan constitution.[e]

[a] [LS note] *Rep. Lac.* I1. Cf. *Hell.* VII 2.1 and *Anab.* I 5.9.

[b] [LS note] *Rep. Lac.* X 8.

[c] [LS note] Cf. *Rep. Lac.* XV 1 and *Ages.* I 4 with *Cyrop.* I 1 and VIII 8.2.

[d] [LS note] Cf. *Rep. Lac.* VIII 4 (the tyrannic power of the ephors) and XV 7–8.

[e] [LS note] See Croiset, loc. cit., pp. 149ff., and Guil[elmus or Wilhelm] Prinz, *De Xenophontis Cyri institutione*, Göttingen, 1911, pp. 8–13.—The following improvements of the Persian constitution upon the Spartan constitution deserve to be emphasized. The Persians have "schools of justice" ([*Education of Cyrus*] (I 2.6), the Spartans have not. Whereas the Spartans teach their children "to steal well," that sort of education is wisely rejected by the Persians (cf. [*Education of Cyrus*] I 6.31–32 with *Rep. Lac.* II 6–9). Whereas the Spartans educate their youths to silence (*Rep. Lac.* III 1), the Persians, by compelling their boys to give and take account of their doings, educate them to a charming talkativeness ([*Education of Cyrus*] I 4.4 and 3.12), which enables them to converse with one another in a way reminding of the manner of Socrates and his friends (see especially [*Education of Cyrus*] I 6 and II 2).—Cf. also [*Education of Cyrus*] IV 2.1, 3.8.

Thus, the question as to what Xenophon's political ideal was must and can be answered on the basis of a single book of his. As a matter of fact, the account of the way in which Cyrus gradually replaced the original Persian constitution by the eventual constitution of his empire is the main thread of the story told in the *Education of Cyrus*. Therefore, the general question as to what Xenophon's political ideal was can be reduced to the more precise question: is the substitution, effected by Cyrus, of the absolute monarchy for an ideal oligarchy considered by Xenophon to be an improvement upon the latter or a deterioration of it?

The surest guide to the answer to this question is implied by the title *Education of Cyrus*, which is, in a sense, inadequate—for the book deals with the whole life of Cyrus and not with his education only—, but which has not been chosen at random: it is by the title that Xenophon gives us the[97] key to the understanding of the whole work. Cyrus, being the son of the king of Persia, i.e., of a king who had to obey the laws, "was educated, it is true, in the laws of the Persians." But so were all other Persian boys of good families. There was, however, an important difference between the education of Cyrus and the education of his fellow boys, a difference which helps to explain why he, and he only, became the founder of an[98] empire. He spent the first twelve years of his life in Persia and in the same ways all other noble Persian boys did; but, thereafter, he stayed for a couple of years with his mother's father, King Astyages of Media. "He was educated, it is true, in the laws of the Persians," but "he was brought up" in Media as well.[a] Thus, his education consists of two parts, of a Persian education and of a Median upbringing. It was the happy and unique combination of these two types of education which largely accounts for the marvelous achievements of Cyrus. This result, a hint of which is given by the title, is confirmed by the story as a whole. For the conception that Cyrus represents the peaceful "synthesis" of the Persian with the Median spirit determines the whole biography of Cyrus as told by Xenophon: this biography is nothing other than a picturesque presentation of that conception. It is with that conception in mind that Xenophon falsifies the most outstanding and recorded facts of Cyrus' career: whereas in fact Cyrus forcibly dethroned Astyages while liberating the Persians from Median subjugation,[b] according to Xenophon he ascends

[a] [LS note] [*Education of Cyrus*] I 2.2 and I 4.1 (IV 2.10).

[b] [LS note] This is indicated by Xenophon in *Anabasis* III 4.8 and 4.11. ["This" replaces "the truth"; several other difficult to decipher alternatives are crossed out, including perhaps: "Xenophon knew, of course, the truth" and "The true story."]

the Median throne in the most peaceful way by marrying Astyages' only other grandchild while being the lawful heir to the Persian throne,[99] and whereas, according to Herodotus,[a] Cyrus was brought up by a shepherd and his wife, he had been given, according to Xenophon, the best education which both Persia and Media knew of.

We are now in a position to repeat our original question in a still more precise fashion.[100] We had reduced the question as to what Xenophon's political teaching was to the question as to whether he judged the substitution, effected by Cyrus, of the eventual constitution of the Persian empire for the original constitution of Persia to be an improvement upon the latter or a deterioration of it. Now, the foundation of the Persian empire, the heart of which was Persia and Media, i.e., the substitution of an absolute monarchy for an ideal oligarchy, was largely due to Cyrus' education, and this education consisted of a Persian education and a Median upbringing. Consequently, the difference between the eventual constitution of the Persian empire and the original constitution of Persia is largely due to the influence on Cyrus' mind of the Median spirit. We have, therefore, to raise the question: is the Median spirit equal in value to, or different in value from, the Persian spirit? In the answer to this apparently very special question, the answer to the general question of what Xenophon's political teaching was is implied.

What was, then, according to Xenophon, the difference between the Persian mode of life, or constitution,[b] and the Median constitution? The Persians enjoy a moral education of exceptionally high standing,[c] but nothing of the kind is met with in Media. The Persians are lovers of toil, and they eat and drink and dress in a most frugal and simple ("Spartan") way, but the Medes are lovers of splendor and luxury.[d] The Persians are free and, in principle, equal; political distinction among them almost entirely depends on distinction as regards education; thus, the actual rule is in the hands of a highly educated minority; the Persian king has to obey the laws and to respect the citizens who are his equals; he is supreme only as regards leadership in war and worship of the gods; the Medes, on the other hand, are ruled by a despot, whose desires are the laws of the community: whereas the principle guiding the Persian king is equality and legality, the principle

[a] [LS note] [Herodotus *Histories*] I 113.3; 122.3; cf. 130.3.

[b] [LS note] Cf. Aristotle, *Politics*, 1295b1.

[c] [LS note] [*Education of Cyrus*] I 2.2ff.

[d] [LS note] [Ibid.] I 3.2ff. and 5.1.

guiding the Median tyrant is "having more than the others" (*pleonexia*).[a] The Persians in accordance with their "Spartan" mode of life and their aristocratic government have an "equal freedom of speech" for all; the Medes enjoy such a dubious freedom only if[101] they and their king are drunk.[b] The Persian education leads to a charming ("Attic") talkativeness which is most becoming for freemen, whereas the despotically ruled Medes do not know to use their tongue.[c102]

Xenophon's descriptions of the (original) Persian constitution and the Median constitution do not leave the slightest doubt that he judged the former to be absolutely superior to the latter: the Median spirit is characterized by a barbarian coarseness and servility; the Persian spirit apparently unites all which is best in both Sparta and Athens. Now, Cyrus' foundation of the Persian empire, i.e., his substitution of an absolute monarchy for an ideal oligarchy, is largely due to the influence on his mind of his partly Median upbringing; therefore, the substitution is definitely a destruction of an excellent political order, a destruction which became visible even to the most short-sighted[103] eyes immediately after the death of Cyrus; for human nature is such, and the difficulties of ruling human beings are so great, that the short-lived success of a tyrant is marveled at as a great feat of wisdom.[d104] Consequently, Xenophon's political ideal was not a vast empire ruled by an absolute monarch, but rather a small, if very powerful, commonwealth ruled by a highly educated minority. The apparent praise of Cyrus' apparently marvelous achievement actually is a most stringent censure of a thoroughly[105] bad management of public affairs: the whole *Education of Cyrus* is thoroughly ironical.

Most readers will not be convinced by considerations based on the title and the general economy of a book and on the general assumption that a good writer is very careful in choosing his[106] title and in arranging the

[a] [LS note] [*Education of Cyrus*] I 1.4; 2.3; 3.18; 5.4–5; II 1.3; VIII 5.22.

[b] [LS note] [Ibid.] I 3.10.

[c] [LS note] [Ibid.] I 4.3 and 4.12.

[d] [LS note] [Ibid.] I 1.1 (cf. I 3.18 with the passages quoted in p. 1, n. 1) and VIII 8.2.—Dakyns makes the following occasional remark on (his translation of) V 5.39–40: "as a matter of philosophic 'historising,' probably Xenophon conceives the Median element as the corruption and sapping one in the Persian empire (*vide* Epilogue), only he to some extent justifies and excuses Cyrus in his imitations of it. That is a difficulty." It is *the* difficulty and, therefore, the key to the understanding of Xenophon's teaching. Cf. *Rep. Lac.* XV 1 and *Ages.* 1.4, passages which contain the epilogue of the *Education of Cyrus in nuce*. [The quotation in this note is from *The Education of Cyrus*, trans. Henry Graham Dakyns (London: J. M. Dent and Sons, 1914), 188.]

economy of his book,[107] if the result of those considerations appears[108] to be in obvious contradiction to every individual statement occurring in the book in question. Thus, our finding is open to the objection that it is based on a mere assumption, on the assumption, that is, that Cyrus actually underwent the debasing[109] influence of the Median spirit to any considerable degree. The assumption seems, besides, flatly contradicted by an express statement of Xenophon, according to which Cyrus, when returning from Media to Persia, still was the same uncorrupted and charming[110] Persian public school boy he was when he left his country. Thus the account of his Median period, far from indicating that he was corrupted by the bad spirit of Media, actually seems to be[111] destined to set forth in the most impressive way how little his excellent nature, strengthened by an excellent education, was susceptible to corruption by the very worst environment. Yet, attractive[112] though this interpretation might be, it cannot be upheld once one takes the trouble of reading somewhat more carefully the statement in question and of considering the context within which it occurs.[a] First of all, it is not Xenophon[113] who finds that Cyrus was not corrupted by Media, but the Persian boys, and it is not likely that Xenophon[114] considers boys of fifteen or so to be sufficiently discerning judges of the true signs;[115] for what impressed[116] those boys most was the fact that Cyrus had not lost his (Persian) frugality and love of toil, i.e., qualities which are characteristic likewise of "noble and just men"[117] and of a certain kind of criminal.[118] And, besides, Xenophon clearly indicates that by staying for a couple of years in Media, Cyrus was prevented from attending[119] his lessons[120] of justice: he interrupted his education in justice. But while learning justice less than his Persian fellows, he learned more,[121] i.e., at a much earlier age than they, the arts of hunting and war, which are the arts related to the virtue of manliness.[b] His strong side was, then, not justice, but manliness, i.e., he had the moral equipment befitting the founder of an empire based on conquest. Or are we to believe that Cyrus was such a born saint[122] that he would interrupt his lessons in justice without any harm being done to his character? This he himself seems to believe,[123] and he even utters this belief when discussing with his mother whether it will be advisable for him to prolong his Median

[a] [LS note] [Ibid.,] I 5.1.

[b] [LS note] Cf. [Ibid.,] I 4.25 with I 3–4. [Strauss appears in this note to suggest comparing a single passage on a moment toward the end of Cyrus' Median education (I 4.25) with the whole period of that education (I 3–4).]

sojourn. To the question of his mother, "But justice, my son, how will you learn it here (sc. in Media), when your teachers are there (sc. in Persia)?," Cyrus replies, "But, mother, I have these things at my fingertips already." And when the twelve-year-old boy[124] repeats this able[125] remark somewhat later on in the same discussion by adding, "If I need anything further (sc. as regards instruction in justice), my grandfather (sc. the tyrant of Media) here will give me an additional instruction," and his mother draws his attention to the fact that, strictly speaking, there is no justice at all to be found in Media—for the desires of the king are the laws of the land—and that what he could possibly learn in Media is the view that he ought to "have more" than others, Cyrus rejoins, "Your father is more clever in teaching people to have less than to have more; for do not you see that he has taught all the Medians to have less than himself?"[126] Can anybody bring himself to believe that any intelligent writer[127] can have written the sentences quoted without ironical intention? Not to mention the fact that Xenophon was, after all, the pupil of Socrates, i.e., of a man who not only taught that justice is knowledge and therefore is acquired exclusively by some specific training,[a] but who likewise was famous for his irony.

But let us be more exact. Let us see what the most important alterations, effected by Cyrus, of the old Persian constitution are, and whether or not[128] these alterations betrayed Median influence. His first public action is a speech which he delivers before the Persian nobility almost immediately after having been elected as a general by the Persian commonwealth. In that speech he points out what he considers to be the fundamental shortcoming of the original constitution, or of the traditional mode of life, of the Persians. He confesses that the former generations of the Persians were not inferior to the present one as far as the actions of virtue themselves are concerned; but he fails to see that they increased by their military virtue their own and the city's wealth and happiness and honors.[b] The Persians of old lacked, then, that taste for "having more" which Cyrus may easily have acquired in Media. At any rate, his first political action is an attempt to instill that taste into the minds of the Persians. That is to say, the relation of Cyrus to the Persians of old is exactly the same as that of the Lacedaemonians of Xenophon's time to the Lacedaemonians of old; for the latter

[a] [LS note] *Memor.* III 9.5 and I 2.19, 2.23 with III 5.24.

[b] [LS note] [*Education of Cyrus*] I 5.7ff.

were interested in being worthy to lead, whereas the former are interested in ruling rather than in being worthy of rule.[a] Cyrus' second public action is the reorganization of the Persian army.

Notes

1. Heinrich Meier, "How Strauss Became Strauss," *Enlightening Revolutions: Essays in Honor of Ralph Lerner*, ed. Svetozar Minkov (Lanham, MD: Lexington Books, 2007), 366.

2. *OT*, 28.

3. Cf. *CM*, 60.

4. My emphasis.

5. My emphasis.

6. Meier, *Leo Strauss and the Theological-Political Problem*, 29.

7. Plato, *Republic* 496d; see *CM*, 79, where Strauss, in his only treatment of this particular discussion of the philosopher minding his own business, pretends that it describes the life of the retiring gentleman rather than that of the retiring philosopher; cf. pp. 122–26.

8. Strauss treats similar issues in an essay written in 1939; see "Exoteric Teaching" in *The Rebirth of Classical Political Rationalism: An Introduction to the Thought of Leo Strauss*, ed. Thomas Pangle (Chicago: University of Chicago Press, 1989).

9. Strauss numbers it "6a," continuing its contents in handwriting on the back of the page.

10. *PAW*, 17–18.

11. The unreadable word could be "übergewicht," German for "preponderant."

12. Crossed out: "destined."

13. The paragraph is on the verso of the page.

14. "and" was inserted by hand.

15. After this sentence, the following sentence was crossed out by hand: "In some cases, that opinion takes on the form of the belief that modern sociology supplies the historian with the indispensable knowledge of the standard."

16. Illegible words were crossed out and are partly missing; "these" was inserted by hand.

17. "whose knowledge of the standard precedes their study of the doctrines of the past" was inserted by hand. Also inserted by hand at the bottom of the page was an alternative formulation: "who as such do not expect to be materially helped in their knowledge of the standard by historical studies."

18. "the" was crossed out and "these" inserted by hand.

19. "of the past" was crossed out by hand after "doctrines."

20. After "by" "modern" was crossed out and replaced by hand with "such"; "such" was then crossed out by hand as well.

21. Strauss wrote "quâ."

[a] [LS note] *Rep. Lac.* XIV 5.

22. After this sentence the following was crossed out by hand: "The fruitfulness of that approach, however, entirely depends on whether "the cultural and social back-"

23. "with reference to their background, before one attempts a sociological explanation of the doctrines, the doctrines themselves must have been understood" was inserted by hand, apparently replacing "and, besides, the doctrines to be explained must, to begin with, be understood," which was not crossed out.

24. "their sociological explanation": initially, "the explanation of it"; then, "the" and "of it" were crossed out by typed X's and "its" was typed above "the," resulting in "its explanation"; finally, "its" was crossed out by hand and "sociological" was added by hand.

25. "gradual" was typed above "the understanding" with a caret insert by hand between "the" and "understanding."

26. Typed quotation marks around "background" were crossed out by hand here and throughout the paragraph.

27. After "But," "this was due to the fact that" was crossed out by hand.

28. "or is it because of their desire" was added by hand to replace "it is mainly because they desired," which was crossed out by hand.

29. Question mark was added by hand.

30. "At any rate," was added by hand, replacing "And," which was crossed out by hand.

31. "from the outset" was added by hand.

32. Strauss wrote "e.g."

33. The next sentence was crossed out by hand: "Is it impossible to attempt, not expressing the 'background' or always changing 'reality,' but understanding eternal truth?"

34. "is" was preceded by "was" crossed out by typed X's.

35. "discussing" was added by hand, replacing "criticizing," which was crossed out by hand.

36. "cannot be denied that" was inserted by hand, replacing "is true," which was crossed out by hand.

37. "rash" was inserted by hand, replacing "absurd," which was crossed out by hand.

38. "less dangerous" was inserted by hand, replacing "more correct," which was crossed out by hand.

39. "essential" was inserted by hand, replacing "important," which was crossed out by hand.

40. "principles" was inserted by hand; another illegible word inserted by hand but crossed out by hand.

41. "others" was typed above "him," which was crossed out with typed X's.

42. "true accounts of what these men actually said" was written by hand and inserted to replace a typewritten "true" which was crossed out; above it were several crossed-out illegible handwritten words.

43. "however" was added by hand.

44. "was, in a sense," was added by hand, replacing "led to a consequence which was," which was crossed out by hand.

45. Followed by "or of any other," was crossed out by hand.

46. "sort" was inserted by hand, replacing "kind," which was crossed out by hand.

47. "is" was inserted by hand, replacing "was," which was crossed out by hand.

48. "is" was inserted by hand, crossing out the "e" in "the" so that "the" became "this."

49. Above "science" is an illegible word inserted by hand.

50. "a" was inserted by hand.

51. An X was inserted by hand at the end of the paragraph, denoting a footnote; another such X was inserted in the margin to the left of the typed footnote contained in note 36 above. At the foot of the page are two handwritten notes, each beginning with an X to indicate they are the footnotes corresponding to the X's written on the page above. The first note refers to the *Parmenides* but is otherwise illegible; the second is illegible.

52. "as such" was typed above the typed line; a handwritten caret indicates insertion here.

53. Between pages 6 and 7 of the typescript was inserted a page labeled by hand "6a" on one side and "6b" on the other. 6a consists of typescript the first paragraph of which was crossed out by hand; it is followed by typescript that breaks off at the bottom of 6a and is picked up at the top of 6b with handwriting. The crossed-out portion of 6a reads: "The study of social or political doctrines of the past is practically identical with the attempt at understanding a finite, if great, number of books. Those of the books in question which are most difficult to understand may be divided into two classes. The first class consists of the works of those thinkers who, for one reason or the other, took no particularly great interest in the literary form in which they transmitted the results of their reflections to posterity: either they left it to other people to collect and to edit the notes which had been put down during the course of decades, or they themselves wrote biggish books within a surprisingly short time. The second class consists of the works of those thinkers who were exceedingly careful writers, who were so careful that, so to speak, not a single word occurs in their works which is not full of significance. Good examples of the first class can be found in the production of the last generations. To find good examples of the second class, we have to go back to earlier ages. This is not a matter of chance." We have included the remainder of 6a and 6b above in the body of the lecture despite the fact that it interrupts the flow of the argument from page 6 to page 7.

54. A repeated "the" was crossed out.

55. "dur-" and "g" of "dur-ing" were crossed out by typed X's, leaving "in."

56. "more or less" was inserted by hand, replacing "most," which was crossed out by hand.

57. Here begins the handwriting on the verso of 6a; it ends with "prejudices" at the end of the first sentence of paragraph 11.

58. Originally: "men like Leibnitz and Voltaire as by men like Herodotus and Plato"; an indecipherable word is written in the margin before the crossed-out "Herodotus."

59. "exoteric writers of classical antiquity" was originally: "classical writers in question."

60. Crossed out: "would have denied that such a possibility exists at all."

61. "to" has been inserted by the editor.

62. Crossed out: "in a disguised way."

63. This sentence, written by hand at the end of page 6a, replaces the following sentence typed at the beginning of page 7: "To begin with, there were two ways open

for teaching the truth in a manner consciously and deliberately adapted to the popular prejudices."

64. "dignity" was inserted by hand, replacing "true happiness," which was crossed out by hand.

65. Repeated "or" was crossed out.

66. Followed by "is immortal" crossed out by hand.

67. "an" was inserted by hand.

68. "of his deeds" was inserted by hand.

69. Followed by a phrase inserted by hand beginning "e.g." but otherwise illegible.

70. "historiography" was inserted by hand, replacing "writing," which was crossed out by hand.

71. Crossed out by hand: "The end always is the refutation of *hybris*. For *hybris* does not see the end, until it has come to it, nor does the mind of the uneducated: the uneducated fall an easy prey to successful *hybris*, since not considering the end, they are impressed by the present only and consequently, overwhelmed by present success, of however short a date. Purification (*katharsis*) from *hybris* will, therefore, not be effected if the teacher of moderation limits himself to showing the end of *hybris*, his first duty is to." The next word in the typescript is "imitate," which was modified by hand to "imitating" two sentences below in the sentence beginning "He will not effect."

72. Written by hand and crossed out by hand was: "Purification (*katharsis*) from *hubris* will not be effected."

73. "ing" was inserted by hand after "let" to make "letting."

74. "us" was inserted by hand, crossing out the "en" in "then" so that "then" became "thus."

75. "to begin with" was inserted by hand, replacing "first," which was crossed out by hand.

76. Followed by "all," crossed out with typed X's.

77. "e.g." was inserted by hand.

78. "or by some other devices" was crossed out by hand.

79. "a" has been inserted by the editor.

80. "classical" was inserted by hand, replacing "three," which was crossed out by hand.

81. "considerable" was inserted by hand, replacing "large," which was crossed out by hand.

82. "only" was inserted by hand.

83. "government" was written above "rule."

84. Crossed out: "by men" written above "over men."

85. "government" written above "rule" was crossed out.

86. The editor has replaced Strauss's question mark with a comma.

87. "government" was written above "rule," which was crossed out.

88. Crossed out after "Cyrus," which was possessive, was: "rule the kind of government exercised by Cyrus eventually was absolute monarch."

89. "Two things are" replaced "One thing is."

90. Alternative to "bestowed high praise upon" was "praised."

91. "Constitution" was crossed out.

92. "assuming the dimensions of" replaced "being adapted to the exigencies of," which was crossed out.

93. "Climate" was crossed out and replaced by "atmosphere."

94. "dynasty which started with" replaced "monarchy founded by," which was crossed out.

95. Alternative written above: "ended with his son."

96. Alternative written above: "changed his political views."

97. Crossed out: "a."

98. "an" replaced "the Persian."

99. For the sake of readability, the editor has changed "he ascends, according to Xenophon" to "according to Xenophon he ascends" and has moved "while being the lawful heir to the Persian throne" to the end of the clause. After "grandchild" Strauss inserted and then crossed out "the daughter of his uncle Cyaxares."

100. This paragraph and the first sentence of the following paragraph, written on the verso, were inserted here, replacing the following, which was crossed out: "Since Cyrus was enabled to found the Persian empire, the central part ["heart" is written above "central part"] of which was Persia and Media, by having combined in himself, thanks to his twofold education, the Persian with the Media spirit, the question of the difference between these two modes of life, or constitutions, becomes truly decisive for the understanding of the teaching of the *Education of Cyrus*. What was, then, that difference? The Persians . . ."

101. Another "if" preceded "only if," perhaps indicating an abbreviation of "if and only if."

102. Crossed out: "There cannot be the slightest doubt that Xenophon judged the Persian mode of life absolutely superior to the Media one." The following paragraph, much of which is reproduced elsewhere in the document, was also crossed out: "We are now in a position to repeat our original question in a still more precise fashion. We had reduced the question of Xenophon's political teaching to the question as to whether he judged the substitution, effected by Cyrus, of the eventual constitution of the Persian empire for the original constitution of Persia to be an improvement upon the latter or a deterioration of it. To answer that question, we must know what Xenophon judged to be a good and a bad constitution. This judgment is implied in his descriptions of the original Persian constitution and the original Median constitution: the Median mode of life is characterized by barbarian coarseness and servility, the Persian spirit apparently unites all that is best in both Sparta and Athens. Now, as is indicated by the title, the foundation of the Persian empire, i.e., the substitution of an absolute monarchy for an oligarchy based on education, is largely due to Cyrus' education, and this education consists of a Persian education which was noble, and a Median upbringing which of necessity was base (for the form of education depends on the form ['kind' is crossed out] of the constitution). We have, therefore, to raise the question ['ask' is crossed out]: was Cyrus actually influenced by his partly Median upbringing? Does the alteration, effected by him, of the original Persian constitution betray any important Median influence? In the answer to this apparently very special question, the answer to the general question of Xenophon's political teaching is implied."

103. "most short-sighted" replaced "least discerning," which was crossed out.

104. "achievement" was crossed out before "feat of wisdom."

105. "Thoroughly" was crossed out and replaced by an illegible word, perhaps "appallingly"; the editor has reinserted "thoroughly" as more certain.

106. "the" was written above "his."

107. Crossed out: "the composition [crossed out: 'planning'] of his book."

108. Written above: "seems."

109. Crossed out: "degrading."

110. Crossed out: "pure."

111. Crossed out: "is."

112. Crossed out: "appealing."

113. "A pupil of Socrates" was crossed out.

114. "Xenophon" replaced "a pupil of Socrates," which was crossed out

115. Written above: "germs."

116. Beneath "for what impressed" was "and, besides," which was crossed out.

117. "'noble and just' men" replaced "the truly virtuous men."

118. In the phrase "certain kind of criminal," "certain" is partly illegible and "criminal" is plural.

119. "at" after "attending" has been dropped by the editor for readability.

120. Crossed out after "lessons": "given in the Persian public schools."

121. Crossed out: "than they."

122. "born saint" replaced "moral genius," which was crossed out.

123. After "believe," the phrase "but obviously not Xenophon" was crossed out.

124. "the twelve-year-old boy" replaced "he."

125. Crossed out: "competent."

126. Crossed out: "Can anybody bring himself to believe that Xenophon who, after all, was a pupil of Socrates, i.e., of a man who not only taught that justice is knowledge and, therefore, requires teaching by speech but who likewise was famous for his irony, has written those sentences in seriousness?" In this crossed-out sentence, the phrase "teaching by speech" had the same note as LS note ff: "*Memor*. III 9.5 and I 2.19, 2.23 with III 5.24"; beneath the same phrase, also crossed out, were "learning justice" and "a certain kind of training."

127. Crossed out: "and especially Xenophon who, after all, was a pupil of Socrates, i.e. of a man who not only taught that justice is knowledge and, therefore, cannot be acquired but by a certain kind of specific training, but who likewise was famous for his irony, can have written the sentences quoted without smiling?" Also crossed out: "can have meant the sentences quoted to be serious?" In this crossed-out sentence, the word "training" has the same footnote to the *Memorabilia* included above in the preceding endnote and in Strauss's note ff.

128. Crossed out: "how far."

5

Modern Natural Right

Hobbes as the Founder of Modern Political Philosophy

SVETOZAR MINKOV

"The Origin of Modern Political Thought"—a lecture likely dating from the late 1930s[1]—can serve as a bridge between Strauss's treatment of Hobbes in the 1936 *The Political Philosophy of Hobbes: Its Basis and Its Genesis* and the discussion of Hobbes in a subchapter of the 1953 *Natural Right and History*, while also showing interesting continuities and discontinuities with the 1954 "On the Basis of Hobbes's Political Philosophy," first published in English in the 1959 *What Is Political Philosophy?* In "The Origin of Modern Political Thought" we see Strauss more openhandedly thinking through objections to his approach to understanding modern political thought (which he here uses interchangeably with modern political philosophy), and we see more directly the reasoning involved in his sleuthing as he searches first for the identity, and then for the deepest thought and intention, of the founder of modern political thought (an honor he accords Hobbes), referring in the process to Driedo, Mariana, Scaliger, Stevin, Fortescue, among many others, and displaying his prodigious erudition. We see him raising and responding to objections, tracing the origin of objections, disentangling principles from rhetorical presentation, discussing the proper point of departure for understanding a thinker, and so on. For these reasons, among others, it is a lecture worth studying; in fact, based on the great number of footnotes, as well as on Strauss's insistence at points, for example, that a new paragraph be marked, it appears to be not a mere talk but an essay planned for publication. One should keep in mind, nevertheless, that Strauss did not completely polish or publish the lecture, and preference should be given to his mature, finished, and published treatments in *Natural Right and History* and *What Is Political Philosophy?*

Strauss had an abiding concern with identifying the true founder, or the precise origin, of modern political philosophy.[2] But he begins "The Origin of Modern Political Thought" by stating some objections to the search for the origin. Someone, such as Dr. Carlyle, might say that there was no radical break in political thought during early modernity. And others might say, making a quasi-Aristotelian point, that modern political thought should be studied in its mature, late-modern or contemporary form rather than in its rudimentary origins. Strauss's first reply, to Carlyle, is that observers who lived in the 1500s themselves believed they were staging, or witnessing, a revival, if not a radical break, in learning and that some slightly later thinkers such as Grotius, Scaliger, and Stevin even thought they needed to go back to a primeval antiquity, thus rolling back both Christianity and the classical tradition. The experience of this revival and the accompanying belief in an unheard-of progress gained "strength and firmness," reaching its climax before and during the French Revolution.

Yet while these reflections respond to Carlyle's view, this line of argument appears to take Strauss away from the period of Hobbes, let alone Machiavelli, and into a later century. And indeed, in his refutation of Carlyle, Strauss relies at first on Condorcet's and Paine's view that while thinkers such as Hobbes and Grotius had not stated or understood the scientific principles of modern political thought, Locke did (in Condorcet's view). Strauss also quotes Burke concerning the unprecedentedly rationalistic character of the French Revolution and its conflict with "old morality." Strauss, however, suggests that while the French Revolution may have been the point at which theoretical innovation conflicted with tradition in the most vivid way, the French Revolution is not the moment at which the theoretical innovation of modern thought was made with the fullest self-consciousness. In fact, the debate around the French Revolution only showed that the forces of "old morality" had already weakened considerably.[3] Thus the struggle between new and old morality was all but forgotten. The "age-long actual experience" of struggling against the old values was replaced by "learned studies made by detached historians." Moreover, Condorcet's assertion that it was Locke who founded modern political thought lends some weight to Carlyle's thesis since Locke himself owes so much to the judicious Hooker who is connected with the classical tradition. Strauss finds these observations sufficient for concluding that there was a definite break "just between Hooker and Locke" or rather in "the period beginning with Machiavelli and ending with Hobbes." The break was concealed by thinkers such as Leibniz and Swift who were "reactionary," but also by Locke's accommodations and the Rousseauian attempts to reconcile as much as possible the new ideas with traditional values.

Who then to study within the chronological band "Machiavelli-Hobbes" as the true founder? While saying that no one among "Machiavelli, Luther,

Calvin, Bodin, Althusius, Bellarmine, Suarez, Grotius, Hobbes" (Strauss adds Mariana shortly) can be neglected safely, Strauss focuses on the most "radical"[4] thinker, Hobbes. He does not focus on the others mentioned since all of them, including Machiavelli, were too interested in returning to some tradition or other (though, as we see, this is not wholly untrue of Hobbes either). Bodin comes closest as a candidate, but only Hobbes succeeded, Strauss says, in laying the foundations for a new political science. In fact, even in the later *Natural Right and History*—that is, after he had seen that it was Machiavelli who "discovered the continent on which Hobbes could erect his structure"[5]—Strauss reaffirms that Hobbes is "indeed the founder" of political philosophy understood as "the most important kind of knowledge" and as a science that one can expect a lot more from than the classics would have;[6] and even in *Natural Right and History*, Hobbes is "the man who was the first to draw the consequences for natural right from this momentous change [the emergence of nonteleological natural science]").[7]

The Foundation of Hobbes's Political Philosophy

Having identified Hobbes as the founder of modern political thought, in the rest of the essay Strauss stages a dramatic search for the real foundation of Hobbes's political philosophy. After two additional preliminary observations,[8] Strauss reduces all of Hobbes's objections to all political philosophy that preceded him to one: all previous political philosophy essentially teaches anarchy. The presentation of anarchy as Hobbes's main target and of the need for obedience as his corresponding emphasis is much more pronounced in "The Origin of Modern Political Thought" (at least in the first half of the treatment of Hobbes) and in Strauss's 1936 Hobbes book than it is in *Natural Right and History*. In fact, in a correlate passage in the latter Strauss says that Hobbes "traces the failure of the idealistic tradition to one fundamental mistake: traditional political philosophy assumed man is by nature a political or social animal," an assumption that is a far cry from teaching anarchy. And the later treatment in *What Is Political Philosophy?* all but begins by distinguishing between what Hobbes sees as the radical deficiency of the traditional doctrine (overestimation of reason) and what he sees as a merely derivative deficiency ("anarchism").[9]

Hobbes's clamorous objection that all previous political philosophy encouraged disobedience, even that political philosophy did this merely by believing in natural standards of justice, may create the impression that

Hobbes's thought is fundamentally biblical, not just in its presentation. And Strauss does point here to Hobbes's respect for Jewish law and states that Hobbes was "fully aware that by being [an exponent of a doctrine of absolute obedience to the laws] he was following another tradition"—"fully aware," not unconsciously guided by hopes for providence as Strauss suggests in the concluding section of the lecture. Here Strauss shows, in relatively short order, that Hobbes's respect for scriptural authority is dubious. Yet, "in spite of his denial of the authority of the Scripture and in spite of his very atheism, it is not a mere matter of chance or prudence that Hobbes attacks the classical tradition in the name of the biblical tradition: as we shall see soon, his own teaching would not have been possible without the Greek tradition having been undermined by the biblical tradition." This problem will prove to be the nub of the lecture, articulated in a way that will not find the same expression, and might even be denied, in the Hobbes subchapter of *Natural Right and History* and the Hobbes chapter in *What Is Political Philosophy?*[10]

Hobbes's adherence to "law" may indeed be even more profound than Aristotle's. But Strauss shows that Hobbes transforms radically the traditional meaning of law. Hobbes replaces the traditional meaning of law with law as the will of the sovereign: "Hobbes replaces God by the Kings, the will of God by the will of the Kings or any other sovereign power." But this is not yet the deepest stratum of Hobbes's thought, as Strauss understands it. To uncover the true foundation, Strauss begins by reexamining the way in which medieval voluntarist theology—God as will rather than intelligence or what might be called the "Euthyphro problem"[11] in the thought of Suarez—prepares the ground for Hobbes's transition from the classical idea of law as rational order to the idea of law as imposed by a superior or more powerful person. The presentation here is more suspenseful than it is in *Natural Right and History* as Strauss keeps alive longer the possibility that Hobbes's ultimate principle is indeed willful authoritarianism. In *Natural Right and History*, Strauss underlines the "supremacy of authority as distinguished from reason" in Hobbes's teaching only after spelling out its root, i.e., the "extraordinary extension of the natural right of the individual";[12] that is, the possibility of divine voluntarism as the ground of Hobbes's thought is no longer given as much play.

Even in "The Origin of Modern Political Thought," however, voluntarism, be it divine or human, is far from being Hobbes's last word. Strauss spotlights an "astonishing contradiction" in Hobbes regarding natural law, one not present in the Hobbes subchapter of *Natural Right and History* (for the reason indicated in the immediately preceding paragraph). On the one hand, Strauss points out, Hobbes presented natural law(s) as merely indicative or suggestive, and as fundamentally uncertain. On the other hand, he presented natural law(s) as immutable and eternal and hence as certain. This contradiction requires that we go to the "real foundation of Hobbes's political philosophy." That foundation is not natural law, for Hobbes himself says that natural law is merely a means. The rock bottom justification of natural law is the legitimacy of the protection of life or the pursuit of peace;[13] that is how the fusty old doctrine of natural law could become, in Hobbes's hands, "much more of a revolutionary force."[14]

The Primacy of Natural Right in Hobbes

This means, then, that the foundation of Hobbes's political thought is a right or a liberty.[15] And, indeed, natural right exists in pre-civil law times, prior to the voluntarist imposition of the sovereign: in the state of nature, there are wrong intentions, if not wrong actions.[16] The problem then becomes how Hobbes—the great proponent of obligation—can generate obligation out of liberty. "There is only one answer possible: if the liberty on which the obligation rests proceeds itself from an obligation, a binding force, a restraint." At the root of Hobbes's political philosophy is the compulsory power of the fear of violent death.[17] "Natural right is the source of natural law. The obligation which is imposed by natural law—and it *is* an obligation, if only for the conscience—is derived from the binding, restraining force of death which justifies natural right."[18] Only now is Strauss able to articulate the real meaning of Hobbes's reliance on obedience and the relation of obedience to the teaching of the Bible. "Fear of God is the irrational, prerational equivalent to fear of death which, in spite of its being prerational, has nevertheless the merit that it is the only means to make man rational." The blind fear of death makes men see their interest more rationally.[19] This Hobbesian use, but ultimate denigration, of the fear of God will not prevent Strauss from raising the theme of Hobbes's indebtedness to the Bible at the end of the lecture in the most forceful way yet. In fact, the focus on this "debt" may be what distinguishes "The Origin of Modern Political Thought" from the treatment in *Natural Right and History* and *What Is Political Philosophy?* As in *The Political Philosophy of Hobbes*, "The Origin of Modern Political Thought" suggests that in some way Hobbes's thought is still laboring under the influence of its opponent, the Bible.[20]

But let us return to natural right. According to Strauss, the primacy of natural right over natural law is what is truly distinctive and innovative in Hobbes's thought. In fact, Strauss suggests that the very sharpness of the distinction between right and law is Hobbes's original contribution. Strauss indeed notes precedents to Hobbes's distinction in Bodin, Driedo, Suarez, Grotius, and Fortescue, but concludes that none of them drew the distinction as sharply as did Hobbes, and they did not because they did not look with Hobbes's intense motivation for an "immanent" foundation of morality or for a middle ground between transcendent law and wild, indefensible human appetite, between the maximum demand of God upon man and the maximum claim of human beings even in the face of other human beings.[21] In *Natural Right and History* Hobbes is still "the classic and the founder of the specifically modern natural law doctrine," but he originates it by "transplanting natural law on the plane of Machiavelli."[22] For Hobbes was "too sensible" not to see that there is a difference between any human appetite and right or good human appetite while at the same time denying the existence of a transcendent, superhuman order or a superhuman will.[23] To be sure, what Strauss will say at the end of "The Origin of Modern Political Thought" suggests that at that point in his studies of Hobbes, Strauss had doubts about the success or depth of Hobbes's denial of the existence of such a will or order, which doubt is importantly different from the concluding doubt in the *Natural Right and History* subchapter, where what Strauss doubts that Hobbes will be able to expel permanently is not God or supernature but nature.[24]

After a digression in which he indicates the effects of Hobbes's weakening of natural law and prioritization of natural right on other thinkers such as Spinoza, Pufendorf, Locke, Montesquieu, and Rousseau, Strauss reiterates and expands on the radical character of Hobbes's defense of rights. Far from denying certain human rights as they were already understood in the eighteenth century, Hobbes by restricting rights to the "single right to defend right and limb" provides a "practically limitless" basis for rights claims. By denying that courage is a virtue, by seeing the root of all injustice in "pride,"[25] "glory," and "honour," by replacing the traditional idea of *beatitudo* with the modern idea of progress, Hobbes supplies the "whole fire and passion" to the claims of freedom and equality.[26] This consequence of Hobbes's teaching is stated clearly in *Natural Right and History* as well, though it is more or less relegated to a footnote whose purpose is to distinguish Hobbes's conventionalism from classical, philosophic conventionalism ("Hobbes's orientation necessitates egalitarianism").[27] In the earlier *The Political Philosophy of Hobbes*, by contrast, there is a whole chapter devoted to Hobbes's critique of aristocratic morality; in this, as in other ways, "The Origin of Modern Political Thought" is a transition or a bridge between *The Political Philosophy of Hobbes* and *Natural Right and History*.

Hobbes and Theology

In the course of spelling out Hobbes's unprecedented emphasis on rights, Strauss again raises the question of Hobbes's theological views. Hobbes fulfills the conditions for a "fundamental change in the conception of natural equality and freedom" with "singular clarity" in denying that the original freedom and equality of biblical man was indeed innocent and by concomitantly asserting that the actual lack of equality and freedom is not due to sin and that it is therefore permissible to attempt to remove it "by merely human efforts."[28] This analysis tallies closely with its correlate in *Natural Right and History*: the "antitheological implication of 'the state of nature' [in Hobbes] can only with difficulty be separated from its intra-philosophic meaning, which is to make intelligible the primacy of rights as distinguished from duties."[29] Even already in "The Origin of Modern Political Thought," however, Strauss suggests strongly that Hobbes's own intention was not to promote freedom and equality but "to prove that actual inequality and dominion is much to be preferred to original equality and freedom," i.e., to the biblical idea of innocent bliss.

That is why Strauss returns in the concluding section of the lecture to the question of Hobbes's atheism. The "ultimate assumption" of the "primacy of Right before Law" goes with a denial of a "superhuman order or will," but it is not necessitated by it, as one can see from the case of premodern atheistic materialism. As in *Natural Right and History*,[30] Strauss uses a quotation from Burke concerning the difference between an "enterprising" and "designing" atheism (Hobbes's) and an "unenterprising" one (the old Epicureans'). It is of considerable interest that, perhaps because he had changed his view, the explanation Strauss gives of Hobbes's enterprising atheism in "The Origin of Modern Political Thought" differs significantly from the one he gives in *Natural Right and History*. In *Natural Right and History*, Hobbes is said to take up "conscious construction," artificial "intellectual tools" in an effort to combat skepticism,[31] though Strauss does express serious doubts about the equation of wisdom with "free construction" and calls "the vision of the City of Man to be erected on the ruins of the City of God" an "unsupported hope."[32] In *Natural Right and History*, Strauss faults Hobbes for allowing the "experience, as well as the legitimate anticipation, of unheard-of progress" to render him "insensitive" to what Pascal called "the eternal silence of those infinite spaces";[33] in "The Origin of Modern Political Thought," on the other hand, he all but says that Hobbes himself is "frightened" by that same silence of those same infinite spaces, as well as by "his fellow men" who "naturally are nothing better than his potential murderers."[34] The Hobbes of the end of "The Origin of Modern Political Thought," or the kind of deism or atheism he represents (his name hardly appears in the concluding pages), proves to be much more Christian, if distortedly so (see the "atheism out of probity" at the end of Strauss's 1962 autobiographical preface): his belief in providence has been shattered, but his hope for help from providence has remained ("accustomed by a tradition of almost two thousand years").[35] The denial of providence no longer went with serene and detached philosophizing but with disappointed and indignant hope. It was no longer merely a theoretical assertion but a practical *revolt* based on the feeling of righteous indignation at the sufferings of human beings.[36] Strauss's lively lecture—full of reversals, sudden deep dives, detective work, and surprises—ends in this dramatic, half-poetic, half-sermonlike manner. The anguished Hobbesian at the end here is a far cry from "that imprudent, impish, and iconoclastic extremist, that first plebeian philosopher, who is so enjoyable a writer because of his almost boyish straightforwardness, his never failing humanity, and his marvelous clarity and force" of *Natural Right and History*.[37]

The Origin of Modern Political Thought (1937)

LEO STRAUSS

The fact that we are seeking for[38] the origin of modern political thought needs some explanation and even justification.[a39] We study the origin of modern political thought in order to arrive at an exact understanding of the essence of modern political thought. But precisely if it is our primary[40] intention to understand the essence of modern political thought,[41] we must ask ourselves whether it would not be easier and at the same time more adequate to study modern political thought in its developed and mature form instead of in its embryonic form. For the essence of a thing shows itself only in its perfect[42] state. True[43] as this principle is, its application in the present case is very doubtful. For it might perhaps be rash to assume that, say, contemporary thought is, as regards the essential questions, more developed than, say, seventeenth century thought. But however this may be, we have to go back to the origin of modern political thought in the first instance not in order to understand that thought *better* than we could do by studying contemporary thought but in order to understand it at all. For it would be a waste of time to ask[44] *what* a thing is before we know *whether* it is. Now, the very existence of something which might justly be termed[45] modern political thought has been called in[46] question. We mean, of course, by modern political thought not merely contemporary thought but the thought of the four centuries since the Reformation. For we are used to divide the history of political thought in particular, just as we do general history, into three parts: ancient, medieval, and modern. And by doing so, we assume that all modern political doctrines, in spite of all their divergences, have something in common which allows us to take them all together, to look on them as a unity in contradistinction to both medieval and ancient doctrines. Now, this very assumption which is accepted, I think, by most students[47] has been

[a] The text can be found in Leo Strauss Papers, box 14, folder 11. This transcription was produced by Svetozar Minkov, revised by J. A. Colen and Scott Nelson, and annotated by Svetozar Minkov; it benefited from a comparison with the transcription included in Emmanuel Patard, *Leo Strauss at the New School for Social Research.*

challenged by one of the most learned men of our age. Dr. A. J. Carlyle has expressed the opinion that "at least from the lawyers of the second century to the theorists of the French Revolution, the history of political thought is continuous, changing in form, modified in content but still the same in its fundamental conceptions."[a] This statement of Dr. Carlyle[48] includes the assertion that seventeenth- and eighteenth-century political thought is *not* fundamentally different from the medieval. This, however, means that the as yet[49] current opinion according to which there is a modern period in the history of political thought, just as there is such a period in general history, is utterly wrong.

By making the statement quoted, Dr. Carlyle attacks the older opinion which says that there was a definite break between modern and medieval political thought. This opinion was based on the remembrance of what had happened since the Renaissance and the Reformation. It is perhaps not amiss to recall briefly the most important stages of this modern development with special regard to the question in hand. People who lived in 1500 had the impression that they were witnessing a revival of learning, that after centuries of barbarism, of useless, and even dangerous, scholasticism, the great inheritance of classical antiquity or of biblical antiquity or of both was being rediscovered. Those people did not merely believe that a break with the Middle Ages was effected—they saw that break with their own eyes. But people could not leave it at a break with the Middle Ages: they became aware that replacing the teaching of the Middle Ages by that of antiquity would not satisfy their needs. As long as they were under the spell if not of actual antiquity, at least of the idea of antiquity, they tried to replace veneration for actual, known antiquity by search for another antiquity which was older than Greek antiquity: scholars like Grotius, Joseph Scaliger, and Stevin were very much interested in the *siècle sage*, compared with which even Greek antiquity was a period of barbarism.[b] Those men attempted[50] a break not only with medieval, but also with classical thought. In doing so,[51] they were bringing forth the time when people dared to look to the future, to hope for a progress beyond all earlier achievements. Progress

[a] [LS note] *A History of Mediaeval Political Thought in the West*, vol. 1, 2nd ed., 1927, p. 2. Dr. Carlyle seems to recognize three great periods of the history of political thought: 1) Plato and Aristotle, 2) from the Stoa to the French Revolution, 3) from Burke onwards. (See loc. cit., pp. 2 and 14.) Compare, however, the somewhat different observation on p. 197.

[b] [LS note] See J. Klein, *Die griechische Logistik und die Entstehung der Algebra, II*, in: *Quellen und Studien zur Geschichte der Mathematik* usw. Vol. III, pp. 196–99.

desired led to progress achieved. By the middle of the seventeenth century, the belief was practically established that a progress beyond all previous epochs had been attained,[52] a progress which was based on the fact that entirely new foundations had been laid. This belief gained in strength and firmness[53] during the following century, and it reached its climax before and during the French Revolution. In the heyday of that belief, the fundamental difference between modern political thought on the one hand, medieval and classical on the other, was recognized with enviable clarity. Condorcet, certainly one of the most important theorists of the French Revolution, held the following opinion about that difference:[a] that[54] modern political philosophy is a true science, whereas the political philosophy not only of the Middle Ages and of the humanists but even of Plato and Aristotle was "a science of matters of fact, and so to say, empiric, rather than a veritable theory based on general principles"; that the true philosophical method—the exact analysis of our ideas and sentiments—has been found only by Locke; that as a consequence of their wrong method, all earlier thinkers, Althusius, Grotius, and Hobbes[55] included, were unable to reach a true, scientific knowledge of the rights of man; that Locke and Rousseau are the most important teachers of the rights of man; that they were the first to deduce the natural rights[56] of man from human nature and to perceive that the sole aim of political societies is the maintaining of those rights; that[57] the object of their political science, in contradistinction to all earlier political thought, is to found a society of equal and free men on the natural rights of man. Thomas Paine expresses the same opinion by saying, "the rights of man were but imperfectly understood at the (English) Revolution,"[b] and by distinguishing between the new system of government and the old one, which latter is that of "such governments as have hitherto existed in the world."[c] This claim of the theorists of the French Revolution that they had attempted and achieved a break with tradition in its entirety was not consented by the leader of the historical movement which came to power as a reaction to that Revolution. As regards this point, there is perfect harmony[58] between Paine and Burke. Paine says: "What we formerly called Revolutions, were little more than a change of persons, or an alteration of local circumstances. They rose and fell like things of course, and had noth-

[a] [LS note] *Esquisse d'un tableau historique des progrès de l'esprit humain*, ed. Prior, pp. 57f., 60f., 74, 110, 113, 130, 132, 149ff., 156, and 164.

[b] [LS note] *Rights of Man*, Everyman's Library, p. 14.

[c] [LS note] Loc. cit., p. 163.

ing in their existence or their fate that could influence beyond the spot that produced them. But what we now see in the world, from the revolutions of America and France, are a renovation of the natural order of things, a system of principles as universal as truth and the existence of man, and combining moral with political happiness and national prosperity."[a] And Burke:[59] "There have been many internal revolutions in the government of countries, both as to persons and forms, in which the neighboring states have had little or no concern;[60] [. . .] the revolution, turning on matter of local grievance, or of local accommodation, did not extend beyond its territory.[61] The present revolution in France seems to me to be quite of another character and description; and to bear little resemblance or analogy to any of those which have been brought about in Europe, upon principles merely political. *It is a revolution of doctrine and theoretic dogma*."[b] Accordingly, Burke, no less than his opponents, stresses the fact that the pupils of Rousseau oppose a new morality ("that new invented virtue") to "the old morality."[c] The fact that the leaders of the French Revolution were determined by a new morality, by a new conception of man, virtue, and State, by a conception basically different from both classical and medieval conceptions was thus not doubted of by competent[62] observers while the struggle was going on. But as soon as this struggle lost its original vehemence, the object of the struggle lost its original lucidity too. Or, to put it more exactly, the opponents of the new morality were themselves so[63] much under the spell of that morality, their principles were so[64] much weakened by it, that they were not able to perceive with sufficient clarity the fundamental principle involved in the struggle. They opposed to the morality not so much the old morality as—"history."[65] While the old morality, not less than the new one, had claimed to be based on reason, the most influential[66] opponents of the new morality appealed not to reason, not even to tradition as based on Divine Revelation, but to tradition pure and simple, to evolution. As a result, historical research gained during the nineteenth century an importance never heard of in earlier ages. This research was guided, at least as far[67] as the more conservative thinkers are concerned, by the idea of slow, unconscious evolution; and seeking such evolution, the historians found it more or less

[a] [LS note] Loc. cit., p. 135.

[b] [LS note] "Thoughts on French Affairs," in *Reflections on the French Revolution & Other Essays*, Everyman's Library, p. 287f.

[c] [LS note] "Letter to a Member of the National Assembly," loc. cit., p. 262 f.—Compare Condorcet's judgment on the Aristotelian Ethics, loc. cit., p. 71ff.

everywhere. When the original struggle between the new morality and the old one, between the new political ideas and the old ones was almost completely forgotten, from the middle[68] of the nineteenth century until the Great War, it became even possible to deny that there ever had been[69] such a struggle at all; it became possible to believe and to state that "at least from the lawyers of the second century to the theorists of the French Revolution, the history of political thought is continuous, changing in form, modified in content, but still the same in its fundamental conceptions."

This statement is thus, indeed, the logical conclusion of the modern development; but it is based on people having forgotten[70] an experience undergone[71] at all earlier stages of the modern development, the experience undergone[72] by the modern mind as long as it had to struggle against the old values.[73] And is not an age-long actual experience of this kind, which in addition is most clearly evidenced, incomparably more trustworthy than the results of the most learned[74] studies made by detached historians?

However, historical evidence will always carry great weight. Now, as regards the historical evidence, there are a number of facts which speak, at first sight, in favor of Dr. Carlyle's thesis. I need not dwell on these facts. It is sufficient for our purpose to emphasize that by collecting those facts, Dr. Carlyle plays havoc with a series of current opinions about the specific difference between modern and medieval (or classical) political thought. But still, the essential thesis, as Condorcet has stated it, remains unshattered: the fundamental difference between modern and earlier political thought consists in this: that only modern political thought is based on the conception of the rights of man. This very[75] conception is the essence of modern political thought.

In order to see this, we must, however, not follow Condorcet too strictly.[76] For his historical assertions are, to some extent, misleading; they are paving the way to Dr. Carlyle's thesis. Condorcet believed that modern political philosophy was founded by Locke. Now, it is well-known how much Locke owed to the judicious Hooker; Hooker, in his turn, follows, as far as principles are concerned, Thomas Aquinas and the Fathers; the latter do nothing other than expound the views of the Bible on the one hand, of Greek and Roman philosophy and of the Roman lawyers on the other. Thus, the statement of so revolutionary a theorist[77] as Condorcet leads almost automatically to the judgment of so conservative an historian as Dr. Carlyle, who states that there is a continuity of the fundamental political conceptions from the Roman lawyers to the theorists of the French Revolution.

It can be shown that this development from Cicero to Condorcet is not so continuous as it seems to be; that there is a definite break of this continuity just between Hooker and Locke. The fact that this break is overlooked is due to[78] a specific fallacy created by the writings[79] of the later seventeenth and the eighteenth century in general, and of this period in England in particular.[a] The thought of this period was already a reaction in the direction[80] of the classical, and even of the theological, tradition against the much more radical first half of the seventeenth century. I need only recall the names of the most original[81] exponents of this movement: Leibniz and Swift:[82] Leibniz who tried to reintroduce the teleological conception of Aristotle into the framework of the mechanistic and determinist modern science as founded by Descartes and Hobbes, and Swift, the author of the battle of the books.[b]

And as regards the most important political philosophers of the period in question—Locke indeed[83] was a rather moderate thinker; and as regards[84] Rousseau, who cannot be said to have been moderate, he found his conception of the State not without going back to Sparta and republican Rome, in opposition to the specifically modern enlightened despotism of the seventeenth and eighteenth centuries.[c] To put it more accurately, we may say: the reaction of the later seventeenth and of the eighteenth centuries took over as a matter of course the specifically modern fundamental conceptions, and, therefore, the thought of this period is definitely modern, but the thinkers concerned attempted to raise on the modern foundations a structure which was in the greatest possible harmony with traditional ideals;[85] as a result, their work can easily create the illusion that there is only a slight difference between their thought and that of the Middle Ages, that no break of continuity had happened in the meantime. What has been said of the eighteenth century holds *mutatis mutandis* of the nineteenth century: [I can here only refer back to what I have indicated[86] about the importance of historical research in the nineteenth century and of the meaning of that importance.] By these considerations we are led to the conclusion that the fundamental principles of modern political thought and, therefore, the essence of modern political thought shows itself in its purity only in the first

[a] [LS note] Burke says in his Letter to a Member etc. (loc. cit., p. 267): "We continue, as in the last two ages, to read, more generally than I believe is now done on the Continent, the authors of sound antiquity."

[b] [LS note] *The Battle of the Books* (1704).

[c] [LS note] This character of [the] enlightened despotism is stressed by Condorcet, loc. cit., p. 148.

period of that thought, i.e., in the period beginning with Machiavelli and ending with Hobbes. This period we must study, not in order to understand modern political thought *better* than we could do by studying nineteenth or twentieth-century thought, but in order to understand modern political[87] thought at all.

None of the great political thinkers of the period in question—Machiavelli, Luther, Calvin, Bodin, Althusius, Bellarmine, Suarez, Grotius, Hobbes—could safely be neglected. But in order that[88] the multiplicity of persons and of points of view may not weaken our understanding[89] of the essential question,[90] I suggest that we study today[91] exclusively only[92] the most radical of the thinkers mentioned.[93] That thinker could rightly claim, more than anybody else, to be the founder of modern political thought in its peculiar character.[94] From this point of view,[95] certainly none of the theological thinkers can be called radical. For even those who did not, like Bellarmine and Suarez, simply continue the medieval tradition, but rejected that tradition, Luther and Calvin in particular, based their political teaching in the last instance on the revealed will of God, and this foundation is certainly not characteristic of modern political thought as such. On the other hand, Machiavelli, who was[96] less than any other of the thinkers mentioned bound by the philosophical and theological tradition, intends more to revive the spirit of the Roman republic than to give a new foundation to political thought. As regards Althusius, he plainly confesses in the preface to his *Politica*[a] that he intends nothing else but to bring into a convenient order the political precepts differently handed down by different types of literature, and that the political precepts which he teaches are mainly taken from the traditional political works.[b] Grotius states in the Prolegomena to his *De jure belli ac pacis* that nobody has up to him treated the law of nations exhaustively and in a clear order, and, besides, that nobody has succeeded in giving to jurisprudence in general the form of an art because nobody has as yet tried to separate those parts of jurisprudence which are

[a] [LS note] *Politica methodice digesta, atque exemplis sacris et profanis illustrata* (1603).

[b] [LS note] "Conatus sum . . . praecepta politica, quae varia a variis literis sunt tradita, in ordinem convenientem revocare . . . Tractarunt vero politicas quaestiones et aphorismos tum Philosophi, tum Jurisconsulti, tum Theologi . . . Eiusmodi ut supervacua in hac arte et aliena rejicienda et ad sedes proprias, quas dictante justitia in aliis scientiis habent, releganda esse putavi. Desideravi in hisce quoque nonnulla. Omiserunt enim quaedam necessaria . . . Praecepta vero politica et exempla quae trado, ex his iisdem politicis magistris, magnam partem sunt desumpta . . ." ed. Friedrich, p. 3f. [*Nonnulla* and *quaedam* have been underlined in pencil.]

based on natural law from those which are merely positive; but as regards the foundation of all doctrine of law, i.e., the natural law, Grotius holds fast to the Stoic tradition, and however[97] much he may criticize Aristotle, he accepts the traditional opinion that Aristotle is *princeps philosophorum*.[a] We come to a different world when we read the statements about the tradition of political science in the preface to Bodin's *Les six livres de la République*. According to Bodin, there are scarcely three or four books dealing with the State; the political works of Plato and Aristotle are much too short to contain a sufficient teaching; in their time, political science was hidden in a dense[98] darkness; and as regards those who have written about the State since, they were even worse: they have profaned the sacred mysteries of political philosophy. Thus Bodin seems to attempt a really new foundation of political science. But how little this is the case one perceives if one remembers that Bodin too, not much[99] less than Machiavelli, Mariana, or Grotius, was a humanist, that historical testimonies carried almost as much weight with him as did the results of his own reflections.[b] No, even Bodin did not succeed in laying a new foundation to political science. The man who did this was none[100] other than Thomas Hobbes.

In order to see this, we have only to compare Hobbes's general and introductory[101] statements on the political tradition with those of Bodin. While Bodin complains that there are but few books dealing with the State, Hobbes complains that there are "infinite volumes" of political philosophy.[c] While Bodin blames only traditional political philosophy in the usual sense of the word, Hobbes extends this judgment to political philosophy in its original sense, i.e., he rejects traditional moral philosophy too.[d] While Bodin says that political philosophy in the times of Plato and Aristotle was hidden in dense[102] darkness, Hobbes says that there was before him no political

[a] [LS note] §§1, 6–8, 30, 36, and 42.

[b] [LS note] "... entre un million de livres que nous voyons en toutes sciences, à pe[i]ne qu'il s'en trouve trois ou quatre de la Repub. qui toutefois est la Princesse de toutes les sciences. Car Platon et Aristote ont tranché si court leurs discours Politiques, qu'ils ont plustost laissé en appetit que rassasié ceux qui les ont leuz: ioinct aussi que l'expérience depuis deux mil ans ou environ qu'ils ont escrit, nous a faict cognoistre au doigt et à l'oeil, que la science Politicque estoit encores de ce temps là cachee en tenebres fort espesse ... ceux qui depuis en ont escrit ... ont prophané les sacrez mysteres de la Philosophie Politicque ..."—Speaking in the Dedication to his "République" of one of his most important propositions, Bodin says he had proved it "cum divinis et humanis legibus, tum etiam rationibus ad assentiendum necessariis."

[c] [LS note] *Elements of Law*, pt. 1, ch. 13, sect. 3. See also ch. 1, sect. 1; and *De cive*, praef.

[d] [LS note] "... nihil profuisse ad scientiam veritatis quae hactenus scripta sunt a Philosophis moralibus." *De cive*, Ep. ded.

science at all,[a] that almost the whole political teaching of classical antiquity was utterly wrong and utterly dangerous: "In these westerne parts of the world, we are made to receive our opinions concerning the Institution, and Rights of Common-wealths, from Aristotle, Cicero, and other men, Greeks and Romanes . . . I think I may truly say, there was never anything so deerly bought, as these Western parts have bought the learning of the Greek and Latine tongues."[b]

Bodin's and Hobbes's general[103] statements on the tradition of political philosophy have, however, in spite of their differences, a further very important feature in common: in the statements quoted they do not even mention the medieval tradition. This fact does not mean that they had a better opinion of the medieval tradition than they have of the classical tradition. Quite the contrary, it means that they rejected medieval tradition even more than the teaching of classical antiquity. That is not to deny that the medieval thinkers were[104] in more than one way preparing the ground for modern political philosophy in general, and the doctrines of Bodin and Hobbes in particular, and that, consequently, from this point of view, medieval political philosophy is nearer to modern political philosophy than is classical political philosophy. But all those very important modifications, made in the Middle Ages, of classical political thought were inserted into the framework of classical thought; they did not lead to a systematic criticism of the classical framework, i.e., of the principles laid down by Plato, Aristotle, and the Stoics. We should never forget that even as radical a work as Marsilius's *Defensor pacis* is, in its philosophical part, at least according to Marsilius's intention, essentially based on Aristotle's *Politics*. And if Marsilius, as some scholars contend, had come under[105] the influence of Averroes, we must further point out that Averroes was the most vigorous medieval exponent of classical thought who was known to Christian Europe. If there was criticism of classical political philosophy in the Middle Ages, the classical tradition was attacked in the name of another *tradition*—of biblical tradition. With reference to this most important fact, we may fairly say that there is at least as deep an affinity between modern political philosophy and classical political philosophy as there is between either of them and

[a] [LS note] ". . . non (est) juris et legum naturalium major scientia hodie quam olim." Ibid.—"Physica ergo res novitia est. Sed philosophia civilis multo adhuc magis; ut quae antiquior non sit . . . libro quem De Cive ipse scripsi." *De corpore*, Ep. ded. In the same sense Hobbes says in his autobiography that *De cive* "novus omnis erat." *Opera Latina*, ed. Molesworth, Vol. I, p. xc.

[b] [LS note] *Leviathan*, ch. 21 (p. 113f., ed. Lindsay).

medieval political philosophy. For both modern and classical political philosophy made at least the attempt to discuss independently of any tradition the principles of politics. Arguments of authority did not carry any[106] great weight either with Plato and Aristotle, or with Hobbes and Rousseau; but they did carry great weight[107] with the medieval thinkers. From this point of view[108] we understand the meaning of the fact that Bodin and Hobbes do not mention in their general[109] statements the medieval tradition: they were fully aware that medieval political philosophy was, as regards the fundamental principles, based on classical political philosophy, and that, therefore, their real opponents were not Thomas Aquinas or Occam[110] but Plato or Aristotle,[111] not the, however original and independent, followers but the first founders. For the discussion of the late sixteenth and the early seventeenth centuries turned on the fundamental principles themselves.

But which are the specifically modern principles opposed by the most radical modern political thinker to those of classical antiquity? Before we ask Hobbes for his answer to this question, we must make[112] two further preliminary observations. (1)[113] The objections which Hobbes raises against the classical tradition, are, to some extent, based on the biblical tradition. Therefore, we have to disentangle Hobbes's own and truly revolutionary principle from[114] its traditional presentation. But we ought not to underestimate that presentation which is, as a matter of fact, the historical presupposition of Hobbes's own teaching. (2) There are certainly some features of Hobbes's doctrine which cannot be said to characterize modern political thought in general. We cannot exclude from the outset the possibility that even those views which are at first sight specifically Hobbian are more congenial to the deepest tendencies of the modern mind than are the opposite views which are more commonly accepted by modern thinkers. But it would not be wise to take this possibility as our point of departure. To begin with, we shall take those specifically Hobbian views at their face value, i.e., as the individual teaching of an outsider; but, by going back from those views to their ultimate assumption, we shall find that that very assumption is at the same time the ultimate assumption of modern political philosophy as such.

[All objections which Hobbes raises against classical political philosophy, as founded by Socrates and carried on by Plato, Aristotle, Cicero, Seneca, "and thousand others," and thus to all political philosophy up to his, may be reduced to one fundamental objection. According to Hobbes, the whole tradition of political philosophy was based on the assumption that private men[a] can know by themselves what is good and evil. Indeed, Socrates and all his followers did make this assumption by raising the question as to what is good and evil. But this very assumption is according to Hobbes[115] "the original error"; for the rules of good and evil are the *laws*, whereas the classical philosophers "make the Rules of Good, and Bad, by their own Liking, and Disliking," by their *passions*. As the true rules are the laws, whatever the lawgiver, the *king*, commands is to be accepted as good and whatever he forbids is to be accepted as bad. The traditional teachers of politics, by trying to answer by their own reason the question as to what is good and bad, tried to set up a standard by which they, and anybody else, were enabled to measure the laws. Thus they became teachers of disobedience, promoters[116] of anarchy, sophists who deceived men by the specious name of liberty.[b] To the traditional political philosophy which was based on independent reflection of private men, which with necessary consequence led to a doctrine of rebellion, anarchy, *freedom*, Hobbes opposes a new political science which intends to establish by cogent reasons that man is obliged to unconditional *obedience*; in opposition to the classical tradition of democratic ideals, Hobbes teaches the preference of absolute monarchy.

Hobbes is thus in opposition to classical thought an exponent of a doctrine of absolute obedience to the laws. He was[117] fully aware that by being this he was following another tradition. In the same texts on which we have mainly based our characterization of Hobbes's primary tendency, he gives us sufficient hints as to that other tradition. He states that when private men claim to have an independent knowledge of good and evil, they wish

[a] [LS note on a separate sheet] Compare in this connection the following statement by Calvin: "Sane valde otiosum esset, quis potissimus sit politiae in eo quo vivunt loco futurus status, a privatis hominibus disputari: quibus de constituenda re aliqua publica deliberare non licet." *Instit.*, IV, cap. 20, §8. Hobbes held the same view: "And of the three sorts (of government), which is the best, is not to be disputed, where any one of them is already established; but the present ought alwaies to be preferred, maintained, and accounted best . . ." *Leviathan*, ch. 42 (p. 299). From this view we have to start in order to understand why Hobbes asserts the preference of monarchy, of which he was fully convinced, not as a demonstrated truth. See *De cive*, praef.

[b] [LS note] *De cive*, praef. and cap. 12 art. 1–4; *Leviathan*, ch. 20 (p. 109), ch. 21 (p. 113) and 46 (pp. 366 and 372); *Opera Latina*, ed. Molesworth, Vol. V, p. 358f.—That Hobbes held the same view even before his philosophical period is shown by his introduction to his translation of Thucydides. There, he judged the behavior of the Athenian general towards the Melians to be unobjectionable, because the former executed a command given to them by their superiors (*English Works*, ed. Molesworth, Vol. VIII, p. xxix), and not because he accepted the doctrines, borrowed from the Sophists, with reference to which the Athenians justified their actions.

to be like kings (*cupiunt esse sicut reges*); and he adds that the oldest of all commandments of God was that man should not eat of the fruit of the[118] tree of knowledge of good and evil, and that the oldest of the temptations of the devil was: You will be as[119] gods, knowing good and evil. Thus Hobbes seems to base and, to some extent, he actually does base[120] his criticism of the classical doctrine of freedom and democracy on the biblical doctrine of obedience and monarchy.[121]

There are other texts which show the same tendency. Hobbes opposes to the Greek schools of philosophy the Jewish schools of law. And whereas he considers the former to have been completely useless, he strongly recommends the latter. In the Jewish schools of law, which were nothing other than congregations of the people, "the Law was every Sabbath day read, expounded, and disputed." In accordance with this model, there should in every commonwealth "times be determined, wherein (the people) may assemble together, and . . . hear those their Duties told them, and the Positive Lawes, such as generally concern them all, read and expounded, and be put in mind of the Authority that maketh them Lawes. To this end had the Jewes every seventh day, a Sabbath, in which the Law was read and expounded . . ."[a] Speaking of his doctrine of the rights of the sovereign power, he says: "But supposing that these (principles) of mine are not such Principles of Reason; yet I am sure they are Principles from Authority of Scripture; as I shall make it appear when I shall come to speak of the Kingdome of God (administered by Moses) over the Jewes, his peculiar people by Covenant."[b] Against the doctrine of "Aristotle, and other *Heathen* Philosophers," who "define Good, and Evill, by the Appetite of men," he makes the objection: "Not the Appetite of Private men, but the Law . . . is the measure. And yet is this Doctrine (sc. of those heathen philosophers) still pracised; . . . and no man calleth Good or Evill, but that which is so in his own eyes."[c] The expression "whatsoever seemeth good in his own eyes"[d] is obviously of scriptural origin. We need only refer to Hobbes's own quotation: "After the death of Joshua, till the time of Saul, the time between is noted frequently in the Book of Judges,

[a] [LS note] *Leviathan*, ch. 30 (p. 181) and 46 (pp. 364–66).

[b] [LS note] *Leviathan*, ch. 30 (p. 179). It may be added that the interpretation, given by Hobbes as well as by other absolutist writers, of the biblical right of kings (1 Sam. 8, 11ff.)—see *Leviathan*, ch. 20 (p. 108) and *De cive*, cap. 11, art. 6—is based on the teaching of the Talmud (B. Sanhedrin 20b; cf. Maimonides, *Hilchoth melakhim* IV). The influence of Jewish law on the political discussions of the 16th and 17th centuries deserves a special study.

[c] [LS note] *Leviathan*, ch. 46 (p. 372).

[d] [LS note] Ibid. (p. 366).

that there was in those dayes no King in Israel; and sometimes with this addition, that every man did that which was right in his own eyes."[a]

[Of course, we must not take Hobbes's quotations from the Scripture too seriously. Far from having been a sincere believer in the Scripture, he may rightly be said to have been the harshest critic of the authority of the Scripture, and even of its specific teaching, among the many violent opponents of the Bible in the seventeenth and eighteenth centuries.] I cannot produce now the proofs[122] of[123] this assertion. On the present occasion, it will be sufficient to quote the following accounts by Hobbes's friend and biographer Aubrey, which can be confirmed by an exact analysis of the *Leviathan*. Aubrey recounts: "When Mr. T. Hobbes was sick in France, the divines came to him, and tormented him (both Roman Catholic, Church of England, and Geneva). Sayd he to them 'Let me alone, or els I will detect all your cheates from Aaron to yourselves.' I thinke I have heard him speake something to this purpose." "Mr. Edmund Waller sayd to me, when I desired him to write some verses in praise of him (Hobbes), that he was afrayd of the Churchmen . . . that, what was chiefly to be taken notice of in his elogie was that he, being but one, and a private person, pulled-downe all the churches, dispelled the mists of ignorance, and layd-open their priest-craft."[b] To these quotations I shall add only one point: Hobbes rewrites the ten commandments by replacing God by kings.[c] The absolute obedience which Hobbes demands has then as its object not divine law, the will of God, but human law, the will of the sovereign power.

But in spite of his denial of the authority of the Scripture and in spite of his very atheism, it is not a mere matter of chance or prudence that Hobbes attacks the classical tradition in the name of the biblical tradition: as we shall see soon, his own teaching would not have been possible without the Greek tradition having been undermined by the biblical tradition.[124]] At a first glance, Hobbes seems to base his political theory on the traditional doctrine of natural law. This impression is, however, proved wrong by Hobbes's emphatic[125] statement that natural laws are not properly laws, that it is uncertain. The real foundation of his political philosophy is the doctrine of natural *right*. This is already proved by the fact that he deduces

[a] [LS note] Ibid., ch. 40 (p. 257); cf. *De cive*, cap. 11, art. 4.

[b] [LS note] *Brief Lives*, ed. Clark, Oxford 1898, I. p. 357f.—"I have heard him (Hobbes) inveigh much against the crueltie of Moyses for putting so many thousands to the sword for bowing to (the golden calf)." Ibid., p. 357.

[c] [LS note] *Leviathan*, ch. 30 (pp. 180–82).

natural law from natural right, that he deals first with natural right and only in the second place with natural law.[126]

The fact that Hobbes opposes the principle of absolute obedience to the laws to the classical principle of freedom might, at a first glance, create the impression that he is a more decided upholder of the rule of[127] law than was Aristotle. But it is just the conception of the rule of law which he most sharply attacks: ". . . this is another Errour of Aristotles Politiques, that in a wel ordered Common-wealth, not Men should govern, but the Laws. What man, that has his naturall Senses, though he can neither write nor read, does not find himself governed by them he fears, and beleeves can kill or hurt him when he obeyeth not? or that beleeves the Law can hurt him; that is, Words, and Paper, without the Hands, and Swords of men?"[a] Not the law is sovereign, but the will of men, of the men in power; and the law, far from being the sovereign, is itself completely subject to the will of the governing men.[b] Thus, Hobbes's stressing absolute obedience to the laws is misleading. His real opinion finds a more adequate expression in the fact that, while his first presentation of his political philosophy was entitled *The Elements of Law*, his final presentation is called *Leviathan, or the Matter, Form and Power of a Common-wealth*; i.e., in the fact that the more Hobbes understood his own[128] intention, the more he put the idea of law into the background in favor of the idea of the sovereign will. Accordingly, when Hobbes opposes to the classical doctrine of freedom, which was, as he himself knew very well, really a doctrine of the rule of law, his own doctrine of absolute[129] obedience to the laws, the conceptions of "law" and "obedience" must have undergone a fundamental change.

Hobbes replaces God by the Kings, the will of God by the will of the Kings or any other sovereign power. The will of the sovereign power, i.e., the civil laws, are, as he says, the only authentic rules of good and evil, of right and wrong.[c] And, therefore, "where there is no Common-wealth, there nothing is Unjust."[d] But this statement is only an inexact[130] expression of what he really means. For he knows too well that when the sovereign power requires absolute obedience, the question arises: on which authority does the sovereign power base its claim? And this question cannot be answered by another command of the sovereign power. A law forbidding questioning

[a] [LS note] *Leviathan*, ch. 46 (p. 373 f.). Cf. also ch. 18 (p. 91f.) and *De cive*, cap. 12, art. 4.

[b] [LS note] *Leviathan*, ch. 26 (p. 141) and *De cive*, praef. and cap. 6, art. 14.

[c] [LS note] *Elements of Law*, Pt. II, ch. 10, sect. 8; *De cive*, praef. and cap. 12, art. 1.

[d] [LS note] *Leviathan*, ch. 15 (p. 74).

the authority of the sovereign, i.e., a law forbidding rebellion, would be ridiculous; for if the subjects are not obliged beforehand to obey, i.e., not to resist and to rebel, any law would be invalid; and, on the other hand, a law which obliges the subjects to something to which they are obliged already is superfluous. Thus the obligation to civil obedience, the obligation to which all civil laws owe their validity, is prior to any civil law.[a] As a result, obedience to the civil laws, to the will of the sovereign,[131] is based not on civil law, but on natural law.

But why then does Hobbes say that there is no distinction between good and bad, between right and wrong, before there are civil laws? As I have already indicated, this is an inexact expression. Hobbes himself has summed up his political teaching by saying that he derived *virtues* and vices from *natural* law, and goodness and badness of the *actions* from the *civil* laws.[b] What he really means and often enough says is then that before there are civil laws, there is no distinction between good and evil *actions*, right and wrong *actions*; the distinction between right and wrong *intentions*, between virtues and vices, is prior to all civil law, depends only on natural law. Generally speaking,[132] the civil laws are concerned only with the actions, while the natural law is concerned only with the intentions.[c] The concrete meaning of the distinction between natural law and civil law is that, before there is a commonwealth,[133] i.e., in the state of nature, nobody is obliged to peaceful actions; but even in the state of nature, everyone is obliged, by the law of nature, to peaceful intentions.[d] Now, this obligation, derived from natural law, to peaceful intentions is the very root of the obligation to absolute obedience to the sovereign, since the sovereign power is established to no other purpose than[134] to secure peace, and since the sovereign must dispose, according to his own discretion, of the wills and faculties of his subjects in order to maintain peace at home and abroad. As thus the final consequence of the law of nature is the obligation to absolute obedience to the sovereign, there can never be a conflict between the natural law and the civil law.[e] Thus Hobbes succeeds in avoiding the difficulty[135] that the idea

[a] [LS note] *De cive*, cap. 14, art. 21; cf. *Leviathan*, ch. 28 (p. 169).

[b] [LS note] "At ille (sc. Hobbes) mores hominum ab humana natura, virtutes et vitia a lege naturali, et bonitatem malitiamque actionum a legibus civitatum, derivavit." *Opera Latina*, Vol. I, p. xix.

[c] [LS note] *Elements*, Pt. II, ch. 6, sect. 3; *Leviathan*, ch. 27 (p. 154f.) and 46 (p. 374). Compare *Leviathan*, Introduction.

[d] [LS note] *Elements*, Pt. I, ch. 17, sect. 10–14; *De cive*, cap. 3, art. 27; *Leviathan*, ch. 15 (p. 82).

[e] [LS note] *De cive*, cap. 14, art. 10; *Leviathan*, ch. 26 (p. 141f.).

of natural law might endanger, as in principle it always had done, absolute obedience to the earthly governors.[136] But, on the other hand, he fully realized that rejecting natural law[137] would have meant rejecting the foundation of all political philosophy, and even denying the very root of all civil law.

Our result so far is that the basis of Hobbes's political teaching is the traditional doctrine of natural law. This impression[138] is, however, contradicted by the fact that Hobbes does all he can in order to depreciate natural law. Almost in the same breath in which he says that the laws of nature *oblige* always and everywhere man's conscience, that "a Law of Nature (*Lex Naturalis*) is a Precept, or generall Rule, found out by reason, by which a man is *forbidden* to do etc.,"[a] he denies the so-called laws of nature the dignity of laws: "the Lawes of Nature . . . are not properly Lawes."[b] Natural law would be a law if it had been imposed by a lawgiver: "the Lawes of Nature . . . are not properly Lawes . . . When a Commonwealth is once settled, then are they actually Lawes, and not before; as being the commands of the Commonwealth; and therefore also Civill Lawes: For it is the Soveraign Power that obliges men to obey them."[c] Independently of *civil* legislation,[139] natural[140] law would be a law only as imposed by God. But this possibility is tacitly denied by Hobbes. It is true, in the earliest presentation of his political philosophy, he said: "And forasmuch as law (to speak properly) is a command, and these dictates (sc. the laws of nature), as they proceed from nature, are not commands; they are not therefore called laws in respect of nature, but in respect of the author of nature, God Almighty." But in the final presentation, he states: "These dictates of Reason, men use to call by the name of the Lawes; but improperly; for they are but Conclusions, or Theoremes . . . But yet if we consider the same Theoremes, as delivered in the word of God, that by right commandeth all things; then are they properly called Lawes."[d] The latter statement implies the denial that divine legislation can be known by natural reason; and as Hobbes denies revelation any authority if it is not made authoritative by the civil sovereign, his final statement[141] amounts to denying divine revelation in any sense. Thus, according to him, natural law is in no sense a *law*. For a law is essentially a command, i.e., a precept which man has to obey merely because it is commanded; the reason for which man

[a] [LS note] *De cive*, cap. 3, art. 27; *Leviathan*, ch. 15 (p. 82) and 14 (p. 66).

[b] [LS note] *Leviathan*, ch. 26 (p. 141); cf. ch. 15 (p. 83) and *De cive*, cap. 3, art. 33.

[c] [LS note] *Leviathan*, ch. 26 (p. 141).

[d] [LS note] *Elements*, Pt. I, ch. 17, sect. 12; *De cive*, cap. 3, art. 33; *Leviathan*, ch. 15 *in fine*.

has to obey a law is the *will* of authority. Thus law is fundamentally different from all precepts the reason of obedience to which is drawn from one's own benefit, from the matter itself which is commanded.[a] Consequently, "the knowledge of all Law, dependeth on the knowledge of the Soveraign Power," i.e., of the lawgiver.[b142] From this conception of law, it necessarily follows that the so-called natural law is no law at all.[143] For natural law is a precept, not imposed by the will of an authority, but "found out by reason"; the obligation to obey it is founded not on the will of a superior, but on insight into the matter, into what is good, what is good to the obeying man: the natural law "are but Conclusions, or Theoremes, concerning what conduceth to the conservation and defence *of themselves*."[c]

In order to understand Hobbes's view aright, we must remember that his whole doctrine is expressly[144] directed against the whole tradition and particularly against[145] the classical doctrine. Accordingly, we have to glance back to the classical conception of law in order to grasp the assumptions underlying Hobbes's thesis that natural law is no law. In the conception of classical philosophy,[146] the idea that law is essentially a command given by a superior is, to say the least, not in the foreground. The conception guiding[147] Plato as well as Aristotle and Cicero may be summed up in the formula: Law is an order, a distribution and assignation of something; it owes its validity to its having emanated from wisdom and understanding; law is right order, found out by reason, and it *is* law not because it is imposed on man by the will of authority, and not in the first instance because it is consented to by the citizens, but because it is founded on perception of what is good.[d] Law is right order, a rule and measure, not imposed on man, but understood by man. This conception had been maintained, when Hobbes was a child, by Hooker in his *Laws of Ecclesiastical Polity*. Hooker says that there are people who "apply the name of Law unto that only rule of working which superior authority imposeth; whereas we somewhat more enlarging the sense thereof term any kind of rule or canon, whereby actions are framed, a law." "A law therefore generally taken, is a directive rule unto goodness of operation." "That which doth assign unto each thing the kind, that which

[a] [LS note] *Elements*, Pt. II, ch. 10, sect. 4; *De cive*, cap. 14, art. 1; *Leviathan*, ch. 25 (p. 136).

[b] [LS note] *Leviathan*, ch. 31 (p. 189) and 26 (p. 140f.).

[c] [LS note] *Leviathan*, ch. 15 *in fine*.

[d] [LS note] Plato, *Laws* IV (714 a) and XII (957 c); *Politicus* 296f., Aristotle, *Eth. Nic.* X 10 (1180a21–23) and *Politics* VII 4.—Cicero, *Legg.* I, 6, 18–19.

doth moderate the force and power, that which doth appoint the form and measure, of working, the same we term a Law."[a] It is the consequence of his adopting this classical conception of law that Hooker can acknowledge, without any qualification, natural law as a law in the proper sense of the word: "the natural measure whereby to judge our doings, is the sentence of Reason, determining and setting down what is good to be done. Which sentence is either *mandatory*, showing what *must* be done; or else permissive . . . or thirdly admonitory . . ."[b]

When Hobbes attacks the classical view according to which law is essentially dependent on understanding, and the consequence of this view that natural law is a real law, he follows a medieval tradition.[c] The theological correspondence to the classical view is the thesis that the ultimate reason of natural law is divine *understanding*. To that thesis, a number of medieval thinkers had opposed the opinion that the ultimate reason of natural law is divine *will*. According to this opinion, natural law is for this reason, and for this reason only, a law because it is commanded by God who can change it or repeal it just as he likes; consequently, no action whatsoever is intrinsically good or bad, but merely as far as it is commanded or forbidden by God. There were other thinkers who could not accept this consequence of the latter opinion because they realized that the actions commanded or forbidden by natural law are intrinsically good or bad; they tried to avoid the danger[148] that the intrinsic validity of the principles[149] of morality would be denied in the name of divine omnipotence; for this purpose, they made natural law absolutely independent of the will of God; but as they had accepted the assumption that law is essentially a command, they could not maintain the classical view that natural law is a real law; they came to the conclusion that natural law is no law in the proper sense of the word, that it does not command, but merely indicate and show what has to be done or omitted. Their teaching is taken over by Hobbes when he says that the natural law, in spite of its intrinsic validity (its eternity and immutability), is not properly a law.[d]

[a] [LS note] Book I, ch. 2, §1; ch. 3, §1; ch. 8, §4.

[b] [LS note] Book I, ch. 8, §8.

[c] [LS note] The following exposition is based on Suarez, *Tr. de legibus ac de Deo legislatore*, lib. II, c. 6, and lib. I, c. 5.

[d] [LS note] Suarez, loc. cit., lib. II, c. 6, §1: ". . . ratio dubitandi . . . Lex . . . propria et praeceptiva non est sine voluntate alicuius praecipientis . . . ; sed lex naturalis non nititur in voluntate

But Hobbes goes much beyond saying that natural law is merely indicative, not perceptive; he even says that it is *uncertain*; the laws of nature "are but theorems, tending to peace, and those uncertain, as being but conclusions of particular men, and therefore not properly laws."[a] It is true, he affirms the contrary often enough: it will be sufficient to note that he accepts the traditional doctrine that the natural laws are immutable and eternal,[b] and consequently certain. This astonishing contradiction compels us to go back from the theory of natural law[150] to the foundation of Hobbes's political philosophy. This foundation is *not* the doctrine of natural law. For, according to Hobbes, natural law is merely a *means* for an end.[c] Consequently, the end for which natural law is necessary cannot be established by natural law; there must be another principle, prior to natural law, which sanctions the end for which natural law is the means. That principle is natural *right*. By studying Hobbes's doctrine of natural right, we shall be enabled to solve the contradiction mentioned; for then we shall see that the natural law, as Hobbes understands it, is in one sense certain, and in another sense uncertain.

Right is distinguished from law by the fact that a right is a liberty to do or forbear, whereas law is a binding obligation. Accordingly, natural right is the liberty which man has by nature to defend his life and limb; and natural law is the obligation, under which man is by nature, to seek peace. This obligation is based on the fact that peace is the universal condition for securing conservation of life and limb; thus, the natural obligation, natural

---

alicuius praecipientis; ergo non est propria lex." §2: "In hac re prima sententia est, legem naturalem non esse legem praecipientem proprie, quia non est signum voluntatis alicuius superioris, sed esse legem indicantem, quid agendum vel cavendum sit, quid natura sua intrinsece bonum ac necessarium, vel intrinsece malum sit. Atque ita multi distinguunt duplicem legem: unam indicantem, aliam praecipientem, et legem naturalem dicunt esse legem prior modo, non posteriori . . . Atque hi auctores consequenter videntur esse concessuri, legem naturalem non esse a Deo ut a legislatore, quia non pendet ex voluntate Dei, et ita ex vi illius non se gerit Deus ut superior praecipiens, aut prohibens; immo ait Gregorius, quem caeteri secuti sunt, licet Deus non esset, vel non uteretur ratione, vel non recte de rebus iudicaret, si in homine esset idem dictamen rectae rationis dictantis, v. g. malum esse mentiri, illud habiturum eamdem rationem legis, quam nunc habet, quia esset lex ostensiva malitiae, quae in obiecto ab intrinseco existit."—Hobbes's earlier view, as expressed in *Elements*, Pt. I, ch. 17, sect. 12, is the same as Suarez's. Cf. ibid., §§11 and 16.

[a] [LS note] *English Works*, Vol. IV, p. 285.

[b] [LS note] *De cive*, cap. 3, art. 29 and *Leviathan*, ch. 15 (p. 82).

[c] [LS note] *De cive*, cap. 3, art. 29; cf. cap. 1, art. 1.

law, is nothing other than the necessary means for safeguarding natural liberty, natural right. More exactly, natural law has no other source but natural right, from which all the dignity of natural law is completely derived.[151] [But how can a liberty create an obligation? There is only [one answer] possible: if the liberty on which the obligation rests proceeds itself from an obligation, a binding force, a restraint. Now, the natural right of man is his liberty to defend his life and limb; this liberty is derived from the fact that everybody flees[152] with inescapable necessity from the first and greatest and supreme evil: death.[a] Thus, the natural right, the natural liberty is not a thing of which man could dispose according to his judgment or pleasure; his natural liberty or right is rather imposed on him: man is *compelled* to his natural right.[b] The power which "compells," restrains, binds[153] man to his right, is "Nature," or, less vaguely, "that terrible enemy of nature, death."[c] By the fear of death, man's natural appetite, which in itself is infinite, is limited, restrained to reasonable care for self-preservation. Out of this care, out of the reflection on the best and necessary means for self-preservation arises the perception of natural law. This perception, a work of reason, is on the one hand certain; for there is no possible doubt that only peace is the best and necessary means for preserving life and limb. However,[154] the perception of natural law is on the other hand uncertain; for it is a work of reason only; and not reason, but only the passion of fear of death has an absolutely binding, restraining power. But natural right, since it immediately proceeds from perceiving and feeling and fearing death, is absolutely certain.[155]

Natural right is the source of natural law. The obligation which is imposed by natural law—and it *is* an obligation, if only for the conscience—is derived from the binding, restraining force of death which justifies natural right.[156] There is another feature of the natural law, as Hobbes sees it, which, too, has its origin in a corresponding feature of natural right. Natural law is primarily prohibitive: "A Law of Nature . . . is a Precept, or generall Rule, found out by Reason, by which a man is *forbidden* to do, that, which is destructive of his life, or taketh away the means of preserving the same; and to omit that, by which he thinketh it may be best preserved."[d] In this prohib-

[a] [LS note] Ibid., cap. 1, art. 7.

[b] [LS note] As a consequence, the virtues are passions, though passions of a particular kind. Compare *Elements*, Pt. I, ch. 16, sect. 4, with ch. 17, sect. 14.

[c] [LS note] Compare *Leviathan*, ch. 27 (p. 160) and *Elements*, Pt. I, ch. 14, sect. 6.

[d] [LS note] *Leviathan*, ch. 14 (p. 66).

itive character of natural law, the fact is reflected that the ultimate reason of natural right, and consequently of all right, law, and morality, is the fear of death, i.e., of the supreme evil, and not a desire for a supreme good: according to Hobbes, there is no supreme good, while there is a supreme evil.[a]

Only now are we in a position to understand the actual meaning of Hobbes's opposing the idea of obedience to the classical idea of freedom. Actually, he opposes to the seeing, understanding obedience to right reason, (the) blind obedience to the will of the sovereign; and that blind obedience is derived from the fear of death which—in spite of the fact that it *makes* man prudent—is itself not prudent, not seeing, but blind.[157] Obedience, as Hobbes understands it, and fear of death are related to each other by the fact that they both are blind. We may take it that the fear of death which is the beginning of all prudence is only the "secularized" form of the fear of God which is the beginning of all wisdom. Indeed, Hobbes coordinates the fear of "Spirits Invisible" or, rather, "the feare of that Invisible Power, which they every one Worship as God" to the natural state, just as he coordinates the fear of the sovereign power to the civil state.[b] This, however, means, as the natural state is essentially irrational, while the civil state is essentially rational,[c] and as men's subjection to a sovereign power arises out of natural fear, of fear of violent death,[d] that, according to Hobbes, fear of God is the irrational, prerational equivalent to fear of death, which, in spite of its being prerational, has nevertheless the merit that it is the only means to make man rational.

The consequence then is:[158] the real principle of Hobbes's political philosophy is the absolutely certain natural right as distinguished from natural law, which is at least[159] in one sense uncertain.[160] Already the distinction between Right and Law is highly significant. It was definitely[161] no[162] usual distinction. Hobbes himself says: "though they that speak of his subject, use to confound Jus, and Lex, Right and Law; yet they ought to be distinguished; because Right, consisteth in liberty to do, or to forbeare; Whereas

[a] [LS note] With this is connected the fact that Hobbes judges on the preference of the several sorts of government with regard not to their virtues but to their defects. See the chapter headings of *Elements*, Pt. II, ch. 5 ("The incommodities of several sorts of government compared") and *De cive*, cap. 10 ("Specierum trium civitatis, quoad incommoda singularum, comparatio").

[b] [LS note] *Leviathan*, ch. 14 (p. 73).

[c] [LS note] *De cive*, cap. 10, art. 1.

[d] [LS note] *De cive*, cap. 1, art. 2 and Ep. ded.

Law, determineth, and bindeth to one of them: so that Law, and Right, differ as much, as Obligation, and Liberty; which in one and the same matter are inconsistent." And as he says:[163] "I find the words Lex Civilis, and Jus Civile, that is to say, Law and Right Civil, promiscuously used for the same thing, even in the most learned Authors; which neverthelesse ought not to be so . . ."[a] The distinction, made by Hobbes, is, to some extent, identical with the distinction, made in German jurisprudence, between right in the subjective sense ("Right") and right in the objective sense ("Law"). What Hobbes understands by "Law" needs no further[164] explanation; what he means by "Right" may be called, less ambiguously, a justified claim, a right which I *have* in contradistinction to a right by which I am *bound*. Accordingly, "natural right," as Hobbes understands it, is the justified claim par excellence, the right which I have under all circumstances.[165]

As far as I can see, the distinction between Right and Law, so that Right means nothing other than justified claim, and Law nothing other than obligation or command, has been introduced by Hobbes. I shall not insist on the fact that the two words were generally[166] used promiscuously, as Hobbes rightly observed. It is more useful to note that the distinction, suggested by Hobbes, was led up to or suggested[167] by more or less similar distinctions, made by earlier writers. We find a distinction between Right and Law in Bodin, who borrowed it from a tradition which can be traced back at least to Isidorus of Sevilla; according to that distinction, Right is equity, Law is written law;[b] that is to say, that distinction has nothing to do with Hobbes's distinction; for what Bodin and his forerunners call "Right" is called by Hobbes "Natural Law" (and what the former call "Law" is called by Hobbes "Civil Law").[c] We find a distinction between different meanings

[a] [LS note] *Leviathan*, ch. 14 (p. 66f.) and 26 (p. 153). Compare *Elements*, Pt. II, ch. 10, sect. 5, and *De cive*, cap. 2, art. 10.

[b] [LS note] Bodin, *République*, I, ch. 8 (ed. Paris, 1583, p. 155: ". . . il y a bien difference entre le droit et la loy: l'un n'emporte rien que l'equité, la loi emporte commandement: car la loy n'est autre chose que le commandement du souverain, usant de sa puissance."—Suarez, *Tr. de legibus*, lib. I, cap. 2 §5: "Addit vero Isidorus . . . ius et legem comparari ut genus et speciem; nam ius vult esse genus, legem vero speciem. Et rationem reddere videtur, quia ius legibus et moribus constat. Lex autem est constitutio scripta . . . Et videtur sequi d. Thomas . . . dicens rationem aequi et iusti, si in scriptum redigatur, esse legem . . ."

[c] [LS note] Hobbes says of equity "that principall *Law* of Nature called Equity"; see *Leviathan*, ch. 26 (p. 150); cf. ch. 15 (p. 80), *De cive*, cap. 3, art. 15 and many other passages. This means that equity is an obligation and, consequently, neither the basis nor the essence of natural right, as Hobbes understands it.—It should, however, be mentioned that Hobbes occasionally characterizes the content of natural *right* as *aequum* (*De cive*, cap. 3, art. 27 annot.).

of "Right" in Driedo,[a] Suarez,[b] and Grotius;[c] on the way from Driedo via Suarez to Grotius, that meaning of "Right," which is, according to Hobbes, its only meaning, comes more and more into the foreground;[d] but all those writers insist on the use of "Right" in the sense of law also, and, besides, they introduce what Hobbes understands as the distinction between "Right" and "Law" as a distinction between two different meanings of "Right," to say nothing of the fact that they do not assert that the two meanings of "Right" which they distinguish are contrary.[e] We find another distinction, closely related to that already mentioned, between "Right" and "Law" in Sir John Fortescue's *De natura legis naturae*;[f] his statements come indeed very near to those of Hobbes, perhaps nearer than those of anybody else; he obviously thinks, when speaking of law, of obligation, and when speaking of right, of justified claim; but he fully agrees with the traditional view[g] that right as derived from justice and as being "all that is equitable and good"[168] is the genus and law the species; thus, he does not reach Hobbes's distinction according to which Right and Law are contraries.

[a] [LS note] Ioannes Driedo (ca. 1480–1535), *De libertate christiana*, Lovanii 1548, lib. I, cap. 10.

[b] [LS note] *Tr. de legibus*, lib. I, cap. 2. Compare also lib. II, cap. 17, §1.

[c] [LS note] *De jure belli ac pacis*, lib. I, cap. 1, §§3–9.

[d] [LS note] While for Driedo the first meaning of "Right" is law, for Suarez its first meaning is the equity which is owed to everybody and, consequently, the right which I have. Grotius goes farther than Suarez. While Suarez treated first (lib. I, cap. 1) the different meanings of *lex*, and only in the subsequent chapter the different meanings of *ius*, Grotius speaks exclusively of the different meanings of *ius*; and, in addition, he names as the first meaning of *ius*: that which is allowed (I am following the interpretation given by Gronovius in his notes to *De jure belli*, lib. I, cap. 1, §3). Here, we must remember that Hobbes, too, characterizes the content of the natural right as something which "ought to be allowed" to man; see *Leviathan*, ch. 13 (p. 64). Compare also the negative characters of natural right as explained in *De cive*, cap. 1, art. 7 and *Elements*, Pt. I, ch. 14, sect. 6, with Grotius's statement concerning the first meaning of *ius*: "jus hic nihil aliud quam quod justum est significat, idque negante magis sensu quam ajente, ut jus sit quod injustum non est."

[e] [LS note] Grotius, when speaking (loc. cit., §5) of the right which I have, says he will call that right afterwards "dus proprie aut stricte dictum," and thus he seems to accept that meaning of *ius* which is, according to Hobbes, its only meaning, at least its proper meaning. This impression is proved wrong by parallel passages (Prolegg. §§8–10 and 41; lib. I, cap. 1, §9; lib. II, cap. 17, §2; lib. III, cap. 10, §1) which show that Grotius speaks of "jus proprie aut stricte dictum" merely in order to distinguish all actions which are related to justice in particular from the actions which are related to virtue in general. Thus, "jus proprie aut stricte dictum," as Grotius understands it, means both Right and Law, as Hobbes understands them.

[f] [LS note] Pt. I, cap. 30: *Differentia inter ius et legem*.

[g] [LS note] See p. 184, n. b, above.

But these[169] [word illegible] earlier writers did not distinguish so clearly between Right and Law as did Hobbes. And they did not[170] solely because they had no interest in such a distinction. For why does Hobbes make that distinction? Because he could not acknowledge a transcendent, superhuman order or a superhuman will as the ultimate reason of all law, right, and[171] morality; and because, on the other hand, he was too sensible not[172] to see that there is a fundamental difference between human appetite as such and between right or good human appetite. Now, he conceived human appetite as such, natural appetite of man, as a striving after ever greater power, or more exactly, as a striving after ever increasing triumph over all other men. Thus, man's natural appetite is nothing other than "the offensiveness of man's nature one to another."[a] That is to say, man's natural appetite is a claim which every man naturally raises against every other man; it is the absolute claim, the maximum claim. Now, this claim cannot be answered for[173] in the face of any other man. For "if we consider how little odds there is of strength or knowledge between men of mature age, and with how great facility he that is the weaker in strength or in wit, or in both, may utterly destroy the power of the stronger, since there needeth but little force to the taking away of a man's life; we may conclude that men considered in mere nature, ought to admit amongst themselves equality; and that he that claimeth no more, may be esteemed moderate."[b] The actual war of every one against every one, which is the necessary consequence of every man's raising the maximum claim, leads to the result that every man is compelled to acknowledge the equality of every other, i.e., to claim no more than the right of defending his life and limbs. Thus, out of the experience of the natural state of war, the minimum claim, the absolutely justified claim, arises; and this claim is absolutely justified because it can be answered for[174] in the face of all other men under all circumstances. In this way Hobbes succeeds in taking into account the fundamental difference between human appetite as such and right human appetite, without having recourse to a transcendent, superhuman order or will;[175] he succeeds in what we may call an "immanent" foundation of morality. But he succeeds in this merely because he was able to discover natural right (namely: the minimum claim) as a medium between transcendent law and human appetite.[176] In order to maintain the fundamental difference between human appetite as such and right appetite,

[a] [LS note] *Elements*, Pt. I, ch. 14, sect. 11.

[b] [LS note] Ibid., sect. 2.

in spite of his denying a transcendent order, he must assert the primacy of Right before Law. And for this very reason, he had, to begin with, to distinguish between Right and Law as clearly as at least no well-known and influential thinker before him had ever attempted to do.[177]

That Hobbes asserts the primacy of Right before Law is shown not only by the fact that he treats natural right before treating natural law, but also by his explanation of the meaning of "justice." "Justice" signifies "the same thing with no injury"; injury is "the breach or violation of covenant, . . . consisting in some action or omission, which is therefore called Unjust. For it is action or omission, without *jus*, or right; which was transferred or relinquished before."[a] That is to say, "justice" is derived from "*jus*," Right, understood as justified claim. What this means becomes fully apparent if one compares with Hobbes's derivation of "justice" from *ius* the two traditional derivations of *ius* from *iubere* or *iustitia*;[b] for according to the latter explanations,[178] the right which I have is derived from a preexisting law or order, while, according to Hobbes's explanation,[179] all law and virtue is derived from[180] the right which I have.

Thus,[181] the primacy of Right before Law was never asserted before Hobbes, either by the idealistic and[182] theological or by the materialistic tradition.[c] As regards the former: as long as God or an eternal order is believed in, the primacy of law before any human claim, and also before any human right, is a matter of course. As regards the materialistic tradition,[183] we can limit ourselves to the Epicurean since it was the only tradition of this kind which played an important role in the sixteenth and seventeenth centuries. But it must be stressed that what I am going to say with regard to Epicurus holds true, *mutatis mutandis*, of[184] all other materialism before Hobbes.[d] Hobbes, as we have seen, distinguishes between man's natural appetite and man's natural right: while natural appetite is the origin of all injustice, natural right is the origin of all justice. Such a distinction could

[a] [LS note] *Elements*, Pt. I, ch. 16, sect. 2 and 4. Cf. *De cive*, cap. 3, art. 3 and 5, as well as *Leviathan*, ch. 14 (p. 68).

[b] [LS note] Suarez, loc. cit., lib. I, cap. 2, §§1–2.

[c] [LS note] As regards the skeptical tradition, I would refer the reader to Hobbes's criticism of Carneades in *Leviathan*, ch. 15 (p. 74f.) and 46 (p. 365). Compare in this connection Grotius, *De jure belli*, Prolegg., §§5, 16 and 18.

[d] [LS note] As regards in particular the teaching of the Sophists, we may recall Hobbes's interpretation of the discussion between Athenians and Melians. This interpretation shows with all clarity the gulf which separates Hobbes's thought from that of the Sophists. See p. 173, n. b, above.

not be accepted by the adherents of the Epicurean tradition, which derived all justice from covenants. For if all justice depends on covenants, then, as Epicurus himself expressly says, "nothing is *just or unjust*" before there are covenants made;[a185] Hobbes, on the contrary,[186] teaches that before there are covenants made, nothing is *unjust*, i.e., every man has a *right* to everything. That, however, means[187] that there is a difference between right and wrong independently of all human legislation and covenants, that there is a *natural* right.[188]

It may fairly be said that at least no well-known and influential thinker before Hobbes asserted the primacy of Right before Law.[189] Thus Hobbes marked an epoch in the history of political thought by this very fact that he was the first to teach that primacy. For the primacy of Right before Law, never heard of in earlier ages, became the characteristic feature of the most important political doctrines of the period after Hobbes.

* * * * 190

Spinoza bases his political doctrine on the *ius naturae*, in the sense of a justified, unblamable liberty or claim: *ius naturae*, as he understands it, is the right which men or other beings *have*.[b] Spinoza goes even farther than Hobbes; he denies the very existence of a natural law in the sense of moral law.[c] With this is connected the fact that, while Hobbes could distinguish between justice, as obedience to civil law, and equity, as obedience to natural law, Spinoza asserts that both justice and equity presuppose[191] civil law.[d] *Pufendorf* deals in his *Elementa Jurisprudentia Universalis*[192] with *ius* as the right which men have, before he treats obligation and law.[e193] *Locke* certainly does not derive natural law from natural right; he even affirms that natural law obliges in the state of nature to right actions. But in spite of his adhering so far to the traditional view, it is easy to see that in his teaching, too, natural law is put into the background in favor of natural right. To perceive this, we need only to follow the hint which he himself gives us: by quoting so emphatically the judicious Hooker, he, as it were, invites us to compare his

[a] [LS note] *Ratae sententiae* XXXII (Diog. Laert., X, 150).

[b] [LS note] *Tract. Theol.-pol.*, XVI, 3–4 and 40; *Tr. Pol.*, II, 3. Cf. *Eth.* IV, prop. 37, schol. 2 and app. c. 24.

[c] [LS note] *Tract. Theol.-pol.*, XVI, 54.

[d] [LS note] Cf. *Leviathan*, ch. 21 (p. 112) with *Tr. Theol.-pol.* XVI, 41–42.

[e] [LS note] *Jus* is dealt with in *Def.* 8, *Obligatio* in *Def.* 12, and *Lex* in *Def.* 13. Compare also *De jure naturae et gentium*, lib. I, cap. 1, §§19–21.

doctrine with that of Hooker. Indeed, we have only to compare the context into which Locke in the second book of his *Two Treatises of Government* inserts his first quotation from Hooker with the context in which the passage quoted occurs in Hooker's work in order to realize that, as regards the fundamental principles, there is no possible continuity between Hooker and Locke. The passage by which Hooker intended to illustrate the natural law which concerns "our duty . . . towards man"[a] is used by Locke to prove the equality of man by nature.[b] The chapter in which the passage in question occurs in Hooker's work is one out of five chapters dealing with natural law, while in Locke's treatise there is no single chapter especially devoted to natural law: the chapter into which Locke inserted the quotation mentioned deals with the *state* of nature. It is true, Locke mentions already in the first section of that chapter the natural law; but he does this only, as it were, parenthetically. The purpose of the two first sections is rather to show that the state of nature is a state of perfect freedom and equality, i.e., to define the natural right. Only the following section is devoted to natural law. The seven subsequent sections, i.e., more than the half of the chapter, deal with the *rights* to punish the transgressors of natural law and to take reparation for damage.[194] The intention of the two concluding sections is to prove that there is or was a state of nature. The least one must infer[195] is that on the way from Hooker to Locke the interest has shifted from the law of nature to the state of nature.[c] This, however, means a shifting of the interest from the law of nature to the right of nature; for the analysis of the state of nature has no other aim but to illustrate "all the *privileges* of the state of nature."[d] *Montesquieu* then[196] asserts against Hobbes most emphatically the existence of laws of nature; but he understands by those laws no rule and measure, but sentiments and desires.[e] Accordingly, he judges the laws of nature to be inferior in value to the positive laws: "(Les bêtes) ont des lois naturelles, parce qu'elles sont unies par le sentiment; elles n'ont point de lois positives, parce qu'elles ne sont point unies par la connaissance."[f] Thus, natural law loses all

[a] [LS note] *Ecclesiastical Polity*, Book I, ch. 8, §7.

[b] [LS note] *Two Treatises of Government*, Book II, ch. 2, §5.

[c] [LS note] "It is not the Law of Nature, but the State of Nature which is now (sc. since Rousseau) the primary subject of contemplation." Maine, *Ancient Law*, ed. C. K. Allen, p. 73.

[d] [LS note] Locke, loc. cit., ch. 9, §127.

[e] [LS note] *L'esprit des lois*, I, ch. 2.

[f] [LS note] Ibid., ch. 1.—The statement quoted recalls Ulpianus's famous distinction between *jus naturale* and *jus gentium*, according to which *jus naturale* is common to all animals, and *jus gentium* to all men. But Ulpianus's definition is based on the Stoic doctrine of the

its dignity. As regards *Rousseau* I need only quote the following sentences from a recent book on his political doctrine: "His argument starts from the traditional theory of natural man and natural rights, ideas to which he clings although he has abandoned the associated idea of natural law . . . The change that Rousseau . . . effects in the theory of Locke is not so much in his view of political society as in his theory of the state of nature, and this is itself the result of abandoning the idea of natural law . . ."[a]

All the thinkers mentioned put natural law into the background in favor of natural right. But[197] we can understand the significance of this tendency which dominates seventeenth- and eighteenth-century political thought only by studying Hobbes's doctrine.[b] For none of the others asserted with clarity with which Hobbes did the primacy of natural right before natural law. [Natural right, as Hobbes understands it, is primarily the right to defend life and limb. It is for satisfying the demands of that right that men unite themselves in political societies. For the necessary means for defending life and limb is peace and union against common enemies; and the end of the State is[198] nothing other than "Peace and Common Defence."[c] In order to found the State, men must renounce their "originall Right"[d] to everything and every action, which in the state of nature was justified as a necessary consequence of the right to defend life and limb. But they need not and they cannot renounce that fundamental right itself: "the right men have by Nature to protect themselves, when none else can protect them, can by no Covenant be relinquished."[e] Men keep this right even against the sovereign power, and it cannot be forfeited by anything, not[199] even by any crime: "If the Soveraign command a man (*though justly condemned*) to kill, wound,

---

principia naturae which are common to all animals; i.e., *jus naturale*, as he understands it, in any case in the distinction mentioned, is meant to be merely the point of departure for arriving at the highest good which is appropriate to *human nature* (see Cicero, *De finibus*, III, 5, 16ff. and V, 9, 24ff.), and, consequently, for arriving at the natural law in the full and usual sense. As it seems to me, it is this natural law which is intended by Ulpianus when he speaks in the definition referred to of *jus gentium*. (Compare, however, the different interpretation given by Carlyle, loc. cit., pp. 39–44. Carlyle does not take into account the Stoic doctrine of the principia naturae.) We may then say that Montesquieu, by coordinating the law of nature to sentiment and the positive law to knowledge, replaces the law of nature in the traditional sense by positive law.

[a] [LS note] A. Cobban, *Rousseau and the Modern State*, London 1934, p. 115.

[b] This and the following sentence appeared initially in reverse order.

[c] [LS note] *Leviathan*, ch. 17 (p. 90); cf. *De cive*, cap. 5, art. 9.

[d] [LS note] *Leviathan*, ch. 14 [15?] (p. 67); cf. *De cive*, cap. 2, art. 4 (*jus primaevum*).

[e] [LS note] *Leviathan*, ch. 21 (p. 116).

or mayme himselfe; or *not to resist those that assault him*; . . . yet hath that man the Liberty to disobey." ". . . in case a great many men together, have already resisted the Soveraign Power unjustly, or committed some Capitall crime, for which every one of them expecteth death, whether have they not the Liberty then to joyn together, and assist, and defend one another? Certainly they have: For they but defend their lives which the Guilty man may as well do, as the Innocent."[a] If the meaning of the doctrine of the rights of man is that the State has no other purpose than safeguarding those rights, which are prior to the State, and that those rights, being inalienable, are the limits to any and every action of the State, we must rank Hobbes among the teachers of the rights of man. One cannot object that Hobbes, by acknowledging the right to defend life and limb only, denied the rights of man as they were understood in the eighteenth century. For Hobbes himself could not leave the matter at the single right to defend life and limb: "As it is necessary for all men that seek peace, to lay down certaine Rights of Nature; that is to say, not to have libertie to do all they list: so is it necessarie for mans life, to retaine some; as right to governe their owne bodies; enjoy aire, water, motion, waies to go from place to place; and all things else without which a man cannot live, or not live well."[b] ". . . There be some Rights, which no man can be understood by any words, or other signes, to have abandoned, or transferred . . . the motive, and end for which this renouncing, and transferring of Right is introduced, is nothing else but the security of a mans person, in his life, and in the means of so preserving life, as not to be weary of it."[c] It would be an easy thing indeed to justify all rights of man in the most extravagant sense of the word by the natural right acknowledged by Hobbes, the right[200] to "all things without which a man cannot live, or not live well," at any rate, if one has replaced, as Hobbes had done, the traditional idea of *beatitudo* by the modern idea of progress, i.e., if the meaning of the claim to living well is practically limitless.

And it is even as easy, by starting from Hobbes's assumptions, to raise the claim that the State ought to be a society founded on the natural rights of man, of equal and free men. That men are naturally equal and free was, indeed, a traditional view. But, according to tradition,[201] original equality and freedom had been forfeited by human fault or even by original[202] sin. Thus

[a] [LS note] Ibid. (p. 114f.); cf. *De cive*, cap. 2, art. 18.

[b] [LS note] *Leviathan*, ch. 15 (p. 80); cf. *De cive*, cap. 3, art. 14.

[c] [LS note] *Leviathan*, ch. 14 (p. 68); cf. ibid. (pp. 71 and 72) and *De cive*, cap. 2, art. 19, as well as cap. 6, art. 13.

the traditional doctrine of natural[203] equality and freedom was combined, at least in its origin, with a systematic refusal of all claims to equality and freedom in the actual society. For the claiming person was not supposed to be in that state of original innocence which was thought to be the condition for enjoying original equality and freedom.[a] Equality and freedom could become the object of a claim, they could become an inalienable *right*—in other words, the traditional conception of natural equality and freedom could take on a revolutionary meaning—only under two conditions: firstly, if original equality and freedom was no longer judged to be bound up with original innocence, or, secondly, if the actual[204] lack of equality and freedom was no longer looked upon as effected by the sin of all men in Adam and, consequently, as not to be removed by merely human efforts. Both conditions necessary for bringing about that fundamental change in the conception of natural equality and freedom have been fulfilled with singular clarity in Hobbes's political philosophy.

For Hobbes, far from asserting any connection between original equality and freedom on the one hand, original innocence on the other, teaches that original equality and freedom is the counterpart of original wickedness. He does this, of course, in order[205] to prove that actual inequality and dominion is much to be preferred to original equality and freedom. But whatever may have been his intention, actually he made equality and freedom being, as it were, inherent qualities of man which were not conditioned by any other qualities (innocence,[b] goodness, or spiritual life). Now, if men even in their original, wicked state, the state of nature, where *homo homini lupus est*, were equal and free, why should they not claim equality and freedom in their actual, at least much better state, the civil state, where[206] *homo homini*

[a] [LS note] It is very significant that the most powerful advocate of equality and freedom was able to say of himself: "Pour moi, je suis toujours demeuré le même; plus ardent qu'éclairé dans mes recherches, mais sincère en tout, même contre moi; *simple et bon*, mais sensible et faible: faisant souvent le mal, et toujours aimant le bien . . ." (Rousseau, Lettre à M. de Beaumont, shortly after the beginning). Rousseau could claim equality and freedom of the natural state because he had, or believed to have, the qualities of the man of that state. Compare, e.g., the following statement in the *Discours sur l'origine de l'inégalité parmi les hommes*: "L'homme sauvage n'a point cet admirable talent; et, faute de sagesse et de raison, on le voit toujours se livrer étourdiment au premier sentiment de l'humanité."

[b] [LS note] See particularly *Leviathan*, ch. 21 (p. 115), quoted on p. 190 above [that is: "the right men have by Nature to protect themselves, when none else can protect them, can by no Covenant be relinquished"].

Deus est? Particularly if just the actual inequality and dominion were the reason, as it sometimes happens, for[207] men becoming weary of life?

No less important is the fact that Hobbes by his doctrine of natural right paved the way for[208] the belief that the people as such is morally better than the higher and governing class as such.[209] According to him, natural right is the source of natural law and, therefore, of all virtues. This means that only those human qualities which are derived from natural right are truly virtues. Now, the root of natural right is fear of death, more exactly, fear of violent death. As a consequence, he must deny that courage is a virtue. The necessity to draw this conclusion was all the more urgent as he sees the root of all injustice in the will to triumph over all other men, in "pride," "glory," or "honour," as honor is related to war, and the virtue in war is courage. What has been said of Hobbes's opinion about courage holds also of his opinion about all other virtues which characterize the aristocracy, the military class, the court. The only virtues which he really esteems are those which can be derived from fear of violent death, i.e., those of the peaceful, law-abiding, industrious, and thrifty subject. We may say, he admits as virtues only those of the bourgeoisie as opposed to the pseudo-virtues of the aristocracy. By this fact, he opens up the way to the belief that the people as such is better than the court as such, i.e., to the belief to which the claim to equality and freedom owed its whole fire and passion. If the people as such is better than the governing class as such, then actual inequality and dominion have no moral justification at all; for then it is obvious to think that actual inequality and dominion have their origin not in the sin or the fault of all men, but rather in the malice of those who profit by the oppression of their fellow men, in the "pride" of the aristocrats: "*Dominantibus propria* est superbia."[a]

It was, then, the new foundation, laid by Hobbes, of political philosophy which made possible the development of the doctrine of the rights of man in the seventeenth and eighteenth centuries, i.e., the development on which all later political thought, however hostile to the gospel of the French Revolution, is based. Therefore, if we want to understand the essence, the ultimate assumption underlying modern political thought in general, we have to study, in the first instance, the political philosophy of Hobbes.

As regards that ultimate assumption, I indicated already that the *conditio sine qua non* for the primacy of Right before Law is the denial of any super-

[a] [LS note] Spinoza, *Tract. polit.* VII, 27.

human order or will. But this negative condition fails to explain fully why the conception of Right, as distinguished from Law, came more and more into the foreground. For there was a materialism in classical philosophy, a materialism which, no less than that of Hobbes, implied the denial of any superhuman order or will, and this classical materialism, as we have seen, did not lead to the conception of natural right. We have, therefore, to seek after the specific difference between premodern and modern materialism, or rather atheism, in order to grasp the ultimate reason of Hobbes's doctrine of the primacy of Right before Law.[210] That there is a fundamental difference between both is evident from the outset. As Burke has put it: "Boldness formerly was not the character of Atheists as such. They were even of a character nearly the reverse; they were formerly like the old Epicureans, rather an unenterprising race. But of late they are grown active, designing, turbulent, and seditious."[a] Why then did atheism become "enterprising" and "designing"?

Premodern atheism was based on knowledge of the limits set to human designs: if man will be happy, he has to seek his happiness in himself, he has, to begin with, to make himself as independent as possible of external goods, of all goods the possession of which does not depend on his will alone. Out of this view, no interest in the[211] conquest of nature and in the[212] revolution of society could possibly arise. Things changed fundamentally when the possibility of such an interior happiness was no longer believed in, when the idea of *beatitudo* was rejected as being incompatible with human life, with its continuous movement and restlessness. Man was, then, no longer judged to dispose of the possibility of self-sufficiency, but to depend essentially, i.e., with regard to the very core of his happiness, on external conditions. While Epicurus could say almost in the same breath that because of death all men are living in an unwalled city, and that death does not concern us,[b] Hobbes's very starting point is that death is the greatest and supreme evil, not counterbalanced by a supreme good. This, however, means that the essential conditions on which happiness rests are not only external, independent of man's will, but even contrary, hostile to it: nature made men not only dependent, with regard to the essence of happiness, on each other, it did even "dissociate"[c] them, make them the enemies of each other. That is to

[a] [LS note] *Thoughts on French Affairs*, loc. cit., p. 314.

[b] [LS note] *Gnomolog. Vatican.*, 2 and 31.

[c] [LS note] *Leviathan*, ch. 13 (p. 65).

say that man does no longer feel helped by nature, but menaced by it: he is frightened by both "le silence éternel de ces espaces infinis"[a] and his fellow men which naturally are nothing better than his potential murderers. Nature is, however, felt as a menace not because man has now discovered natural evils either in the world or in himself which were unknown to classical philosophy, but because man had been accustomed by a tradition of almost two thousand years to believe himself or to be[213] protected by Providence. When this belief became shattered, he could not immediately cease to hope for Providence, to expect help from it. Denial of Providence was thus from now on related not[214] to serene and detached philosophizing, but rather to disappointed hope[215] in Providence. What was in earlier times nothing more than the complaint of suffering, not yet enlightened Job became now, as it were, the keystone of philosophy. No classical philosopher could have said what Voltaire put into verses on the occasion of the earthquake of Lisbon:

> Croyez-moi, quand la terre entr'ouvre ses abîmes,
> Ma plainte est innocente et mes cris légitimes.
> . . .
> Je respecte mon Dieu, mais j'aime l'univers.
> Quand l'homme ose gémir d'un fléau si terrible
> Il n'est point orgueilleux, hélas, il est sensible.[b]

When reading these verses, we understand best the fundamental change in political thought which lies at the root of the modern doctrine of the rights of man. In the seventeenth and eighteenth centuries, men—whether they were as yet deists or already outspoken atheists, is not important—believing themselves justified by their *sufferings*,[c] began to raise claims not only, and not in the first instance, against their crowned or uncrowned fellow men, but against Providence. Being as yet under the spell of the traditional idea of Providence, they felt the menace to their happiness, this menace which was and is always felt, much stronger than classical philosophers could do; but no longer believing in the existence of Providence, they were

[a] [LS note] Pascal, *Penseés*, Brunschvicg, fr. 206.

[b] From "Poème sur le désastre de Lisbonne, ou examen de cet axiome: 'tout est bien'" (1756).

[c] [LS note] In this they were following the lead which Hobbes had given by justifying natural right by the fear of the greatest and supreme evil. Compare, besides, Locke, *Essay on Human Understanding*, Book II, ch. 20, §6.

enabled by this very unbelief to fight that menace. Their denial of Providence was not merely a theoretical assertion but a practical revolt against Providence. Fighting the superhuman, inhuman menace to human happiness, however, meant conquering nature, i.e., both boundlessly producing external goods and revolutionizing society. It was in this way that atheism became "enterprising," that the principles leading to the French Revolution came into being.[216]

Notes

1. One sign that this is the approximate date of the lecture is that Machiavelli is not regarded yet by Strauss as the founder of modern political philosophy, a shift in Strauss's views most likely finding its first expression in the 1942 "What Can We Learn from Political Theory?" found in this volume; another sign is a reference to a 1934 book as "recent." More generally, as we will see, the lecture is closer on several substantive points to the treatment in the 1936 *The Political Philosophy of Hobbes* than it is to the analyses in the 1953 *Natural Right and History* or in the 1953/1954 *What Is Political Philosophy?* I include frequent comparison to the treatment of Hobbes in *What Is Political Philosophy?* since, during a 1953 seminar on Hobbes, Strauss revised his understanding of the thinker, a revision that found its first expression in the Polin review (the chapter on Hobbes in *WIPP*). I wish to thank Brian Bitar, Rafael Major, and Devin Stauffer for a number of good suggestions.

2. See the 1952 preface to the American edition of *The Political Philosophy of Hobbes* in which he indicates he has settled the question to his satisfaction in naming Machiavelli as that founder and provides an explanation of his error.

3. See *NRH*, 15: the historicist objection to the theory-based revolutionariness of the French Revolution is itself a "much more extreme form of modern this-worldliness than the French radicalism of the eighteenth century had been."

4. Strauss has *three* formulations of what he means by "radical" here, all of which he has crossed out: (1) "[b]y most radical thinker I understand that man who, being a deep and at the same time influential thinker, effected the break with tradition in its entirety in the most visible, the most profound and the most ample way"; (2) that man who "had the clearest intention and the clearest consciousness that he gave an essentially new foundation to political [science], and who, therefore, expressed most precisely the opinion that traditional political science was fundamentally wrong"; (3) he who, "being a reasonable and sincere person, intended with the greatest energy to give *an essentially* new foundation to political science, who had at the same time the clearest consciousness that he *did* give it such a foundation."

5. *NRH*, 177.

6. Ibid.; see the concluding paragraph below.

7. *NRH*, 166. Incidentally, Strauss makes a passing comment that in a sense there is a greater affinity between modern and classical political philosophy than between ei-

ther one of them and medieval, authority-based political philosophy—a comment all the more striking since he has just said that modern political philosophy rejected medieval political philosophy even more radically than it rejected classical political philosophy and also said that medieval political philosophy, despite its innovativeness, especially in Averroes and Marsilius, relied on "classical thought."

8. On the need to disentangle Hobbes's revolutionary principle from his traditional, biblical presentation and a more subtle one about not taking it as one's point of departure that even Hobbes's idiosyncratic elements may in fact be more "congenial to the deepest tendencies of the modern mind" than their more common opposites.

9. *WIPP*, 173. See the end of chapter 3 of *NRH* with pp. 130 and 141, and p. 187n30; see *WIPP*, 194: "by trying to give reasons for unqualified submission to authority, Hobbes makes impossible unqualified submission to authority" and "is forced to repeat what he regarded as Socrates' fatal mistake, 'anarchism'"; see *SPPP*, 66.

10. One important difference between the treatment of Hobbes in OMPT and that in *NRH*, a difference that prepares the even more significant difference between OMPT and the Hobbes chapter in *WIPP*, is that the discussion in *NRH* begins and ends with the theoretical problem of nature's intelligibility; "[w]hile Hobbes's political science cannot be understood in the light of his natural science, it can also not be understood as simply independent of his natural science or as simply preceding it" (*WIPP*, 180). This transition to taking Hobbes's natural science more seriously on its own terms is also evident in the treatment of Hobbes in Strauss's 1941 course "Political Philosophy in the Age of Reason."

11. "There cannot be knowledge if there is no primacy of the ideas. Therefore if one denies the primacy of the ideas, one denies the possibility of knowledge. If the ideas are not the primary beings, the primary beings or the first things cannot be knowing beings. Their action must be blind. They will collide, they will fight. In other words, if the primary beings are the gods, and not the ideas, whatever is good or just will be good or just because the gods love it, and for no other reason, for no intrinsic reason. The primary act is not knowledge or understanding but love without knowledge or understanding, i.e., blind desire. But is this alternative not overcome in monotheism? It is impossible to decide this question on the basis of the Euthyphron, in which I believe the singular 'god' never occurs. Still the Euthyphron seems to suggest that even the oldest god must be conceived of as subject to the ideas." "An Untitled Lecture on Plato's *Euthyphron*," *Interpretation* 24, no. 1 (Fall 1996): 17.

12. *NRH*, 186.

13. *NRH*, 179, 187, 190nn30 and 33.

14. *NRH*, 183; see OMPT.

15. A. P. Martinich, in his "Leo Strauss's Olympian Interpretation: Right, Self-Preservation, and Law in the Political Philosophy of Hobbes" (*Reading Between the Lines: Leo Strauss and the History of Early Modern Philosophy*, ed. Winfried Schroeder [Berlin: De Gruyter, 2015], 77–97), is not justified in either his denial that Strauss connected rights and liberty or his claim that Hobbes's rights are "liberty rights" (not "claims rights") and "nonnormative." Martinich's suggestion that Strauss's supposed misinterpretation of Hobbes is based on a preconceived schema in which the moderns are to be rejected because they believe in will is untenable on the basis of any of Strauss's works on Hobbes, in-

cluding OMPT, and that is where the voluntarist interpretation gets even more play than elsewhere. Strauss's reading is flexible, full of reversals, and radical problematizations—a far cry from Martinich's dogmatic caricature of a dogmatic schematizer.

16. OMPT; *PPH*, 24.

17. OMPT; *NRH*, 181: death "takes the place of *telos*."

18. OMPT.

19. See the unpublished notes from Strauss's 1953 course on Hobbes: fear of violent death wakes up men to their true situation of abandonment (October 12, 1953 session), Leo Strauss Center; and the *WIPP* treatment of Hobbes: "Once he realizes his true situation . . . he becomes filled with fear indeed, but with a kind of fear which points the way toward its overcoming: the stupendous whole which oppresses him lacks intelligence" (181).

20. *PPH*, 28, and Strauss's Lubienski review in *Hobbes's Critique of Religion*, 135.

21. OMPT; the formulations are very similar to *PPH*, 155n2.

22. *NRH*, 182.

23. See David Leibowitz's "The Section on Hobbes in Leo Strauss's *Natural Right and History*: The Meaning of Hobbes's Claim to be the Founder of Political Philosophy" (http://www.revue-klesis.org/pdf/Strauss-9-Klesis-Leibowiz.pdf); Devin Stauffer's "Leo Strauss's 'On the Basis of Hobbes's Political Philosophy,'" in Major, *Leo Strauss's Defense of the Philosophical Life*; and Timothy Burns's "Leo Strauss on the Origin of Hobbes's Natural Science and Its Relation to the Challenge of Divine Revelation," in *Reorientation: Leo Strauss in the 1930s*, ed. Martin D. Yaffe and Richard S. Ruderman (Basingstoke, UK: Palgrave, 2014).

24. *NRH*, 201–2.

25. Strauss states in the 1971 seventh printing of *NRH* and earlier in the 1964 German foreword to *PPH* that it was only in the *WIPP* discussion (n. 2 on p. 176) that he finally identified the nerve or simple leading thought of Hobbes's argument. In the January 15, 1964 session of his Hobbes course (https://leostrausscenter.uchicago.edu/sites/default/files/courses/4-Hobbes-4-1964-01-15.mp3), Strauss gives an accessible account of that thought: "Hobbes's fundamental change: man is not a social animal by nature. But man remains the rational animal. But this rationality of man is too redefined. The specifically human rationality consists in considering things as causes of effects, and therefore of course in considering himself as a cause of effect. If you consider a stone as a possible cause of effect, by implication you consider yourself, by throwing the stone or doing something with it, as a cause of effect. Therefore, man is the being capable or consciously capable of power, becoming concerned with power, and therefore also secondarily, but not unimportantly, losing himself in the mere contemplation of his power; of his superiority to other man and his power. Pride. This, I believe, is the fundamental thought of Hobbes and it took me about thirty years until it became clear to me [referring to his efforts to understand Hobbes as early as the mid-1920s in *Spinoza's Critique of Religion*]. In the last seminar on Hobbes [1953] I saw it, but it is not entirely my fault because Hobbes himself has never set forth clearly this thought." In a letter to Yasonobu Fujiwara from April 29, 1971, Strauss remarks: "I would like to help you place Hobbes's political philosophy in his whole philosophy. For that you need to identify the *principle* underly-

ing the distinction between political philosophy and all other philosophy: that principle is far from being clear . . . The first chapters of *Leviathan* (as of *Elements of Law*) make it quite clear that the whole physiological account of sense-perception, desire, etc. is presupposed. Nevertheless, he treats political philosophy as independent of the *whole* theoretical philosophy in *De cive*. I do not believe that Hobbes succeeded in extricating himself from this difficulty—a difficulty by no means peculiar to him . . ." In a letter to Seth Benardete from October 30, 1956, Strauss remarks that his continued study of the *Leviathan* is his "most simple example of the 'infinity' of interpretation." "Only now did I discern H's definition of man which clarifies many things which hitherto were obscure, but is it not strange that H. never sets forth the definition *eo nomine* nor explicitly deduces (as he could have done) his whole moral-political doctrine from it?" Leo Strauss Papers, box 4, folder 19.

26. Incidentally, this may be a case in which what may appear to be a backwardness or sternness specific to Hobbes is in fact more expressive of the fundamental tendency of the modern spirit (see 197n8 above and OMPT, p. 172).

27. *NRH*, 184–85n23.

28. This and similar statements in *PPH*, *NRH*, and *WIPP* make Martinich's claim that Strauss engages in hermeneutic contortions to *assert* that Hobbes was "committed to the sinfulness of human nature" especially bizarre.

29. *NRH*, 184.

30. *NRH*, 169.

31. *NRH*, 169–75.

32. This does not mean that Strauss characterizes Hobbes in *NRH*, as he comes close to doing in OMPT, as secretly hoping for providential protection. See *NRH*, 198: "There was only one fundamental objection to Hobbes's basic assumption which he felt very keenly and which he made every effort to overcome. In many cases the fear of violent death proved to be a weaker force than the fear of hell fire or the fear of God."

33. *NRH*, 175.

34. "Frightened," however, in an inadequately sobering way; in *WIPP*, the "eternal silence" is mentioned as engendering the "true mood, or the true view" about the universe (181).

35. Contrast *WIPP*, 181: "*By nature* man is blind concerning his situation. He regards himself as somehow taken care of by the first cause or causes, by spirits invisible, not to say as a favorite of Providence" (emphasis added). See Strauss to Karl Löwith, June 23, 1935 (*Gesammelte Schriften*, 3: 649). In this connection, consider David Bolotin's suggestion: "In the case of Hobbes, then, as well as Callicles, the conviction that the world is at odds with justice weakens the attachment to justice, at least as justice first presents itself to our ordinary understanding, i.e., as a restriction on our freedom of action in relation to other human beings, and as a restriction that does not depend on our own consent. Hobbes and Callicles even come to assert that they have rejected, and with good reason, the belief that justice in this primary sense has any real existence. But in fact, this belief continues to live on in them. And these two men are not the only ones for whom the denial that there is any higher support for the cause of justice in its primary sense leads to what presents itself as a sound decision to abandon it as an illusion, whereas in fact it

continues to live an underground life." "Is There a Life to Live As We Please (So Long As We Respect the Life of Others to Do the Same)," in Minkov, *Enlightening Revolutions*, 326.

36. Cf. Richard Kennington's comment: Baconian humanitarianism "did not require, and never possessed, the new natural science, nor a new metaphysics, neither of which are found in Bacon's writings, except in nascent form. Its basis lies in no epistemology, but only in the human knowledge of misery, especially of death, and the conviction that it is ignoble not to avenge our subjugation at the hands of a niggardly nature, by the exaltation of the power of man" ("Descartes and the Mastery of Nature," in *On Modern Origins: Essays on Early Modern Philosophy*, ed. Pamela Kraus and Frank Hunt [Lanham, MD: Lexington Books, 2004], 128). By 1946, in the "Natural Right" lecture (included in this volume), in which Strauss uses the same verses from Voltaire, on the occasion of the Lisbon earthquake ("I respect God, *but* I love the universe"), that he uses in OMPT, this lingering hope in providence, accompanied by a shattered belief in providence, is only a part of a "spiritual climate." Moreover, the formulation of this new relation to God is quite different: "we may venture to say that the rights of man came to the fore in a world that tried to preserve all the privileges of man's being created by God while making light of the burdens which so noble an origin must be presumed to entail. This, however, cannot be the last word on the subject. For there are reasons to suppose that the theological garb owing to which the doctrine of the rights of man achieved its victory was really not more than the protective coloring of an essentially untheological effort." Strauss's 1964 *City and Man* has a passage that harks back, if faintly, to this interpretation of the root of the fundamental change represented by modern political thought: "What is peculiar to modern thought is not this conclusion by itself [that nature is not a kind mother but a harsh stepmother to man, i.e., that the true mother of man is not nature], but the consequent resolve to liberate man from that enslavement by his own sustained effort." "Own sustained effort" does not suggest as much indignation, or as much underground hope for providence, as does the end of OMPT.

37. *NRH*, 166.

38. "The question of" was replaced by "The fact that we are seeking for." (Only the more significant corrections by Strauss have been noted.)

39. "is far from being clear in itself" was replaced by "needs some explanation and even justification."

40. "it is our primary" was inserted, replacing "we have this."

41. "to understand the essence of modern political thought" was inserted by hand.

42. Strauss had handwritten "complete" over "perfect" but then crossed it out.

43. "As" was crossed out by hand before "True," capitalized by hand.

44. "we cannot understand" was replaced by "it would be a waste of time to ask."

45. "call" was crossed out.

46. "into" was in part crossed out by hand.

47. The remainder of the paragraph was crossed out; however, the following paragraph continues discussing Carlyle's statement so we have kept the passage.

48. "of Dr Carlyle" was inserted by hand.

49. "as yet" was added by Strauss.

50. "believed" had been replaced by "endeavored" which in turn was replaced by "attempted."

51. "By this fact" was crossed out and replaced by hand with "In doing so."

52. "was reached" was replaced by "had been attained."

53. "firmity" was replaced by "strength and firmness."

54. "that" was inserted by hand.

55. "and Hobbes" was added.

56. A page numbered 3a had been inserted with alternative phrasing, replacing the text underlined and then crossed out by pen. The text crossed out reads: "based on general principles'; that as a consequence of their wrong method, all earlier thinkers, Grotius and Althusius included, were unable to reach a true, scientific knowledge of the rights of man; that the true philosophical method—the exact analysis of our ideas and sentiments—has been found only by Locke; that Locke and Rousseau are the most important teachers of the rights of man; that they were the first to deduce the natural rights."

57. "that" was inserted by hand

58. "a" before "perfect harmony" was crossed out by hand.

59. Following the colon, "The present revolution" was crossed out.

60. Strauss crossed out and omitted Burke's "Whatever the government might be, with respect to these persons and these forms, the stationary interests of the nation concerned have most commonly influenced the new governments in the same manner in which they influenced the old; and"

61. Note written by hand: "No paragraph!"

62. "any" before "competent" was crossed out.

63. "too" was replaced by "so."

64. "too" was replaced by "so."

65. "that is to say, a definitely modern conception" was crossed out.

66. "most influential" was added.

67. "as far" was inserted by hand above the line.

68. "in the last decades" was replaced by "from the middle."

69. "ever" was typed above the line and followed by hand with "had been."

70. "the oblivion of" was replaced by "people having forgotten."

71. "made" was replaced by "undergone."

72. "made" was replaced by "undergone."

73. "*in statu militant[d?]i*" was replaced by "as long as it had to struggle against the old values."

74. "the most learned" was added.

75. "very" was added.

76. "keep too strictly to Condorcet's words" was replaced by "follow Condorcet too strictly."

77. "thinker" was x'ed out and "theorist" typed above the line.

78. "I shall speak of it later. Now I shall stress only one point. There is" was replaced by "The fact that this break is overlooked is due to."

79. "the writings of" was added.

80. “sense” was replaced by “direction.”

81. “genial” was replaced by “original.”

82. The portion of the sentence after the colon was added by hand in the margin.

83. “indeed” was inserted by hand and the same word crossed out by hand after “thinker.”

84. “as regards” was inserted by hand.

85. “with materials borrowed from tradition” was replaced by “which was in the greatest possible harmony with traditional ideals.”

86. “said” was replaced by “indicated” typed above the line. The square brackets were inserted by hand.

87. “modern political thought,” abbreviated, replaced “it.”

88. “in order that” by hand replaced “lest.”

89. “perception” was replaced by “understanding.”

90. “point” was replaced by “question.”

91. “primarily, i.e., for the present occasion” was replaced by “today [to-day].”

92. “only” was added.

93. “in question” was replaced by “mentioned.”

94. This sentence, however, was crossed out. Also crossed out was the sentence preceding this one: “By most radical thinker I understand that man who, being a deep and at the same time influential thinker, effected the break with tradition in its entirety in the most visible, the most profound and the most ample way.” Also crossed out was a handwritten version of that same statement: that man who “had the clearest intention and the clearest consciousness that he gave an essentially new foundation to political [science], and who, therefore, expressed most precisely the opinion that traditional political science was fundamentally wrong.” Finally, also crossed out was yet a third formulation: “being a reasonable and sincere person, intended with the greatest energy to give an essentially new foundation to political science, who had at the same time the clearest consciousness that he did give it such a foundation.”

95. The passage from “From this point of view” up to and including “political precepts which” was crossed out in red, but the continuation of the passage requires the crossed-out passage.

96. “perhaps” was crossed out.

97. “however” was added by hand.

98. “deep” was replaced by “dense” by hand.

99. “scarcely,” was replaced by hand by “not much” with “more” crossed out.

100. “none” replaced “nobody” which was crossed out.

101. “programmatic” was replaced by “general and introductory.”

102. “dense” was inserted by hand.

103. “programmatic” was replaced by “general.”

104. “preparing” was crossed out by hand after “were” and “preparing the ground” added after “one way.”

105. “undergone” was replaced by “come under.”

106. “any” was inserted by hand.

107. We have deleted the article "a" before "great weight" to be consistent with its deletion by Strauss in other passages.

108. "From this point of view," typed above the line, replaced "Thus," crossed out.

109. "programmatic" was replaced by "general."

110. "Duns Scotus" was replaced by "Occam."

111. "Or Cicero" was deleted.

112. An alternative text was crossed out by hand, from "we must make" to "modern political philosophy as such."

113. In the crossed-out passage Strauss speaks of "one" preliminary observation and does not list what became observation "1)."

114. Strauss replaced "out of" by "from."

115. "according to Hobbes" was inserted.

116. "fautors" was replaced by "promoters."

117. "himself" was crossed out.

118. "fruit of the" was added.

119. "as" in pencil replaced "like."

120. "bases" was corrected by hand.

121. The paragraph that follows was crossed out in red pencil, perhaps, as in cases above, an indication that the passage should be skipped during delivery but not struck from the lecture itself.

122. Strauss crossed out with a red pencil the passage beginning "I cannot now produce the proofs" up to and including the sentence further in the same paragraph that ends with "will of the sovereign power."

123. "for" was replaced in pencil by "of."

124. The rest of this paragraph was added.

125. "repeated" was replaced by "emphatic."

126. Strauss had mistakenly written "right" instead of "law." The passage from "At first glance" to the end of the paragraph was handwritten in the margin.

127. The portion of the paragraph up to this point was crossed out in red pencil, perhaps to indicate that it should be skipped during delivery, perhaps to underscore it.

128. "became conscious of his" was x'ed out and replaced by "understood his own."

129. "the conceptions of law and" was x'ed out and replaced by "his own doctrine of absolute

130. We have corrected "unexact" to inexact in the text in all instances.

131. ", to the will of the sovereign," was added by hand.

132. "On the other hand" was replaced by "Generally speaking."

133. The passage beginning "before there is a commonwealth" up to and including the first sentence of the next paragraph was crossed out (or underlined) in red pencil.

134. "but" was replaced by "than," by hand.

135. "the difficulty" was added by hand.

136. "to the earthly governors" was added.

137. "the" was crossed out before "natural law."

138. "result" was replaced by "impression."

139. The passage beginning "Independently of *civil* legislation" and ending with the sentence "Thus, according to him, natural law is in no sense a *law*" was crossed out in pencil.

140. "the" before natural was crossed out by hand.

141. "opinion" was x'ed out and replaced by "statement."

142. The point made in this sentence was marked as "1" in pencil.

143. The point made in this sentence was marked as "2" in pencil. The rest of this paragraph was crossed out in red pencil.

144. "expressly" was added by hand.

145. "whole tradition and particularly against" was inserted by hand.

146. Strauss replaced "In the classical conception," with "In the conception of classical philosophy."

147. "which is" before "guiding" was crossed out.

148. "the danger" was added by Strauss.

149. "precepts" was x'ed out and replaced by "principles" above the line.

150. Strauss replaced "cannot be solved but by going back to the real" with "compels us to go back from the theory of natural law [to the]."

151. The two sentences that follow were crossed out in pencil.

152. "flies" was replaced by "flees."

153. "obliges" was crossed out.

154. "However" was added over a "but," which was not crossed out.

155. The following paragraph was crossed out in red pencil.

156. "which justifies natural right" was added in the margin by hand.

157. The rest of this paragraph was added by hand.

158. "The consequence then is:" was added by hand above the line.

159. "at least" was added by hand.

160. "in one sense certain, in another sense uncertain" was replaced by "at least in one sense uncertain."

161. "to say the least" was replaced by "definitely" (the word "certainly" was written in pencil and then put in square brackets).

162. We have corrected "not" to "no."

163. "And as he says" [?] was added.

164. "further" was added.

165. Here, near the bottom of p. 27 of the original typescript, there is a note in pencil saying, "*Folgt*: 30," perhaps indicating that Strauss intended to skip (in his delivery) to p. 30 of the typescript, which begins with "But these earlier writers did not distinguish." The following three sentences were crossed out in red pencil.

166. "mostly" was replaced by hand by "generally" by hand.

167. "prepared" was replaced, though seemingly not in Strauss's handwriting, by "led up to or suggested."

168. "as derived from justice and as being 'all that is equitable and good'" was added by hand.

169. "But these" was added. We have lowercased "Earlier" accordingly.

170. "And they did not" was added and made the beginning of a new sentence.

171. "and" was inserted by hand.

172. "as" before "not" was crossed out.

173. "answered for" had been replaced by "justified" but was then restored.

174. "answered for" had been replaced by "justified" but was then restored.

175. "power" was replaced by "will."

176. An alternative ordering of this sentence was indicated by penciled arrows: "But he succeeds in this merely because he was able to discover a medium between transcendent law and natural appetite: namely, natural right (the minimum claim)."

177. The paragraph that follows was crossed out in red pencil.

178. "for the latter derivations imply in any case that" was replaced by "for according to the latter explanations."

179. "Hobbes's derivation implies that the ultimate reason of" was replaced by ", according to Hobbes's explanation."

180. "derived from" was added.

181. "Thus" was inserted by hand.

182. "or" was crossed out and replaced by typed "and."

183. After "As regards the materialistic tradition," Strauss inserted by hand "it was never sufficiently interested in political and legal problems" and crossed out in red pencil the discussion of Epicureanism that follows here. Contrary to the rule we followed in the book, precedence has been given to the typed text and not to Strauss's corrections of it, since we are not sure of the meaning of the sections crossed out in red pencil.

184. "of" written by hand replaced "with regard to."

185. Alternative version corrected by penciled arrows: "as Epicurus himself expressly says, if there are no covenants made, 'nothing is *just or unjust*.'"

186. "other hand" was x'ed out and "contrary" typed above the line.

187. "that there is a difference between everybody's right and everybody's appetite and thus" was crossed out.

188. "that there is a natural right" was inserted by hand, with a note: "[paragraph!]."

189. This sentence was crossed out or underlined in red pencil.

190. Before the paragraph starting "*Spinoza*," in the area where we have inserted asterisks, there are some barely legible words, including "First" and "Only Locke."

191. "presuppose" was typed over "are related" that was crossed out.

192. "*Elementa Jurisprudentia Universalis*" was added and underlined.

193. "and law" was added.

194. "for damage" was added by hand in the margin.

195. "say" was crossed out and "infer" inserted by hand.

196. "then" was added by Strauss.

197. "But" was inserted by hand to mark the beginning of the sentence.

198. A repeated "is" was crossed out by hand.

199. "not" was added by hand.

200. "the right" was inserted by hand.

201. "the" before "tradition" was crossed out.

202. "the" before "original" was crossed out.

203. "original" was x'ed and "natural" typed above the line.

204. "present" was x'ed and "actual" typed above the line.

205. "the intention" was replaced by "order."

206. "when" was handwritten above "where."

207. "for" by hand replaced "that."

208. "for" by hand replaced "to."

209. Following the period, "He did this by his" was x'ed out.

210. The first four sentences of this paragraph were crossed out in red pencil (possibly because Strauss may have intended to omit them from his oral delivery), but since the rest of the section depends on the setup of these sentences, they have been retained.

211. "the" was inserted by hand.

212. "the" was inserted by hand.

213. "or to be" by hand replaced "being."

214. "not" was inserted by hand.

215. "disappointed hope" by hand replaced "deceived belief."

216. The final sentence was added by hand.

6

The Crisis of Natural Right

Recovering Natural Right

J. A. COLEN

"Natural Right" is the simple title of a typescript, with handwritten corrections and additions, that Leo Strauss composed to give two lectures in Annapolis, Maryland, in January of 1946. This text was not composed much earlier than what would become the Walgreen Lectures of 1949—and in fact Strauss included it, in modified form, in *Natural Right and History*. Most of its ideas reappear in the later text, but some were abridged, and many more were expanded.

There is a riddle, subject of much speculation, that shows up immediately: why does Strauss seem to endorse Aristotle's view—despite not being an Aristotelian—and to reject or nuance Aquinas's? While describing the different approaches adopted by the classics in *Natural Right and History* Strauss devotes barely two pages to Aquinas, the "classic of natural right" in the 1940s. In these two pages, despite the "unambiguity," "definiteness and noble simplicity" that make Aquinas's teaching surpass even "the mitigated Stoic Natural Law teaching,"[1] Strauss nonetheless deems it "reasonable to assume" that the "profound changes" that the Aquinas teaching represents with respect to his classic predecessors are due "to the influence of biblical revelation," and we are, therefore, "forced to wonder" if this doctrine is accessible to the "unassisted human mind," that is, without the light of Divine Revelation.[2]

A riddle compounded by the fact that although Strauss usually presents the "classical solution" to the problem of natural right as a unity, as opposed to the variety of modern solutions,[3] the classics were almost as much in disagreement between themselves as the moderns in this matter. Why are the classics the solution for the problem of natural right, since prior to the Stoics very little is said by the classics, namely, Plato and Aristotle, about natural right? And why does he take Aristotle's side against Aquinas, considering that he disagrees head-on with Aristotle, not only with regard to cosmology, but on other more important matters—even taking into account that the writings by Aristotle that have reached us are exoteric[4]—while in this lecture he merely seems to seek a middle way between Thomas's and Averroes's interpretations of Aristotle?

The almost boyish candor and the freshness of this lecture by Strauss may help to solve the puzzle. In his 1946 lecture, Strauss often, if not always, speaks in his own name, dispensing with the "immunity" of a commentator, and clearly makes judgments on several "untenable," "misleading," or "confused" approaches to the problem.

Most older (and even recent) interpretations of Strauss's approach to classical natural right focus solely on the question of its changeability and the implicit problem of the "state of exception,"[5] as well as on the resulting outrage against or approval of Strauss's hidden Machiavellianism. This essay will contend that such a focus distracts us from what is at the heart of Strauss's thought on natural right: the unfinished dialogue between the conventionalist and the classical proponents of nature as a standard for what is just.[6]

For this we need to present the three main lines of argument that he pursues during the lecture, within the framework of his thought as a whole: (1) the forgetting, not to say obfuscation, of the question of natural right due to positivism and historicism; (2) the delineation of the differences between modern and classical natural right; (3) the solution to the puzzle of Plato and Aristotle's relative silence about natural right and, finally, Leo Strauss's own singular proposal that natural right consists of more a hierarchy of virtues or goods than any set of rules.

Forgetting

Strauss says that natural right is the most pressing philosophical question of our time, but also that it is now concealed, a conundrum that forces us to study history and go to the roots—that is, to return to the classics. Strauss's 1946 lecture begins with the observation that the concept of natural right, once taken for granted, is now widely rejected—except among Catholics—and that it is no longer even understood. This forgetting of a question that is no longer at the center of discussion, this consideration of it as a mere "delusion," was also put forward in the Walgreen Lectures and in the introduction to the 1953 book.

The question of natural right is urgent because a right "independent of human arbitrariness" is the only alternative to positive right. Without recourse to natural right we do not have at our disposal any ground on which to criticize a given positive law for being unjust. Indeed, without natural right there is not even a firm ground for the legitimacy of positive law itself. Positive law, as now generally understood, derives its force from the will of the majority, yet such a will cannot be taken to be necessarily just, Strauss suggests, unless it in turn derives from some kind of natural right, the natural right of the majority to rule. Otherwise any reason to "respect, and not merely fear, laws enacted democratically as distinguished from laws enacted by the rubberstamp parliament of a dictator" would vanish.

Strauss would argue, moreover, that simply saying that the surest grounds we have to uphold such convictions are "ideals" fails to tackle the problem, for ideals are simply "objects of aspiration" that lack the force of duty implied by the concept of a natural right. Ideals are ultimately commendable or praiseworthy, but they lack a binding power. Furthermore, "are we not compelled to question the ideals of our society? To wonder whether our society plus its ideals is civilized or barbaric?"

The choice between civilization and barbarism is reinforced in 1949 and 1953 by the alternative between liberals and cannibals,[7] but the same reasoning applies. If the possibility of knowledge of right is excluded and arbitrariness rules, the argument continues, then we are doomed to blindness and to acting in ignorance of what is actually right, and this implies that all things are ultimately permissible for us. Furthermore, Strauss explains that to exalt expediency or usefulness as a guiding principle does not solve the problem either: "Everything expedient or useful is expedient or useful *for* something." Similar objections could be raised against other ultimately arbitrary standards that might be suggested in place of natural right, such as "social cohesion and durability," or "the idea of justice"—unless justice is taken in "the sense of Plato or that of Kant," which equates, "for all practical purposes," to natural right. So the slippery intruder that has just been kicked out by the door climbs back in through the window. Strauss recalls that most of our contemporaries in fact believe in a natural right to self-achievement for each individual, treating it as something that not only is guaranteed by American law, say, but that ought to be guaranteed universally, even though this was not widely recognized to be the case until recently in world history. The same applies "if one asserts that freedom is to be preferred to oppression," since this statement implies that "every human being has a just claim to liberty." The attention Strauss devoted to the U.S. Constitution in his classes at the New School, followed by his reference to the noble words of the Declaration of Independence and compounded by references to Lincoln's second inaugural address and the letter of Horace to Augustus[8] conveys in the Walgreen Lectures of 1949 additional support for the same argument.

Strauss subsequently identifies the primary reasons for the contemporary rejection of natural right and the arguments typically offered against its existence.[9] The first reason for the rejection of natural right, he says, is a desire to ensure total allegiance to the law of the land. This is a desire for "legal security," since appealing to a standard of justice more universal than a given regime's positive law opens the way to civil disobedience, and this naturally poses problems for the given regime. This motive was underlined previously and explored more fully by him in an early text from 1931.[10]

The second reason Strauss identifies for the rejection of natural right is the attitude of historicism, or "the historical consciousness": the belief that all conceptions of natural right are functions of the cultural *milieu* in which they are expressed, and as such necessarily lack the nonarbitrary universality to which they aspire. Historicism provides the first prominent argument against natural right: the sheer number of competing conceptions of natural right that have been asserted across eras and cultures undermines the conviction that any single one of these conceptions is correct. Any points of agreement one could identify as common to all natural right theories would be too general to prove that there is any meaningful, substantive consensus on the matter.[11] Strauss argues that such a position is problematic insofar as the nineteenth-century thinkers who began to challenge natural right by appealing to History were merely attacking modern versions of natural right theories and therefore neglected to consider seriously the legitimacy of the doctrine in its ancient and medieval forms. In other words, they failed to consider the idea of natural right in its original and not in its derivative form. This neglect of premodern natural right theories was itself based simply on an unchallenged acceptance of the Hegelian assumption that history always builds upon previous human achievements, or on the acceptance of "a law of progress," and therefore on the assumption that a modern theory must necessarily be superior to the ancient theory it replaces.

Strauss claims that a serious study of ancient and medieval natural right does not support the conclusion that the modern theory constitutes an improvement upon its forebears. Indeed, the most formidable criticism of natural right, he surprisingly declares, is not based on historicism; it rather starts with the problem that all claims of morality or justice ultimately belong to convention rather than nature. The very distinction between nature and convention—between natural and positive right—was rejected by nineteenth-century historicists owing to their belief that all law is ultimately historical in character. This formidable but unsatisfying account takes the political or ethnic group to be "a natural unit, an organism," and the alternative would be to draw a novel distinction between the historical and the natural, with all right claimed to be historical rather than natural.

This is tantamount to the traditional conventionalist view: to say that all right is historical in nature is to claim that it arises out of a given political or social group's inner feeling of historical necessity. Historicism is then akin to conventionalism insofar as it ascribes all right to a kind of convention or agreement between the members of a society about that society's needs; conventionalism's advantage over historicism is that it does not make the problematic claim that a given group always and necessarily identifies its needs correctly; it does not preclude the possibility of error on the part of society. In the oral delivery of the Walgreen Lectures Strauss is perhaps more vocal about the insufficiency of social needs as the basis of natural right:

> This standard cannot be found in the needs of the society concerned. So that one could reject cannibalism, for example, on the ground that it is not really needed for the societies that practice it, or that the practice is based on demonstrably erroneous beliefs, for society and man have many needs which frequently conflict with each other.
>
> The problem of priorities arises . . . Is there no support for the view that the interests which arise out of the bodily needs are divisive, whereas beliefs—agreements regarding fundamentals—have a unifying effect?[12]

In granting the possibility of error by society, we are, however, brought back to the search for natural right, since the conventionalist and the historicist both reject justice because each believes it to be ultimately arbitrary, in the sense that "all right, including the trans-legal standards of right and wrong, owes its being, i.e. its being *right*, to the fact that it has been agreed upon, or accepted, by a given society and to nothing else." But Strauss seems to say that conventionalism is more resilient than and superior to historicism. There is a handwritten addition in this lecture: "Not the soft cushion of historicism, but the hard rock of conventionalism is *the* alternative to natural right."

In short, it is nearly impossible for us to avoid an implicit appeal to some "notion, correct or mistaken, clear or hazy, of natural right." Nevertheless, as he often reasserts later, this does not prove that there is *a* natural right: "A wish is not a fact."[13] The need for a natural right does not prove that there is a natural right: all right may depend entirely on social *fiat*. As he explains in 1949:

> This does not contradict the fact that the public dogma is from another point of view necessary. It may be necessarily caused by the ignorance or bias of the society concerned, but this necessity does not do away with the fact that in the decisive respect the public dogma is arbitrary or accidental, and hence conventional.[14]

The alternative between conventionalism and natural right might be clearer if the question were not obfuscated in our era by positivism and historicism "on the most popular level."[15]

The Contrast between Modern and Classic Natural Right

We are in a situation, Strauss argues, in which to claim a proper understanding of the idea of natural right, we must study anew its history. Henceforth, Strauss asserts, to achieve "*some* degree of clarity" on "the problematic character of natural right" we must turn to history. This does not surprise any reader of his previous texts, where he avers that we live in a cave below the cave[16] and, in particular, another text also composed in 1946, where he explains both why the classics at large ignored history, and how today research "becomes necessary whose purpose is to keep alive the recollection, and the problem, of the foundations hidden by progress."[17]

In the lecture that follows, he proceeds to sketch the history of natural right theory as commonly narrated. While natural right had been recognized by Plato and Aristotle, among others, the concept was first emphasized by the Stoics, and in turn by the Roman jurists. It was then brought into harmony with Christian teaching by the Church Fathers, becoming "the backbone of Western social philosophy," of which modern natural law is more or less the secularized version.

Strauss, however, rejects the notion that modern natural right theory, a product of the seventeenth century, was radical in its secularization; the independence of natural right from theology was denied by neither the ancients nor the medievals, but on the contrary was "a foregone conclusion."

Rather, he suggests, there is a fundamental break of a different nature. The heart of the difference between the traditional and modern conceptions of natural right is that the former was essentially conservative and the latter essentially revolutionary.

The revolutionary character of modern natural right is closely connected to the fact that unlike its premodern counterpart, which mainly prescribed duties, it clearly distinguishes rights from duties and identifies the goal of government as the protection of the former rather than the cultivation of the latter. Hobbes, Rousseau, Spinoza, Paine, Kant, and Fichte all professed conceptions of natural right that gave rights, understood in this way, rather than duties to man.[18]

Strauss proceeds in 1946 to list the characteristics of modern natural right doctrines. The first distinctive element of modern natural right is that it is largely public rather than private. Before modernity, natural right was not conceived primarily as a political matter. It advised against tyranny, but otherwise allowed conventional right to determine much of a government's power. With Hobbes, Locke, and Rousseau, natural right came to be seen as a universally binding law governing the conduct and indeed the very legitimacy of all sovereign political rule in any time or place. Premodern natural right never claimed to determine anything so absolute as the legitimacy of a given regime. It was modern natural right that gave rise to phenomena such as the American and French revolutions, assemblies, and constitutions.

The second distinctive element of modern natural right is that it is conceived of as completely independent from any positive right, and therefore as something to be expounded comprehensively and systematically, something whose tenets can be precisely and absolutely enumerated.

Third, the modern idea of natural right is bound up with the idea of a "state of nature," a human condition characteristic of a time prior to the establishment of civil society. The distinction between a state of nature and the civil state replaced the traditional Christian distinction between the state of nature and the state of grace; modern natural right theorists sought to diminish the import of the fall of Adam and to provide the grounds for the claim that properly ordered government rather than divine grace is the primary corrective for the deficiencies of the state of nature. Or to state it differently, moderns sought to dispel the biblical understanding of man or his origins altogether. Sin should be replaced by mistakes or even tendencies, which should not necessarily be corrected so much as directed toward better or more productive results by the right kind of institutions.

Modern natural right also requires that a regime be easily achievable and primarily characterized by either efficiency (as with Machiavelli) or "legitimacy." Both alternatives depart from the classical conviction that a political order is inextricably bound up with the character of its citizens. Modern political philosophers seek a political regime effective regardless of the character of its citizens as the right political order. Ancient thinkers tend to seek rather the government most likely to cultivate the virtue of its citizens—a quest deemed too uncertain by the moderns, who consequently seek a sort of citizen-proof government. In keeping with this approach to the question of political order, the ancient sense that the right thing to do in any given situation should be determined by men of practical wisdom is discarded, again because it leaves too much to uncertainty or chance. Instead, discerning a natural right with specific and absolute legal requirements obviates the difficulty of determining just who possesses the prudence to fulfill the classical role of the statesman. Yet it is the prudence of the ancient statesman that allows him to determine on a case-by-case basis the specifics that natural right does not suggest by rules. Modern natural right, being systematic and geometrical, offers the "attraction of making wisdom superfluous."[19]

Strauss does not deny that this "attempt has had a remarkable success: the combination of universal freedom and social stability which has been achieved for some time in certain parts of the Western world surpasses everything which in this respect had ever been achieved in the past." Yet "because this is a very high achievement, a high price had to be paid for it. The price which man had to pay for the modern blessings of a high degree of general happiness was the lowering of the peaks, the lowering of man's ultimate aim."

As the reader will notice immediately, Strauss's précis of the history of natural right in this lecture is significantly different from the one that he presents in 1949 and 1953: it is mainly based on a comparison of the tenets of premodern and modern natural right.

Aristotle's Silence and the Three Versions of Classic Natural Right

Finally, Strauss asserts, "We cannot judge properly of modern natural right if we do not understand premodern natural right." However, "[t]he classic of premodern natural right is Thomas Aquinas. But . . . because his solution is so perfect, so elegant, it is very difficult to become aware of the *problem* of natural right if one starts from Thomas's teaching." But in order to retrieve the problem as seen by the classics, we need to address the puzzle of Plato and Aristotle's silence about natural right. To do so, Strauss seeks to explain Aristotle's strangely terse treatment of the subject. The typical answer to the question of why both Plato and Aristotle pay so little explicit attention to natural right is based on Hegel's reading of Greek political philosophy.

As Strauss stated before, Hegel replaced the nature-convention distinction with a distinction between the subjective mind and the objective mind, the latter of which reflects a higher order of reasoning and takes shape in institutions. In this framework, Plato and Aristotle are taken to have articulated the Greek city as embodying this kind of objective reason, leaving natural right as something to be realized in the Greek city and not in need of articulation apart from it. Hegel's reading of Plato and Aristotle, however, is "untenable"; for the great Greek philosophers concerned themselves precisely with prescribing for the city what it ought to be as distinct from what it is, a distinction Hegel himself does not countenance.

Noting this, Strauss offers another explanation for the relative silence of the ancient Greeks on natural right: they recognized that natural right cannot in itself organize society justly, but rather must be filtered to some degree through positive right or convention. To radically and universally implement the dictates of natural right would undermine social order and result in chaos—as would be the case, for instance, with the radical redistribution of goods based on the ultimate needs of each. Such an action would violate the consent of many, whose opinion of what is right does not always correspond to what is right in fact. Recognition of the extent to which the many rely on opinion leads to caution and restraint in implementing the dictates of what is truly right by nature when this would encounter the kind of opposition from the many that would destroy the equilibrium of society.

In this lecture, Strauss more or less glosses over the differences between the three versions of classic natural right teaching, Socratic-Platonic-Stoic, Aristotelian, and Thomist, which he indicates but does not expand on in the Walgreen Lectures in 1949.[20]

What Strauss identifies in the fourth chapter of *Natural Right and History* as the "Socratic-Platonic-Stoic natural right teaching"[21] is founded upon the tension between the two prevailing assumptions about the nature of justice: that it demands giving each man his due, and that it is good. Civil law decides what is each man's due; but civil law can err in deciding thus, in which case it fails to be good and thus fails to be just. In order to be good, justice must, therefore, be defined independently of civil law, namely, as the giving to each what is in fact, or by nature, his due. Giving each his due in turn entails benefiting all, giving each what is good for him. Only wise men can determine what is truly good for each person, and a city can therefore meet this criterion of justice only if it is run by wise men.

But a philosopher must be willing to compromise with the opinion of the city—to allow a compromise between wisdom and consent, between natural right and conventional right. Natural right must be diluted if it is to inform the laws of the city.[22] This is the philosophical stance that is attributed to Strauss, which is quite different from that of Aristotle. So we must be on guard against equating Strauss and Aristotle when the former proceeds to address Aristotle's doctrine of natural right, the thematic treatment of which, as Strauss notes, is confined to less than a page of the *Nicomachean Ethics*.[23] We cannot say this distinctive feature of Aristotle corresponds to Leo Strauss's own voice.[24]

A warning should nonetheless be given regarding Strauss's suggestion of a middle way of interpreting Aristotelian natural right, which appears clearly in the 1946 Annapolis lecture below, as well as in chapter 4 of *Natural Right and History*. For while Strauss considered the classical approach more sound,[25] he also chose to illustrate it with its most shocking applications: natural right of slavery and money[26] (and, despite everything which has been said of Strauss, nobody has yet accused him of defending slavery).

Strauss's Middle Way

Aristotle's more disturbing claim about natural right is that it is changeable.[27] Saint Thomas Aquinas interprets this statement with the qualification that it is changeable only at the level of more specific injunctions; the more general precepts of natural right are themselves unchangeable.[28] Yet such a view derives from the Church Fathers rather than Aristotle, who plainly says that *all* right (and not only natural right) is changeable. The Averroistic interpretation of Aristotle seems to stay closer to this element of his teaching: it claims that, for Aristotle, natural right actually refers to "legal natural right," which is in fact contingent upon civil law and is raised above the status of mere positive right only by virtue of the ubiquity of its acceptance; natural right is thus not purely natural, strictly speaking. A basic set of dictates of justice is recognized and considered necessary almost universally, but it remains a matter of convention because of the periodic development of conditions in which these dictates no longer apply; nonetheless, the normal rules of justice do apply with such overwhelming frequency that they must be taught as immutable in order to be effective, even though this teaching thereby makes the doctrine of natural right false. This interpretation is thus ultimately un-Aristotelian, insofar as it maintains that natural right does not, strictly speaking, exist.

Strauss suggests an alternative to the two extreme interpretations of Aristotelian natural right described above. Action is concerned with particular decisions, not with general principles, and thus natural right does not in fact dispense with general principles but rather exists on the level of the particular circumstance; it justifies or condemns specific actions rather than universal rules of actions. A consideration of each particular scenario or dilemma will point to a particular solution that may be more desirable than the straightforward application of a general rule. In this sense, natural law is unchangeable. Yet each decision is implicitly guided by more general principles. Aristotle himself acknowledges the existence of such general guiding principles, such as commutative and distributive justice. Yet these principles of justice are themselves ultimately subservient to a still more basic requirement of justice, namely, the common good; and the common good requires not simply a just distribution of goods, but also the maintenance of the very existence of the political society that is able to oversee that distribution. For this reason, when the application of true commutative or distributive justice would threaten the continued existence of the political society, it is better for the sake of the common good to temporarily dispense with these particular demands of justice. In war, for instance, there is no general law prescribing exactly what constitutes acceptable behavior in any circumstance; one nation's acceptable behavior in a given war depends upon which particular tactics the enemy is able or willing to resort to, and there is no general rule that can be given in advance to govern such unpredictable circumstances, which depend on the enemy's resourcefulness or creativity.

Ultimately, "justice has two different principles or sets of principles: the requirements of public safety, or what is necessary in extreme situations to preserve the mere existence or independence of society, on the one hand, and the rules of justice in the more precise sense, on the other."[29] There is no absolute rule to determine when the one principle must be upheld more urgently than the other; it is up to the prudent statesman to make that determination in the moment of conflict. This point defines the difference between Aristotelian idealism and Machiavellian cynicism: whereas Machiavelli takes the exceptions to the norm of justice to be the defining moments of politics, Aristotle accepts the usual requirements of justice as paradigmatic and only reluctantly and cautiously countenances deviations therefrom when the situation demands it.

Strauss identifies a common thread running through both the Platonic and the Aristotelian doctrines of natural right, a principle he expresses as follows: "There is a universally valid hierarchy of ends, but there are no universally valid rules of action."[30] The universal hierarchy of ends cannot itself be altered, and it provides the standard of nobility for actions, individuals, and regimes; but it does not define the whole range of possible contingent circumstances, or what is the best response to any such particular circumstance; the universal hierarchy of ends does not come with a universal rule of application.

Aquinas's elegant solution represents, therefore, a significant change, in that all doubts about the harmony of the city and natural right are dissipated and "likewise . . . the immutable character of the fundamental propositions of natural law" is upheld. Strauss points to modern natural law as a "reaction to this absorption of natural law by theology."[31] Strauss's reservations, however, are more clear as regards the "modern followers of Thomas Aquinas, among others, [who] are forced to take a position which implies a radical break with the thought of Aristotle, as well as that of Thomas Aquinas himself," as he says in 1949: "Religious faith, faith in Biblical revelation no doubt solves the difficulty, but religious faith is not rational knowledge."[32]

As Strauss asserts elsewhere in this volume, the classical tradition founded by the trio of Socrates Plato and Aristotle had something in common: they took their bearings from the perfection of human nature. But the Platonic teaching that points more clearly beyond the city to the philosophical life is superior because it supports the not unproblematic return of the philosopher to man's "cave," while acknowledging the partially conventional nature of the *polis* and its laws. Strauss, therefore, only seemingly sides with Aristotle. Despite Aristotle's sober approach, Strauss supports Socrates and Plato's presentation—to which he adds the Stoic teaching—because only such a presentation properly addresses the objection of the conventionalists that the city exists by convention and not by nature, while Aristotle attempts to justify the *polis* by nature.

Natural Right (1946)[a]

LEO STRAUSS

Lecture to be delivered on January 9, 1946, in the General Seminar and in February 1946 in Annapolis

I propose to discuss certain aspects of the *history* of *natural right*. The problem of natural right is, of course, a *philosophic* and *not* a historical problem. But we are today in the unfortunate position that before we can even *think* of a philosophic discussion of natural right, we have to engage in historical studies. Our position is this: Natural right is no longer taken for granted; it is generally considered, at least among non-Catholics, a delusion; it is no longer in the center of discussion, of philosophic discussion, it is more or less despised; as a consequence, it is no longer really *known*. But it *was* in the center of discussion, it was known in the past. We are in need of a return to the past, of some sort of historical investigation, if we want to familiarize ourselves with the philosophic problem of natural right.

That natural right is a *problem*, a most *serious* problem, can be seen directly, i.e., without historical reflection. Natural right is right that is independent of human arbitrariness. The alternative to the view that there is a natural right seems to be[33] the assertion that all right depends on human arbitrariness, or is man-made, i.e., positive right. This assertion known as legal positivism is difficult to maintain. For: if there is no right but positive right, or positive law, we cannot speak any longer of unjust laws. But we are frequently compelled to speak of unjust laws. The most ruthless exponent[b] of legal positivism was finally compelled to admit that while no positive law or right can be wrong, it may be erroneous. More than that: positive law cannot guarantee its own[34] obligatory character; it cannot answer the

[a] This typescript can be found in Leo Strauss Papers, box 6, folder 15. It was transcribed and annotated by J. A. Colen.

[b] Strauss has inserted "Bergbohm" by hand in the margin. Cf. *NRH*, 10n3: "The legal positivism of the nineteenth and twentieth centuries cannot be simply identified with either conventionalism or historicism. It seems, however, that it derives its strength ultimately from the generally accepted historicist premise (see particularly Karl Bergbohm, *Jurisprudenz und Rechtsphilosophie*, I [Leipzig, 1892], 409ff.)."

question why we ought to obey it irrespective of the policeman around the corner. Why do we respect, and not[35] merely fear, laws enacted democratically as distinguished from laws enacted by the rubberstamp parliament of a dictator? Ultimately because we believe that only the will of the majority has a just claim to our obedience. The justice of majority rule is not and cannot be the product of democratic or nondemocratic legislation; it is derived from principles higher than positive law. That we need such principles, that human life would be impossible without them, is fairly generally admitted. But, some people say, those principles are not a natural right, but the ideals of our society. This is evidently insufficient:[36] are we not compelled to question the ideals of our society? To wonder whether our society plus its ideals is[37] civilized or barbaric? To measure those ideals by ideals[38] which are independent of any parochial or[39] regional predilections or prejudices? But it does not suffice to appeal from the ideals of our society to ideals simply. For we usually understand by ideals: objects of aspiration to which we may, or may not, aspire without any consequence other than that in the first case we are idealists and in the second case something else; we do *not* understand by ideals objects of plain duty which oblige us in our conscience: this obligatory character which is blurred by the term ideals is squarely set forth by the term natural *right*. Besides, ideals are frequently understood as objects of faith; but faith is not knowledge; the Nazis have as much faith in their ideals as democrats have in theirs; there is an indefinite variety of faiths which are mutually exclusive; we cannot help wondering which faith, if any, is the right faith; we are compelled to go beyond the realm of faith into the realm of reasoned discussion in order to acquire, if we can, *knowledge*. The problem of natural right is as serious as our need for standards, accessible to the knowledge of man as man, which are natural, i.e., which are independent of human arbitrariness. If there are no such standards, all human action is blind, because it does not *know* whether its ultimate aims are *right*. If there are no such standards, *everything* is permitted or legitimate.[40]

One merely evades the issue if one says that our translegal standards are expediency or utility. Everything expedient or useful is expedient or useful *for* something. For society, as most people would say. But what is expedient or useful for one section of society may be hurtful to others. Must we consider all sections of society equally, or must we consider, most of all, its most respectable part, or its[41] most numerous part? And does expediency mean chiefly expediency for a higher standard of living, or expediency for moral and spiritual welfare? Others have suggested as the standard "social cohesion and durability." But one may have social cohesion and durability on the most different levels: on the level of Indian caste society, of China, of Sparta, of Venice, of Britain. Is social cohesion and durability based on oppression as good as the social cohesion and durability of a free society? And if one asserts that freedom is to be preferred to oppression, does one not tacitly appeal to justice, to right, to a right that is not established arbitrarily, but intrinsically right? For does one not imply that every human being has a just claim to liberty?

One equally blurs the issue if one speaks of the idea of justice. For if one understands "idea of justice" in a precise sense, in the sense of Plato or that of[42] Kant, it is identical at least for all practical purposes with natural right. And if one understands "idea of justice"[43] in a vague sense, one certainly blurs the issue. I believe it was Fr. J. Stahl,[a] the founder of the Prussian conservative party, who replaced natural right by the idea of justice, or the ideas of right (*Rechtsideen*). In order to exclude absolutely any right to revolution, in order to prevent any appeal from positive laws however unjust or unreasonable to a higher law, he asserted that the translegal standards of laws have the character, not of right or law, but of ideas: I would say, he asserted that the translegal standards of laws have the character *merely* of ideas.

If these remarks are substantially correct, it would follow that we are necessarily guided by some notion, correct or mistaken, clear or hazy, of natural right. In our time, many people in this country actually believe, whether they know it or not, in the natural right of each to self-realization. For when they demand that everyone be given the opportunity of realizing his self, they do not appeal to any *legal* right; they do not appeal to any particular *American* aspiration which as such would concern only Americans; they do not appeal to a principle of *our* society: for they apply it to all societies by calling societies of the present or past which do not recognize self-realization, backward or reactionary societies. Nor do they appeal to a mere ideal: for they consider those who object to self-realization, in theory or in practice, not merely unidealistic, but unjust or vicious. They appeal then to something that is intrinsically right, if ignored until a very short time ago. What is true of self-realization is true of the rule "From everyone

[a] Friedrich Julius Stahl is not so much the founder as the inspirer of the *Deutschkonservative Partei*, a political party of the German Empire, founded in 1876, which disappears at the end of the World War I, composed mainly by *Junker*, which defended constitutional monarchy but opposed parliamentarianism, the principle of equality of citizens, natural right, and rationalism.

according to his capacity and to everyone according to his needs"[a] and of every other rule of this kind.

Our *need* for natural right does not guarantee, of course, that there *is* a natural right. According to the view that obtains in our age, there is none. The usual arguments adduced in support of this view are as strong as usual arguments usually are. They are usually refuted with the equally formidable arguments of the Saint Georges or Don Quixotes who sally forth on the noble steeds of idealism in order to fight the dragons or sheep called the relativists. I beg leave to follow a more pedestrian course. Present-day opposition to natural right has two main motives. First, an interest in legal security, a desire to secure absolute obedience to the law of the land. Civil obedience seems to be fundamentally endangered if one may have recourse to a law higher than the law of the land. The second motive is "the historical consciousness," i.e., the conviction that all ideas are essentially relative to given nations, classes, epochs, etc. The typical present-day arguments against natural right are: (1) the anarchy, the indefinitely large variety, the disgraceful variety of natural law doctrines proves the shortcomings of all: if there were knowledge, there would be agreement. This anarchy ceases to be a stumbling block, once one admits that all alleged natural right is merely an expression of specific historical situations. (2) If there are certain principles common to every natural law doctrine, these principles are too general, too formal, to be of any significance. The present-day rejection of natural right is usually traced to the alleged discovery made in the nineteenth century of History, of what was formerly called the historical process and what is now being called the historicity of man. This is correct inasmuch as the decisive change was brought about by the attack of the historical school of jurisprudence on natural right jurisprudence (Savigny[b] in Germany and

[a] Karl Marx, slogan is in his 1875 *Critique of the Gotha Program*. The same phrase is used in *NRH*, 148. Strauss appears to translate from the German, "Jeder nach seinen Fähigkeiten, jedem nach seinen Bedürfnissen!," since common English translations are slightly different. In *NRH*, 148, Strauss actually says, "from everyone according to his capacity and to everyone according to his merits."

[b] Friedrich Carl von Savigny (1779–1861) was a nineteenth-century jurist and historian who belonged to the historical school of jurists founded by Gustav Hugo. The works for which Savigny is best known are the *Recht des Besitzes* and the *Beruf unserer Zeit für Gesetzgebung*. Savigny argued in the latter that law is part and parcel of national life. He opposed the idea, common to both French eighteenth-century jurists and Bentham, that law can be arbitrarily imposed on a country irrespective of its state of civilization and history.

Sir Henry Summer Maine in England[a]). But in so far as this is the case, the present-day rejection of natural right rests on very shaky foundations. For the historical school took issue with *modern* natural right, with the natural right of the eighteenth century; it did not really consider the natural right of the Middle Ages and of classical antiquity. The historical school tacitly assumed of course that premodern natural right had been disposed of by modern natural right. This assumption was based on the common belief in a law of progress or else on Hegel's philosophy of history according to which the true elements of each significant position are necessarily preserved in the succeeding positions. Sanguine assumptions of this kind are not borne out by a sober analysis of the criticism of premodern natural right by the originators of modern natural right.

As far as present-day criticism of natural right has any value, it does not presuppose the so-called discovery of History. It is merely a repetition of the age-old criticism of natural right, of the criticism that culminates in the thesis that all notions of justice or morality are conventional. This statement evidently requires some explanation. The notion of conventional belongs to the fundamental dichotomy *natural*-conventional which is implied in the distinction between natural and positive law. The distinction natural and conventional is *not*, as some people believe, a specialty of the sophists and their spiritual descendants, but of course fundamental for Plato and Aristotle as well. It is implied, e.g., in Aristotle's distinctions between natural and positive right, between natural and legal slavery, between the natural sounds and the conventional words. Now, the distinction between natural and conventional was gradually abandoned in the nineteenth century. The historical school raised the claim of having finally dissolved the old bifurcation of law into natural and positive law, of having resolved natural and positive law in a higher unity, by understanding *all* law as historical (Gierke, *Althusius*, 338).[b] How far it succeeded can be seen perhaps from

[a] Sir Henry James Sumner Maine (1822–88) was an English jurist and historian. He maintained that law and society developed "from status to contract." According to the thesis, in the ancient world individuals were bound by status to traditional groups, while in the modern world, in which individuals are viewed as autonomous agents, they are free to make contracts and form associations with whomever they choose. Cf. *Ancient Law: Its Connection with the Early History of Society, and Its Relation to Modern Ideas* (London: John Murray, 1861).

[b] The reference is to Otto Gierke, *Johannes Althusius und die Entwicklung der naturrechtlichen Staatstheorien: zugleich ein Beitrag zur Geschichte der Rechtssystematik* (Breslau: Verlag Marcus, 1902 [ed. orig. 1880]). Strauss appears to be using the 1939 English translation by

the admission by its last exponent (Gierke) that "the philosophic elaboration of this thought remains imperfect to this day." For what the historical school actually did was *not* to replace the old bifurcation of law into natural and positive by the higher unity of the historical, but to assert the *natural* character of things which had been previously considered fundamentally conventional or dependent on human institution. For the historical school could not understand all law as historical but by understanding all law as the "expression of an organic group-consciousness"; it had to interpret the nation, the ethnic group in particular, as a natural unit, as an organism. The difficulties to which this attempt is exposed could not be solved but by introducing a novel distinction, the distinction between the natural and the historical: human *groups* in particular were eventually conceived of as historical and not as natural. It is the distinction between the natural and the historical which underlies all present-day orientation. So much so that today *the* alternative to the assertion of natural right seems to be the view that all right is *historical.* I contend that this view, the historicist view, ultimately leads back to the conventionalist view of old. Let me explain this.

The conventionalist thesis is to the effect that no right is natural, but that all right, including the translegal standards of right and wrong, owes its being, i.e., its being *right,* to the fact that it has been agreed upon, or accepted, by a given society and to nothing else. The *historicist* thesis is to the effect that no right is natural, but all right owes its being to something more fundamental, or less arbitrary, than the decree of society. Savigny, for example, asserted that all right owes its being primarily and fundamentally, not to conscious legislation or arbitrary decision, but to the "common conviction of the people, to the equally and commonly shared feeling of inner necessity."[a] The common conviction of a people or a people's feeling of inner necessity is from any philosophic point of view nothing but generally accepted opinion which owes its validity, not to its truth, but to the fact that it is generally accepted or agreed upon. Today, historicists usually assert that

Bernard Freyd, *The Development of Political Theory.* Otto Friedrich von Gierke (1841–1921) specialized in the study of the antecedents of German law. His view of the rule of law and his emphasis on the federal nature of medieval states were famous and controversial. In fact, he asserted that society grows because people associate in groups and groups of groups, from families to the state. He was an opponent of civil law interpretation and theorizing. He was a major influence on the British historian of law F. W. Maitland, who translated as *Political Theories of the Middle Ages* some of Gierke's major works, and on John Neville Figgis.

[a] The reference is to Friedrich Carl von Savigny, *System des heutigen Römischen Rechts* (Berlin: Veit, 1840), 19.

the translegal standards of right which are adopted by a given society are determined by the specific character, or the specific *needs*, of that society. The question of course is whether the standards of the various societies are *really* determined by their *needs*, and not rather by their *opinions* about their needs, or by the opinion of the ruling groups about their needs, and hence above all by their opinions about God, world, and man. As far as this is the case, as far as the standards rest on opinion as distinguished from knowledge, they are essentially arbitrary or conventional: opinions have no stability of their own; they have to be stabilized by convention. Conventionalism is superior to historicism because it does not gratuitously assume that each society knows what it needs or that the general will cannot err. It is with a view to difficulties such as these to which the older type of historicism is exposed that the more sophisticated historicists of our time trace all translegal standards of right to "historical *decisions*." But by tracing them to decisions, they almost openly proclaim the arbitrary, the conventional character of all standards.

The choice with which man always was and still is confronted is then that between natural right and the view that all notions of justice are conventional. Not the cushion of historicism but the hard rock of conventionalism is *the* alternative to natural right.[44] Precisely because this is the case, the problem of natural right is our *most* serious problem.

To reach *some* degree of clarity about the *problem*, i.e., the problematic character, of natural right, we turn to the *history* of natural right. That history is presented in the popular literature as well as in a part of the scholarly literature[a] as follows. Natural right or natural law came to the fore with the Stoics, especially the Roman Stoics. The Stoic natural law was adopted by the Roman lawyers, and it was reconciled with the teaching of the Bible by the Church Fathers. The Stoic-Christian natural law is the backbone of Western social philosophy. The natural law of the seventeenth and eighteenth centuries is merely the secularized version of the Stoic-Christian natural law. No error is more grave than that of earlier generations which considered the seventeenth and eighteenth centuries the heyday of natural law, and believed that Hugo Grotius was the father of natural law. The importance of the secularization of natural law in the modern centuries is differently evaluated by different scholars. The late A. J. Carlyle, who is gen-

[a] Cf. the reference to Carlyle below, and the more explicit unpublished text on the state of the literature in Leo Strauss Papers, box 14, folder 9.

erally considered the greatest authority on the subject, apparently did not consider it *very* important. For he said that "at least from the lawyers of the 2nd century to the theorists of the French revolution, the history of political thought is continuous, changing in form, modified in content, but still the same in its fundamental conceptions,"[a] and he understood by these fundamental conceptions primarily the notion of natural right and its corollaries.

Now, a word or two of criticism. It is not necessary to dwell on the obvious fact that natural right was recognized long before the Stoics, e.g., by Aristotle, by Plato, by many sophists. One is justified in saying that natural right is as old, not indeed as philosophy in general, but as *political* philosophy.

It is more important for our immediate purpose to lay the ghost of the so-called secularization of natural right in the modern era. What does secularization mean in this context? Separation of natural right from divinely revealed right? That separation was a foregone conclusion for all classical philosophy, and it was not rejected by medieval philosophy. Or does secularization mean separation of natural right from *natural* theology, from a doctrine concerning God which is based on reason, and not on revelation? There is no necessary or obvious connection between Plato's and Aristotle's natural right and any theology, and Grotius's declaration that natural right would be valid even if there were no God is of scholastic ancestry. The transformation of natural right in the seventeenth century can*not* be described as a secularization of natural right.

This does not mean that there is an unbroken continuity in the history of natural right. Without any question, the seventeenth century witnessed a break with the tradition of natural right. This is indicated with sufficient clarity by the following facts. Firstly, we observe in the seventeenth and eighteenth centuries a most vocal dissatisfaction with the whole traditional doctrine of natural right: certain outstanding men demand an entirely *new*

[a] Strauss refers to A. J. Carlyle, *A History of Mediaeval Political Theory in the West*, vol. 1: *The Second Century to the Ninth* (Edinburgh and London: William Blackwood and Sons, 1903), 2. The context is of the quotation is this: "There are, no doubt, profound differences between the ancient mode of thought and the modern;—the civilisation of the ancient world is very different from that of the modern; but just as it is now recognised that modern civilisation has grown out of the ancient, even so we think it will be found that modern political theory has arisen by a slow process of development out of the political theory of the ancient world,—that, at least from the lawyers of the second century to the theorists of the French Revolution, the history of political thought is continuous, changing in form, modified in content, but still the same in its fundamental conceptions."

doctrine of natural right. Secondly, traditional natural right had been, in the main, a *conservative* doctrine; from the seventeenth century on, natural right became a *revolutionary* doctrine. Whereas the rebellion of the Low Countries against Spain was based on *positive* right, the English civil war, the Glorious Rebellion of 1689, the American Declaration of Independence and the French Revolution were at least partly based on principles of *natural* right. There is no need to trace this change from a conservative doctrine to a revolutionary doctrine to a change in the social circumstances; for it is perfectly intelligible from the change which the meaning of natural right itself underwent in that period. The change which natural right underwent in the seventeenth century is *the* epoch-making event in the history of natural right.

Let us first enumerate the characteristics of modern natural right, of the natural right of the seventeenth and eighteenth centuries.

a) Modern natural right is to a[45] much higher degree than, say, medieval natural right *constitutional* natural right, or *public* natural right. The distinction between public right which orders the commonwealth and its relation to the citizens, and private right which regulates the relation among the citizens, goes back to the Greeks. But only since the seventeenth century do we find a new discipline called *jus publicum universale sive natural*: a public right valid for *all* states, and hence based, not on customs, precedent, or positive law, but on natural reason alone (the Dutchman Ulrich Huber[a] published in 1672 *De iure civitatis libri tres novam*[46] *disciplinam iuris publici universalis continentes*). Works such as Hobbes's *Leviathan*, Locke's *Civil Government*, and Rousseau's *Social Contract* are works devoted to universal, i.e., natural, *public* right. The alternative title of the *Social Contract* is "principles of political right"—of course of the political right of *every* society. Natural right was described by Ulpianus as a part of *private* right. As a rule, however, natural right was considered in premodern times to have certain implications regarding constitutional right. But these implications were of a very general, and hence fairly innocuous, character: they did not go beyond establishing the illegitimacy of tyranny. In modern natural right,

[a] Ulrich (or Ulrik) Huber (1636–94) was a professor of law at the University of Franeker and a political philosopher. His major work, *De jure civitatis libri tres*, was published initially in 1672 and continued to be revised until 1694. Huber considered captivity in war, criminal conviction, voluntary renunciation of liberty, and birth from a female slave legal as grounds for slavery. Apart from this work, he was known for his studies on Roman law. He is a typical representative author of the Dutch theory of the conflict of law.

however, the constitutional implications are much more incisive. The first in time is the doctrine of sovereignty; for the whole doctrine of sovereignty, i.e., of the *rights* of the sovereign, is of course a doctrine of natural constitutional right: the rights of the sovereign are determined, not by the customs or precedents or laws of a given society, but universally with a view to the nature of political society as such. As a consequence, the legitimacy, and not merely the expediency, of all sorts of mixed government or of any constitutional limitations of the sovereign is contested: it is contested on grounds of natural constitutional right. Other modern teachers of natural right, Locke in particular, deny the legitimacy of *any* absolute government on[47] grounds of natural right. Rousseau asserts as a doctrine of natural right that only republican government is legitimate. Thomas Paine asserts for all practical purposes that according to natural right only democracy is legitimate. The practical bearing of such doctrines is manifest: there is all the difference in the world between saying that monarchy, for example, is not the best form of government, or that it is undesirable or inexpedient, *and* saying that it is illegitimate. The former assertion does not justify revolution, but the latter does—most emphatically. Natural *public* right is at the bottom of the Declaration of Independence, and above all of the French Declaration of the Rights of Man of 1789, of 1793, and 1795. It is at the bottom of the idea of the necessity of a constituent assembly and of written constitutions: it[48] *prescribes* constituent assemblies and written constitutions. People sometimes are at a loss to understand why the great enemy of the principles of the French Revolution, Burke, could base his opposition to those principles on natural right. The answer of course is that Burke's natural right is one which does not entail incisive consequences for constitutional right, or that is fundamentally the premodern natural right.

b) The *second* characteristic of specifically modern natural right is the *form* in which it is presented. It is presented in complete independence of positive right. In premodern times, the distinction between natural and positive right did not lead to the establishment[49] of a separated *discipline* of natural right, and still less of university chairs exclusively for natural right. It evidently was felt that a complete and self-contained treatment of natural right was either impossible or else[50] of no great value or importance. Only in modern times does natural right take on the form of a *system*—of a *deductive* system. All the great teachers of modern natural right do at least tend toward a natural right demonstrated *more geometrico*. In the lower regions this tendency led to the elaboration of complete *codes* of natural right, covering even the natural right of fiefs, natural feudal right. "Natural law was treated (sc. in this period) as a code of laws taught by reason, and positive law as a system of ordinances issued for its enforcement" (Gierke, *Althusius* 353).

c) The *third* characteristic of specifically modern natural right is its connection with the idea of a *state of nature*: of a human life prior to the establishment of civil society. In premodern time, there is no such a connection. Premodern natural right was rather the framework of all positive codes than a complete code for a particular status, the state of nature. In the literature, one frequently finds accounts of the state of nature in the teaching of the sophists, of Lucretius, of Mariana, etc. But there is nothing of a state of nature in the texts themselves. The very term state of nature stems, not from reflections on natural right, but from Christian theology. The state of nature is distinguished from the state of grace, and it is normally subdivided into a state of pure nature, prior to Adam's fall, and a state of corrupted nature, the state after the fall. The immediate purpose of the term state of nature in the seventeenth and eighteenth centuries is precisely to deny the significance of the distinction between the state of pure nature and the state of corrupted nature, i.e., to deny the significance, if not the historicity, of the fall of Adam. The traditional theological view of man and society was based on the biblical view of the origins of mankind; the purpose of the modern doctrine of the state of nature was to supply a nonbiblical, rational basis for the new view of man and society. The modern doctrine of the state of nature is in a sense[51] the early form of what today is called anthropology, as appears with particular clarity from Rousseau's discourse on the origin of inequality. On the other hand, by replacing the distinction state of nature–state of grace by the distinction state of nature–civil state, men like Hobbes, Locke, and Rousseau expressed the view that the cure for the deficiencies or inconveniences of the state of nature is, not grace, but orderly government. The term state of nature in this sense takes on central significance for the first time in Hobbes, who still excuses himself for this apparently novel usage.

d) The *fourth* and most important characteristic of specifically modern natural right is that it is, or tends to be, a doctrine of *rights* rather than of *duties*. Premodern natural right was essentially a doctrine of duties. Only very late, in the second half of the sixteenth century, did scholasticism start to speak emphatically of natural rights as distinguished from natural duties or obligations. In Thomas Aquinas's thematic treatment of natural right, and even in that of Richard Hooker at the end of the sixteenth century, natural rights as distinguished from natural duties are not even mentioned. In the seventeenth century we observe a radical shift of emphasis from duties to rights, a shift of emphasis which determines political and social thought up to the present day. First of all, the very distinction between right and duty becomes much more emphatic than in former ages. Above all, the political society is now conceived of for the first time chiefly or exclusively as serving the purpose of guaranteeing natural *rights*, and not of guaranteeing the performance of man's natural duties. This fundamental change finds its most striking expression in the teaching of Hobbes. It is equally visible in the teaching of Rousseau, whose social contract is preceded exclusively by natural rights, and not at all by duties, or in the teaching of Spinoza, for whom natural right means exclusively the right which man *has* as distinguished from the right which *binds* man. Paine expressed this view most clearly by the title of his book, *Rights of Man*. Kant's and Fichte's doctrines of natural right are essentially doctrines of the *rights* of man. For Kant it is already a *problem* why moral philosophy is usually called the doctrine of duties and not also of rights. Regarding Locke, one merely has to compare his statements based on Hooker with what Hooker himself says in the context of his[52] work in order to see that there is no real continuity between the natural right of Locke and that of Hooker. As to Descartes, he does not mention duties in his ethical treatises: he does speak, in the central passage, of rights.

This characteristic of modern natural right is recognized somewhat obliquely by those who call modern natural right individualistic or subjectivistic. It is less ambiguous to describe modern natural right as concerned primarily with rights as distinguished from duties.

The first step toward an understanding of modern natural right would consist in ascertaining its *origin*. For once we know the man or type of men who originated modern natural right, we know its *spirit*. For the sake of brevity and simplicity, I shall limit myself to the question of the origin of the emphasis on rights rather than on duties. At least since Hegel it has become customary to trace the doctrine of the rights of man to Christianity as such, to the discovery of what was called "the infinite value of the individual soul." Gierke in particular found the thought "that every individual by virtue of his eternal destiny is in his inmost nature sacred and inviolable" "not merely suggested but more or less clearly expressed" everywhere in medieval literature. I have the impression that it is rather less clearly expressed there. It seems to me that one can easily detect the rights of man in medieval times, if one makes one or more of the following mistakes. Firstly, if one mistakes for a natural *right* something which is *permitted* by the law of nature as either not punishable or even decent. Secondly, if one mistakes for a natural right of A what B is commanded or forbidden by natural law to do to A (e.g., a natural law prohibition against murder does not yet constitute a natural right of each to life, a natural law command to give alms to the needy does not yet constitute a natural right of the needy to alms). Thirdly, if one mistakes for a natural right what is actually a natural duty. E.g., what is sometimes referred to in modern literature as a right to resistance is frequently in earlier times a duty to resistance, or at least something that "is allowed only as a form of obedience" (Figgis);[a] what is in modern times frequently called a right to resistance was originally the duty to obey God rather than man. Or[53] self-preservation is for medieval natural right a duty rather than a mere[54] right, whereas in modern times it is a right and not necessarily a duty. Ritchie in England[b] and Jellinek[c] in Germany have traced the rights of man with greater justice to the English Puritans. Indeed, one merely has to read the Clarke papers or Cromwell's speeches in order to come across natural rights. But is one justified in saying that "Puritan England has produced the theory of natural rights" (Ritchie)? The thesis of Ritchie is inseparably connected with his view of the Reformation as a whole: "The theory of natural rights is simply the logical outgrowth of the Protestant revolt against

[a] John Neville Figgis (1866–1919) was a historian and political philosopher who translated and adapted some ideas from Otto von Gierke. The reference is from *The Divine Right of Kings* (Cambridge: Cambridge University Press, 1914), 221.

[b] Probably David George Ritchie (1853–1903), a Scottish philosopher influenced by Thomas Hill Green and Arnold Toynbee. While he was in Oxford the foundations were laid both for his interest in idealistic philosophy, namely, Hegel, and also for his strong bent toward practical politics. He wrote a book called *Natural Rights* in 1895 and several on Darwinism and politics. Georg Jellinek (1851–1911) was a German public lawyer, considered to be of Austrian origin, who along with Hans Kelsen and the Hungarian Félix Somló belonged to the group of Austrian legal positivists and was considered to be *the* exponent of public law in Austria.

[c] Jellinek is best known for his essay *The Declaration of the Rights of Man and the Citizen* (1895), which argues for a universal theory of rights, as opposed to the culturally and nationally specific arguments then in vogue (particularly that of Émile Boutmy). Jellinek argued that the French Revolution, which was the focal point of nineteenth-century political theory, should be thought of not as arising from a purely French tradition (namely, the tradition stemming from Jean-Jacques Rousseau) but as a close analogue of revolutionary movements and ideas in England and the United States.

the authority of tradition, the logical outgrowth of the Protestant appeal to private judgment, i.e., to the reason and conscience of the individual." As untenable as this view of the Reformation, untenable is the attempt to trace the rights of man to Puritanism. In addition, the more exact investigations of Figgis have shown that the doctrine of natural rights occurs considerable time before English Puritanism in certain Spanish Jesuits and Dominicans of the late sixteenth and of the early seventeenth centuries. However this may be, one thing is the explicit admission of, and even emphasis on, natural rights, and an entirely different thing is the explicit or implicit *preference* given to natural rights as compared with natural duties or obligations. The problem of the origin of modern natural right is the problem of the origin of the orientation by rights rather than by duties. If we formulate, as we must, the question in this way,[55] there can be no doubt as to its answer: *the* originator of modern natural right is none other than Thomas Hobbes. Not only does Hobbes with a clarity and emphasis unusual in former times distinguish between natural right and natural law, i.e., between natural right and natural duty; he even makes the natural right as distinguished from the natural duties the very basis, and hence the limits, of all obligations. The natural right, which he recognizes, the right to one's life, is truly inalienable; it cannot be forfeited by any crime whatsoever. It, and it alone, is necessary and sufficient for determining the nature of political society, its purpose and its absolute limits. To secure man's natural, unalienable right, and for no other purpose, Hobbes's Leviathan is instituted among men. It is a right which every human being has regardless of sex, color, creed, age, merit or sin, not only against every other human being, but against every sovereign and against every society.

It is a right which every human being has even against God—as one is tempted to say, going beyond the letter but hardly beyond the spirit of Hobbes's teaching. Indeed, the principle of modern natural right cannot be understood if one does not take into account its theological implications. The primacy of right over duty presupposes the denial of any superhuman order or will. On the other hand, the complete absence or at least relative weakness of the doctrine of rights of man prior to the seventeenth century is doubtless due to the overwhelming influence of the biblical teaching. The biblical view has been formulated by Cardinal Newman as follows: "the simple absence of all rights and claims on the part of the creature in the presence of the Creator; the illimitable claims of the Creator on the service of the creature" (*The Idea of a University*, 183).[a] It suffices to refer to the book of Job and the insistence in the Bible on the need for divine mercy. "Behold, as the eyes of slaves look unto the hand of their master, and as the eyes of a maid unto the hand of her mistress, so our eyes wait upon the Lord our God, until he have mercy upon us" (Psalm 123). There is no right against God, because there is no right to mercy. There cannot be rights of man against God, if man owes his whole being to the free act of creation by God, and especially if man's moral being is as it were constituted by duties imposed on him by God. For if this is the case, man's practical concern is not so much with the dignity of his original or natural status as man as with his actual sinfulness (with his being sold to sin) or with his being redeemed from sin, on account, not of his merits, but of the free grace of God. The spiritual climate favorable to the insistence on the rights of man is characterized by an entirely different, by an entirely unbiblical view of the relation of man to God. It is characterized in the first place by the fact that the consciousness of man's sinfulness receded into the background. In dogmatic terms, Adam's fall ceased to be of crucial and even of great significance. The modern concept of the state of nature with its neutrality to the difference between the state of pure nature and that of corrupted nature took care of that.[b] The rights of man took on practical and popular significance for the first time with the English Puritans, whose greatest poet does not seem to have attached exaggerated importance to the fall: "some natural tears" Adam and Eve "dropped, but wiped them soon; The world was all before them."[c] The world ceased to be the valley of tears: it became the best of all possible worlds, seeing that in the worst case sin had affected only the earth which is but a minor planet in an infinite universe not polluted by sin. Even the earth soon became a potential paradise. For the stern justice of God and his glory made place for his unqualified loving kindness, for[56] his sugary sweetness—a kind father would give his children sugar rather than rod, as Bayle points out in one of his arguments against the biblical tradition.[d]

[a] The reference is to John Henry Newman, *The Idea of a University* (London: Basil Montagu Pickering, 1873), 183.

[b] [LS note] cf. my Hobbes 123, n. 2. (The reference is to *PPH*. The quoted note is from *Leviathan*, chap. 13, p. 65, and asserts "Nature [should not] . . . dissociate, and render men apt to invade, and destroy one another," in the context of the presentation of the state of nature.)

[c] John Milton, *Paradise Lost*, 12.645–46.

[d] Probably Pierre Bayle, *Historical and Critical Dictionary*, article on Origen, remark E, part IV.

Those who preferred a sterner language interpreted the age-old view of man as a citizen of the world to mean that man, being a citizen of the world, has rights against the sovereign of the world, against God. It was Leibniz who said that in the ideas of God every monad has a right to demand that God in ordering the other monads have regard to it. In this respect, there is no fundamental difference between Leibniz and his most famous antagonist, Voltaire. On the occasion of the earthquake of Lisbon, Voltaire wrote the following lines which I have to render in prose: "Believe me, if the earth opens its abysses, my complaint is innocent, and my cries are legitimate . . . I respect my God, *but* I love the universe. If man dares to complain about a misery so terrible, he is not proud—*hélas*, he is sensitive."[a] The fact that God has created man a feeling being gives man a right to protest against God's providence, to insist on his rights against God himself. For what possibly is the strongest statement, we have to turn to Kant. It is by virtue of the fall, Kant holds, that man became the equal of angels and of God himself: as regards the *claim* to be an end in himself; in other words, man's owes his very dignity[57] and the rights deriving from it, not to his creation, but to his revolt, to the fall; the expulsion from paradise is a "change" which is perilous indeed, but no less honorable. To sum up this point, we may venture to say that the rights of man came to the fore in a world that tried to preserve all the privileges of man's being created by God while making light of the burdens which so noble an origin must be presumed to entail.—This, however, cannot be the last word on the subject. For there are reasons to suppose that the theological garb owing to which the doctrine of the rights of man achieved its victory was really not more than the protective coloring of an essentially untheological effort.[58]

Before saying something about this effort, I would like to illustrate modern[59] natural right by looking at its moral implications. Whereas premodern natural right was a doctrine of obedience, or at least of conformity with an order not originating in the human will, modern natural right is a doctrine of freedom. But freedom is an ambiguous term. It may mean the liberty to that only which is good, just, and honest, and it may mean the liberty to other things as well. The type of freedom which was fostered by modern natural right can be recognized from the following examples. The natural right to property as interpreted by Locke is the right not limited by

[a] The reference is to Voltaire, "Poème sur le désastre de Lisbonne, ou examen de cet axiome: 'tout est bien'" (1756).

any duties of charity to the unlimited accumulation of capital. The natural right to communicating one's thoughts as interpreted by Kant is the right to speak or to make promises to others whether truthfully and sincerely or untruthfully and insincerely: freedom of speech not limited by the duty of truthfulness. The natural right to publish one's thoughts as interpreted by Milton justifies the claim to liberty of unlicensed printing not only of moral and orthodox books, but likewise of books which are likely to "taint both life and doctrine."[a] Freedom in the sense of the doctrine of the rights of man is a liberty to evil as well as to good, a liberty limited only by the recognition of the same liberty in all other men. It is a liberty, not only for reason, but also for unreason. Nor must we overlook the fact that the limitation of this kind of liberty by the recognition of the same liberty in others is very tenuous, as almost everyone admits today in regard to the liberty of the acquisitive instincts: those endowed by their creator with strong acquisitive faculties will gladly grant the same liberty to indulge their acquisitive inclinations to others which they demand for themselves; they will not lose anything by this deal.

These aspects of modern natural right must remain paradoxical and bewildering, as long as one does not consider them in a broader context: in the context of the attempt made at the beginning of the modern period to establish a *new* science of politics. That attempt followed from the conviction that traditional political science, i.e., fundamentally *classical* political science, had utterly failed. Classical political science had been the attempt to bring to light the best political order as that political order which lives up, within the limits of the possible, i.e., without the assumption of a miraculous or nonmiraculous change of human nature, to the requirements of virtue, of human excellence, *and* whose actualization is a matter of chance. The revolt of modern political philosophy, which was originated by Machiavelli, was directed against what we may call the *utopian* character of classical political philosophy: against its orientation by what would be the best possible solution under the most favorable conditions, *and* against its inability or unwillingness to expect the actualization of the best possible from anything else but chance. Modern political philosophy as such, i.e., in so far as it does not merely continue the classical tradition, is a quest for a political order whose actualization is *probable*, if not even *certain*. It is

[a] Reference to John Milton, "A Speech for the Liberty of Unlicensed Printing," *The Prose Works of John Milton*, ed. Charles Symmons (London: T. Bensley, Bolt Court, 1806), 1: 302.

concerned with a *guarantee* of the actualization of the desirable political order or with the *conquest* of chance. Both the classics and the moderns understand by the desirable order the *natural* order. But whereas for the classics the actualization of the natural order is a matter of chance, for the moderns it is a necessity, or almost a necessity: it would come into being everywhere, by itself, but for the foolish human intervention or ultimately for ignorance. Hence *knowledge* of the natural order, and *diffusion* of that knowledge, is the decisive means for actualizing the natural order of society. And if diffusion of knowledge is not the decisive means, it is at least indispensable. Adam Smith's invisible hand does not produce the natural economic order without the influence of Adam Smith's teaching—just as Rousseau's natural man in the *Emile* does not come into being but with the help of Rousseau.[60] Whereas according to Plato, evil will not cease in the cities if the philosoph*ers* do not rule, according to the moderns, evil will not cease in the cities if philosoph*y* does not rule, i.e., if *non*philosophers who have been apprised of the results of philosophy or science do not rule. In the course of time, people became ever more skeptical as regards the results of enlightenment; but they did not abandon the attempt of getting a *guarantee* of the actualization of the desirable order. In the nineteenth century, it was no longer enlightenment but "History" which was expected to supply that guarantee—or again *Nature* in her progressive process which by means of the survival of the fittest would lead to the desirable end. Present-day view rather expects the[61] emergence of truth by the free market of ideas.[62]

If one wants to discover the desirable political or social order whose actualization is probable, or *everywhere* possible, one has to take one's bearings by men as they actually are, and not by men as they ought to be; by how men mostly are and not by how men rarely are.[a] Now, men are less rarely seekers of pleasures, riches, and honors than they are seekers of truth and justice. Accordingly, modern political philosophy tried to establish an aim considerably *lower* than that of premodern philosophy or theology: an aim which can be reached by man as he mostly is. This attempt has had a remarkable success: the combination of universal freedom and social stability which has been achieved for some time in certain parts of the Western world surpasses everything which in this respect had ever been achieved in the past. Yet exactly because this is a very high achievement, a high price

[a] [LS note in the margin] Cf. *Leviathan*, p. 77, and *Contrat social*: reconciliation of justice and interest.

had to be paid for it. The price which man had to pay for the modern blessings of a high degree of general happiness was the lowering of the peaks, the lowering of man's ultimate aim.

Only from this point of view can one understand the characteristics of modern natural right.

a) In order to have a goal which was likely to be reached, one had to replace the quest for the best order either by the quest for *efficient* government regardless of its level, or by the quest for *legitimate* government. The first alternative led to Machiavellianism and reason of state. The second led to natural constitutional law. In other words, the classical notion of the best political order is inseparable from the conviction that that order stands and falls with a very high development of *character*, of the *moral* character of *all* the citizens. The modern notion of natural constitutional law implies that properly constructed institutions would take care wholly, or decisively, of the problem of political order.

The sternest moral philosopher of modern times, Kant, protested against the view that the right political order would presuppose a nation of *angels*: no, he says, the right political order can be established in a nation of *devils* provided they have sense. The classics were far from being blind to the importance of institutions: the classical origin of the mixed government is a sufficient proof for *that*. But: for the classics the institutions were nothing but devices for *establishing* or *securing*[63] the rule of the virtuous; they were not meant to be a *substitute* for virtue. If the emphasis is on character, one admits the crucial importance of chance: on how many accidents does the formation of character depend! If the emphasis is on institutions, there is a much greater prospect of conquering chance.

b) According to the premodern view, the more specific rules of natural right cannot be *deduced* from the axioms of natural right, for all more specific rules permit of exceptions; whether the specific rule or the exception is in order in a given case can be decided only on the basis of the knowledge of the *circumstances*, and the decision as to whether the rule or the exception must obtain in the circumstances is to be decided by *prudence* or practical wisdom. The question of what would be just in a given case can mostly find no general answer other than this: that would be just what a sensible man would choose in the circumstances. Now, practical wisdom requires maturity, experience of all sorts and conditions of men and situations, the experience of many years; it is normally the preserve of older men. Hence in order to be guided well regarding what is just in more specific cases, one has to listen to what old men say or write. Thus the distinction between natural right *proper* and *ius gentium*, i.e., the right accepted by civilized peoples in particular, cannot be very rigid in practice, and an independent treatment of natural right is out of the question. From the modern standpoint, the premodern point of view seems to admit elements of extreme arbitrariness, uncertainty, and chance. Who is going to decide, the moderns object, as to who is a sensible man? And what should be done in the conceivable case in which two or more sensible men disagree? In order to get rid of this uncertainty, of the apparent *vagueness* of the principle "how a wise man would determine," natural right transforms itself in the modern period into a deductive system: what is by nature right in specific cases can be found out by *everyone* by means of simple deduction from the axioms of natural right—or, if not, it would not be natural right and the question would have to be decided arbitrarily by the sovereign. Thus the element of chance and uncertainty which is implied in the unpredictably unequal natural distribution of wisdom and folly is eliminated by the geometrical and systematic character of modern natural right. *Method* does not merely bridge the gulf between the wise and the fools by equalizing opportunities to know, as Bacon and Descartes had stated: it offers the additional attraction of making wisdom superfluous.

c) Now let us try to understand the modern concept of a state of nature. What characterizes this concept is *not* the implication that man's nature is *complete* without his actually living in society or his being subject to social discipline. When Aristotle says that man is by nature a political animal, he seems to reject by implication the idea that there could be human life outside of civil society; actually, however, he merely means by his famous saying that man is by nature *capable* of living in society; a man who does not actually live in society is, according to Aristotle, not necessarily a mutilated human being. Since this is so, it is legitimate even from the Aristotelian point of view to distinguish between man's natural status and his civil status, between what he owes to nature and what he owes to human institution. The difference between the moderns and Aristotle is rather this: that Aristotle determines man's natural status with a view to man's natural perfection,[a] whereas the moderns determine it with exclusive regard to qualities which[64] normal human being necessarily possesses. Now, if man's

[a] [LS note] Consider here: according to the moderns the average man is complete outside of society; according to Aristotle, only superior man is complete outside of society.

natural status is defined in terms of human perfection, very high demands on men follow even for the state of nature; but if man's natural status is defined in terms of the natural qualities actually possessed by every human being, the bare minimum demands, if any demands at all, follow, and thus the way is paved for the delineation of a social order whose actualization does not seem to be too difficult or improbable.[a]

The modern concept of the state of nature was decisively prepared by Machiavelli. Apparently, Machiavelli was still more convinced than were the classics of the power of chance: he does not tire of speaking of *fortuna*. Yet he understands by chance no longer exclusively something essentially exempt from any human control, but also something which not merely may be used, but actually be *mastered*. To master chance is something much greater than to make use of chance, greater even than to make the *best* use of chance. Accordingly, for Machiavelli the great statesman is no longer in the best case a man who establishes, under favorable circumstances, the best political order, but the man who establishes *any* political order thanks to his mastering of chance. For this reason, as well as for his distrust of the utopianism of the classics, his chief concern is with the establishment of political order as such, i.e., of efficient government regardless of its level. For this purpose he has to go back behind every established order and to understand how, or by means of what human qualities, the great man can produce order out of chaos. The result is that the great man cannot do this but by making use of such moral qualities and of committing such actions as are necessarily condemned by him after the order has been established. What Machiavelli arrives at is then the view that the morality of the condition antedating civil society is essentially and legitimately lower than the normal morality of civil society, and the lower morality of what we may call the state of nature or, more precisely, of the period of founding[65] influences in various ways the morality suggested by Machiavelli of civil society itself. The orientation by the idea of conquest of chance is a decisive reason for the lowering of standards in modern times.

d) The best political order as conceived by premodern political philosophy was defined in terms of *duties*. Hence, premodern political philosophy

[a] [LS note in the text in parentheses] This interpretation of Aristotle implies that morality as such which necessarily presupposes social discipline, do *not* belong to man's natural perfection. Difference between Thomist and Averroist interpretation. Cf. *E. N.* X; Hayy ibn Yuqdhân; Ibn Bagga [Bâjja], Tadbîr al-mutawahhid. See below, p. XXXff." [LS note in margin] *Republic*, 558b3ff. and 496c3–5.

was utopian insofar as man's duties in the comprehensive sense of the term are not likely to be performed. In order to delineate a social order whose actualization would be probable, nothing was more helpful than the decision to take one's bearings by rights rather than by duties. For man's rights are very close to his self-interest, to his self-interest as everyone can understand it; whereas the kinship between man's duties and his self-interest does not meet everyone's eye. Hence, man can be depended upon to fight for his rights—much more than he can be[66] depended upon to do his duty. "The catechism of the rights of man is easily learned, the conclusions are in the passions" (Burke).[a] The catechism of the duties of man is less easily learned, insofar as the conclusions are not in the passions. From here we understand the revolutionary character of modern natural right as compared with the conservative character[67] of premodern natural right. As long as men took their moral bearings by duties, they were driven to search themselves rather than others as regards the fulfillment of duties; they were not primarily and essentially concerned with the misdeeds of their rulers; in addition, there was always the question as to whether the subjects had the right of punishing their ruler for his transgression of natural law; besides, the subjects might not worry particularly about their ruler's immorality. A ruler's transgression of his duties did not automatically call forth punishment; his keeping within the bounds of natural law was not automatically guaranteed. Premodern natural right was not self-enforcing. An entirely different situation develops once people take their moral bearings by their natural rights. Once this is the case, the ruler's transgressing the boundaries of natural law means nothing but infringement of the subjects' rights, and this is practically identical with touching them where it hurts. Hence there is as it were an automatic guarantee of[68] the enforcement of the punitive clauses of natural right. Modern natural right is, almost, self-enforcing.

There is probably no element of modern natural right which is so important as the interpretation which it gave to the natural right of self-preservation. The right to self-preservation implies the right to the means of self-preservation—of course. But there is a question as to what are the proper means of self-preservation. Or as to who has the right to decide regarding the propriety of various means. According to the premodern view, the decision rests with the wise. This thought, if followed up to its ulti-

[a] The text is found in "Thoughts on French Affairs," in Edmund Burke, *The Works of the Right Honorable Edmund Burke*, rev. ed., (Boston: Little, Brown, 1866), 4: 342.

mate conclusion, leads to the admission of the legitimacy of absolute and irresponsible rule of the wise. Modern natural right gives the diametrically opposed answer. The right to the choice of the means of self-preservation belongs by nature to everyone, regardless of wisdom or stupidity. The reason can be stated as follows: while the fools must be presumed to make foolish choices, they must be presumed also to care more for themselves, to have a greater interest in their own preservation than any wise adviser of them would. In other words, self-interest may supply the want of wisdom. The idea that for all practical or political purposes everyone is a better judge of his true interests than any wise guardian of his would be necessarily leads to democratic consequences. I believe that this idea, probably the most important result of modern natural right, is still the strongest argument, the most sober argument in favor of the democratic principle which we have. We owe that argument to Hobbes and Rousseau.

Modern natural right came into being in opposition to the alleged or real utopianism of premodern natural right. It intended to be emphatically "realistic." There can be no doubt as to the fact that the appeal to the rights of life, liberty, property, etc., had a much stronger attraction and effect than the appeal to that so frequently and so easily ridiculed virtue. What we must start wondering about is whether the modern, realistic, hard-boiled world which as Rousseau noted has replaced virtue by economics has not developed a much more destructive utopianism of its own. For is it not utopian to believe that by lowering one's aims, one guarantees their realization? Is it not more utopian to expect social harmony from enlightened self-interest or either enlightened or unenlightened self-realization than from self-denial? Is it really true that man is so averse to virtue as[69] the modern argument assumes? "Les hommes, fripons en détail, sont en gros de très honnêtes gens: ils aiment la morale" (Montesquieu).[a]

We cannot judge properly of modern natural right if we do not understand premodern natural right. The classic of premodern natural right is Thomas Aquinas. But precisely because he is the classic, because his solution is so perfect, so elegant, it is very difficult to become aware of the *problem* of natural right if one starts from Thomas's teaching. To understand the problem of natural right, one must look at the Thomistic doctrine as one possibility of interpreting the Aristotelian doctrine of natural right.

Aristotle's doctrine is certainly in need of interpretation. For Aristotle

[a] Strauss quotes *L'Esprit des Lois*, book 25, chap. 2.

has devoted to this grave subject barely one page of his work. Hence the first question which comes to our mind is this: why does Aristotle say so little, so *very* little about natural right? The same question arises in regard to Plato and indeed to all the other pre-Stoic philosophers. Why does natural right play such a comparatively negligible role, at least apparently, in pre-Stoic philosophy?

The usual answer is based on the usual, i.e., the Hegelian, interpretation of Plato and Aristotle. Hegel may be said to have replaced the classical distinction between natural and conventional by the distinction between the subjective mind and its[70] reflective reasoning on the one hand, and the objective mind which expresses itself in living institutions on the other. What was formerly called conventional was interpreted by Hegel as the work of the objective mind, of Reason, of a higher form of Reason than that which manifests itself in the reflections of individuals. The discovery of the objective mind distinguished Hegel from Kant and seventeenth/eighteenth-century rationalism. On the basis of this view, Hegel interpreted Plato and Aristotle: Hegel : eighteenth century = Plato and Aristotle : sophists.[a] Accordingly, the political philosophy of Plato and Aristotle was understood as an attempt to understand the life of the Greek city as the embodiment of Reason or the Idea. There cannot be a natural right in Plato and Aristotle which is different from the living order of the Greek city. Only after the collapse of the Greek city (Alexander) did natural right become severed from the city and become a disembodied norm.

This view of Plato and Aristotle is not tenable. For Hegel, the best political order is necessarily identical with some actual order, whereas for Plato and Aristotle the best political order is possibly, and even normally, different from, and transcendent to, any actual order. For Hegel, it is foolish to prescribe to the state how it ought to be as distinguished from understanding it in its intrinsic reasonableness; but Plato and Aristotle have, so to say, no other concern but to prescribe to the city how it ought to be. In this decisive aspect, Plato and Aristotle are at one with seventeenth/eighteenth-century rationalism and Kant against Hegel. We have therefore to explain the relative silence about natural right in pre-Stoic philosophy along different, along non-Hegelian lines.

The reason for[71] that silence may be stated as follows: it is due decisively

[a] That is, Hegel was related to the eighteenth century as Plato and Aristotle were related to the sophists.

to the conviction that natural right is of a very problematic character as a norm of social conduct; natural right is not only not *sufficient* for ordering society, it would even be *destructive* of society, if it were not *diluted* by a fundamentally conventional right.

In Xenophon's *Education of Cyrus* the following story is told.[a] The boy Cyrus attended, as all other Persians boys did, a school of justice. One day, he was given the following case to decide: a big boy had a small coat, and a small boy had a big coat; the big boy took the small boy's big coat and gave the small boy his small coat; Cyrus decided that this was well done. He was refuted by the argument which is still generally used to refute jurisprudence of welfare: he got a spanking, and his teacher told him that he had not been asked to decide what was most *fitting* but what was *just*, i.e., in this particular case who was the rightful owner of the big coat. The implication is obvious: the naturally right is precisely the fitting, but the orientation by that natural right would play havoc with all settled life. Plato's *Republic* as a whole is an indirect representation of how what is naturally right would be destructive of almost everything which we cherish and consider just: property, monogamous family, prohibitions against incest, privileges of old age, etc. The natural right in the strict sense would be that the truly wise have absolute and irresponsible power and allot on this basis to everyone what he truly deserves, what is truly fitting for him, i.e., what would make him a better man. Naturally, right is the rule of the naturally superior; but this natural right is in conflict with what people generally *believe* to be right; they believe that it is right that every social order should be based on consent, regardless of the wisdom or folly of those consenting. The only practicable solution is the *dilution* of the *naturally* right principle of rule of wisdom by the *supposedly* right principle of consent (*Legg.* 757, cf. *Rep.* 501b); of the naturally right principle of inequality by the conventionally right principle of equality or ruling and being ruled in turn of all (*E.E.* 1242b28 ff.). Or, to take a more specific example, Aristotle distinguishes slavery according to natural right from slavery according to conventional right; a man may be naturally a freeman and yet a slave according to conventional right; his being a slave is against natural right, and yet just. The underlying idea is that the appeal to natural right from a conflicting conventional right would be destructive of settled social life. The difficulty goes even deeper: natural

[a] Leo Strauss explains this story in *NRH*, 147–48. It is taken from Xenophon's *Cyropaedia* 1.3.16–17.

right is the right of the wise to absolute rule; of course, to rule in the interest of the less wise or the unwise. But here the formidable question arises as to whether it can be naturally right that the better *serve* the worse, that the higher *serve* the lower (cf. RMbM *Comm. on Mishna*—Heinemann, *Uebermensch*; *Politics* 1254b33ff.).[a] Natural right could be in itself a norm of social conduct, if social life could dispense with fictions, myths, or noble lies; but the opposite is the case: not truth but opinion is the element of social life (cf. apart from *Rep.*: Rousseau, *p. m.*,[b] 331, p. 2 ff.).[c]

Aristotle reconciled this difficulty with the evident need for natural right by a radical limitation of the subject matter of natural right. According to him, natural right is that right which by nature obtains among the full members of a political society; it is essentially limited to the members of that group, a *Binnenmoral*. But this apparently creates new difficulties. This is shown most simply by the fact that Aristotle's natural right is interpreted in diametrically opposite ways by Thomas Aquinas on the one hand, and by the Islamic-Jewish philosophers on the other. According to Thomas, Aristotle taught that there is a natural right and that the principles of that natural right are immutable, i.e., not open to any exceptions. According to the Islamic-Jewish philosophers, Aristotle taught that there is no natural right strictly speaking, but that there is a kind of conventional right which is a *necessary* convention of all political societies, and that this quasi-natural right is radically changeable, i.e., subject to exceptions. The "Averroist" interpretation is in manifest conflict with Aristotle's explicit statement that there is a natural right. The Thomist interpretation, on the other hand, is in manifest conflict with Aristotle's explicit[72] statement that *all* natural right is changeable. I suggest this interpretation.

Aristotle does not understand by natural right any *rules*, but those just determinations of given cases which are based exclusively on principles of

[a] RMbM is the acronym for Rabbi Moses ben Maimon or Maimonides. Leo Strauss inserted by hand a note: "no wise man would choose to rule" (*Rep.* 1). The quotation from Plato's *Republic* is in 347d6–8.

[b] This may be a reference to the *First Discourse*: "p. m." means "in my possession" (see Strauss, *Gesammelte Schriften*, ed. Meier, 1: 356.

[c] [LS note typed inside the text, but separated by two lines] Gierke, *Althusius* engl. [translation], 337 n. 25: "the very existence of lordship and ownership involved a breach of the pure law of nature." 114 n. 12. Aegidius Collonna III 1 c. 6 supposes 3 possible origins of the state: the purely natural way of the outgrowth from the family, the partly natural of *concordia constituentium civitatem vel regnum* and lastly mere force and conquest. Purely natural = simply just. [The reference to Aegidius Collonna or Giles of Rome is to *De regimine principum*.]

either commutative or distributive justice, i.e., which do not presuppose any positive right. E.g., a positive law which does not contain any arbitrary element, that solves justly without including any arbitrary element the problems arising in a given country at a given time, *is* natural right.[73] Naturally right therefore are the equality of the price of a thing with the value of the labor and expense of the producer of the thing; or the proper proportion between crime and punishment; or the distribution of income from a common enterprise according to the proportion of the shares of the capital contributed by each; or the distribution of ruling offices according to merit, etc. Or, if one wants to have *rules* of natural right, such rules as the prohibition against murder, theft, etc., would be rules of natural right. But: the application of the principles of commutative and distributive justice or of any general or particular rule of natural right is subject to one crucial limitation: that application must not seriously conflict with, i.e., really endanger, the existence of the community as a whole. *All* rules of natural right are subject to the clause: *salus publica suprema lex.* As *a rule*, the principles of natural right must obtain; but *exceptionally* they are *justly* overridden by considerations of *salus publica.* Since those principles obtain as a rule, all *teaching* must proclaim those principles and nothing else; to do this effectively, the rules of natural right must be taught *without qualifications*, without ifs and buts (e.g., thou shalt not kill—period). But the omission of all qualifications, which makes the principles of natural right *effective*, makes them at the same time *untrue*. Regarding *any* unqualified rules of natural right, Averroes is right, these unqualified rules are not natural right, but conventional right, if a necessary convention of all civil societies.

The difference between Thomas and Aristotle will appear less great if we consider the fact that Thomas could allow for exceptions to the rules of natural right by falling back on *divine* dispensation. Thomas can afford to assert the immutability of the principles of natural right *merely* because he admits a *divine* right in addition to natural right (*S. th.* II 2, q. 64 a. 6 ad 1; cf. Gierke, 340 n. 39: "For the benefit of the omnipotent Council, Randorf teaches that, if the welfare of the Council requires it, the Council may dispense with the moral law").[a]

[a] Aquinas in the II-II q. 64 a. 6 ad 1 in fact says: "Respondeo dicendum quod aliquis homo dupliciter considerari potest, uno modo, secundum se; alio modo, per comparationem ad aliud. Secundum se quidem considerando hominem, nullum occidere licet, quia in quolibet, etiam peccatore, debemus amare naturam, quam Deus fecit, quae per occisionem corrumpitur. Sed sicut supra dictum est, occisio peccatoris fit licita per comparationem ad bonum com-

All rules of natural right are open to exceptions. But there is no general rule enabling us to decide in advance what cases would call for the rule and what cases would demand the exception. This can only be decided on the basis of knowledge of the *circumstances* ("which with certain people count for nothing"), and the decision can be made rightly only by men of practical wisdom.

Examples of exceptions to natural right: Ostracism, i.e., punishment of innocent, even virtuous men (cf. *Esprit des Lois* 26.16 f.); assassination of potential tyrants; espionage which is impossible without lying, deceit, incitement to treason, at least! One may also think here of the word of Montesquieu that there are cases where one has to *veil* for one moment liberty for the *sake* of liberty (12.19).

Aristotle's doctrine of natural right may be stated in the form of an answer to the question as to whether the end justifies the means, i.e., *any* means, *unjust* means. As a rule, Aristotle suggests, the end, i.e., the common good, justifies only just means; as a rule, the *salus publica* as the remoter purpose of the state is swallowed up completely in its proximate purpose which is justice; but in exceptional cases, the end, i.e., the common good, justifies, i.e., makes truly just, the very transgression of justice proper. But just as we do not entrust the dispensation of poison but to skilled and honest physicians, we must reserve the dispensation of this political poison for the most skilled physician of the body politic, i.e., the true statesman.[74]

Notes

1. *NRH*, 163.
2. Ibid.
3. See *WIPP*. Cf. Michael P. Zuckert and Catherine H. Zuckert, *Leo Strauss and the Problem of Political Philosophy* (Chicago: University of Chicago Press, 2014), p. 147.
4. See *PAW*.
5. See Tony Burns and James Connelly, eds., *The Legacy of Leo Strauss* (Charlottesville, VA: Imprint Academic, 2010). William Clare Roberts, "All Natural Right Is Changeable: Aristotelian Natural Right, Prudence, and the Specter of Exceptionalism," *Review of Politics* 74 (2012): 261–283, notes on p. 264 and in note 17 of the same page how wrong it is to assert that Strauss is not merely noting that in extreme situations the preservation of the state requires suspension of the rules—and is endorsing injustice like Machiavelli.

---

mune, quod per peccatum corrumpitur. Vita autem iustorum est conservativa et promotiva boni communis, quia ipsi sunt principalior pars multitudinis. Et ideo nullo modo licet occidere innocentem."

Some, it seems, take Strauss's claim that the "exceptions are as just as the rules" to allow any injustice. The obvious reading is rather that rules cannot foresee all situations and that the supreme rule is the common good.

6. Despite the magnificent presentation of this issue by Devin Stauffer, "On 'Classic Natural Right' in *Natural Right and History*," in *Brill's Companion to Leo Strauss' Writings on Classical Political Thought*, ed. Timothy W. Burns (Leiden: Brill, 2015), we need to consider Strauss's explicit statement in this text: "The choice with which man always was and still is confronted is then that between natural right and the view that all notions of justice are conventional. Precisely because this is the case, the problem of natural right is our *most* serious problem."

7. *NRH*, 3.

8. See *NRH*, 2, with Horace, Letters to Augustus, Epistle 2.1. This reference was called to our attention by Pierre Manent.

9. Cf. WL, lecture 1, p. 6, and *NRH*, 8.

10. "An Introduction to Natural Right" (1931) in Strauss, *Hobbes's Critique of Religion and Related Writings*, ed. Gabriel Bartlett and Svetozar Minkov (Chicago: University of Chicago Press, 2011).

11. These "principles common to every natural law doctrine, these principles [that] are too general, too formal, to be of any significance," are no different from the morality of a gang of robbers. See *PAW*, 112 and ff., especially 116.

12. WL, lecture 1, pp. 1–2.

13. *NRH*, 6.

14. WL, lecture 1, p. 6.

15. Ibid.

16. *PL*, Pref.

17. In the same year, Strauss explains this need for a "fusion" between philosophy and history. See "Political Philosophy and History."

18. For Kant it is a problem, on which he is a far cry from Hobbes: "*the* originator of modern natural right is none other than Thomas Hobbes. Not only does Hobbes with a clarity and emphasis unusual in former times distinguish between natural right and natural law, i.e., between natural right and natural duty; he even makes the natural right as distinguished from the natural duties the very basis, and hence the limits, of all obligations." This passage echoes the chapter on Hobbes in *Natural Right and History*.

19. NR 1946.

20. WL, lecture 5, p. 5. We need to consider that chapters 4 and 6 of *NRH* are the only ones that were not published in academic journals immediately after the lectures (between 1950 and 1952), and may have been edited later. However, the chapter on Rousseau (6A), unlike that on Burke, seems to have been completely written down and diverges from his other 1946 paper on Rousseau's intention.

21. *NRH*, 146.

22. In some of his writings, in particular passages from his *Republic* and *Laws*, Cicero presents a version of the Stoic conception of natural right in which it is not at odds with the requirements of civil society. For this reason, the theory of natural right is typically attributed to Cicero, whose work is the earliest surviving extensive articulation of the

typical premodern natural right theory. Yet Strauss observes that a careful reading of Cicero does not clearly bear out the attribution to Cicero personally of such an approach to natural right. Cicero was himself an Academic skeptic, and the articulation of natural law theory in question here is expressed in his dialogues by adherents of Stoicism; in his *Republic*, Philus, an Academic skeptic, challenges the notion of natural right, and in the same dialogue Scipio strongly suggests that civil law can only be a diluted version of natural law. As Strauss notes, "it is then misleading to call Cicero an adherent of the Stoic natural law teaching" (*NRH*, 156).

23. However, Strauss considers not just this page but Aristotle's philosophy as a whole: "It is in accordance with the general character of Aristotle's philosophy that his teaching regarding natural right is much closer to the ordinary understanding of justice than is Plato's." Cf. Strauss, "Natural Law," in *International Encyclopedia of the Social Sciences*, ed. David L. Sills (New York: Macmillan and Free Press, 1968), 11: 81. He also mentions, besides the famous single page in the *Ethics*, Aristotle's *Rhetoric* 1373b4–18.

24. Strauss does not here make the crucial distinction he makes in the note on Riezler ("Note on 'Some Critical Remarks on Man's Science of Man,'" Leo Strauss Papers, box 14, folder 9) between "human nature," which can be studied through theoretical natural science, and "human things," which are the subject of political philosophy. Nor does he raise, at this point, the possibility of an Aristotelian political science, which is "nothing other than the fully conscious form of the common sense understanding of political things" (*CM*, 12, 25; "Aristotle's cosmology, as distinguished from Plato's, is unqualifiedly separable from the quest for the best political order," *CM*, 21).

25. Leo Strauss, seminar on Aristotle's *Politics*, 1960, lecture 1, p. 1, and more explicitly at pp. 6–7: "The historical reflections are only secondary, by which I implied, although out of a justifiable cowardice—I didn't say at the beginning—I implied that Aristotle's (p. 9) approach is the sound approach, and that is what I meant. And we must—of course, that is an absolutely paradoxical assertion and I beg you to be as resistant to that proposition as you can. But I would like now to say something more simple—the hypothesis that the Aristotelian understanding of social matters is fundamentally superior to our present-day understanding is necessary as a heuristic device. That one—I believe one can prove, as follows. We are perfectly open to the possibility that Aristotle was wrong, and maybe wholly wrong, but we cannot know this, we cannot know that his teaching was wrong if we do not know first what his teaching was. That seems to be absolutely necessary. Otherwise you talk about perhaps a figment of your imagination." Idem, p. 9: Aristotle "is superior," considering the failure of the moderns, p. 21. There would be an advantage replacing the framework of modern science with Aristotle's framework (pp. 214–15). https://leostrausscenter.uchicago.edu/course/aristotle-politics-spring-quarter-1960

26. Cf. "Progress or Return" (*RCPR*, 227–70).

27. Saint Thomas's doctrine of natural right is considerably more straightforward in this regard than that of either Plato or Aristotle: for Thomas, "the principles of the moral law, especially as formulated in the Second Table of the Decalogue, suffer no exception, unless possibly by divine intervention" (*NRH*, 163). In the Thomistic view, conscience is the means whereby the dictates of natural law are made known to all, probably due to the eventually widespread acceptance of biblical revelation. Yet if it is faith in divine revela-

tion that is the key element here, we are faced with the concern that what Saint Thomas considers to be natural law does not in fact qualify as natural law on the classical criterion of ability to be discerned by the reasoning of the unaided human mind; the knowledge of the Thomistic absolute natural right depends to an extent upon divine communication. Furthermore, Thomas accepts a twofold picture of the natural aim of man, encompassing both intellectual and moral perfection; but, in order to account for the importance of moral virtue, he argues that man's natural aim is in itself insufficient and points beyond itself; natural law is only perfected by divine law. Natural right thus becomes inherently bound up with theology and, in particular, revealed theology. The modern theory of natural law was formulated in part as a reaction to the Thomistic theory, as a return to a conception of natural law as something that ought to be more obviously compelling, more truly self-evident, than contentious points of revealed theology. Modern natural right theorists such as Montesquieu intended to restore to the statesman the deliberative responsibility and autonomy he possessed in the ancient model. The best analysis of conscience is in *TOM*, 149: "[Machiavelli's] destructive analysis of . . . conscience" shows possible later reservations on Strauss's part.

28. A balanced survey of the question can be found in Douglas Kries, *The Problem of Natural Law* (Lanham, MD: Lexington Books, 2008). An overview of the evidence can be found on pp. 29–44. Harry V. Jaffa, *Thomism and Aristotelianism: A Study of the Commentary by Thomas Aquinas on the Nicomachean Ethics* (Chicago: University of Chicago Press, 1952), radicalized Strauss's view as presented in *NRH*.

29. *NRH*, 161.

30. *NRH*, 162. See Strauss to Helmut Kuhn, undated, *Independent Journal of Philosophy* 2 (1978). Strauss avers in these letters that "what Aristotle and Plato say about man and the affairs of men makes infinitely more sense to me than what the moderns have said or say." In addition, he states, even more assertively, that the "whole Platonic doctrine of the order of the soul and of the order of the virtues is the doctrine of natural right"—if justice is correctly understood, that is, "if it is true that 'justice' does not necessarily mean one of the many virtues but the all-comprehensive virtue" (24).

31. *NRH*, 64; see also 202 and ff.

32. See WL, lecture 1, p. 6.

33. "seems to be" was inserted by Strauss.

34. "own" was inserted by hand.

35. "not" was inserted by hand.

36. "in-" before "sufficient" was inserted by hand.

37. Strauss wrote "are."

38. "standards" was crossed out and "ideals" inserted by hand.

39. An "o"[r] in the margin was crossed out. Many other letters were added by hand in this typescript at the end of the lines, where the typewriter failed. We do not mention in notes these frequent insertions by hand.

40. "or legitimate" was inserted by hand.

41. Strauss wrote "it."

42. "that of" was inserted by hand.

43. The quotation marks are ours.

44. This sentence was handwritten in the margin.

45. "a" was inserted by hand.

46. The word "*novam*" is both underlined and italicized in the typescript.

47. "the" was crossed out.

48. There is an error that was not corrected in the typescript: "as it we," instead of "it."

49. The word "establishment" was typed above a crossed-out word.

50. "either impossible or else" was inserted by hand.

51. "in a sense" was inserted by hand and "merely" was crossed out.

52. We have inserted "his."

53. "is" instead of "or" was not corrected by Strauss.

54. The word "mere" was typed and inserted above the line.

55. "way" was inserted by hand.

56. We have changed "of" to "for."

57. Several words were crossed out in the typescript.

58. Several words crossed out in the typescript were replaced by "effort."

59. "modern" was inserted by hand.

60. This sentence was written in Strauss's hand in the margin.

61. We have inserted "rather expects the."

62. The sentence "Present day: the emergence of truth by the free trade of ideas" was inserted by Strauss's hand in the margin.

63. "or *securing*" was typed above the line.

64. Following "which," the word "every" was crossed out.

65. "or, more precisely, of the period of founding" was inserted by hand in the margin.

66. We have inserted "be," missing in the text.

67. Two words were crossed out, "natural" and an illegible one; "character" was inserted by hand.

68. The handwritten "of" replaced the typed words "as to."

69. "as" was inserted and "than" was crossed out.

70. We have changed "his" to "its."

71. We have changed "of" to "for."

72. The word "manifest" was crossed out.

73. Strauss inserted this sentence by hand in the margin.

74. The final part of this sentence was handwritten by Strauss, "political poison for the most skilled physician of the body politic, i.e., the true statesman."

An Afterword

Toward Strauss's Intention and Teaching in *Natural Right and History*

J. A. COLEN

The very character of *Natural Right and History* is controversial. As noted in the introduction to this volume, it is obvious to any reader that the historical studies that compose *Natural Right and History* do not represent conventional historical scholarship. But it is also obvious to any reader that most of the book indeed comprises historical studies. To state the terms of the controversy directly, it will suffice to raise a few questions: What was Leo Strauss's understanding of historical scholarship? And how did Strauss understand the relation between a historical study and a philosophical study? Since the philosophical study of historical thinkers implies a philosophical engagement with them, the difference between the claims that Strauss reveals his own teaching in *Natural Right and History* and that the book is a collection of historical studies is probably no more than a nuance—but it is an important nuance nonetheless.

The short answer to this difficult question is probably as follows: according to Strauss, a historical study conducted in a nonhistoricist vein must assume, as a starting point, that it is approaching the views of an earlier author as the "true doctrine" which, so to speak, must "answer back," that is, must meet our refutations and objections. That is how we learn from a philosopher. A thorough treatment of this point was perhaps never articulated as clearly by Strauss as in his 1941 lecture on historicism, in which he developed the following arguments: (1) The movement to replace philosophy by history, that is, "the tendency on the part of philosophers to devote their attention to the past or to the present or to the future rather than to what is always or the eternal" is impoverishing and hence undesirable—what once was a liberating force is now "a blinder, for it has become a prejudice itself." According to Strauss's understanding, the study of a doctrine should counteract the conflation of history and philosophy, the reduction of philosophy to history. (2) The examination of some, if not all, forgotten philosophical questions requires us to engage in historical studies, "for there does not exist any longer any significant philosophic position which is not tinged by historicism"; "as matters stand today, in our time, one is unable to elaborate, and to answer, a fundamental philosophic question without actually becoming a historian of philosophy," but this connection between philosophy and history is accidental and not necessary. (3) To be true to a philosophical doctrine, one must consider it possible that it is or may be "the true doctrine; one must familiarize oneself with the outlook of the author by practicing it," which is to say that "one has not understood an author of the past as long as one does not know from intimate knowledge how he would have reacted to our modern refutations of his doctrine." (4) This familiarity and real engagement are far more important than, say, the impossible rules of an "exact" historian. These rules can be ignored if they constitute an obstacle to the search for the truth. Strauss's expositions in *Natural Right and History* of Plato, Locke, or Rousseau, for example, ignore some of these putative rules: that a historical period "must not be judged by standards alien to it"; that an adequate interpretation is not the ultimate goal but rather "the indispensable prerequisite for judgment or explanation" by other factors; that any claims about an earlier author "are ultimately borne out by explicit statements of the author himself,"[1] taken at face value; and that no terminology "must be used in the interpretation of an author which cannot be literally translated into the language of the author, and which has not been used by the author himself or which was not in fairly common use in his time."

Natural Right and History is not only a collection of historical studies. It has a subtext suggested with "pedagogical reserve"; Strauss presents, for instance, his own view of justice, his unique "philosophical anthropology" based on a conception of human nature capable of dismissing "pseudo-human sciences" that explain man by subhuman factors, an original solution to the Humean-Kantian problem of the absolute separation of facts and values, and an exposition of the relation between reason and revelation. Further, it conveys Leo Strauss's view of the most important philosophical problem of our time, and the only political concept which is certainly of philosophical origin, i.e., natural right. If the approach suggested here is correct, *Natural Right and History* includes a defense of philosophy within a historical-political framework, and this framework sheds light on political teaching and on philosophical teaching proper. This afterword will merely underline the coherence of the whole book and point to some questions clarified by these early drafts. Considering how soon after his departure from the New School Strauss delivered the Walgreen Lectures, in the fall of 1949, it is hardly surprising to find that most if not all of his distinctive philosophical stances had already taken shape a long time before his arrival at the University of Chicago; indeed, these had been developed in his courses and writings as far back as 1937. In spite of—or even because of—Strauss's surprising attention to "great books" of metaphysics or anthropology on which he commented, such as *De Anima* or *The Passions of the Soul*, among others, the philosophical positions he articulated during the New York period are represented not only in the 1953 book but also (often more fully) in many of his later writings. In particular, there is evidence in *Natural Right and History* of his reading of Plato's *Republic* as an ancient experiment in utopianism, which Plato devised as if he were "organizing an insane asylum," yet which has more than antiquarian interest because as "genuine political philosophy" it aims essentially at "reminding us of the limits set to all human hopes and wishes."[2] There is also evidence in the writings of the New School period of his polemical treatment of modern philosophy, from Machiavelli to Locke and Hobbes or Rousseau, as presenting an alternative "historical" account to the biblical account of the origins of society. The same could be said of his view of political philosophy as the "eccentric core" of philosophy, or of the quarrel between philosophy and poetry or between philosophy and revelation. But no insights about *Natural Right and History* or these later texts should assume that they represent Strauss general stance or his final view, considering how restless a philosopher Strauss was, always ready to start his inquires anew. It is more prudent to limit the scope of this brief summary to the controversies surrounding the 1953 book's origins.

Strauss's Intention in *Natural Right and History*

It is therefore time to venture an interpretation of Strauss's intention and the main teachings in *Natural Right and History*. Is *Natural Right and History* an apology for philosophy or is it primarily moral and political in its intention?[3] One would do well to begin with the most obvious markers Strauss has given about the intention of a philosopher writing a book. One such indication is commonsensical: "An author may reveal his intention by the titles of his books," and subordinately, by their chapter headings as well, "which occupy an intermediate position between the titles of the books and their substance."[4] Even the rhetorical force of the introduction to the 1953 book is significant. It is significant because Strauss says elsewhere that while reading an author, even the "most obvious and explicit, if initial and provisional statement concerning his intention guides us towards the adequate understanding of his intention, provided 'we put 2 and 2 together' or do some thinking on our own."[5] The title mentions not only "Natural Right" but also "*History*."

Strauss faces the stark possibility that historicism's contention—all is historical, there are no permanent problems—is a "deadly truth," as Tanguay says. The courage to face this truth cannot be reduced to, or even based on, a "moral condemnation." Instead Strauss proposes presenting historicism's arguments as honestly and as strongly as possible as well as critically examining its philosophical assumptions, because historicism leads to the denial of the possibility of philosophy.

Nonetheless, in addition to the threat that historicism poses to philosophy Strauss also stresses that the moral and political consequences of forgetting natural right can be disastrous; that without natural right "life would be impossible," or at least that the decent life which free societies take for granted would be impossible. The confrontation between the authority of History and natural right appears to be the essential theme of the book, as revealed by the title, whose words contain "*Natural Right*" first—and not only "History."

Consequently, while some have emphasized a philosophical teaching in *Natural Right and History*, assigning only secondary importance to its moral and political intention, others have proposed just the opposite. Both are plausible on the basis of the author's explicit statements and subtle hints. These differences, however, seem to have deeper roots that point to the fundamental intention of the 1949 Walgreen Lectures. A third way, pursued here, is to approach the book as a very compressed summary of Strauss's philosophical teaching within a historical framework that also puts forward part of his political teaching. In this interpretation Strauss is not unlike Plato, who also presented his deepest apology for philosophy as a way of life in a political setting.

This volume takes these texts as supplements to the version he chose to make public in 1953, and no interpretation of *Natural Right and History* should discard the "paradoxes" that pervade the book, as pointed out in the introduction to the volume, unless Strauss's own standards are abandoned. The book should be read as one of the "works of those thinkers who were exceedingly careful writers, who were so careful that, so to speak, not a single word occurs in their works which is not full of significance."[6] Strauss's own "exoteric" writing or "pedagogical reserve"[7] should not, however, be insurmountable.

Let me articulate the three key points that these texts and essays add to the understanding of Strauss's intention and teaching in his Walgreen Lectures. Pervading all these earlier essays in this volume and all "historical" studies in the 1953 book, we find these constants: (1) He navigates between the Scylla of Kantian-style justifications of morality or justice as a set of universal principles or rules—that are either dependent on divine revelation or the residues of morality based on revealed religion—and the Charybdis of altogether denying natural right in the face of eternally mutable answers to specific historical situations; (2) he puts forward the view that human "morality" at its noblest can flourish only in the best political settings; (3) he gives a glimpse of the core of his philosophical teaching, based on the notion of nature and science as presented to man.

Strauss's Negative Political Teaching: The Status of the Rights of Man

Let me try first a negative approach, since it is often easier to describe something by tracing its boundaries from the outside. In fact, familiarity breeds habituation among Straussian scholars, while a liberal finds himself in uncharted territory (to avoid any misunderstanding: I am one myself, trying to grasp Strauss's thought in the 1953 book in the current idiom of someone versed in liberal political science). After all, we need to separate ourselves from the object of our attention, which comes with a price, in order to see the overall picture. This interpretation therefore begins by examining what Strauss's political teaching is *not*.

Today, "theories of justice" are the center of attention. Take, for instance, the conceptions of justice that Strauss discards. Note: I speak of "justice" because Strauss himself states that "if one understands the idea of justice in a precise sense, in the sense of Plato or that of Kant, it is identical at least for all practical purposes with natural right."[8]

Why then is Kantianism discarded? Strauss barely mentions Kant in the book,[9] but it is clear that although Kant addresses the same problem, Strauss thinks that his proposal, according to which morality is identified with or reduced to a "good intention," is very weak. Now, in Kantian terms, justice is based on the respect for man *qua* man, based on "the infinite value of the individual soul,"[10] such as taking man as an end in himself, or shaping individual behavior based on rules deemed universal. Moral motivation, according to Kant and all of Rawls's heirs, should exclude any reference to passions or pleasure in order to be qualified as truly "moral."[11]

Nor can a just ordering of society rest solely in "institutions." As Strauss recalls, "[t]he sternest moral philosopher of modern times, Kant, protested against the view that the right political order would presuppose a nation of *angels*: no, he says, the right political order can be established in a nation of *devils* provided they have sense."[12]

One might, therefore, observe the additional weakness of Kantian constructivism: "modern utopianism naturally forgets the existence of the 'forces of evil' and the fact that these forces cannot be fought successfully by enlightenment."[13] As he asserts, "at least some people want more: power, precedence, dominion. And these dangerous people, even if few in number, are able to counteract the whole effort of enlightenment by employing various devices, which sometimes are more effectual than the quiet voice of enlightening reason."[14]

He apparently dismisses (through Aristotle's voice) the attempts to combine in a set of rules what is by nature just in a precise sense. Kant and Kantians of any brand—including Rawls and his heirs—are today by far the most influential proponents of a morality based on universal rules or principles. Strauss acknowledges that there are some principles of justice that apply to man as man, say, to Robinson Crusoe facing Friday—that is, a man on a desert island—such as basic principles of commutative and distributive justice *in the absence of human laws*. He points out some that Aristotle mentions: "Naturally right therefore are the equality of the price of a thing with the value of the labor and expense of the producer of the thing; or the proper proportion between crime and punishment."[15]

Nonetheless, ethics by rules can be grounded only on a view of human nature that is mere "basic nature,"[16] and these rules are in fact universal or "almost" universal. But even basic rules such as "the prohibition against murder, theft, etc."[17] are not in fact rules but "just determinations of given cases . . . based exclusively on principles of either commutative or distributive justice."[18]

Nor, according to Strauss, is natural right defined by "social cohesion and durability,"[19] a standard that may not be very different from the mere morality of a gang of robbers—if there is honor among thieves, that is.

However necessary for life in society "in normal circumstances," all rules of natural right still lack universality except as an intuition of the prephilosophical idea of divine law, or as part of a revealed theology as in Aquinas. While Strauss asserts that he prefers such a notion of natural right to the historicist or positivist alternatives,[20] if taken as an inflexible set of rules natural law has two important flaws. On the one hand, it makes natural right dependent on revelation, while natural right is purported to be more accessible than natural theology. On the other hand, such inflexibility hampers the latitude of statesmen, who eventually discard ethical principles as naïve; and once rules have been dismissed by politically minded men, it leads to Machiavelli's position, a cure that proves worse than the disease.[21] Furthermore, the inflexibility of any set of rules eventually becomes inconsistent, because rules cannot predict every circumstance in which action or inaction occurs. Even Aquinas has recourse to divine exemptions.

Conspicuously absent in Strauss's acknowledged forms of justice is also the notion that the principles of justice should be based on the (subjective) rights of man or on the expression of "individuality." According to Strauss the most significant characteristic of modern natural right is that it identifies the goal of government as the protection of man's rights rather than the cultivation of his duties.

Basing justice on self-interest, that is, utilitarianism, is equally futile: "One merely evades the issue [of the principles of justice] if one says that our translegal standards are expediency or utility,"[22] for utility may favor some and yet harm others—and curiously this remark seems to settle the issue.

Nor is justice merely an "ideal" of our society that cannot serve as the foundation of duty. So what, then, may serve as this foundation?

Strauss's Positive Political Teaching: "Morality" and Polity

To attempt to fill in the content of Strauss's political teaching, one could begin by saying that Strauss upholds both in these texts and in the Walgreen Lectures that philosophy is able to show what is good for man by nature and it can even establish a hierarchy of these goods: external goods, goods for the body, and goods for the soul—that is, as concerns individuals. But Strauss also teaches that the real basis of what is by nature just is, paradoxically, presented by the ancients in the form of the "best regime," that is, in political life.

Most moral and political thinkers today, on the other hand, tend to think that ethics should be more permanent or universal than regimes.[23] Today, "[t]he central significance of the phenomena called 'regimes' has become somewhat blurred."[24] Strauss argues that only with Christianity and egalitarian natural right does the problem of the best regime "lose its crucial significance."[25] According to him, "[t]he best regime as the classics understood it ceases to be identical with the perfect moral order."[26] And this is the understanding he is trying to retrieve.

However peculiar, this proposal is certainly rich in consequences and deserves careful consideration even by someone versed in liberal political science. In a political setting, ethics takes a very different shape. Political authority is not an artificial construct or "social contract," purportedly established to assure a set of individual rights, but a deep human necessity. Only in a polity can one find the full density of human life and therefore of ethics.

Outside a polity, in fact, moral law can be no more than a law of reason or a framework for the codes of law.[27] Even in the simplest of societies, some customs or law enforcement would soon prove to be necessary, so everywhere murder is outlawed and theft condemned as destructive.[28] Such "basic" ethical rules are a far cry from a "gentleman's" ethics: a man of great heart, so to speak, does not limit himself to abiding by the law; he is generous, magnificent, and patriotic, that is, he contributes with his best efforts to the flourishing of the city, takes up arms to defend the polity, and cultivates all forms of human excellence or virtue.

The gentleman's magnanimity or citizens' "moral virtues" do not yet constitute a philosophical ethics; rather they are a mere image or a popular morality, because to keep their compelling force they must go unquestioned. The discovery of nature by the first conventionalists was unfortunate for the *polis* and destructive to society. Questioning casts doubt on the naturalness of the polity and jeopardizes all forms of human allegiance and all human bonds, even or especially the most apparently sacred ones, such as family ties, property, or the sacredness of the inherited lot—the rationale behind the biblical epigraphs in the 1953 book.

According to yet another lecture in this volume, a philosopher, once the idea of nature has been discovered, can no longer ignore the fundamental difference between nature and convention. Strauss supports the ancients in the idea that ethical behavior is based naturally on "awe."[29] Nature has a power in itself: if you expel nature with a hayfork, it returns with a vengeance.[30] But the discovery of nature changed everything: "philosophy is *the* anti-traditional force; the liberation from the opinions of the past, the opening up of new vistas is, and always has been, of the essence of philosophy."[31]

Conventionalist philosophers share with the proponents of natural right the belief that nature is a higher standard than convention, but err in thinking that the sole human principle of human good is pleasure.[32] The ancients, however, did not stop at conventionalism. Conventionalists were confronted with classic natural right proponents. In these lectures Strauss considers the list of the goods derived from the classical tradition (Socrates, Plato, and Aristotle), supplemented by the biblical virtues of mercy and humility, to be a fundamentally sound guide.

If ethics takes its shape in a political setting, however, man's duties to his fellow citizen cannot be extended to all humanity without the loss of their moral weight.[33] Certainly no hierarchy of goods suffices to make wise decisions about the here and now.

In the 1953 book, Strauss returns, after presenting the common features of classic natural right, to the different branches of classic natural right to address this issue. Only in its Socratic-Platonic-Stoic version is one confronted with the true demands of natural right or justice: every man should receive what is good for him, which implies that any actual distribution of property or family bonds is partly based on convention. Undiluted natural right, in its extreme form, implies the abolition of irrelevant differences between man and woman, the abolition of the family and all property rights, etc.; and the resulting social standard would lead to the absolute rule of the wise over the unwise many.

Now such perfect justice as designed by infinitely "generous men" would face the opposition of the many and the indifference of the wise. The principles of justice must therefore, in practice, be objects of compromise or dilution, and they imply a mixture of wisdom and consent, which will lead to the mixed regime.

The Historical Framework: Lessons from the Ancients

As mentioned before in this volume, even the ancients who upheld natural right against the conventionalists thought that natural right in its undiluted form was an insufficient guide to political action. The hierarchy of goods for man, the right proportion of which remains a problem, must be sometimes bracketed with a superior principle, namely, the common good of the polity. The existence of the polity is a necessary condition for the flourishing of human excellence, which cannot exist in a void, for as Strauss says, "[i]n order to reach his highest stature, man must live in the best kind of society, in the kind of society that is most conducive to human excellence. The classics called the best society the best *politeia*." The best life is possible only in the best polity.[34] "Polity"—a word that Strauss used in his teaching as a synonym for the ancient *polis*—may perhaps today take the form of the nation that allows both freedom and civilization. At the heart of Leo Strauss's concern about the problem of natural right since 1931 is the purpose of the modern state as opposed to the ancient *polis*.[35]

Starting in the early 1940s, Strauss upheld that the best regime is "utopian" but not in the modern sense:[36] the ancients upheld the best regime, whose goal was fostering human virtue or excellence, as a standard. Modern utopianism assumes that human nature is infinitely flexible. Modern utopianism requires a "new man," since those currently in existence resist fitting into the model. There is room for a legitimate utopianism, which is the very heart of the philosophy of Socrates, Plato, and Aristotle and is not "pie in the sky" but a standard by which to measure or perfect all existing regimes. The fundamental lesson that Strauss derives from the ancients is, therefore, that their legitimate utopianism is the best cure for political idealism: if you seek perfect justice, what you get is not the best regime but a true nightmare.

Why such a sharp contrast between these two forms of utopianism? The "legitimate utopianism" of Plato and Aristotle's philosophy differs from the modern kind because the ancients did not expect that a perfect society could be achieved *by political means*. That a prudent statesman would design sensible policies without obvious recourse to political philosophy is of course not unthinkable—almost all political ideas or words have their origin in common sense or in political life, but philosophy becomes politically useful when "political truth" is clouded by erroneous teachings. It is then necessary as a kind of apologetic that protects political action from the "infinitely more generous" utopian illusions about human nature by recalling the "limits of all human hopes and desires."[37]

Despite any apparent "shortcomings" on the part of Aristotle,[38] the common features among the ancients are by far more important than their differences, because it is nowadays more urgent to reinstate political philosophy as the queen of the social sciences than to settle the question of the relative importance of philosophy and religion.[39] Every one of the classic trio (Socrates, Plato, and Aristotle) had this in common, even Plato: they took their bearings from the perfection of human nature, or man's *telos*, and not from the basic nature of man, or from man as he mostly is. Since the conventionalists conflated human nature with hedonism, Socrates, Plato, and Aristotle fought them in hedonistic terms, but that was not the core of their vision: they pointed to the ceiling or to human excellence.

A vision of man and man's nature is indeed the basis of classic natural right as a whole,[40] which in fact takes its bearings from what man may be at his best. But the Platonic teaching that points more clearly beyond the city to the philosophical life is superior because it supports the not unproblematic return of the philosopher to man's "cave," despite acknowledging the partially conventional nature of the *polis* and its laws. Strauss supports Socrates and Plato's presentation—to which he adds Stoic teaching—because only such a presentation addresses properly the objection of the conventionalists that the city exists by convention and not by nature, while Aristotle attempts to justify the *polis* by nature.

Since philosophy implies questioning, the philosopher must question (and thereby endanger) this ideal, only later to return to the "cave" of the city in a more thoughtful state of mind. In fact, Strauss consistently encouraged, albeit in a way that was no longer unquestioned and naïve, allegiance to home and country—yet without dismissing the tension between philosophy and the city.

This reading of Strauss's thought, conveyed by the "historical" studies in *Natural Right and History*, anticipated by the essays in this volume, assumes that he ultimately identified himself with the classical proposal, and Plato in particular, having dismissed the more generous modern utopianism. Political philosophy is absolutely necessary[41] as a cure for political idealism, that is, to clearly point out the limits to changing political life through political means.

In short, the role of political philosophy in the modern view is very different from that of the Socratics and their classical and medieval followers which Strauss endorses:

> [T]raditional political philosophy, or moral philosophy, frequently took on the form of exhortation, or moral advice. For if you do not believe that the perfect condition can be brought about by political action, you cannot hope for more than that one or the other of those in power might be induced, by moral appeal, by advice, by exhortations, by *sermons*, to do his best in

> his station along the lines of decency and humanity. This approach was underlying one special genre of political literature in particular, the mirrors of princes.[42]

Fostering human flourishing within the darkness of the cave that is political society but in the light of the superior standard represented by nature, and at the same time maintaining the decent standards seemingly inherent in the bonds of affection that exist between fellow citizens, was the way of Socratic-Platonic political philosophy. In that it does not prevent philosophical questioning, maintaining the bonds between humans is a truer account of political life than fostering human excellence or virtue as mere moral virtues by habituation, which was the way of Aristotelian political philosophy. However, despite Aristotle's sober approach, any considerations of the philosophers about the best regime can be incorporated in the polity only through some dilution or compromise of the standards of man's nature at its best.[43]

The Historical Framework: Lessons from the Moderns

Now, even if the classics take center stage in *Natural Right and History*, one should not hastily dismiss Strauss's approach to modern philosophy as the mere presentation of the history of the decadence of ancient philosophy. There is no doubt that some kind of decay in fact took place in the modern development: "The founding fathers of modern philosophy, while being no doubt genuine philosophers, conceived of philosophy in such a way that a degeneration of philosophic thought became unavoidable." But there is much to learn from the modern venture.

The moderns in fact take up the second half of the 1953 book, where Strauss sketches the history of the modern rights of man. But both here and in the earlier (1946) lecture, he rejects the idea that modern natural right theory, a product of the seventeenth century, was radical in its secularization; for—as he recalls—the independence of natural right from theology was denied neither by ancient philosophers nor by medieval ones. Nonetheless, traditional conceptions of natural right were essentially conservative while modern ones were essentially revolutionary.

There is nonetheless a negative lesson to be learned from the moderns' ultimate failure:

> By erecting the proud edifice of modern civilization, and by living within that comfortable building for some generations, many people seem to have forgotten the natural foundations, not dependent on human will and not changeable, which are buried deep in the ground and which set a limit to the possible height of the building.[44]

Modern philosophy is philosophy nonetheless. If the question of the ancients and the moderns is still "a *question*," according to Strauss it follows that we cannot take either answer for granted. The modern solution was not a small feat and was successful for a long time (at a price); and it is still Hobbes who provides the best argument for democracy to Strauss. Hobbes is the originator of modern philosophy, which is based in a "historical" account alternative to the biblical account of the origins of society. Strauss's final note in the last text in this volume avers that the character of modern natural right is related to its conception of the state of nature: whereas, for Plato and Aristotle, human nature is defined in reference to human perfection, modern political theorists define human nature in terms of the naturally possessed—basic or universal—traits of man. The latter conception obviously lends itself to setting a more easily achievable political goal, or at the least it so seemed to them, as to most contemporary liberals.[45]

Moreover, as he avers in 1949,

> Today natural right is frequently rejected as reactionary. In the 19th century natural right was rejected by continental reactionaries as revolutionary . . . [but] natural right is and always has been revolutionary in the most fundamental sense . . . For this reason, we were forced to pay some attention to the tremendous effort that was required so that the very idea of natural right could emerge.[46]

Which leads to the core of his philosophical teaching in *Natural Right and History*: the idea of nature and science as seen by man.

The Philosophical Teaching in *Natural Right and History*

Natural Right and History unwinds as a compelling narrative of political thought that should be read as an apology for the philosophical life within a political-historical framework. While it is the case that Strauss wrote a history of political philosophy, as opposed to a history of metaphysics or epistemology,[47] one should not hastily infer from this that the whole of Strauss's thought excluded such reflections. He himself warns against mistaking the starting point for the substance of someone's thought.[48]

Some thoughtful scholars have argued that because the human good can flourish only in the best political setting, Leo Strauss, focusing only on political philosophy as the introduction to philosophy proper,[49] dispensed entirely, or at least did not deal thematically, with natural philosophy or metaphysics (or what was in fact prior to the modern break a kind of natural theology), and that those interested in such matters should continue their search "after Strauss," i.e., look beyond his thought.

This decoupling of the cosmic and human realms is sometimes understood to be the deepest meaning of his concentration upon[50] and even identification with "the change in thought that was effected by Socrates."[51] Following this line of argument still further, Strauss, like Socrates, is said to have been unconcerned with "first principles" (*archê*) of nature.

Since he claimed that no consistent explanation of Plato's theory of ideas had ever been presented,[52] it has been inferred, for example, that in Strauss's interpretation, Plato's "world of ideas" was not something to be taken seriously. Plato himself, according to Strauss, did not believe in the world of ideas. But this interpretation is patently refuted by Strauss's unambiguous statements, e.g., in his 1957 course on the *Republic*, where he explains at length why Plato thought it reasonable to infer the existence of something like true ideas.[53] Even in *The City and Man*, although he almost ignores the final part of books 6 and 7 of the *Republic* and the famous images of the sun, the divided line, and the cave, he asserts that "the part of the *Republic* which deals with philosophy is the most important part of the book."[54]

But one should expect no more than hints of Strauss's deepest philosophical thought from *Natural Right and History*—exactly as one should not expect Plato's deepest philosophy in his presentation of the political-minded gentleman, who is, after all, "not identical with the wise man [but merely] the political reflection, or imitation, of the wise man."[55] It is easy to see, for this reason, why the book appealed to traditionalist "gentlemen," as the success of Strauss's own lectures testifies. But as Nathan Tarcov's essay makes clear in commenting on Strauss's claim, even in a political setting it is impossible to disregard a philosophical view of the cosmos. True prudence is equated with obeying the law of the cosmos ruled by God, which is the only true city.[56]

Strauss's Negative Philosophical Teaching: Dispelling Erroneous Theories

What if any philosophical teaching is consistently conveyed by the "historical" studies in the book, as seen under the light of these essays and drafts? Despite the complexities inevitable in deciphering Strauss's philosophy, it is clear that he was no positivist or historicist.[57] One way, then, of explaining his distinctive philosophical approach is to contrast it with the empiricism or positivism present in today's philosophy departments. Leo Strauss notes that the rejection of natural right is made in the name of History and on behalf of the distinction between facts and values.[58]

Positivism is barely mentioned in the 1953 book. It is described in passing as "the school which held that theology and metaphysics had been superseded once and for all by positive science or which identified genuine knowledge of reality with the knowledge supplied by the empirical sciences. Positivism proper had defined 'empirical' in terms of the procedures of the natural sciences."[59] The lectures presented here leave no doubt that Strauss was not a positivist, but they also leave no doubt that he was not unwilling to countenance the "demarcation" between or separation of philosophy and science. "One may try, and people did try, to seclude from the realm of philosophy the questions which do not seem to permit of a universally acceptable answer, but in doing so, one is merely *evading* the questions, not answering them."[60] Consequently, Wittgenstein and those responsible for all the elucubrations of the Vienna Circle, which are the foundation of modern analytical philosophy, are dismissed by Strauss as so many species of intellectual indolence.

Strauss is no more forgiving when it comes to historicism, and the thrust of his argument has important consequences for the philosophy of science, especially social science, and the philosophy of nature. The historicist reasons thus: natural law should be universally recognized by human reason, but the social sciences—i.e., history, anthropology, sociology—show that there is a great variety of conceptions of right, and that there are, therefore, no immutable principles of justice.[61] Strauss goes to the point of saying that this reasoning is "irrelevant": in other words, if natural right implies a process of discovery by reason, it is one thing to assert that there is perhaps no principle of justice that has not been denied in some society or culture at some point in time, and a totally separate thing to show that this denial is justified or reasonable.[62] This is precisely the main purpose of the first section of the Walgreen Lectures as he asserts it in 1949:

> I tried to show that contrary to a widespread view, the strictly historical evidence, the evidence based upon the indefinitely large variety of notions regarding right and wrong in different countries and at different times, is utterly irrelevant as far as the possibility and the existence of natural right is concerned.[63]

According to him, the critique of natural right presented by positivism and historicism has deep philosophical roots—a disbelief in the very possibility of a knowledge of any immutable principles. *Nolens volens* positivism and historicism require a denunciation of reason that proves the impossibility of any access to metaphysics or ethics. The authority of positive science, the critical philosophy that continues that of Hume or Kant, leads to skepticism,[64] to the idea that all ideas are arbitrary; but radical historicism ups the ante by adding that all ideas are not only arbitrary but derive from a specific context, which limits the validity of any principles.[65] The modern opponents of natural right are also the enemies of philosophy, since they reject the very possibility of capturing something that is perennial, because every thought is seen as historical.

Obviously, the rejection by Strauss of important contemporary philosophical theories is not the same as conveying a consistent philosophical theory and a coherent explanation of the world, man, and God. It is certainly much more difficult to capture the core of his philosophical teaching in *Natural Right and History* in a few lines, if only because Strauss refused to conflate philosophy with any "system of philosophy."[66] But an indication that his "negative teaching" is not his entire view is that it is on metaphysical grounds that he rejects Aristotle's teaching: "I am not an Aristotelian since I am not satisfied that the visible universe is eternal, to say nothing of other perhaps more important reasons."[67] Strauss's preference for Plato among the ancients, and not Aristotle, is based not merely on a single page of the *Ethics*, but on his interpretation of Aristotle's philosophy as a whole, that taking each level of being as having a consistency in itself defuses the tension between nature and the city.[68] Again, these lectures and early drafts shed some light on the core philosophical message of *Natural Right and History*.

Strauss's Positive Philosophical Teaching: Awe toward Nature

To grasp the full import of what the opponents of natural right have wrought, let us turn to Strauss's idea of nature. In a text presented here, Strauss claims that "'nature' is *the* fundamental philosophic discovery. Truth, Being, even World, and all other terms designating the object of philosophy are unquestionably older than philosophy, but the first man who used the term 'nature' . . . was the first philosopher."[69] There is, therefore, a fundamental political concept that is of purely philosophical origin: the idea of natural right. Philosophy and with it the discovery of nature changed the landscape. The idea of nature is at the center of Strauss's philosophical inquiry. But the idea of nature would be devoid of content if it were not opposed to divine and man-made things. Moreover, nature is the concept that allows a philosopher to examine political notions and man's nature without conflating history and the eternal. There is much left to be explained, as Nathan Tarcov notes. The difference between philosophy and common sense is substantial because Strauss assumes knowledge of human nature that arises from seeing political things "*sub specie aeternitatis*"—in contrast to what is "essentially perishable."[70]

In Strauss's eyes, as stated in *Natural Right and History*, the transformation carried out by Socrates was a return to sobriety after the madness of his predecessors, because Socrates did not separate wisdom from moderation. In modern language, it was a return to common sense. Disregarding opinions about the nature of things (and especially of human things) amounted to abandoning the most important source of access to reality, which is in opinions or common sense. The starting point is the shape or form or character of a thing, its *eidos*, that which is first visible to us and not that which is intrinsically. The art of ascending from opinions to the nature of things is the friendly art of conversation, dialectic.[71] Strauss puts Plato's contention in more general terms: "All knowledge, however limited or 'scientific,' presupposes a horizon, a comprehensive view within which knowledge is possible. All understanding presupposes a fundamental awareness of the whole: prior to any perception of particular things, the human soul must have had a vision of the ideas, a vision of the articulated whole."[72] These are almost the same words used to refer to the "frame of reference,"[73] whose meaning was clarified in the text included in this volume: such a frame of reference is "a conceptual scheme that mirrors or articulates the essential structure of society as such, and therefore of every possible society. This essential structure would be defined by the purpose of society, or by the natural hierarchy of its purposes."[74]

What is Strauss's vision of the articulated whole? In his later lectures on the "Socratic problem" Strauss gives a more thorough exposition of "noetic heterogeneity"[75] and the natural articulation of the cosmos, but the core of his approach is already summarized in the center of the 1953 book. One thus returns to the real meaning of the Socratic turn to human things: when Socrates raises the question "What is X?" (courage, justice, etc.), he is forced also to raise the question of the *ratio rerum humanarum* and to approach the study of human things as such, which in turn requires understanding the essential difference between human things and divine or natural things, which finally presupposes an understanding of divine or natural things as such.[76] "The thing itself, the completed thing, cannot be understood as a product of the process leading up to it."[77] On the contrary, the process can be understood only through its *telos* or accomplishment. It was this principle that the positivists and historicists eschewed.

In short: one needs to start from opinions or the "shape" of things as they appear to man. Strauss later made clear that this indeed implied what some may call "metaphysical claims." According to him, unlike Heidegger, being for Plato was not the same as "being always."[78] "Being" is not univocal; there are many ways of being. Strauss's philosophy of science, and especially of the science of man, rests, on the one hand, on noetic differences or the "many" articulated shapes of things, and, on the other, on the avoidance of every kind of reductionism, from Freud and Darwin or the sociology of knowledge to the mechanistic view of the atomists or Epicureans—a reduction that would entail explaining the higher by reference to the lower. Now, something that cannot be found explicitly anywhere in Plato's dialogues[79] but that certainly clarifies Strauss's own view is that "Plato, as it were, says: Take any opinion about right, however fantastic or 'primitive,' that you please; you can be certain prior to having investigated it that it points beyond itself, that the people who cherish the opinion in question contradict that very opinion somehow and thus are forced to go beyond it in the direction of the one true view of justice, provided that a philosopher arises among them."[80]

"Philosophical Anthropology" at the New School and Strauss's Distinctive Proposal

As an essay in this volume points out, in the New School Strauss co-taught several courses in "philosophical anthropology." Strauss's sober metaphysical claims in the texts paving the way to the Walgreen Lectures and in *Natural Right and History* are indeed deep enough to provide him with a distinctive "anthropology." In our time, ethics and social or political philosophy must initially consist in a Socratic examination of the classical works that constitute the history of philosophy because they are the sources of our confused, contradictory current opinions.[81]

Strauss stresses that for all the classics, including Plato, man is by nature a social animal. He is constituted in such a way that he cannot live well without other men, because it is *logos*—speech or reason—that distinguishes him from the other animals and this presupposes communication.[82] In fact, man is so much more radically social than the other animals that sociability is humanity itself, i.e., all actions—social and antisocial—refer to others, not from a calculation of the pleasures to be derived from association, but because the mere association is pleasurable. All members of the same species are related, but in man this relationship is deepened by his radical sociability. Procreation is only partly a way to preserve the species; there is no relation between men that is totally free, and everyone is aware of this. Men differ from brutes through speech or reason (*logos*), so the good life is the life of reason or the examined life. Man is by nature social and cannot live well except when living with others; he refers to others in every human act. Love, affection, friendship, and piety are as natural for him as his own self-interest. Men are free but have a sense that the unrestrained exercise of that freedom is not right.

No Naked Human Nature and the Nature of Values

Man, however, as stated before, cannot, with rare exceptions, reach perfection except in the best civil society, or in the city, and "the city is the only whole within the whole or the only part of the whole whose essence can be wholly known,"[83] which is why Strauss wrote a history of political philosophy and not, say, a history of epistemology. Perhaps, after all, Strauss's most important teaching is the need for political philosophy.

Strauss asserts that only modern natural right is conceived of as completely independent from any positive right, and therefore as something to be expounded comprehensively and systematically, something whose tenets can be precisely and absolutely enumerated. The alternative, however, is not a comprehensive and systematic exposition of premodern natural right principles as independent of conventional right. Such an exposition would be conducive to a parochial view of what is by nature just, conflating the "natural man" with any present view of man as eternal. (This is the reason why no other book followed the Walgreen Lectures with such an exposition.)

But man is never outside all cultural frames of reference. We should not discard the existence of such a thing as human nature, as Strauss asserts in the essay "Historicism," but all that can ever be found are the variants of the "text of man"; we cannot lay bare the text of man. This is the additional reason for engaging in historical studies in a philosophical vein, which Leo Strauss maintained as his primary task until the end.

The bonds of society can exist "on the most different levels: on the level of Indian caste society, of China, of Sparta, of Venice, of Britain," and, according to Strauss, it is also clear that a polity based on oppression is not "as good as the social cohesion and durability of a free society."[84] Of course, today the very idea that there is a hierarchy of goods and a hierarchy of societies (even that liberalism is preferable to cannibalism) is disturbing, so ingrained is the idea that all values are equal. Obviously, as he asserts in 1949,

> The distinction between values and facts would not have found the wide acceptance which it did find if there were not some foundation for it. It is akin to the old distinction between questions of fact and questions of right, and similar distinctions. What we have to wonder about is whether the circumstance that the distinction between facts and values is reasonable within the certain limits justifies the radical separation of disciplines, at least to the extent that social science is declared to be fundamentally limited to the study of facts.

According to Strauss, however, values are not something we "posit," our own creations beyond the power of reason. Quite the contrary, value judgments belong together with any reasonable description of man's affairs,[85] for we are not condemned to wholesale madness.[86] As Strauss keeps repeating later, there is no "good reason for abandoning the attempt to acquire clarity about what is preferable or less preferable"—that is, the possibility of evaluating man's ends or distinguishing between goods. For even "[i]f one cannot say which of two high mountains covered by clouds is higher, we could still say that a mountain is higher than a molehill."[87]

This contention carries the consequence that even if fire burns the same in both Persia and Greece, while justice, or burials, or human sacrifices, or the answer to who should rule is not the same everywhere, reason is not as powerless as most social sciences and active politicians tend to think.

New Vistas: The Discovery of Natural Right and Its Character

Natural Right and History remains controversial to this day. To begin with, any interpretation of Strauss's teaching clashes with the repeated assertions by scholars that Strauss had no philosophical teaching *per se*. There is more than a grain of truth in this assertion, since, as Strauss himself says in one of the texts in this volume, Philosophy is at best possession of clear knowledge of the *problems*—it is not possession of clear knowledge of the *solutions* to the problems. The basic questions in all branches of philosophy are as unsolved today as they were at all times; new questions have been raised from time to time, the interest has shifted from one type of question to others, but the most fundamental, the truly philosophic questions remain unanswered.[88]

One cannot leave it at that, however, because he adds almost immediately: "Deeper study shows that this impression is misleading. It would be absurd to say that deeper study shows us all political philosophers in perfect agreement; it does show us however that there was a tradition of political philosophy whose adherents were in agreement as regards the fundamentals"—that is, as he says in another essay, despite specific differences among their teachings.[89]

Moreover, it is not unreasonable, considering both his constant return to the problem of natural right in different contexts and through different approaches, to infer that despite his initial disclaimer that the need for natural right does not imply its existence, he does, in the Walgreen Lectures, uphold the possibility of real knowledge of natural right: "the concept of a natural law, or of a natural order, is coeval with philosophy itself." Moreover, he continues, this is the "very soul of Plato's and Aristotle's political philosophy, whose primary and guiding purpose is to discover that 'constitution,' that order of civil society, which is 'natural.' Even if such perfect order is never found in any actual order, it is the object of the wish 'of all decent people.'"

Such knowledge of natural right, however, is not the kind that can be expounded *more geometrico*, as a system or a set of rules, as in modern natural right; rather it is the kind upheld by the classics. Strauss chose to present it within what appears to some as an "idiosyncratic" *précis raisonné* of natural right, his fourth presentation of such a history since 1931.[90]

Now the idea of natural right, according to Strauss, may surprise those who think it necessarily supports a "conservative" view of society. As he states in 1949:

> If we approach the issue of natural right in an impartial manner, we note that . . . the very idea of natural right presupposes the doubt of all authority; that is to say, man's inner independence of all authority.
>
> Natural right is a standard higher than all authority, a standard by which all authority is to be measured, and this standard is in principle accessible to man as man . . . The present-day discussion of natural right suffers from the fact that the idea of natural right is taken too much for granted by its adherents as well as by its opponents.[91]

We acknowledge that, its tentative character notwithstanding, this afterword may come off as rather polemical or sometimes even slapdash, and in the process simplifies positions that are really much more sophisticated. It is therefore appropriate for more than one reason, considering Strauss's initial allusions in the Walgreen Lectures to Lincoln's words, to close this volume of essays by assuring the reader that it is presented "with malice toward none, with charity for all," but also with no "firmness in the right"—on the contrary, with merely a reminder of how tempting all forms of polemic are—and in the hope that it will not only contribute to giving *Natural Right and History* the place it deserves in the canon of great philosophical works, but also foster studies of the book as a whole.

Notes

1. All previous quotations are taken from H 1941 in this volume, pp. XXX–XX.
2. See WCL.
3. See Tanguay's essay in this volume.

4. *TOM*, 37. Leo Strauss in *TOM* acknowledges, "The titles of Machiavelli's two books are most unrevealing in this respect. The same is almost equally true of the chapter headings . . . We have noted that the chapter headings of the *Discourses*, to say nothing of those of the *Prince*, reveal hardly anything of the daring quality of his thought," therefore suggesting the way to grasp "the daring quality" of his own thought.

5. Note to *TOM*, 36.

6. OSCPP. See *NRH*, 127. Susan Shell states in her unpublished lecture "Natural Right in the Face of History" that "the work expresses itself less in outright dissembling and self-contradiction—let alone obscurely coded riddles—than in a studied ambiguity or imprecision, which resolves itself to the degree that Strauss is read with adequate attention. Precision is the prize or offshoot of reader alertness, or what Strauss elsewhere calls being wide awake."

7. Cf. Zuckert and Zuckert, *Leo Strauss and the Problem of Political Philosophy*, 7.

8. NR 1946.

9. See *NRH*, 15n, 20, 43, 60n, 77, 96n, 182n, 193–94, 255n, 263n, 279, 316. But "[t]hat justice in contradistinction to courage and moderation cannot be misused is an important ingredient of the first paragraph of the text of Kant's *Foundations of the Metaphysics of Morals*—Cf. *Republic* 491 b7–10 and *Meno* 88 a6–e4" ("On the *Euthydemus*," *SPPP*, 76n8). See Susan Shell, introduction to Leo Strauss's Kant Seminars (unpublished).

10. Or maybe in Christian terms as understood by Hegel. Cf. NR 1946.

11. Cf. *Groundwork for the Metaphysics of Morals* in *Kant: Practical Philosophy*, ed. Mary Gregor (Cambridge: Cambridge University Press, 1996); and Rawls, "Kantian Constructivism in Moral Theory," in *Collected Papers*, ed. Samuel Freeman (Cambridge: Harvard University Press, 1999), 303–58, as well as its criticism in Michael Sandel, *Liberalism and the Limits of Justice* (Cambridge: Harvard University Press, 1997).

12. NR 1946.

13. WCL. See also Susan Shell, "Taking Evil Seriously," in *Leo Strauss: Political Philosopher and Jewish Thinker*, ed. Kenneth Deutsch and Walter Nicgorski (Lanham, MD: Rowman and Littlefield, 1994), 175–93.

14. WCL.

15. NR 1946.

16. Cf. *NRH*, 150n24.

17. NR 1946.

18. Ibid.

19. Ibid.

20. *NRH*, preface.

21. *WIPP*, 41–47.

22. NR 1946.

23. On this crucial connection between the best regime and natural right, cf. Strauss's comments on Plato in "Natural Law" in Sills, *International Encyclopedia of the Social Sciences*, 11: 80: "Natural right in Plato's sense is in the first place the natural order of the virtues as the natural perfections of the human soul (cf. *Laws* 765E–766A), as well as the natural order of the other things that are by nature good. But assigning to each what

is good for him by nature is impossible in any society. Such assigning requires that the men who know what is by nature good for each and all, the philosophers, be the absolute rulers and that absolute communism (communism regarding property, women, and children) be established among those citizens who give the commonwealth its character; it also requires equality of the sexes. This order is the political order according to nature, as distinguished from and opposed to the conventional order (*Republic* 456B, C; cf. 428E). Thus natural right in Plato's sense also determines the best regime, in which those who are best by nature and training, the wise men, rule the unwise with absolute power, assigning to each of them what is by nature just, i.e., what is by nature good for him. The actualization of the best regime proves indeed to be impossible or at least extremely improbable; only a diluted version of that political order which strictly corresponds to natural right can in reason be expected."

24. *NRH*, 138

25. *NRH*, 144.

26. *NRH*, 144. Strauss contends "that the predominance of that belief prevents the emergence of the idea of natural right or makes the quest for natural right infinitely unimportant: if man knows by divine revelation what the right path is, he does not have to discover that path by his unassisted efforts" (*NRH*, 90).

27. Cf. *PAW*, 126ff.

28. On these minimum conditions for living in a polity, Strauss refers to Aristotle: "If this interpretation is correct, natural right is that right which must be recognized by any political society if it is to last and which for this reason is everywhere in force. Natural right thus understood delineates the minimum conditions of political life, so much so that sound positive right occupies a higher rank than natural right. Natural right in this sense is indifferent to the difference among regimes, whereas positive right is relative to the type of regime—positive right is democratic, oligarchic, etc. (cf. *Politics* 1280a8–22)." "Natural Law," in Sills, *International Encyclopedia of the Social Sciences*, 11: 140. Yet "Aristotle concludes his laconic statement on natural right, 'one regime alone is by nature the best everywhere.' This regime, 'the most divine regime,' is a certain kind of kingship, the only regime that does not require any positive right (*Politics* 1284a4–15; 1288al5–29). The flooring and the ceiling, the minimum condition and the maximum possibility of political society, are natural and do not in any way depend on (positive) law." (Ibid.)

29. *NRH*, 130.

30. Cf. H 1941.

31. WCL.

32. As Strauss explains elsewhere: "Is all right conventional (of human origin), or is there some right which is natural (*physei dikaion*)? This question was raised on the assumption that there are things which are by nature good (health, strength, intelligence, courage, etc.) . . . Yet the conventionalists could not deny that justice possesses a core that is universally recognized, so much so that injustice must have recourse to lies or to 'myths' in order to become publicly defensible. The precise issue then concerned the status of that right which is universally recognized: is that right merely the condition of the living together of a particular society (i.e., of a society constituted by covenant or

agreement, with that right deriving its validity from the preceding covenant), or is there a justice among men as men which does not derive from any human arrangement? In other words, is justice based only on calculation of the advantage of living together, or is it choiceworthy for its own sake and therefore 'by nature'?" "Natural Law," in Sills, *International Encyclopedia of the Social Sciences*, 11: 80.

33. *NRH*, 139–44. Devin Stauffer seems to make a similar point. "On 'Classic Natural Right' in *Natural Right and History*," 140 and ff.

34. *NRH*, 135.

35. I thank Susan Shell for her comments on this question. See "An Introduction to Natural Right (1931)" in Strauss, *Hobbes's Critique of Religion*.

36. But cf. *SPPP*, 139.

37. WCL.

38. OSCPP. See, however, *PAW*, 28 and ff., on the exoteric nature of Aristotle's presentation of Plato's teaching. I thank Timothy Burns for calling my attention to this problem.

39. See this idea expanded and clarified in Leo Strauss, "An Epilogue," *Essays on The Scientific Study of Politics*, ed. Herbert Storing (New York: Holt, Rinehart, and Winston, 1962), 305–27.

40. But see John Finnis, *Natural Law and Natural Rights* (Oxford: Clarendon Press, 1980), vi.

41. See "Why Political Philosophy Is Absolutely Necessary," Leo Strauss Papers, box 18, folder 9.

42. WCL. Despite being a mere footnote in the book (*NRH*, 150n24), Stauffer, "On 'Classic Natural Right' in *Natural Right and History*," made a similar passage central to his essay on chapter 4 of *NRH*.

43. An indication of this preference is that Strauss almost completely ignores the first book of Aristotle's *Politics* in the text of *NRH*.

44. WCL.

45. Cf. NR 1946.

46. WL, lecture 1.

47. Meier, *Leo Strauss and the Theologico-Political Problem*, 55.

48. Cf. *NRH*, 120–21.

49. Cf. *WIPP*, 93.

50. Cf. *NRH*, vii.

51. *NRH*, 120.

52. See *CM*, and *HPP*, 53.

53. Cf. *HPP*, 53 and ff. Elsewhere Strauss also asserts leisurely: "The subject matter is very difficult and presupposes an understanding of the doctrine of ideas as a whole. By this I mean this simple thing on which we got into troubles—that Plato introduces the whole discussion by saying that what is intelligible (476c2–480a13). Then he goes on to say that everything that is intelligible" (139). And later: "But let me give you a much better example. There was a being which the Greeks called Victory. Now there was a victory at Marathon and many other places, but there was also Victory with a capital V. Now Glaucon would immediately understand that Victory with a capital V is something

different from the victory at Marathon. He would understand without any difficulty that Victory herself or itself would be something quite different from this statue of Victory. And if he were still more clever, he could even see that Victory herself, the Goddess of Victory, is something altogether different from all statues everywhere. All statues are only imitations of that. If you can presuppose that, then it is clear that such a man would understand immediately what an idea is. We do not have such gods, for example Victory, whose every inch, every finger and so on is victory. If you look at such a statue you see that. Once you can presuppose such a thing, it is no longer difficult to understand the thought of ideas . . . Plato's ideas are really meant to take the place of the gods. I think this is safe to say." Seminar on the *Republic*, Spring 1957, p. 163. https://leostrausscenter.uchicago.edu/course/republic (accessed May 8, 2016).

54. *CM*, 123; *HPP*, 59; see Seth Benardete, "Leo Strauss' *The City and Man*," *Political Science Reviewer* 8 (1978): 20. Seminar on the *Gorgias*, Winter 1957, p. 199. https://leostrausscenter.uchicago.edu/node/113 (accessed May 8, 2016). In his seminar on the *Gorgias* in 1957, Strauss explains: "What does Plato's idea mean? [In *Republic* X] [i]t is a model, a model which cannot be in the way in which this [tangible] chair is. The human soul is distinguished from the soul of brutes by the fact that, in mythical language, the human soul has seen the ideas prior to birth. In nonmythical language, it is [that] man, prior to making any sense perception, has already [some] understanding of these forms. Otherwise, he would not have sense perception in a human way. In present day language, one could state this, perhaps, as follows: there is never pure sense perception; sense perception is always interpreted; the categories precede the perception. Plato does not speak of categories, but of ideas. The ideas, we can say, are the natural framework in which everything is perceived. This is in the essence of man . . . The philosopher is concerned with the ideas as ideas, but every human being has some understanding of the ideas."

55. *NRH*, 142.

56. See Tarcov's essay in this volume with *NRH*, 150.

57. But we must not underestimate the importance and influence of Heidegger. See the letter to Löwith where Strauss "takes Heidegger's side." Strauss to Löwith, March 15, 1962, *Gesammelte Schriften*, 3: 686); also December 13, 1960, *Gesammelte Schriften*, 3: 684–85.

58. *NRH*, 8.

59. *NRH*, 16.

60. H 1941.

61. *NRH*, 9.

62. *NRH*, 10.

63. WL, lecture 2, p. 1.

64. *NRH*, 20.

65. Cf. Karl Popper, *The Poverty of Historicism* (Abingdon, UK: Routledge, 1957): "Are generalizations confined to periods?" (89 and ff.).

66. See Strauss to Gadamer (February 26, 1961): "In passing, I note that your rendering of Aristotle's understanding of time is decisively incomplete. Strictly speaking time is not the cause of decay rather than of the opposite (*Physics* 222 b25–26); time can be said

to be with equal justice the discoverer or a good helper of knowledge (EN. 1098 a 22–26)." Strauss adds: "I would speak of a negatively absolute situation: the awakening from *Seinsvergessenheit* belongs to the *Erschütterung alles Seienden*, and what one awakens to is not the final truth in the form of a system but rather a question which can never be fully answered . . ." "Correspondence concerning *Wahrheit und Methode*," *Independent Journal of Philosophy* 2 (1978), 7.

67. Strauss to Kuhn in *Independent Journal of Philosophy* 2 (1978): 5.

68. The most comprehensive examination of why Strauss was not an Aristotelian can be found in Zuckert and Zuckert, *Leo Strauss and the Problem of Political Philosophy*, 144–66.

69. WCL.

70. WCL.

71. *NRH*, 124.

72. *NRH*, 125.

73. *NRH*, 26.

74. FRSS.

75. "The Origin of Political Science and the Problem of Socrates: Six Public Lectures," *Interpretation* 23, no. 2 (Winter 1996): 171, 177.

76. *NRH*, 122.

77. *NRH*, 123.

78. See chaps. 4 and 5 of Catherine H. Zuckert, *Postmodern Platos* (Chicago: University of Chicago Press, 1996), as well as Richard Velkley, *Heidegger, Strauss, and the Premises of Philosophy: On Original Forgetting* (Chicago: University of Chicago Press, 2011).

79. This is not to deny that this is the fundamental thrust of every Platonic dialogue.

80. *NRH*, 125. Some may be disappointed by the commonsensical character of Strauss's metaphysics. But let us listen to a man who never eschewed simple common sense, Thomas More, commenting on "scholasticism": "I wonder, by Jove, how these petty adepts ever reached the conclusion that those propositions should be understood in a way no one on earth but themselves understands them. Those words are not technical terms on which these men can claim a monopoly . . . Such expressions are actually common language . . . They have borrowed words from the public domain, they abuse public property." Thomas More, *Yale Edition of the Complete Works of St. Thomas More*, vol. 15: *In Defense of Humanism: Letters to Dorp, Oxford, Lee, and a Monk*, ed. Daniel Kinney (New Haven: Yale University Press, 1986), 35.

81. I thank Catherine Zuckert for this remark.

82. *NRH*, 129.

83. *CM*, 29.

84. NR 1946.

85. See seminar on natural right, 1962, lectures 1–4.

86. *NRH*, 4.

87. Quoted from Strauss's 1962 seminar on natural right, session 2. Cf. also *WIPP*, 23.

88. See WCL; cf. also *WIPP*, 115–16.

89. See H 1941.

90. On natural right in Strauss as a problem, see Victor Gourevitch, "The Problem of Natural Right and the Fundamental Alternatives in *Natural Right and History*," in *The Crises of Liberal Democracy*, ed. Kenneth Deutsch and Walter Soffer (Albany: SUNY Press, 1987), 30–47; and Stewart Umphrey, "Natural Right and Philosophy," in Deutsch and Nicgorski, *Leo Strauss: Political Philosopher and Jewish Thinker*, 275–295.

91. WL, lecture 1.

Appendix

Leo Strauss: Courses at the New School for Social Research

COMPILED BY SVETOZAR MINKOV

VII. Greek and Roman Political Philosophy. Wednesdays, 5:10–7 p.m. Plato and His Predecessors. 1. The Greek city: its parts and its structure. 2. Survey of Greek political thought before Plato. 3. The *History* of Thucydides. 4. Xenophon's *Education of Cyrus*. 5. Plato's political philosophy. (Fall 1938)

VIII. Seminar: Plato's *Laws*. Hours to be arranged. Interpretation of this relatively neglected work with regard to the question of the relation between state and religion; the *Laws* as the precursor of the Middle Ages. (Fall 1938)

VII. Greek and Roman Political Philosophy: Aristotle and Later Ancient Political Thought. Wednesdays, 5:10–7 p.m. 1. Aristotle's Ethics and Politics. 2. Stoa and Epicureanism. 3. Polybius. 4. Cicero. 5. Seneca. 6. The conception of the Emperor. 7. Philo and Josephus. (Spring 1939)

IX B. Utopias and Political Science. Fridays, 8:10–10 p.m. Open course. While surveying the most outstanding Utopias of both ancient and modern times the following problems will be discussed: Utopias and prognosticizing science; Utopias and the Golden Age; Utopias and eschatology; Utopias and natural man; Utopias and satire; Utopias and genuine political science. (Spring 1939)

405-G. Political Philosophy from Hooker to Spinoza. Wednesdays, 5:10–7 p.m. The political and moral doctrines of the following authors will be discussed: Hooker, Bacon, Grotius, Descartes, Hobbes, Petty, Milton, Harrington, and Spinoza. The theological and scientific background of their doctrines will be considered. Stress will be laid on the following trends characteristic of the period in question: the gradual substitution of the ideas of the sovereign state and of the natural rights of man for the traditional idea of a state subordinate to natural and divine law; the search for and the elaboration of a new method of political science; the beginnings of national economy ("political arithmetic"), the transition from the ideal of the courtier to a middle class ideal. (Fall 1939)

409-O. Persecution of Freedom of Thought in Classical Antiquity. Fridays, 8:10–10 p.m. Down to very nearly the end of the 18th century, persecution was, in a manner of speaking, natural atmosphere to which free thought or the expression of free thought had to adapt itself. In order to understand the ultimate reasons underlying the struggle between the forces of persecution and independent thinking as well as the original meaning of the devices by the use of which independent thinking succeeded in defeating barbarism, it is helpful to refer back to the classical example of that struggle, the trial of Socrates; its meaning will be discussed on the basis of the writings of Xenophon and Plato. (Fall 1939)

407-S. Political Philosophy (elsewhere listed as "Political Science") and the Study of History in Antiquity. Hours to be arranged. The problem of the connection between political science and historical studies will be discussed on the basis of classical passages in the works of Herodotus, Thucydides, Plato, and Aristotle. (Fall 1939)

408-S. Political Philosophy (elsewhere listed as "Political Science") and the Study of History in the Modern World. Hours to be arranged. The problem of the connection between political science and historical studies will be discussed on the basis of classical passages in the works of Hume, Rousseau, Condorcet, Burke, Hegel, Nietzsche, and Bergson. (Spring 1940)

410-O. Continental Champions of Freedom of Thought. Fridays, 8:10–10 p.m. The events of the last decades have heightened our interest and increased our understanding of the fight waged by such men as Bayle, Voltaire and Lessing for freedom of thought. What did they understand by freedom of thought? How did they conceive of its political and institutional implications? To what extent is their view of freedom of thought tinged by the peculiar prejudices of their age? And how did it influence the literary form of their writings? (Spring 1940)

406-G. European Political Thought from Locke to Burke. Wednesdays, 5:10–7 p.m. The political and moral doctrines of the following authors will be discussed: Locke, Leibniz, Montesquieu, Voltaire, Gibbon, Hume, Rousseau, Burke, and Paine. The theological and scientific background of their doctrines will be considered. The emphasis will be laid on the emergence of the ideas underlying the Declaration of Independence and the American Constitution, as well as on the struggle between the rationalistic and the historical approach to political and social problems. (Spring 1940)

537-S. Seminar: The Origin of Economic Science. Saturdays, 10 a.m. The texts to be discussed are Xenophon's economic treatises and the economic parts of Aristotle's *Politics*. (Fall 1940)

535-G. Plato's *Republic* and the Problems of Political Philosophy. Thursdays, 5:10–7 p.m. The following topics are discussed on the basis of Plato's *Republic*: morals and politics; the various meanings of justice; family and political community; private and public ownership; equality and its limits; peace and war; the political function of science and freedom of thought; poetry and political life; origin and decline of political communities. (Fall 1940)

533-O. Persecution and Freedom of Thought. Tuesdays, 8:10–10 p.m. Down to very nearly the end of the 18th century persecution was, in a manner of speaking, the natural atmosphere to which free thought or the expression of free thought had to adapt itself. In order to understand the ultimate reasons underlying the struggle between the forces of persecution and of independent thinking, as well as the devices by the use of which independent thinkers succeeded in defeating persecution, it is helpful to refer back to the classical example of that struggle, the trial of Socrates; its meaning is discussed on the basis of the writings of Xenophon and Plato. (Fall 1940)

538-S. Seminar: Political Science and the Study of History. The various aspects of the connection between political science and historical studies are dealt with on the basis of classical passages in the works of ancient philosophers and historians. (Spring 1941)

536-G. Political Philosophy of the 17th Century (titled "Political Philosophy in the Age of Reason" in the spring catalogue, as opposed to the annual one). The political and moral teachings of the following authors are discussed: Bacon, Grotius, Descartes, Hobbes, Milton, the Clarke Papers, Harrington, Spinoza, Petty, and Locke (in the spring catalogue the list is: Hobbes, Spinoza, Locke, Montesquieu, and Rousseau). The scientific and theological background of their teachings are [*sic*] considered. Stress is laid on the following characteristic trends of the period in question: gradual substitution of the ideas of the sovereign state and of the natural rights of the individuals for the traditional idea of natural and divine law; the search for and elaboration of a new method of political science; the beginnings of national economy ("political arithmetic"); the transition from the ideal of the courtier to middle class ideals. (Spring 1941)

534-O. Reading in Philosophy. Hours to be arranged. Study of philosophy in general and of political philosophy in particular consists to an important extent in reading and understanding philosophic and political literature. The purpose of the course is to give beginners elementary training in the technique of reading philosophic and political classics. Two short texts, an ancient and a modern one, are discussed thoroughly. Choice of the texts is determined by interests of the students. (The spring catalogue specifies a text: "One comparatively short text, Descartes' *Discourse on Method,* is discussed thoroughly.") (Spring 1941)

76. Seminar (the official course number is unavailable): The Influence of Politics on Literature. Saturdays, 10 a.m.–12 p.m. What is the meaning of poetic or fictional presentation of political problems? How do the constant and changing features of political life affect various forms of literature? These questions are discussed on the basis of Voltaire's *Candide,* Swift's *Tale of a Tub,* Shakespeare's *Julius Caesar,* and, more fully, a work of antiquity. (Spring 1941)

7. Philosophy and Sociology of Knowledge. Tuesdays and Thursdays, 9:10–11:00 a.m. The course consists of a preliminary, general discussion of the relations of philosophy and sociology of knowledge, applying the results of that discussion to specific historical material. In the first part the views of Max Scheler, the American discussion of German sociology of knowledge, and the relation of pragmatism to the sociology of knowledge are considered. The second part centers on the phenomenon of utopias. (Summer 1941)

403-B. History of Political Ideas. Mondays, 6–7:50 p.m. I. The Greek City: its parts and its parties. II. Survey of Greek political thought before Plato. III. The comedies of Aristophanes. IV. The History of Thucydides. V. Xenophon's *Education of Cyrus.* VI. Plato's *Republic.* VII. Aristotle. VIII. Polybius. IX. Cicero. X. Seneca. XI. Philo and Josephus. XII. St. Augustine's *City of God.* XIII. Thomas Aquinas and Dante. XIV. Marsilius of Padua. XV. Thomas More's *Utopia.* (Fall 1941)

107-S. Joint Seminar: History of Psychology and the Doctrine of Man. Albert Salomon, Leo Strauss. Wednesdays, 6–7:50 p.m. Psychological trends in Greek and Roman thought. Science of man in scholasticism and Renaissance. Montaigne. Hobbes and the Aristotelian Rhetoric. Descartes's contribution to psychology. Pascal and Loyola. Bacon and Gracian. La Rochefoucauld and St. Evremond. La Bruyère and Theophrastus. Temple and Mandeville. Shaftesbury, Adam Smith, Hume. (Fall 1941)

407-G. Absolutism and Constitutionalism, Ancient and Modern. Thursdays, 5:10–7 p.m. The constant and changing aspects of the conflict between absolutism and constitutionalism are studied with reference to the doctrines of Plato, Aristotle, Xenophon, Cicero, Machiavelli, Hobbes,

Locke, Montesquieu. Required reading: C. H. MacIlwain, *Constitutionalism, Ancient and Modern.* (Fall 1941)

404-B. History of Political Ideas. Mondays, 6–7:40 p.m. I. Machiavelli. II. Luther and Calvin. III. Hooker. IV. Hobbes. V. Spinoza. VI. Locke. VII. Montesquieu. VIII. Rousseau. IX. Burke. X. *The Federalist.* XI. Kant. XII. Fichte. XIII. Hegel. XIV. John Stuart Mill. XV. The origins of totalitarianism. (Spring 1942)

408-G. The Political Philosophy of Aristotle. Thursdays, 5:10–7 p.m. I. The aim of Aristotle's political philosophy. II. Method. III. Happiness and virtue. IV. Justice and the other virtues. V. Friendship. VI. Society and science. VII. The political community. VIII. The constitution. IX. The question of the best constitution. X. The good and the defective constitutions. XI. The change of constitutions. XII. Politics, education, rhetoric and poetry. (Spring 1942)

410-S. Readings in Political Philosophy. Saturdays, 11 a.m.–1 p.m. The seminar is devoted to a discussion of the intention of Rousseau. His *Discours sur l'origine de l'inégalité* and his *Lettre à d'Alembert* are studied closely. (Spring 1942)

7. Research in the History of Ideas. Tuesdays and Thursdays, 9:10–11:00 a.m. The aim of this course is to introduce students to the techniques of research in the history of ideas. The first part of the course is devoted to a preliminary general discussion of the aims and methods of such research. In the second and major part, the results of the general discussion are illustrated by their application to three specific historical questions: 1) Machiavellianism and its sources; 2) the historical position of Hobbes; 3) the significance of the Socratic question. (Summer 1942)

403-B. History of Political Philosophy. Mondays, 6–7:50 p.m. I. The Greek City: its parts and its parties. II. Survey of Greek political thought before Plato. III. Sophocles' *Antigone.* IV. The comedies of Aristophanes. V. The *History* of Thucydides. VI. Xenophon's *Education of Cyrus.* VII. Plato's *Republic.* VIII. Aristotle. IX. Polybius. X. Cicero. X. Seneca. XI. Philo and Josephus. XII. St. Augustine's *City of God.* XIII. Thomas Aquinas and Dante. XIV. Marsilius of Padua. XV. Thomas More's *Utopia.* (Fall 1942)

409-G. Natural Law and the Rights of Man. Thursdays, 6–7:50 pm. After a preliminary discussion of the historicist and positivist criticism of the ideas of "natural law" and "rights of man," the natural law doctrines of the following thinkers are discussed: Cicero and the Roman lawyers; Thomas Aquinas and the Aristotelian tradition; Hooker; Grotius; Hobbes; and

Locke. Special attention is given to these questions: natural law and natural right; natural law and rational law; natural law and moral law; natural law and the state of nature. (Fall 1942)

411-S. Readings in Political Philosophy: Reason of State and the Absolutist Concept of Government. Fridays, 8:20–10:10 p.m. Analysis of selected passages from Machiavelli, Hobbes, and Hegel. (Fall 1942)

106-S. Religion and the Rise of Modern Capitalism: The Weber-Tawney Controversy. Mondays, 8:20–10:10 p.m. C. Mayer, L. Strauss. The question of the relationship between the origin of modern capitalism and nascent Protestantism constitutes a subject matter of investigation in which cooperation between the various branches of the social sciences can most fruitfully be practiced. The seminar carefully considers and analyzes the positions concerning this question held respectively by Max Weber (*The Ethics of Protestantism and the Spirit of Capitalism*) and by R. H. Tawney (*Religion and the Rise of Capitalism*). (Spring 1943)

404-B. Modern Political Philosophy (also announced as "History of Political Philosophy"). Mondays, 6–7:50 p.m. I. Machiavelli. II. Luther and Calvin. III. Hooker. IV. Hobbes. V. Spinoza. VI. Locke. VII. Montesquieu. VIII. Rousseau. IX. Burke. X. *The Federalist*. XI. Kant. XII. Fichte. XIII. Hegel. XIV. John Stuart Mill. XV. The origins of totalitarianism. (Spring 1943)

*406-G. Political Theory: Selected Problems. Thursdays (evening). Title changed. The course will deal with the scope of political theory, its place within political science, sovereignty and the rule of law, utopianism and realism, law of nations and eternal peace. (Spring 1943)

412-S. Readings in Political Philosophy: Rule of Law and Constitutionalism. Fridays, 8:20–10:10 p.m. Analysis of selected passages from Cicero, Locke, and Montesquieu. (Spring 1943)

**412-S. Readings in Political Philosophy. Fridays (night). (Spring 1943)

410-G. Utopias and Political Science. Thursdays, 6–7:50 p.m. After a preliminary discussion of the idea of "neutral" (*wertfreie*) political and social science utopias are discussed with a view to the following questions: utopias and prognosticating science; utopias and the Golden Age; utopias and eschatology; utopias and ideals; utopias and natural man; utopias and satires; utopias and genuine political science. (Spring 1943)

401-B. History of Political Philosophy. Basic course. Thursdays, 6–7:50 p.m. Two points of credit. I. The beginnings of political philosophy. II. Plato. III. Aristotle. IV. Cicero. V. Augustine. VI. Thomas Aquinas. VII.

Machiavelli. VIII. Hobbes. IX. Locke. X. Montesquieu. XI. Rousseau. XII. Burke. XIII. Hegel. XIV. John Stuart Mill. XV. The origins of totalitarianism. (Fall 1943)

403-G. The Political Philosophy of Plato and Aristotle. Graduate course. Mondays, 6–7:50 p.m. Three points of credit. Interpretation of Plato's *Statesman* and of the third book of Aristotle's *Politics*. (Fall 1943)

551-S. The Philosophy of Aristotle and the Teaching of the Bible. Seminar. Mondays, 8:20–10:10 p.m. Three points of credit. For a proper understanding of the problems involved in the relation of philosophy, or science, and religion, one has to consider the classical discussion of that relation, viz., the mediaeval discussion of the relation of Aristotelian philosophy and the teaching of the Bible. The purpose of this seminar is to introduce students into that mediaeval discussion by means of the interpretation of selected passages from Maimonides' *Guide of the Perplexed* and from Thomas Aquinas's *Summa Theologica*. The passages to be interpreted will deal with the following questions: philosophy and theology; Plato's perfect polity and the divine law; ethics and the natural law; divine will and divine knowledge; creation of the world and eternity of the world; providence and miracles. (Fall 1943)

412-G. Political Theory: Selected Problems. Graduate course. Mondays, 6–7:50 p.m. Three points of credit. I. Political theory, political philosophy, social philosophy, and the social sciences. II. The attack on the concept of "the state." III. Methodological questions. IV. The structure and the purpose of the political community. V. Political community and law. VI. The problem of sovereignty. VII. The principles of democracy. VIII. Utopianism and realism. IX. Law of nations and eternal peace. (Spring 1944)

418-G. The Declaration of Independence. Graduate course. Thursdays, 6–7:50 p.m. Three points of credit. Analysis of the political ideas underlying the Declaration of Independence. (Spring 1944)

532-O. Readings in Philosophy: Philosophy and Politics. Open course. Mondays, 8:20–10:10 p.m. Two points of credit. The purpose of this course is to introduce beginners into philosophy by a discussion of what may fairly be called the most elementary problem of philosophy: the problem of its political or social function. The texts to be studied will be taken from Plato, Cicero, Descartes, Hobbes, and Nietzsche. (Spring 1944)

Political Philosophy: Its Problems and Its Development. Mondays and Tuesdays, 8:30–10:10 p.m. June 12–August 1. Political philosophy and political science. Origins of political philosophy. The question of the best form of government. Natural law. "Realism." Sovereignty. Rights of man. Nationalism and Internationalism. War and peace. (Summer 1944)

103-S. Joint Seminar: Religion and the Rise of Modern Capitalism. C. Mayer and L. Strauss. Mondays, 8:30–10:10 p.m. Three points of credit. The question of the relationship between the origins of modern capitalism and nascent Protestantism constitutes the subject matter of investigation in which cooperation between the various branches of the social sciences is most fruitfully practiced. This seminar carefully analyzes the positions concerning the question held respectively by Max Weber (*The Protestant Ethic and the Spirit of Capitalism*) and by R. H. Tawney (*Religion and the Rise of Capitalism*). (Fall 1944)

107-S. Joint Seminar: Theory of Knowledge. A. Koyré, K. Riezler, L. Strauss. Fridays, 6:20–8 p.m. Three points of credit. Idealism and empiricism on the basis of Plato's dialogue *Theaetetus*. (Fall 1944)

401-O. History of Political Philosophy. Open course. Mondays, 6:20–8 p.m. Two points of credit. The beginnings of political philosophy. Plato. Aristotle. Cicero. Augustine. Thomas Aquinas. Machiavelli. Hobbes. Locke. Montesquieu. *The Federalist*. Rousseau. Burke. Hegel. John Stuart Mill. (Fall 1944)

403-S. Readings in Political Philosophy: Basic Problems in Democracy. Seminar. Fridays, 8:30–10:10 p.m. Three points of credit. Reading and discussion of Rousseau's *Social Contract*. (Fall 1944)

404-S. Readings in Political Philosophy: Justice and Political Necessity. Seminar. Fridays, 8:30–10:10 p.m. Three points of credit. Reading and discussion of selected passages from Aristotle's *Ethics* and *Politics*. (Spring 1945)

420-G. The Constitution of the United States: Philosophical Background. Graduate course. Mondays, 6:20–8 p.m. Three points of credit. Analysis of the political ideas underlying the United States Constitution and the Bill of Rights. (Spring 1945)

540-O. Readings in Philosophy: An Introduction to Philosophy in General and Political Philosophy in Particular. Open course. Mondays, 8:30–10:10 p.m. Two points of credit. The primary aim of this course is to show students how to read a classic. Through intensive reading in class, students are made aware of the factors involved in the process of understanding a great work. Discussion turns on the relationship of scientific and political (rhetorical) argumentation as set forth in Plato's *Gorgias* and in other texts chosen by the students. (Spring 1945)

104-S. Joint Seminar: The Forerunners of Modern Psychology. S. E. Asch, K. Riezler, L. Strauss. Fridays, 6:20–8 p.m. Three points of credit. Critical examination of the doctrines of Aristotle (*On the Soul*) and Descartes (*The Passions of the Soul*) with respect to their bearing on fundamental questions of modern psychology. (Spring 1945)

422-O. The United States Constitution: Theory (new) and Practice. Phillips Bradley and Leo Strauss. Open course. Mondays, 6:20–8 p.m. Two points of credit. (Spring 1945)

404-S. Readings in Political Philosophy: Justice and Political Necessity. Seminar. Fridays, 8:30–10:10 p.m. (Spring 1945)

7. Classical Political Philosophy. Mondays, Tuesdays, Wednesdays, and Thursdays, 8:30–10:10 p.m. June 11–July 5. Political philosophy and history of ideas. The place of politics in classical philosophy. Nature and convention. Law and political power. Politics and morals. Politics and economics. (Summer 1945)

401-O. History of Political Philosophy. Open course. Mondays, 6:20–8 p.m. Two points of credit. The origins of political philosophy. Plato. Aristotle. Cicero. Augustine. Thomas Aquinas. Machiavelli. Hobbes. Locke. Montesquieu. *The Federalist*. Rousseau. Burke. Hegel. John Stuart Mill. (Fall 1945)

403-S. Readings in Political Philosophy; Utopias and Political Science. Seminar. Fridays, 8:30–10:10 p.m. Three points of credit. Interpretation of Plato's *Republic*. (Fall 1945)

417-G. Political Philosophy: Its Problems and Its Development. Graduate course. Fridays, 6:20–8 p.m. Three points of credit. Political philosophy and political science. Political philosophy and history. Political philosophy and authority. The problem of the best political order: Utopias. Natural right. Sovereignty. Constitutionalism. Majority rule. General will. Nationalism. (Fall 1945)

404-S. Readings in Political Philosophy: The Social Philosophy of Early Capitalism. Seminar. Fridays, 8:30–10:10 p.m. Three points of credit. Analysis of Locke's *Civil Government*. (Spring 1946)

104-S. Human Nature in Politics. Solomon E. Asch, Alexander H. Pekelis, and Leo Strauss. Seminar. Mondays, 6:20–8 p.m. Three points of credit. Are all political theory and practice based on a definite view of human nature? The "optimistic" view (Rousseau). The "pessimistic" view (Machiavelli and Hobbes). Perfectibility and its limits. "Utopian" and "scientific" politics. Common sense and its limits. (Spring 1946)

506-O. Readings in Philosophy: An Introduction to Philosophy, Especially Political Philosophy. Open course. Mondays, 8:30–10:50 p.m. Two points of credit. The primary aim of this course is to show students how to read the philosophical classic. Through intensive reading in class, students are made aware of the factors involved in the process of understanding a great work. Discussion of the relations between morals and politics in Plato's *Protagoras*. (Spring 1946)

542-G. Moral Philosophy: Its Problems and Its Development. Graduate course. Fridays, 6:20–8 p.m. Three points of credit. Nietzsche's attack on traditional morality. The moral problem as stated by Socrates and Plato. The Aristotelian solution. Utilitarianism and hedonism, ancient and modern. Kant's formalistic ethics. Self-preservation and self-realization. (Spring 1946)

105-G. Human Nature and Human Institutions I. Solomon E. Asch, Alexander H. Pekelis, and Leo Strauss. Graduate course. Wednesdays, 6:20–8 p.m. Three points of credit. I. Psychological foundations of society; II. The nature of the law-making process; III. Economic behavior: human needs and human desires. (Fall 1946)

401-O. History of Political Philosophy. Open course. Mondays, 6:20–8 p.m. Two points of credit. The subject matter of political philosophy. The origin of political philosophy. Plato. Aristotle. Cicero. Augustine. Thomas Aquinas. Machiavelli. Hobbes. Locke. Montesquieu. Rousseau. Burke. Hegel. (Fall 1946)

403-S. Readings in Political Philosophy: Political Liberty and Separation of Powers. Leo Strauss, assisted by Howard B. White. Seminar. Mondays, 8:30–10:10 p.m. Three points of credit. Discussion of Montesquieu's *Spirit of Laws*. (Fall 1946)

547-G. Socrates and the History of Philosophy. Graduate course. Fridays, 6:20–8 p.m. Three points of credit. "The problem of Socrates" as a philosophic and historical problem. Interpretation of the most important classical texts related to Socrates' teaching. (Fall 1946)

402-S. Readings in Political Philosophy: The Social Philosophy of Thomas Aquinas. Leo Strauss, assisted by Howard B. White. Seminar. Mondays, 8:30–10:10 p.m. Three points of credit. Analysis of selected passages from the *Summa theologica*. (Spring 1947)

532-O. Readings in Philosophy: An Introduction to Philosophy, Especially Political Philosophy. Open course. Mondays, 6:20–8 p.m. Two points of credit. The primary aim of this course is to show students how to read a philosophic classic. Discussion of selected passages from Aristotle's writings. (Spring 1947)

422-G. The Declaration of Independence. Graduate course. Fridays, 6:20–8 p.m. Three points of credit. (Spring 1947)

402-S. Readings in Political Philosophy: The Social Philosophy of Thomas Aquinas. Seminar. Mondays, 8:30–10:10 p.m. Three points of credit. (Spring 1947)

401-O. History of Political Philosophy. Open course. Mondays, 6:20–8 p.m. Two points of credit. The subject matter of political philosophy. Origins of political philosophy. Socrates. Plato. Aristotle. Cicero. Augustine. Thomas Aquinas. Machiavelli. Hobbes. Locke. Montesquieu. Rousseau. Burke. Hegel. (Fall 1947)

405-S. Readings in Political Philosophy: Principles of Liberal Democracy. Seminar. Mondays, 8:30–10:10 p.m. Three points of credit. Analysis of Spinoza's political writings. (Fall 1947)

553-S. Philosophy and Revelation. Seminar. Fridays, 6:20–8 p.m. Three points of credit. The following authors will be considered: Maimonides, Thomas Aquinas, Calvin, Pascal, Spinoza, Kierkegaard and Newman. (Fall 1947).

402-G. Plato's Political Philosophy and Its Metaphysical Foundations. Graduate course. Fridays, 6:20–8 p.m. Three points of credit. Interpretation of Plato's *Republic*. (Spring 1948)

404-S. Readings in Political Philosophy: The Aristotelian Principles. Seminar. Mondays, 8:30–10:10 p.m. Three points of credit. Analysis of selected passages from the *Politics*. (Spring 1948)

502-O. Readings in Philosophy: An Introduction to Philosophy, Especially Political Philosophy. Open course. Mondays, 6:20–8 p.m. Two points of credit. The primary aim of this course is to show students how to read a philosophic classic. Interpretation of two of the smaller Platonic dialogues. (Spring 1948)

404-S Readings in Political Philosophy: The Aristotelian Principles. Seminar. Mondays, 8:30–10:10 p.m. Three points of credit. (Spring 1948)

8. Research in the History of Political Ideas. Mondays and Tuesdays, 8:20–10 p.m. June 7–August 2. The aim of this course is to introduce students to the techniques of research in the history of political and social

ideas. The first part of the course will be devoted to a general discussion of the aims and methods of such research. In the second and major part, the results of the general discussion will be applied to specific questions. Suggestions of students with regard to the second part of the course will be considered within the limits of the feasible. (Summer 1948)

401-O. History of Political Philosophy. Open course. Mondays, 6:20–8 p.m. Two points of credit. The subject matter of political philosophy. The origins of political philosophy. Socrates. Plato. Aristotle. Cicero. Augustine. Thomas Aquinas. Machiavelli. Hobbes. Locke. Montesquieu. Rousseau. Burke. Hegel. (Fall 1948)

405-S. Readings in Political Philosophy: The Problem of Equality. Seminar. Mondays, 8:30–10:10 p.m. Three points of credit. Analysis of Rousseau's *Discourse on the Origins of Inequality* and *Social Contract.* (Fall 1948)

421-S. The Moral Principles of Politics. Seminar. Tuesdays, 8:30–10:10 p.m. Three points of credit. The purpose of the seminar is to clarify the relation between the principles of modern politics on the one hand and of classical politics on the other. (Fall 1948)

502-O. Readings in Philosophy: An Introduction to Philosophy, Especially Political Philosophy. Open course. Mondays, 6:20–8 p.m. Two points of credit. Interpretation of a Platonic dialogue. (Spring 1949)

406-S. Readings in Political Philosophy: The Problem of Theory and Practice. Seminar. Mondays, 8:30–10:10 p.m. Three points of credit. Analysis of selected writings and speeches by Edmund Burke. (Spring 1949)

584-G. The Philosophy of Spinoza. Graduate course. Tuesdays, 8:30–10:10 p.m. Three points of credit. Analysis of Spinoza's principles. (Spring 1949)

References

Arendt, Hannah. "Martin Heidegger at Eighty." In *Heidegger and Modern Philosophy*, ed. Michael Murray, 293–303. New Haven: Yale University Press, 1978.

Aron, Raymond. *Liberté et égalité*. Paris: Editions de l'EHESS, 2013.

———. *La philosophie critique de l'histoire*. Paris: Vrin, 1970.

Behnegar, Nasser. *Leo Strauss, Max Weber and the Scientific Study of Politics*. Chicago: University of Chicago Press, 2003.

Benda, Julien. *La trahison des clercs*. Paris: Grasset, 1927. Translated as *The Treason of the Intellectuals* by Richard Aldington. New York: William Morrow, 1928.

Berlin, Isaiah. "Democracy, Communism and the Individual." In *The Isaiah Berlin Virtual Library*, ed. Henry Hardy. Accessed May 2, 2016. http://berlin.wolf.ox.ac.uk/lists/nachlass/demcomind.pdf.

Bloom, Allan. "Aron: The Last of the Liberals." In *Giants and Dwarfs: Essays 1960–1990*, 256–267. New York: Simon & Schuster, 1990.

———. *The Closing of the American Mind*. New York: Simon & Schuster, 1983.

Bolotin, David, Christopher Bruell, Leo Strauss, and Thomas Pangle. "An Untitled Lecture on Plato's *Euthyphron*." *Interpretation* 24, no. 1 (1996): 3–23.

Burke, Edmund. *The Works of the Right Honorable Edmund Burke*. Revised ed. Vol. 4. Boston: Little, Brown, 1866.

Burns, Timothy. "Leo Strauss on the Origin of Hobbes's Natural Science and Its Relation to the Challenge of Divine Revelation." In *Reorientation: Leo Strauss in the 1930s*, ed. Martin D. Yaffe and Richard S. Ruderman. Basingstoke: Palgrave, 2014.

———. "Leo Strauss' Recovery of Classical Political Philosophy." In *Brill's Companion to Leo Strauss' Writings on Classical Political Thought*, ed. Timothy W. Burns. Leiden: Brill, 2015.

Burns, Tony, and James Connelly. *The Legacy of Leo Strauss*. Charlottesville, VA: Imprint Academic, 2010.

Churchill, Robert P. "Liberal Toleration." In *The Bloomsbury Companion to Political Philosophy*, ed. Andrew Fialla, 139–51. London: Bloomsbury, 2015.

Colen, José and Svetozar Minkov. "A Controversy about the Natural Frame of Reference and a Universal Science: Leo Strauss and Kurt Riezler." *Kairos*, 10 (2014): 25–48.

———. "Two Essays by Leo Strauss on Social and Natural Science." *Review of Politics* 76, no. 4 (2014): 619–33.

Gierke, Otto von. *Natural Law and the Theory of Society*. Trans. Ernest Barker. Cambridge: Cambridge University Press, 1934.

Gourevitch, Victor. "The Problem of Natural Right and the Fundamental Alternatives in *Natural Right and History*." In *The Crises of Liberal Democracy*, ed. Kenneth Deutsch and Walter Soffer, 30–47. Albany: SUNY Press, 1987.

Grathoff, Richard. *Philosophers in Exile: The Correspondence of Alfred Schutz and Aron Gurwitsch, 1939–1959*. Bloomington: Indiana University Press, 1989.

Hallam, Henry. *The Constitutional History of England from the Accession of Henry VII to the Death of George II*. New York: A. C. Armstrong and Son, 1880.

Hayek, Friedrich von. *The Road to Serfdom*. London: Routledge, 2001.

Husserl, Edmund. *The Crisis of the European Sciences and Transcendental Phenomenology: An Introduction to Phenomenological Philosophy*. Evanston, IL: Northwestern University Press, 1970.

———. "Die Frage nach dem Ursprung der Geometrie als intentional-historisches Problem." *Revue internationale de philosophie* 1, no. 2 (1939): 203–25.

———. "Philosophy as Rigorous Science." In *Phenomenology and the Crisis of Philosophy*, 71–147. New York: Harper and Row, 1965.

Iggers, George G. *The German Concept of History: The National Tradition of Historical Thought from Herder to the Present*. Middletown, CT: Wesleyan University Press, 1983.

———. "Historicism: The History and Meaning of the Term." *Journal of the History of Ideas* 56, no. 1 (1995): 129–52.

Jaeger, Werner. *Humanistische Reden und Vorträge*. Berlin/Leipzig: Walter de Gruyter, 1937.

Jaffa, Harry V. *Thomism and Aristotelianism: A Study of the Commentary by Thomas Aquinas on the Nicomachean Ethics*. Chicago: University of Chicago Press, 1952.

Janssens, David. *Between Athens and Jerusalem*. New York: SUNY Press, 2008.

Kahn, Charles H. *The Art and Thought of Heraclitus: An Edition of the Fragments with Translation and Commentary*. Cambridge: Cambridge University Press, 1979.

Kant, Emmanuel. *Groundwork for the Metaphysics of Morals*. In *Kant: Practical Philosophy*, ed. Mary Gregor. Cambridge: Cambridge University Press, 1996.

Kennington, Richard. *On Modern Origins: Essays on Early Modern Philosophy*, edited by Pamela Kraus and Frank Hunt. Lanham: Lexington Books, 2004.

———. "Strauss's Natural Right and History." *Review of Metaphysics* 35, no. 1 (September 1981): 57–86.

Klein, Jacob. *Greek Mathematical Thought and the Origin of Algebra*. Cambridge: MIT Press, 1968.

Koyré, Alexandre. *Études galiléennes*. Paris: Hermann, 1939.

Kries, Douglas. *The Problem of Natural Law*. Lanham, MD: Lexington Books, 2008.

Kukathas, Chandran, and Philip Pettit. *Rawls: A Theory of Justice and Its Critics*. Stanford: Stanford University Press, 1990.

Leibowitz, David. "The Section on Hobbes in Leo Strauss's *Natural Right and History*: The Meaning of Hobbes's Claim to Be the Founder of Political Philosophy." *Klesis* 19 (2011): 129–41.

Maine, Henry James Sumner. *Ancient Law: Its Connection with the Early History of Society, and Its Relation to Modern Ideas*. London: John Murray, 1861.

Martinich, Aloysius P. "Leo Strauss's Olympian Interpretation: Right, Self-Preservation, and Law in the Political Philosophy of Hobbes." In *Reading between the Lines: Leo Strauss and the History of Early Modern Philosophy*, ed. Winfried Schroeder, 77–98. Berlin: De Gruyter, 2015.

Mayer, Carl. Review of *A History of Social Philosophy*, by Charles A. Ellwood. *Social Research* 5, no. 4 (1938): 490–93.

McIlwain, Charles Howard. *The Growth of Political Thought in the West, from the Greeks to the End of the Middle Ages*. New York: Macmillan, 1932.

Meier, Heinrich. "How Strauss Became Strauss." In *Enlightening Revolutions: Essays in Honor of Ralph Lerner*, ed. Svetozar Minkov, 363–82. Lanham, MD: Lexington Books, 2006.

———. *Leo Strauss and the Theological-Political Problem*. Cambridge: Cambridge University Press, 2006.

Minkov, Svetozar. *Leo Strauss on Science*. Albany: SUNY Press, 2016.

Minowitz, Peter. *Straussophobia*. Lanham, MD: Rowman and Littlefield, 2009.

More, Thomas. *Yale Edition of the Complete Works of St. Thomas More*, vol. 15: *In Defense of Humanism: Letters to Dorp, Oxford, Lee, and a Monk*. Ed. Daniel Kinney. New Haven: Yale University Press, 1986.

Nietzsche, Friedrich. *Untimely Meditations*. Cambridge: Cambridge University Press, 1983.

Nozick, Robert. *Anarchy, State, and Utopia*. New York: Basic Books, 1974.

Oexle, Otto G. *Geschichtswissenschaft im Zeichen des Historismus: Studien zur Problemgeschichten der Moderne*. Göttingen: Vandenhoeck & Ruprecht, 1996.

Patard, Emmanuel, ed. *Leo Strauss at the New School for Social Research (1938–1948): Essays, Lectures, and Courses on Ancient and Modern Political Philosophy*. N.d., n.p. Translation of a doctoral dissertation: *Leo Strauss à la New School for Social Research (1938–1948). Essais, conférences et cours sur la philosophie politique ancienne et moderne*, Université Paris I (Panthéon-Sorbonne), March 2013.

Popper, Karl. *The Open Society and Its Enemies*. Princeton: Princeton University Press, 2013.

———. *The Poverty of Historicism*. Abingdon, UK: Routledge, 1957.

Ranke, Leopold von. *Das Briefwerk*. Ed. Walther P. Fuchs. Munich: Hoffmann und Campe, 1949.

———. *Sämtliche Werke*. Ed. Alfred Dove. Leipzig: Duncker & Humblot, 1867–90.

———. *The Theory and Practice of History*. Indianapolis: Bobbs-Merrill, 1973.

Rawls, John. "Kantian Constructivism in Moral Theory." In *Collected Papers*, ed. Samuel Freeman, 303–58. Cambridge: Harvard University Press, 1999.

Rickert, Heinrich. *Grundprobleme der Philosophie*. Tübingen: Mohr, 1934.

Riezler, Kurt. "Some Critical Remarks on Man's Science of Man." *Social Research* 12, no. 4 (1945): 481–505.

Roberts, William Clare. "All Natural Right Is Changeable: Aristotelian Natural Right, Prudence, and the Specter of Exceptionalism." *Review of Politics* 74 (2012): 261–83.

Rutkoff, Peter M., and William B. Scott. *New School: A History of the New School for Social Research*. New York: Free Press, 1986.

Sandel, Michael. *Liberalism and the Limits of Justice*. Cambridge: Harvard University Press, 1997.

Shell, Susan. "'Kurt Riezler: 1882–1955' and the 'Problem' of Political Philosophy." In *Leo Strauss's Defense of the Philosophic Life*, ed. Rafael Major, 191–214. Chicago: University of Chicago Press, 2013.

———. "Taking Evil Seriously." In *Leo Strauss: Political Philosopher and Jewish Thinker*, ed. Kenneth Deutsch and Walter Nicgorski, 175–93. Lanham, MD: Rowman and Littlefield, 1994.

Sheppard, Eugene R. *Leo Strauss and the Politics of Exile*. Hanover, NH: University Press of New England, 2006.

Smith, Steven B. "Leo Strauss: The Outlines of a Life." In *The Cambridge Companion to Leo Strauss*, ed. Smith, 13–40. Cambridge: Cambridge University Press, 2009.

Spengler, Oswald. *The Decline of the West*. New York: Alfred A. Knopf, 1937.

———. *The Predicament of Modern Politics*. Ed. Harold Spaeth. Detroit: University of Detroit Press, 1964.

Stauffer, Devin. "Leo Strauss's 'On the Basis of Hobbes's Political Philosophy." In *Leo Strauss's Defense of the Philosophical Life: Reading "What Is Political Philosophy?"* Chicago: University of Chicago Press, 2013.

Strauss, Leo. *The Argument and the Action of Plato's "Laws."* Chicago: University of Chicago Press, 1975.

———. *The City and Man*. Chicago: Rand McNally, 1964.

———. Courses, lectures, and archives. http://leostrausscenter.uchicago.edu and http://leostrausscenter.uchicago.edu/library-finding-aid.

———. "Existentialism." *Interpretation* 22, no. 3 (1995): 301–20.

———. *Faith and Political Philosophy: The Correspondence between Leo Strauss and Eric Voegelin, 1934–1964*. Trans. and ed. Peter Emberley and Barry Cooper. Columbia: University of Missouri Press, 2004.

———. "Farabi's Plato." In *Louis Ginzberg: Jubilee Volume on the Occasion of his 70th Birthday*, ed. Saul Lieberman, Shalom Spiegel, Solomon Zeitlin, and Alexander Marx, 357–93. New York: American Academy for Jewish Research, 1945.

———. *Gesammelte Schriften*, vol. 1. Ed. Heinrich Meier and Wiebke Meier. Stuttgart: J. B. Metzler, 1996.

———. *Gesammelte Schriften*, vol. 2: *Philosophie und Gesetz—Frühe Schriften*. Ed. Heinrich Meier and Wiebke Meier. Stuttgart: J. B. Metzler, 1997.

———. *History of Political Philosophy*. 3rd ed. Chicago: University of Chicago Press, 1987. First published 1962.

———. *Hobbes's Critique of Religion and Related Writings*. Ed. Gabriel Bartlett and Svetozar Minkov. Chicago: University of Chicago Press, 2011.

———. *Jewish Philosophy and the Crisis of Modernity*. Ed. Kenneth Hart Green. Albany: SUNY Press, 1997.

———. *Leo Strauss on Moses Mendelssohn*. Ed. Martin D. Yaffe. Chicago: University of Chicago Press, 2012.

———. Letter to Helmut Kuhn. *Independent Journal of Philosophy* 2 (1978): 5–12.

———. *Liberalism Ancient and Modern*. New York: Basic Books, 1968.

———. "The Living Issues of German Postwar Philosophy." Leo Strauss Papers, University of Chicago Library, box 8, folders 14. Published in Heinrich Meyer, *Leo Strauss and the Theologico-Political Problem,* Cambridge: Cambridge: University Press, 2006.

———. "Natural Law." In *International Encyclopedia of the Social Sciences,* vol. 11, ed. David L. Sills, 11: 80–90. New York: Macmillan, 1968.

———. *Natural Right and History*. Chicago: University of Chicago Press, 1953.

———. "Natural Right and History: Six Lectures Delivered at the University of Chicago, Autumn 1949, under the Auspices of the Charles R. Walgreen Foundation for the Study of American Institutions." University of Chicago Library.

———. "On Collingwood's Philosophy of History." *Review of Metaphysics* 5, no. 4 (June 1952): 559–86.

———. *On Tyranny: An Interpretation of Xenophon's* Hiero. Glencoe, IL: Free Press, 1963.

———. "The Origin of Political Science and the Problem of Socrates: Six Public Lectures." *Interpretation* 23, no. 2 (Winter 1996): 125–207.

———. "The Origin of the Idea of Natural Right." *Social Research* 19, no. 1 (1952): 23–60.

———. *Persecution and the Art of Writing*. Glencoe, IL: Free Press, 1952.

———. *Philosophy and Law: Contributions to the Understanding of Maimonides and His Predecessors*. German original published 1935.Trans. Eva Brann. Albany: SUNY Press, 1995.

———. *Plato's Symposium*. Ed. Seth Benardete. Chicago: University of Chicago Press, 2001.

———. *The Political Philosophy of Hobbes: Its Basis and Its Genesis*. Chicago: University of Chicago Press, 1952.

———. *The Rebirth of Classical Political Rationalism*. Ed. Thomas Pangle. Chicago: University of Chicago Press, 1988.

———. *Socrates and Aristophanes*. New York: Basic Books, 1966.

———. *Spinoza's Critique of Religion*. New York: Schocken, 1965.

———. *Studies in Platonic Political Philosophy*. Ed. Thomas Pangle. Chicago: University of Chicago Press, 1983.

———. *Thoughts on Machiavelli*. Glencoe, IL: Free Press, 1958.

———. "An Untitled Lecture on Plato's *Euthyphron*." *Interpretation* 24, no. 1 (Fall 1996): 4–23.

———. *What Is Political Philosophy?* Glencoe, IL: Free Press, 1959.

———. *Xenophon's Socrates*. Ithaca: Cornell University Press, 1972.

———. *Xenophon's Socratic Discourse*. Ithaca: Cornell University Press, 1970.

Swift, Jonathan. *A Tale of a Tub with Other Early Works, 1696–1707*. Oxford: Basil Blackwell, 1965.

Tanguay, Daniel. *Leo Strauss: An Intellectual Biography*. New Haven: Yale University Press, 2011.

Tarcov, Nathan. "Will the Real Leo Strauss Please Stand Up?" *American Interest* 2, no. 1 (2006): 120–28.

Troeltsch, Ernst. *Der Historismus und seine Probleme*. Tübingen: J. C. B. Mohr–Paul Siebeck, 1922.

Velkley, Richard. *Heidegger, Strauss, and the Premises of Philosophy: On Original Forgetting*. Chicago: University of Chicago Press, 2011.

Weber, Max. *Gesammelte Aufsätze zur Wissenschaftslehre*. Tübingen: Mohr, 1973.

Zuckert, Catherine H. *Postmodern Platos*. Chicago: University of Chicago Press, 1996.

Zuckert, Michael P. *Natural Rights and the New Republicanism*. Princeton: Princeton University Press, 1994.

Zuckert, Michael P., and Catherine H. Zuckert. *Leo Strauss and the Problem of Political Philosophy*. Chicago: University of Chicago Press, 2014.

Index